THOMAS LANIER (TENNESSEE) WILLIAMS was born in 1911 in Columbus, Mississippi, the second of three children. He attended the University of Missouri from 1929 until 1932, when he was forced by his family to drop out and work in a shoe company. After suffering a heart attack in 1935 he was allowed to reenroll in college; he graduated from the University of Iowa in 1938. The previous year had seen two pivotal events in his life: his play *Candles in the Sun* had been staged in St. Louis, and his beloved older sister Rose was forced to undergo a lobotomy.

After graduation, Williams moved to New Orleans, where he began sending manuscripts out under the pen name "Tennessee." During this period he worked at odd jobs and traveled frequently between New Mexico, California, and New York.

The Battle of Angels was staged by the Theatre Guild in Boston in 1940. In the following years he worked as a teletypist for the War Department and as a scriptwriter for MGM. He also completed work on the plays *The Glass Menagerie* (produced on Broadway in 1945) and *A Streetcar Named Desire* (produced on Broadway in 1947). *Streetcar* won the New York Drama Critics' Circle Award and the Pulitzer Prize, and after this time Williams never needed to worry again about money. Many of Williams' best plays followed soon after: *Summer and Smoke* was produced in 1948, *The Rose Tattoo* in 1951, *Camino Real* in 1953, and *Cat on a Hot Tin Roof* in 1955. *Cat* ran for 694 performances and also received the Drama Critics' Circle Award and a Pulitzer.

During his prolific career Williams published over 60 plays, including *Sweet Bird of Youth* (1956), *Orpheus Descending* (1957), *The Night of the Iguana* (1961; Drama Critics' Award), *The Milk Train Doesn't Stop Here Anymore* (1962), *Small Craft Warnings* (1972), and *Creve Coeur* (1979). He also published two books of poetry; two novels, notably *The Roman Spring of Mrs. Stone;* four short story collections; a book of essays; and in 1975, an autobiography, *Memoirs.* Tennessee Williams died in New York on February 24, 1983.

THE GLASS MENAGERIE

A STREETCAR NAMED DESIRE

CAT ON A HOT TIN ROOF

SUDDENLY LAST SUMMER

....

By TENNESSEE WILLIAMS

PLAYS

Baby Doll (a screenplay)
Camino Real
Cat on a Hot Tin Roof
Dragon Country
The Glass Menagerie
A Lovely Sunday for Creve Coeur
Small Craft Warnings
Stopped Rocking & Other Screenplays
A Streetcar Named Desire
Sweet Bird of Youth
THE THEATRE OF TENNESSEE WILLIAMS, VOLUME I
   Battle of Angels, A Streetcar Named Desire, The Glass Menagerie
THE THEATRE OF TENNESSEE WILLIAMS, VOLUME II
   The Eccentricities of a Nightingale, Summer and Smoke,
   The RoseTattoo, Camino Real
THE THEATRE OF TENNESSEE WILLIAMS, VOLUME III
   Cat on a Hot Tin Roof, Orpheus Descending, Suddenly Last Summer
THE THEATRE OF TENNESSEE WILLIAMS, VOLUME IV
   Sweet Bird of Youth, Period of Adjustment, The Night of the Iguana
THE THEATRE OF TENNESSEE WILLIAMS, VOLUME V
   The Milk Train Doesn't Stop Here Anymore, Kingdom of Earth
   (The Seven Descents of Myrtle), Small Craft Warnings,
   The Two-Character Play
THE THEATRE OF TENNESSEE WILLIAMS, VOLUME VI
   27 Wagons Full of Cotton and Other Short Plays
THE THEATRE OF TENNESSEE WILLIAMS, VOLUME VIII
   In the Bar of a Tokyo Hotel and Other Plays
27 Wagons Full of Cotton and Other Plays
The Two-Character Play
Vieux Carré

POETRY

Androgyne, Mon Amour
In the Winter of Cities

PROSE

Collected Stories
Eight Mortal Ladies Possessed
Hard Candy and Other Stories
The Knightly Quest and Other Stories
One Arm and Other Stories
The Roman Spring of Mrs. Stone
Where I Live: Selected Essays

TENNESSEE WILLIAMS

THE GLASS MENAGERIE

A STREETCAR NAMED DESIRE

CAT ON A HOT TIN ROOF

SUDDENLY LAST SUMMER

Quality Paperback Book Club
New York

Contents

THE GLASS MENAGERIE

Nobody, not even the rain, has such small hands.
E. E. CUMMINGS

The Glass Menagerie was first produced by Eddie Dowling and Louis J. Singer at the Civic Theatre, Chicago, Ill., on December 26, 1944, and at the Playhouse Theatre, New York City, on March 31, 1945. The setting was designed and lighted by Jo Mielziner; original music was composed by Paul Bowles; the play was staged by Eddie Dowling and Margo Jones. The cast was as follows:

THE MOTHER	LAURETTE TAYLOR
HER SON	EDDIE DOWLING
HER DAUGHTER	JULIE HAYDON
THE GENTLEMAN CALLER	ANTHONY ROSS

SCENE: *An Alley in St. Louis*

Part I. Preparation for a Gentleman Caller.
Part II. The Gentleman calls.

Time: Now and the Past.

THE CHARACTERS

AMANDA WINGFIELD (*the mother*)

A little woman of great but confused vitality clinging frantically to another time and place. Her characterization must
be carefully created, not copied from type. She is not para-
noiac, but her life is paranoia. There is much to admire in
Amanda, and as much to love and pity as there is to laugh at.
Certainly she has endurance and a kind of heroism, and
though her foolishness makes her unwittingly cruel at times,
there is tenderness in her slight person.

LAURA WINGFIELD (*her daughter*)

Amanda, having failed to establish contact with reality, continues to live vitally in her illusions, but Laura's situation is
even graver. A childhood illness has left her crippled, one leg
slightly shorter than the other, and held in a brace. This defect need not be more than suggested on the stage. Stemming
from this, Laura's separation increases till she is like a piece
of her own glass collection, too exquisitely fragile to move
from the shelf.

TOM WINGFIELD (*her son*)

And the narrator of the play. A poet with a job in a warehouse. His nature is not remorseless, but to escape from a trap
he has to act without pity.

JIM O'CONNOR (*the gentleman caller*)

A nice, ordinary, young man.

PRODUCTION NOTES

Being a "memory play," *The Glass Menagerie* can be presented with unusual freedom of convention. Because of its considerably delicate or tenuous material, atmospheric touches and subtleties of direction play a particularly important part. Expressionism and all other unconventional techniques in drama have only one valid aim, and that is a closer approach to truth. When a play employs unconventional techniques, it is not, or certainly shouldn't be, trying to escape its responsibility of dealing with reality, or interpreting experience, but is actually or should be attempting to find a closer approach, a more penetrating and vivid expression of things as they are. The straight realistic play with its genuine Frigidaire and authentic ice-cubes, its characters who speak exactly as its audience speaks, corresponds to the academic landscape and has the same virtue of a photographic likeness. Everyone should know nowadays the unimportance of the photographic in art: that truth, life, or reality is an organic thing which the poetic imagination can represent or suggest, in essence, only through transformation, through changing into other forms than those which were merely present in appearance.

These remarks are not meant as a preface only to this particular play. They have to do with a conception of a new, plastic theatre which must take the place of the exhausted theatre of realistic conventions if the theatre is to resume vitality as a part of our culture.

THE SCREEN DEVICE: There is *only one important difference between the original and the acting version of the play* and that is the *omission* in the latter of the device that I tentatively included in my *original* script. This device was the use of a screen on which were projected magic-lantern slides bearing images or titles. I do not regret the omission of this device from the original Broadway production. The extraordinary power of Miss Taylor's performance made it suitable to have the utmost simplicity in the physical production. But I think it may be interesting to some readers to see how this device was conceived. So I am putting it into the published manuscript. These images and legends, projected from behind, were cast on a section of wall between the front-room and dining-room areas, which should be indistinguishable from the rest when not in use.

The purpose of this will probably be apparent. It is to give accent to certain values in each scene. Each scene contains a particular point (or several) which is structurally the most important. In an episodic play, such as this, the basic structure or narrative line may be obscured from the audience; the effect may seem fragmentary rather than architectural. This may not be the fault of the play so much as a lack of attention in the audience. The legend or image upon the screen will strengthen the effect of what is merely allusion in the writing and allow the primary point to be made more simply and lightly than if the entire responsibility were on the spoken lines. Aside from this structural value, I think the screen will have a definite emotional appeal, less definable but just as important. An imaginative producer or director may invent many other uses for this device than those indicated in the present script. In fact the possibilities of the device seem much larger to me than the instance of this play can possibly utilize.

THE MUSIC: Another extra-literary accent in this play is provided by the use of music. A single recurring tune, "The Glass Menagerie," is used to give emotional emphasis to suitable passages. This tune is like circus music, not when you are on the grounds or in the immediate vicinity of the parade, but when you are at some distance and very likely thinking of something else. It seems under those circumstances to continue almost interminably and it weaves in and out of your preoccupied consciousness; then it is the lightest, most delicate music in the world and perhaps the saddest. It expresses the surface vivacity of life with the underlying strain of immutable and inexpressible sorrow. When you look at a piece of delicately spun glass you think of two things: how beautiful it is and how easily it can be broken. Both of those ideas should be woven into the recurring tune, which dips in and out of the play as if it were carried on a wind that changes. It serves as a thread of connection and allusion between the narrator with his separate point in time and space and the subject of his story. Between each episode it returns as reference to the emotion, nostalgia, which is the first condition of the play. It is primarily Laura's music and therefore comes out most clearly when the play focuses upon her and the lovely fragility of glass which is her image.

THE LIGHTING: The lighting in the play is not realistic. In keeping with the atmosphere of memory, the stage is dim. Shafts of light are focused on selected areas or actors, sometimes in contradistinction to what is the apparent center. For instance, in the quarrel scene between Tom and Amanda, in which Laura has no active part, the clearest pool of light is on her figure. This is also true of the supper scene, when her silent figure on the sofa should remain the visual center. The light upon Laura should be distinct from the others, having a peculiar pristine clarity such as light used in early religious

portraits of female saints or madonnas. A certain correspondence to light in religious paintings, such as El Greco's, where
the figures are radiant in atmosphere that is relatively dusky,
could be effectively used throughout the play. (It will also
permit a more effective use of the screen.) A free, imaginative
use of light can be of enormous value in giving a mobile,
plastic quality to plays of a more or less static nature.

Tennessee Williams

THE CATASTROPHE OF SUCCESS

[This essay was first published in "The New York Times," later reprinted in "Story," and is now included, as an introduction, in The New Classics edition of this play.]

This winter marked the third anniversary of the Chicago opening of "The Glass Menagerie," an event that terminated one part of my life and began another about as different in all external circumstances as could well be imagined. I was snatched out of virtual oblivion and thrust into sudden prominence, and from the precarious tenancy of furnished rooms about the country I was removed to a suite in a first-class Manhattan hotel. My experience was not unique. Success has often come that abruptly into the lives of Americans. The Cinderella story is our favorite national myth, the cornerstone of the film industry if not of the Democracy itself. I have seen it enacted on the screen so often that I was now inclined to yawn at it, not with disbelief but with an attitude of Who Cares! Anyone with such beautiful teeth and hair as the screen protagonist of such a story was bound to have a good time one way or another, and you could bet your bottom dollar and all the tea in China that that one would not be caught dead or alive at any meeting involving a social conscience.

No, my experience was not exceptional, but neither was it quite ordinary, and if you are willing to accept the somewhat eclectic proposition that I had not been writing with such an experience in mind—and many people are not willing to believe that a playwright is interested in anything but popular success—there may be some point in comparing the two estates.

The sort of life that I had had previous to this popular

success was one that required endurance, a life of clawing and scratching along a sheer surface and holding on tight with raw fingers to every inch of rock higher than the one caught hold of before, but it was a good life because it was the sort of life for which the human organism is created.

I was not aware of how much vital energy had gone into this struggle until the struggle was removed. I was out on a level plateau with my arms still thrashing and my lungs still grabbing at air that no longer resisted. This was security at last.

I sat down and looked about me and was suddenly very depressed. I thought to myself, this is just a period of adjustment. Tomorrow morning I will wake up in this first-class hotel suite above the discreet hum of an East Side boulevard and I will appreciate its elegance and luxuriate in its comforts and know that I have arrived at our American plan of Olympus. Tomorrow morning when I look at the green satin sofa I will fall in love with it. It is only temporarily that the green satin looks like slime on stagnant water.

But in the morning the inoffensive little sofa looked more revolting than the night before and I was already getting too fat for the $125 suit which a fashionable acquaintance had selected for me. In the suite things began to break accidentally. An arm came off the sofa. Cigarette burns appeared on the polished surface of the furniture. Windows were left open and a rain storm flooded the suite. But the maid always put it straight and the patience of the management was inexhaustible. Late parties could not offend them seriously. Nothing short of a demolition bomb seemed to bother my neighbors.

I lived on room service. But in this, too, there was a disenchantment. Some time between the moment when I ordered dinner over the phone and when it was rolled into my living room like a corpse on a rubber-wheeled table, I lost all interest in it. Once I ordered a sirloin steak and a chocolate sundae, but everything was so cunningly disguised on the table that

I mistook the chocolate sauce for gravy and poured it over the sirloin steak.

Of course all this was the more trivial aspect of a spiritual dislocation that began to manifest itself in far more disturbing ways. I soon found myself becoming indifferent to people. A well of cynicism rose in me. Conversations all sounded as if they had been recorded years ago and were being played back on a turntable. Sincerity and kindliness seemed to have gone out of my friends' voices. I suspected them of hypocrisy. I stopped calling them, stopped seeing them. I was impatient of what I took to be inane flattery.

I got so sick of hearing people say, "I loved your play!" that I could not say thank you any more. I choked on the words and turned rudely away from the usually sincere person. I no longer felt any pride in the play itself but began to dislike it, probably because I felt too lifeless inside ever to create another. I was walking around dead in my shoes and I knew it but there were no friends I knew or trusted sufficiently, at that time, to take them aside and tell them what was the matter.

This curious condition persisted about three months, till late spring, when I decided to have another eye operation mainly because of the excuse it gave me to withdraw from the world behind a gauze mask. It was my fourth eye operation, and perhaps I should explain that I had been afflicted for about five years with a cataract on my left eye which required a series of needling operations and finally an operation on the muscle of the eye. (The eye is still in my head. So much for that.)

Well, the gauze mask served a purpose. While I was resting in the hospital the friends whom I had neglected or affronted in one way or another began to call on me and now that I was in pain and darkness, their voices seemed to have changed, or rather that unpleasant mutation which I had suspected earlier in the season had now disappeared and they sounded now as they had used to sound in the lamented days of my obscurity. Once more they were sincere and kindly voices with the ring of truth in them and that quality of understanding for which I had originally sought them out.

As far as my physical vision was concerned, this last operation was only relatively successful (although it left me with an apparently clear black pupil in the right position, or nearly so) but in another, figurative way, it had served a much deeper purpose.

When the gauze mask was removed I found myself in a readjusted world. I checked out of the handsome suite at the first-class hotel, packed my papers and a few incidental belongings and left for Mexico, an elemental country where you can quickly forget the false dignities and conceits imposed by success, a country where vagrants innocent as children curl up to sleep on the pavements and human voices, especially when their language is not familiar to the ear, are soft as birds'. My public self, that artifice of mirrors, did not exist here and so my natural being was resumed.

Then, as a final act of restoration, I settled for a while at Chapala to work on a play called "The Poker Night," which later became "A Streetcar Named Desire." It is only in his work that an artist can find reality and satisfaction, for the actual world is less intense than the world of his invention and consequently his life, without recourse to violent disorder, does not seem very substantial. The right condition for him is that in which his work is not only convenient but unavoidable.

For me a convenient place to work is a remote place among strangers where there is good swimming. But life should require a certain minimal effort. You should not have too many people waiting on you, you should have to do most things for yourself. Hotel service is embarrassing. Maids, waiters, bellhops, porters and so forth are the most embarrassing people in the world for they continually remind you of inequities which we accept as the proper thing. The sight of an ancient woman, gasping and wheezing as she drags a heavy pail of water down a hotel corridor to mop up the mess of some drunken overprivileged guest, is one that sickens and weighs upon the heart and withers it with shame for this world in which it is not only tolerated but regarded as proof positive that the wheels of Democracy are functioning as they should without interference from above or below. Nobody should have to clean up anybody else's mess in this world. It is terribly bad for both parties, but probably worse for the one receiving the service.

I have been corrupted as much as anyone else by the vast number of menial services which our society has grown to expect and depend on. We should do for ourselves or let the machines do for us, the glorious technology that is supposed to be the new light of the world. We are like a man who has bought a great amount of equipment for a camping trip, who has the canoe and the tent and the fishing lines and the axe and the guns, the mackinaw and the blankets, but who now, when all the preparations and the provisions are piled expertly together, is suddenly too timid to set out on the journey but remains where he was yesterday and the day before and the day before that, looking suspiciously through white lace curtains at the clear sky he distrusts. Our great technology is a God-given chance for adventure and for progress which we are afraid to attempt. Our ideas and our ideals remain exactly what they were and where they were three centuries ago. No. I beg your pardon. It is no longer safe for a man even to declare them!

This is a long excursion from a small theme into a large one which I did not intend to make, so let me go back to what I was saying before.

This is an oversimplification. One does not escape that

easily from the seduction of an effete way of life. You cannot arbitrarily say to yourself, I will now continue my life as it was before this thing, Success, happened to me. But once you fully apprehend the vacuity of a life without struggle you are equipped with the basic means of salvation. Once you know this is true, that the heart of man, his body and his brain, are forged in a white-hot furnace for the purpose of conflict (the struggle of creation) and that with the conflict removed, the man is a sword cutting daisies, that not privation but luxury is the wolf at the door and that the fangs of this wolf are all the little vanities and conceits and laxities that Success is heir to—why, then with this knowledge you are at least in a position of knowing where danger lies.

You know, then, that the public Somebody you are when you "have a name" is a fiction created with mirrors and that the only somebody worth being is the solitary and unseen you that existed from your first breath and which is the sum of your actions and so is constantly in a state of becoming under your own violation—and knowing these things, you can even survive the catastrophe of Success!

It is never altogether too late, unless you embrace the Bitch Goddess, as William James called her, with both arms and find in her smothering caresses exactly what the homesick little boy in you always wanted, absolute protection and utter effortlessness. Security is a kind of death, I think, and it can come to you in a storm of royalty checks beside a kidney-shaped pool in Beverly Hills or anywhere at all that is removed from the conditions that made you an artist, if that's what you are or were or intended to be. Ask anyone who has experienced the kind of success I am talking about— What good is it? Perhaps to get an honest answer you will have to give him a shot of truth serum but the word he will finally groan is unprintable in genteel publications.

Then what is good? The obsessive interest in human affairs,

plus a certain amount of compassion and moral conviction, that first made the experience of living something that must be translated into pigment or music or bodily movement or poetry or prose or anything that's dynamic and expressive— that's what's good for you if you're at all serious in your aims. William Saroyan wrote a great play on this theme, that purity of heart is the one success worth having. "In the time of your life—live!" That time is short and it doesn't return again. It is slipping away while I write this and while you read it, and the monosyllable of the clock is Loss, loss, loss, unless you devote your heart to its opposition.

SCENE ONE

The Wingfield apartment is in the rear of the building, one of those vast hive-like conglomerations of cellular living-units that flower as warty growths in overcrowded urban centers of lower middle-class population and are symptomatic of the impulse of this largest and fundamentally enslaved section of American society to avoid fluidity and differentiation and to exist and function as one interfused mass of automatism.

The apartment faces an alley and is entered by a fire escape, a structure whose name is a touch of accidental poetic truth, for all of these huge buildings are always burning with the slow and implacable fires of human desperation. The fire escape is part of what we see—that is, the landing of it and steps descending from it.

The scene is memory and is therefore nonrealistic. Memory takes a lot of poetic license. It omits some details; others are exaggerated, according to the emotional value of the articles it touches, for memory is seated predominantly in the heart. The interior is therefore rather dim and poetic.

At the rise of the curtain, the audience is faced with the dark, grim rear wall of the Wingfield tenement. This building is flanked on both sides by dark, narrow alleys which run into murky canyons of tangled clotheslines, garbage cans, and the sinister latticework of neighboring fire escapes. It is up and down these side alleys that exterior entrances and exits are made during the play. At the end of Tom's opening commentary, the dark tenement wall slowly becomes transparent and reveals the interior of the ground-floor Wingfield apartment.

Nearest the audience is the living room, which also serves as a sleeping room for Laura, the sofa unfolding to make her

1

bed. Just beyond, separated from the living room by a wide arch or second proscenium with transparent faded portieres (or second curtain), is the dining room. In an old-fashioned whatnot in the living room are seen scores of transparent glass animals. A blown-up photograph of the father hangs on the wall of the living room, to the left of the archway. It is the face of a very handsome young man in a doughboy's First World War cap. He is gallantly smiling, ineluctably smiling, as if to say "I will be smiling forever."

Also hanging on the wall, near the photograph, are a type-writer keyboard chart and a Gregg shorthand diagram. An upright typewriter on a small table stands beneath the charts.

The audience hears and sees the opening scene in the dining room through both the transparent fourth wall of the building and the transparent gauze portieres of the dining-room arch. It is during this revealing scene that the fourth wall slowly ascends, out of sight. This transparent exterior wall is not brought down again until the very end of the play, during Tom's final speech.

The narrator is an undisguised convention of the play. He takes whatever license with dramatic convention is convenient to his purposes.

Tom enters, dressed as a merchant sailor, and strolls across to the fire escape. There he stops and lights a cigarette. He addresses the audience.

TOM: Yes, I have tricks in my pocket, I have things up my sleeve. But I am the opposite of a stage magician. He gives you illusion that has the appearance of truth. I give you truth in the pleasant disguise of illusion.

To begin with, I turn back time. I reverse it to that quaint period, the thirties, when the huge middle class of America was matriculating in a school for the blind. Their eyes had failed them, or they had failed their eyes, and so they were having their fingers pressed forcibly down on the fiery Braille alphabet of a dissolving economy.

In Spain there was revolution. Here there was only shouting and confusion. In Spain there was Guernica. Here there were disturbances of labor, sometimes pretty violent, in otherwise peaceful cities such as Chicago, Cleveland, Saint Louis . . .

This is the social background of the play.

[*Music begins to play.*]

The play is memory. Being a memory play, it is dimly lighted, it is sentimental, it is not realistic. In memory everything seems to happen to music. That explains the fiddle in the wings.

I am the narrator of the play, and also a character in it. The other characters are my mother, Amanda, my sister, Laura, and a gentleman caller who appears in the final scenes. He is the most realistic character in the play, being an emissary from a world of reality that we were somehow set apart from. But since I have a poet's weakness for symbols, I am using this character also as a symbol; he is the long-delayed but always expected something that we live for.

There is a fifth character in the play who doesn't appear except in this larger-than-life-size photograph over the mantel. This is our father who left us a long time ago. He was a telephone man who fell in love with long distances; he gave up his job with the telephone company and skipped the light fantastic out of town . . .

The last we heard of him was a picture postcard from Mazatlan, on the Pacific coast of Mexico, containing a message of two words: "Hello—Goodbye!" and no address.

I think the rest of the play will explain itself. . . .

3

[*Amanda's voice becomes audible through the portieres.*]

[*Legend on screen:* "Ou sont les neiges."]

[*Tom divides the portieres and enters the dining room. Amanda and Laura are seated at a drop-leaf table. Eating is indicated by gestures without food or utensils. Amanda faces the audience. Tom and Laura are seated in profile. The interior has lit up softly and through the scrim we see Amanda and Laura seated at the table.*]

AMANDA [*calling*]: Tom?

TOM: Yes, Mother.

AMANDA: We can't say grace until you come to the table!

TOM: Coming, Mother. [*He bows slightly and withdraws, reappearing a few moments later in his place at the table.*]

AMANDA [*to her son*]: Honey, don't *push* with your *fingers*. If you have to push with something, the thing to push with is a crust of bread. And chew—chew! Animals have secretions in their stomachs which enable them to digest food without mastication, but human beings are supposed to chew their food before they swallow it down. Eat food leisurely, son, and really enjoy it. A well-cooked meal has lots of delicate flavors that have to be held in the mouth for appreciation. So chew your food and give your salivary glands a chance to function!

[*Tom deliberately lays his imaginary fork down and pushes his chair back from the table.*]

TOM: I haven't enjoyed one bite of this dinner because of your constant directions on how to eat it. It's you that make me rush through meals with your hawklike attention to every bite I take. Sickening—spoils my appetite—all this discussion of—animals' secretion—salivary glands—mastication!

4

AMANDA [*lightly*]: Temperament like a Metropolitan star!

[*Tom rises and walks toward the living room.*]

You're not excused from the table.

TOM: I'm getting a cigarette.

AMANDA: You smoke too much.

[*Laura rises.*]

LAURA: I'll bring in the blanc mange.

[*Tom remains standing with his cigarette by the portieres.*]

AMANDA [*rising*]: No, sister, no, sister—you be the lady this time and I'll be the darky.

LAURA: I'm already up.

AMANDA: Resume your seat, little sister—I want you to stay fresh and pretty—for gentlemen callers!

LAURA [*sitting down*]: I'm not expecting any gentlemen callers.

AMANDA [*crossing out to the kitchenette, airily*]: Sometimes they come when they are least expected! Why, I remember one Sunday afternoon in Blue Mountain—

[*She enters the kitchenette.*]

TOM: I know what's coming!

LAURA: Yes. But let her tell it.

TOM: Again?

LAURA: She loves to tell it.

[*Amanda returns with a bowl of dessert*].

5

AMANDA: One Sunday afternoon in Blue Mountain—your mother received—*seventeen!*—gentlemen callers! Why, sometimes there weren't chairs enough to accommodate them all. We had to send the nigger over to bring in folding chairs from the parish house.

TOM [*remaining at the portieres*]: How did you entertain those gentlemen callers?

AMANDA: I understood the art of conversation!

TOM: I bet you could talk.

AMANDA: Girls in those days *knew* how to talk, I can tell you.

TOM: Yes?

[*Image on screen*: Amanda as a girl on a porch, greeting callers.]

AMANDA: They knew how to entertain their gentlemen callers. It wasn't enough for a girl to be possessed of a pretty face and a graceful figure—although I wasn't slighted in either respect. She also needed to have a nimble wit and a tongue to meet all occasions.

TOM: What did you talk about?

AMANDA: Things of importance going on in the world! Never anything coarse or common or vulgar.

[*She addresses Tom as though he were seated in the vacant chair at the table though he remains by the portieres. He plays this scene as though reading from a script.*]

My callers were gentlemen—all! Among my callers were some of the most prominent young planters of the Mississippi Delta—planters and sons of planters!

[*Tom motions for music and a spot of light on Amanda.
Her eyes lift, her face glows, her voice becomes rich and
elegiac.*]

[*Screen legend*: "Ou sont les neiges d'antan?"]

There was young Champ Laughlin who later became vice-
president of the Delta Planters Bank. Hadley Stevenson who
was drowned in Moon Lake and left his widow one hundred
and fifty thousand in Government bonds. There were the
Cutrere brothers, Wesley and Bates. Bates was one of my
bright particular beaux! He got in a quarrel with that wild
Wainwright boy. They shot it out on the floor of Moon Lake
Casino. Bates was shot through the stomach. Died in the
ambulance on his way to Memphis. His widow was also well
provided-for, came into eight or ten thousand acres, that's all.
She married him on the rebound—never loved her—carried
my picture on him the night he died! And there was that boy
that every girl in the Delta had set her cap for! That beautiful,
brilliant young Fitzhugh boy from Greene County!

TOM: What did he leave his widow?

AMANDA: He never married! Gracious, you talk as though
all of my old admirers had turned up their toes to the daisies!

TOM: Isn't this the first you've mentioned that still survives?

AMANDA: That Fitzhugh boy went North and made a fortune—came to be known as the Wolf of Wall Street! He had
the Midas touch, whatever he touched turned to gold! And I
could have been Mrs. Duncan J. Fitzhugh, mind you! But—I
picked your *father!*

LAURA [*rising*]: Mother, let me clear the table.

AMANDA: No, dear, you go in front and study your typewriter chart. Or practice your shorthand a little. Stay fresh

7

and pretty!—It's almost time for our gentlemen callers to start arriving. [*She flounces girlishly toward the kitchenette*] How many do you suppose we're going to entertain this afternoon?

[*Tom throws down the paper and jumps up with a groan.*]

LAURA [*alone in the dining room*]: I don't believe we're going to receive any, Mother.

AMANDA [*reappearing, airily*]: What? No one—not one? You must be joking!

[*Laura nervously echoes her laugh. She slips in a fugitive manner through the half-open portieres and draws them gently behind her. A shaft of very clear light is thrown on her face against the faded tapestry of the curtains. Faintly the music of "The Glass Menagerie" is heard as she continues, lightly:*]

Not one gentleman caller? It can't be true! There must be a flood, there must have been a tornado!

LAURA: It isn't a flood, it's not a tornado, Mother. I'm just not popular like you were in Blue Mountain. . . .

[*Tom utters another groan. Laura glances at him with a faint, apologetic smile. Her voice catches a little:*]

Mother's afraid I'm going to be an old maid.

[*The scene dims out with the "Glass Menagerie" music.*]

SCENE TWO

On the dark stage the screen is lighted with the image of blue roses. Gradually Laura's figure becomes apparent and the screen goes out. The music subsides.

Laura is seated in the delicate ivory chair at the small claw-foot table. She wears a dress of soft violet material for a kimono—her hair is tied back from her forehead with a ribbon. She is washing and polishing her collection of glass. Amanda appears on the fire escape steps. At the sound of her ascent, Laura catches her breath, thrusts the bowl of ornaments away, and seats herself stiffly before the diagram of the typewriter keyboard as though it held her spellbound. Something has happened to Amanda. It is written in her face as she climbs to the landing: a look that is grim and hopeless and a little absurd. She has on one of those cheap or imitation velvety-looking cloth coats with imitation fur collar. Her hat is five or six years old, one of those dreadful cloche hats that were worn in the late Twenties, and she is clutching an enormous black patent-leather pocketbook with nickel clasps and initials. This is her full-dress outfit, the one she usually wears to the D.A.R. Before entering she looks through the door. She purses her lips, opens her eyes very wide, rolls them upward and shakes her head. Then she slowly lets herself in the door. Seeing her mother's expression Laura touches her lips with a nervous gesture.

LAURA: Hello, Mother, I was— [*She makes a nervous gesture toward the chart on the wall. Amanda leans against the shut door and stares at Laura with a martyred look.*]

AMANDA: Deception? Deception? [*She slowly removes her hat and gloves, continuing the sweet suffering stare. She lets the hat and gloves fall on the floor—a bit of acting.*]

LAURA [*shakily*]: How was the D.A.R. meeting?

[*Amanda slowly opens her purse and removes a dainty white handkerchief which she shakes out delicately and delicately touches to her lips and nostrils.*]

Didn't you go to the D.A.R. meeting, Mother?

AMANDA [*faintly, almost inaudibly*]: —No.—No. [*then more forcibly:*] I did not have the strength—to go to the D.A.R. In fact, I did not have the courage! I wanted to find a hole in the ground and hide myself in it forever! [*She crosses slowly to the wall and removes the diagram of the typewriter keyboard. She holds it in front of her for a second, staring at it sweetly and sorrowfully—then bites her lips and tears it in two pieces.*]

LAURA [*faintly*]: Why did you do that, Mother?

[*Amanda repeats the same procedure with the chart of the Gregg Alphabet.*]

Why are you—

AMANDA: Why? Why? How old are you, Laura?

LAURA: Mother, you know my age.

AMANDA: I thought that you were an adult; it seems that I was mistaken. [*She crosses slowly to the sofa and sinks down and stares at Laura.*]

LAURA: Please don't stare at me, Mother.

[*Amanda closes her eyes and lowers her head. There is a ten-second pause.*]

AMANDA: What are we going to do, what is going to become of us, what is the future?

[*There is another pause.*]

LAURA: Has something happened, Mother?

[*Amanda draws a long breath, takes out the handkerchief again, goes through the dabbing process.*]

Mother, has—something happened?

AMANDA: I'll be all right in a minute, I'm just bewildered —[*She hesitates.*]—by life. . . .

LAURA: Mother, I wish that you would tell me what's happened!

AMANDA: As you know, I was supposed to be inducted into my office at the D.A.R. this afternoon.

[*Screen image*: A swarm of typewriters.]

But I stopped off at Rubicam's Business College to speak to your teachers about your having a cold and ask them what progress they thought you were making down there.

LAURA: Oh. . . .

AMANDA: I went to the typing instructor and introduced myself as your mother. She didn't know who you were. "Wingfield," she said, "We don't have any such student enrolled at the school!"
I assured her she did, that you had been going to classes since early in January.
"I wonder," she said, "If you could be talking about that terribly shy little girl who dropped out of school after only a few days' attendance?"
"No," I said, "Laura, my daughter, has been going to school every day for the past six weeks!"
"Excuse me," she said. She took the attendance book out and there was your name, unmistakably printed, and all the dates you were absent until they decided that you had dropped out of school.

I still said, "No, there must have been some mistake! There must have been some mix-up in the records!"

And she said, "No—I remember her perfectly now. Her hands shook so that she couldn't hit the right keys! The first time we gave a speed test, she broke down completely—was sick at the stomach and almost had to be carried into the wash room! After that morning she never showed up any more. We phoned the house but never got any answer"—While I was working at Famous–Barr, I suppose, demonstrating those—

[*She indicates a brassiere with her hands.*]

Oh! I felt so weak I could barely keep on my feet! I had to sit down while they got me a glass of water! Fifty dollars' tuition, all of our plans—my hopes and ambitions for you—just gone up the spout, just gone up the spout like that.

[*Laura draws a long breath and gets awkwardly to her feet. She crosses to the Victrola and winds it up.*]

What are you doing?

LAURA: Oh! [*She releases the handle and returns to her seat.*]

AMANDA: Laura, where have you been going when you've gone out pretending that you were going to business college?

LAURA: I've just been going out walking.

AMANDA: That's not true.

LAURA: It is. I just went walking.

AMANDA: Walking? Walking? In winter? Deliberately courting pneumonia in that light coat? Where did you walk to, Laura?

LAURA: All sorts of places—mostly in the park.

AMANDA: Even after you'd started catching that cold?

LAURA: It was the lesser of two evils, Mother.

[*Screen image*: Winter scene in a park.]

I couldn't go back there. I—threw up—on the floor!

AMANDA: From half past seven till after five every day you mean to tell me you walked around in the park, because you wanted to make me think that you were still going to Rubicam's Business College?

LAURA: It wasn't as bad as it sounds. I went inside places to get warmed up.

AMANDA: Inside where?

LAURA: I went in the art museum and the bird houses at the Zoo. I visited the penguins every day! Sometimes I did without lunch and went to the movies. Lately I've been spending most of my afternoons in the Jewel Box, that big glass house where they raise the tropical flowers.

AMANDA: You did all this to deceive me, just for deception?

[*Laura looks down.*] Why?

LAURA: Mother, when you're disappointed, you get that awful suffering look on your face, like the picture of Jesus' mother in the museum!

AMANDA: Hush!

LAURA: I couldn't face it.

[*There is a pause. A whisper of strings is heard. Legend on screen*: "The Crust of Humility."]

AMANDA [*hopelessly fingering the huge pocketbook*]: So what are we going to do the rest of our lives? Stay home and

13

watch the parades go by? Amuse ourselves with the glass menagerie, darling? Eternally play those worn-out phonograph records your father left as a painful reminder of him? We won't have a business career—we've given that up because it gave us nervous indigestion! [*She laughs wearily.*] What is there left but dependency all our lives? I know so well what becomes of unmarried women who aren't prepared to occupy a position. I've seen such pitiful cases in the South— barely tolerated spinsters living upon the grudging patronage of sister's husband or brother's wife!—stuck away in some little mousetrap of a room—encouraged by one in-law to visit another—little birdlike women without any nest—eating the crust of humility all their life!

Is that the future that we've mapped out for ourselves? I swear it's the only alternative I can think of! [*She pauses.*] It isn't a very pleasant alternative, is it? [*She pauses again.*] Of course—some girls *do marry.*

[*Laura twists her hands nervously.*]

Haven't you ever liked some boy?

LAURA: Yes. I liked one once. [*She rises.*] I came across his picture a while ago.

AMANDA [*with some interest*]: He gave you his picture?

LAURA: No, it's in the yearbook.

AMANDA [*disappointed*]: Oh—a high school boy.

[*Screen image*: Jim as the high school hero bearing a silver cup.]

LAURA: Yes. His name was Jim. [*She lifts the heavy annual from the claw-foot table.*] Here he is in *The Pirates of Penzance.*

AMANDA [*absently*]: The what?

14

LAURA: The operetta the senior class put on. He had a wonderful voice and we sat across the aisle from each other Mondays, Wednesdays and Fridays in the Aud. Here he is with the silver cup for debating! See his grin?

AMANDA [*absently*]: He must have had a jolly disposition.

LAURA: He used to call me—Blue Roses.

[*Screen image*: Blue roses.]

AMANDA: Why did he call you such a name as that?

LAURA: When I had that attack of pleurosis—he asked me what was the matter when I came back. I said pleurosis—he thought that I said Blue Roses! So that's what he always called me after that. Whenever he saw me, he'd holler, "Hello, Blue Roses!" I didn't care for the girl that he went out with. Emily Meisenbach. Emily was the best-dressed girl at Soldan. She never struck me, though, as being sincere . . . It says in the Personal Section—they're engaged. That's—six years ago! They must be married by now.

AMANDA: Girls that aren't cut out for business careers usually wind up married to some nice man. [*She gets up with a spark of revival.*] Sister, that's what you'll do!

[*Laura utters a startled, doubtful laugh. She reaches quickly for a piece of glass.*]

LAURA: But, Mother—

AMANDA: Yes? [*She goes over to the photograph.*]

LAURA [*in a tone of frightened apology*]: I'm—crippled!

AMANDA: Nonsense! Laura, I've told you never, never to use that word. Why, you're not crippled, you just have a little defect—hardly noticeable, even! When people have some

15

slight disadvantage like that, they cultivate other things to make up for it—develop charm—and vivacity—and—*charm!* That's all you have to do! [*She turns again to the photograph.*] One thing your father had *plenty of*—was *charm!*

[*The scene fades out with music.*]

SCENE THREE

Legend on screen: "After the fiasco—"

Tom speaks from the fire escape landing.

TOM: After the fiasco at Rubicam's Business College, the idea of getting a gentleman caller for Laura began to play a more and more important part in Mother's calculations. It became an obsession. Like some archetype of the universal unconscious, the image of the gentleman caller haunted our small apartment. . . .

[*Screen image*: A young man at the door of a house with flowers.]

An evening at home rarely passed without some allusion to this image, this specter, this hope. . . . Even when he wasn't mentioned, his presence hung in Mother's preoccupied look and in my sister's frightened, apologetic manner—hung like a sentence passed upon the Wingfields!
Mother was a woman of action as well as words. She began to take logical steps in the planned direction. Late that winter and in the early spring—realizing that extra money would be needed to properly feather the nest and plume the bird—she conducted a vigorous campaign on the telephone, roping in subscribers to one of those magazines for matrons called *The Homemaker's Companion,* the type of journal that features the serialized sublimations of ladies of letters who think in terms of delicate cuplike breasts, slim, tapering waists, rich, creamy thighs, eyes like wood smoke in autumn, fingers that soothe and caress like strains of music, bodies as powerful as Etruscan sculpture.

[*Screen image*: The cover of a glamor magazine.]

[*Amanda enters with the telephone on a long extension cord. She is spotlighted in the dim stage.*]

AMANDA: Ida Scott? This is Amanda Wingfield! We *missed* you at the D.A.R. last Monday! I said to myself: She's probably suffering with that sinus condition! How is that sinus condition?
Horrors! Heaven have mercy!—You're a Christian martyr, yes, that's what your are, a Christian martyr!
Well, I just now happened to notice that your subscription to the *Companion*'s about to expire! Yes, it expires with the next issue, honey!—just when that wonderful new serial by Bessie Mae Hopper is getting off to such an exciting start. Oh, honey, it's something that you can't miss! You remember how *Gone with the Wind* took everybody by storm? You simply couldn't go out if you hadn't read it. All everybody *talked* was Scarlett O'Hara. Well, this is a book that critics already compare to *Gone with the Wind*. It's the *Gone with the Wind* of the post-World-War generation!—What?—Burning?—Oh, honey, don't let them burn, go take a look in the oven and I'll hold the wire! Heavens—I think she's hung up!

[*The scene dims out.*]

[*Legend on screen*: "You think I'm in love with Continental Shoemakers?"]

[*Before the lights come up again, the violent voices of Tom and Amanda are heard. They are quarreling behind the portieres. In front of them stands Laura with clenched hands and panicky expression. A clear pool of light is on her figure throughout this scene.*]

TOM: What in Christ's name am I—

AMANDA [*shrilly*]: Don't you use that—

18

TOM: —supposed to do!

AMANDA: —expression! Not in my—

TOM: Ohhh!

AMANDA: —presence! Have you gone out of your senses?

TOM: I have, that's true, *driven* out!

AMANDA: What is the matter with you, you—big—big—
IDIOT!

TOM: Look!—I've got *no thing,* no single thing—

AMANDA: Lower your voice!

TOM: —in my life here that I can call my OWN! Everything
is—

AMANDA: Stop that shouting!

TOM: Yesterday you confiscated my books! You had the
nerve to—

AMANDA: I took that horrible novel back to the library—
yes! That hideous book by that insane Mr. Lawrence.

[*Tom laughs wildly.*]

I cannot control the output of diseased minds or people who
cater to them—

[*Tom laughs still more wildly.*]

BUT I WON'T ALLOW SUCH FILTH BROUGHT INTO MY HOUSE!
No, no, no, no, no!

TOM: House, house! Who pays rent on it, who makes a
slave of himself to—

AMANDA [*fairly screeching*]: Don't you DARE to—

19

TOM: No, no, *I* mustn't say things! *I've* got to just—

AMANDA: Let me tell you—

TOM: I don't want to hear any more!

[*He tears the portieres open. The dining-room area is lit with a turgid smoky red glow. Now we see Amanda; her hair is in metal curlers and she is wearing a very old bathrobe, much too large for her slight figure, a relic of the faithless Mr. Wingfield. The upright typewriter now stands on the drop-leaf table, along with a wild disarray of manuscripts. The quarrel was probably precipitated by Amanda's interruption of Tom's creative labor. A chair lies overthrown on the floor. Their gesticulating shadows are cast on the ceiling by the fiery glow.*]

AMANDA: You *will* hear more, you—

TOM: No, I won't hear more, I'm going out!

AMANDA: You come right back in—

TOM: Out, out, out! Because I'm—

AMANDA: Come back here, Tom Wingfield! I'm not through talking to you!

TOM: Oh, go—

LAURA [*desperately*]: —Tom!

AMANDA: You're going to listen, and no more insolence from you! I'm at the end of my patience!

[*He comes back toward her.*]

TOM: What do you think I'm at? Aren't I supposed to have any patience to reach the end of, Mother? I know, I know. It seems unimportant to you, what I'm *doing*—what I *want* to

20

do—having a little *difference* between them! You don't think that—

AMANDA: I think you've been doing things that you're ashamed of. That's why you act like this. I don't believe that you go every night to the movies. Nobody goes to the movies night after night. Nobody in their right minds goes to the movies as often as you pretend to. People don't go to the movies at nearly midnight, and movies don't let out at two A.M. Come in stumbling. Muttering to yourself like a maniac! You get three hours' sleep and then go to work. Oh, I can picture the way you're doing down there. Moping, doping, because you're in no condition.

TOM [*wildly*]: No, I'm in no condition!

AMANDA: What right have you got to jeopardize your job? Jeopardize the security of us all? How do you think we'd manage if you were—

TOM: Listen! You think I'm crazy about the *warehouse?* [*He bends fiercely toward her slight figure.*] You think I'm in love with the Continental Shoemakers? You think I want to spend fifty-five *years* down there in that—*celotex interior!* with—*fluorescent—tubes!* Look! I'd rather somebody picked up a crowbar and battered out my brains—than go back mornings! I *go!* Every time you come in yelling that God-damn *"Rise and Shine!" "Rise and Shine!"* I say to myself, "How *lucky dead* people are!" But I get up. I *go!* For sixty-five dollars a month I give up all that I dream of doing and being *ever!* And you say self—*self's* all I ever think of. Why, listen, if self is what I thought of, Mother, I'd be where he is—GONE! [*He points to his father's picture.*] As far as the system of transportation reaches! [*He starts past her. She grabs his arm.*] Don't grab at me, Mother!

AMANDA: Where are you going?

TOM: I'm going to the *movies!*

AMANDA: I don't believe that lie!

[*Tom crouches toward her, overtowering her tiny figure. She backs away, gasping.*]

TOM: I'm going to opium dens! Yes, opium dens, dens of vice and criminals' hangouts, Mother. I've joined the Hogan Gang, I'm a hired assassin, I carry a tommy gun in a violin case! I run a string of cat houses in the Valley! They call me Killer, Killer Wingfield, I'm leading a double-life, a simple, honest warehouse worker by day, by night a dynamic *czar* of the *underworld, Mother.* I go to gambling casinos, I spin away fortunes on the roulette table! I wear a patch over one eye and a false mustache, sometimes I put on green whiskers. On those occasions they call me—*El Diablo!* Oh, I could tell you many things to make you sleepless! My enemies plan to dynamite this place. They're going to blow us all sky-high some night! I'll be glad, very happy, and so will you! You'll go up, up on a broomstick, over Blue Mountain with seventeen gentlemen callers! You ugly—babbling old—*witch.* . . . [*He goes through a series of violent, clumsy movements, seizing his overcoat, lunging to the door, pulling it fiercely open. The women watch him, aghast. His arm catches in the sleeve of the coat as he struggles to pull it on. For a moment he is pinioned by the bulky garment. With an outraged groan he tears the coat off again, splitting the shoulder of it, and hurls it across the room. It strikes against the shelf of Laura's glass collection, and there is a tinkle of shattering glass. Laura cries out as if wounded.*]

[*Music.*]

[*Screen legend*: "The Glass Menagerie."]

LAURA [*shrilly*]: *My glass!*—menagerie. . . . [*She covers her face and turns away.*]

22

[*But Amanda is still stunned and stupefied by the "ugly witch" so that she barely notices this occurrence. Now she recovers her speech.*]

AMANDA [*in an awful voice*]: I won't speak to you—until you apologize!

[*She crosses through the portieres and draws them together behind her. Tom is left with Laura. Laura clings weakly to the mantel with her face averted. Tom stares at her stupidly for a moment. Then he crosses to the shelf. He drops awkwardly on his knees to collect the fallen glass, glancing at Laura as if he would speak but couldn't.*]

[*"The Glass Menagerie" music steals in as the scene dims out.*]

SCENE FOUR

The interior of the apartment is dark. There is a faint light in the alley. A deep-voiced bell in a church is tolling the hour of five.

Tom appears at the top of the alley. After each solemn boom of the bell in the tower, he shakes a little noisemaker or rattle as if to express the tiny spasm of man in contrast to the sustained power and dignity of the Almighty. This and the unsteadiness of his advance make it evident that he has been drinking. As he climbs the few steps to the fire escape landing light steals up inside. Laura appears in the front room in a nightdress. She notices that Tom's bed is empty. Tom fishes in his pockets for his door key, removing a motley assortment of articles in the search, including a shower of movie ticket stubs and an empty bottle. At last he finds the key, but just as he is about to insert it, it slips from his fingers. He strikes a match and crouches below the door.

TOM [*bitterly*]: One crack—and it falls through!

[*Laura opens the door.*]

LAURA: Tom! Tom, what are you doing?

TOM: Looking for a door key.

LAURA: Where have you been all this time?

TOM: I have been to the movies.

LAURA: All this time at the movies?

TOM: There was a very long program. There was a Garbo picture and a Mickey Mouse and a travelogue and a newsreel and a preview of coming attractions. And there was an organ solo and a collection for the Milk Fund—simultaneously—

24

which ended up in a terrible fight between a fat lady and an usher!

LAURA [*innocently*]: Did you have to stay through everything?

TOM: Of course! And, oh, I forgot! There was a big stage show! The headliner on this stage show was Malvolio the Magician. He performed wonderful tricks, many of them, such as pouring water back and forth between pitchers. First it turned to wine and then it turned to beer and then it turned to whisky. I know it was whisky it finally turned into because he needed somebody to come up out of the audience to help him, and I came up—both shows! It was Kentucky Straight Bourbon. A very generous fellow, he gave souvenirs. [*He pulls from his back pocket a shimmering rainbow-colored scarf.*] He gave me this. This is his magic scarf. You can have it, Laura. You wave it over a canary cage and you get a bowl of goldfish. You wave it over the goldfish bowl and they fly away canaries. . . . But the wonderfullest trick of all was the coffin trick. We nailed him into a coffin and he got out of the coffin without removing one nail. [*He has come inside.*] There is a trick that would come in handy for me—get me out of this two-by-four situation! [*He flops onto the bed and starts removing his shoes.*]

LAURA: Tom—shhh!

TOM: What're you shushing me for?

LAURA: You'll wake up Mother.

TOM: Goody, goody! Pay 'er back for all those "Rise an' Shines." [*He lies down, groaning.*] You know it don't take much intelligence to get yourself into a nailed-up coffin, Laura. But who in hell ever got himself out of one without removing one nail?

25

[*As if in answer, the father's grinning photograph lights up. The scene dims out.*]

[*Immediately following, the church bell is heard striking six. At the sixth stroke the alarm clock goes off in Amanda's room, and after a few moments we hear her calling: "Rise and Shine! Rise and Shine! Laura, go tell your brother to rise and shine!"*]

TOM [*sitting up slowly*]: I'll rise—but I won't shine.

[*The light increases.*]

AMANDA: Laura, tell your brother his coffee is ready.

[*Laura slips into the front room.*]

LAURA: Tom!—It's nearly seven. Don't make Mother nervous.

[*He stares at her stupidly.*]

[*beseechingly*:] Tom, speak to Mother this morning. Make up with her, apologize, speak to her!

TOM: She won't to me. It's her that started not speaking.

LAURA: If you just say you're sorry she'll start speaking.

TOM: Her not speaking—is that such a tragedy?

LAURA: Please—please!

AMANDA [*calling from the kitchenette*]: Laura, are you going to do what I asked you to do, or do I have to get dressed and go out myself?

LAURA: Going, going—soon as I get on my coat!

[*She pulls on a shapeless felt hat with a nervous, jerky movement, pleadingly glancing at Tom. She rushes awk-*

26

wardly for her coat. The coat is one of Amanda's, inaccurately made-over, the sleeves too short for Laura.]

Butter and what else?

AMANDA [*entering from the kitchenette*]: Just butter. Tell them to charge it.

LAURA: Mother, they make such faces when I do that.

AMANDA: Sticks and stones can break our bones, but the expression on Mr. Garfinkel's face won't harm us! Tell your brother his coffee is getting cold.

LAURA [*at the door*]: Do what I asked you, will you, will you, Tom?

[*He looks sullenly away.*]

AMANDA: Laura, go now or just don't go at all!

LAURA [*rushing out*]: Going—going!

[*A second later she cries out. Tom springs up and crosses to the door. Tom opens the door.*]

TOM: Laura?

LAURA: I'm all right. I slipped, but I'm all right.

AMANDA [*peering anxiously after her*]: If anyone breaks a leg on those fire-escape steps, the landlord ought to be sued for every cent he possesses! [*She shuts the door. Now she remembers she isn't speaking to Tom and returns to the other room.*]

[*As Tom comes listlessly for his coffee, she turns her back to him and stands rigidly facing the window on the gloomy gray vault of the areaway. Its light on her face with its aged but childish features is cruelly sharp, satirical as a Daumier print.*]

27

[*The music of "Ave Maria," is heard softly.*]

[*Tom glances sheepishly but sullenly at her averted figure and slumps at the table. The coffee is scalding hot; he sips it and gasps and spits it back in the cup. At his gasp, Amanda catches her breath and half turns. Then she catches herself and turns back to the window. Tom blows on his coffee, glancing sidewise at his mother. She clears her throat. Tom clears his. He starts to rise, sinks back down again, scratches his head, clears his throat again. Amanda coughs. Tom raises his cup in both hands to blow on it, his eyes staring over the rim of it at his mother for several moments. Then he slowly sets the cup down and awkwardly and hesitantly rises from the chair.*]

TOM [*hoarsely*]: Mother. I—I apologize, Mother.

[*Amanda draws a quick, shuddering breath. Her face works grotesquely. She breaks into childlike tears.*]

I'm sorry for what I said, for everything that I said, I didn't mean it.

AMANDA [*sobbingly*]: My devotion has made me a witch and so I make myself hateful to my children!

TOM: *No,* you *don't.*

AMANDA: I worry so much, don't sleep, it makes me nervous!

TOM [*gently*]: I understand that.

AMANDA: I've had to put up a solitary battle all these years. But you're my right-hand bower! Don't fall down, don't fail!

TOM [*gently*]: I try, Mother.

28

AMANDA [*with great enthusiasm*]: Try and you will *succeed!* [*The notion makes her breathless.*] Why, you—you're just *full* of natural endowments! Both of my children— they're *unusual* children! Don't you think I know it? I'm so —*proud!* Happy and—feel I've—so much to be thankful for but— promise me one thing, son!

TOM: What, Mother?

AMANDA: Promise, son, you'll—never be a drunkard!

TOM [*turns to her grinning*]: I will never be a drunkard, Mother.

AMANDA: That's what frightened me so, that you'd be drinking! Eat a bowl of Purina!

TOM: Just coffee, Mother.

AMANDA: Shredded wheat biscuit?

TOM: No. No, Mother, just coffee.

AMANDA: You can't put in a day's work on an empty stomach. You've got ten minutes—don't gulp! Drinking too-hot liquids makes cancer of the stomach. . . . Put cream in.

TOM: No, thank you.

AMANDA: To cool it.

TOM: No! No, thank you, I want it black.

AMANDA: I know, but it's not good for you. We have to do all that we can to build ourselves up. In these trying times we live in, all that we have to cling to is—each other. . . . That's why it's so important to— Tom, I— I sent out your sister so I could discuss something with you. If you hadn't spoken I would have spoken to you. [*She sits down.*]

29

TOM [*gently*]: What is it, Mother, that you want to discuss?

AMANDA: *Laura!*

[*Tom puts his cup down slowly.*]

[*Legend on screen*: "Laura." *Music*: *"The Glass Menagerie."*]

TOM: —Oh.—Laura . . .

AMANDA [*touching his sleeve*]: You know how Laura is. So quiet but—still water runs deep! She notices things and I think she—broods about them.

[*Tom looks up.*]

A few days ago I came in and she was crying.

TOM: What about?

AMANDA: You.

TOM: Me?

AMANDA: She has an idea that you're not happy here.

TOM: What gave her that idea?

AMANDA: What gives her any idea? However, you do act strangely. I—I'm not criticizing, understand *that!* I know your ambitions do not lie in the warehouse, that like everybody in the whole wide world—you've had to—make sacrifices, but— Tom—Tom—life's not easy, it calls for—Spartan endurance! There's so many things in my heart that I cannot describe to you! I've never told you but I—*loved* your father. . . .

TOM [*gently*]: I know that, Mother.

AMANDA: And you—when I see you taking after his ways! Staying out late—and—well, you *had* been drinking the night you were in that—terrifying condition! Laura says that you hate the apartment and that you go out nights to get away from it! Is that true, Tom?

TOM: No. You say there's so much in your heart that you can't describe to me. That's true of me, too. There's so much in my heart that I can't describe to *you!* So let's respect each other's—

AMANDA: But, why—*why,* Tom—are you always so *restless?* Where do you *go* to, nights?

TOM: I—go to the movies.

AMANDA: Why do you go to the movies so much, Tom?

TOM: I go to the movies because—I like adventure. Adventure is something I don't have much of at work, so I go to the movies.

AMANDA: But, Tom, you go to the movies *entirely* too *much!*

TOM: I like a lot of adventure.

[*Amanda looks baffled, then hurt. As the familiar inquisition resumes, Tom becomes hard and impatient again. Amanda slips back into her querulous attitude toward him.*]

[*Image on screen*: A sailing vessel with Jolly Roger.]

AMANDA: Most young men find adventure in their careers.

TOM: Then most young men are not employed in a warehouse.

AMANDA: The world is full of young men employed in warehouses and offices and factories.

TOM: Do all of them find adventure in their careers?

31

AMANDA: They do or they do without it! Not everybody has a craze for adventure.

TOM: Man is by instinct a lover, a hunter, a fighter, and none of those instincts are given much play at the warehouse!

AMANDA: Man is by instinct! Don't quote instinct to me! Instinct is something that people have got away from! It belongs to animals! Christian adults don't want it!

TOM: What do Christian adults want, then, Mother?

AMANDA: Superior things! Things of the mind and the spirit! Only animals have to satisfy instincts! Surely your aims are somewhat higher than theirs! Than monkeys—pigs—

TOM: I reckon they're not.

AMANDA: You're joking. However, that isn't what I wanted to discuss.

TOM [*rising*]: I haven't much time.

AMANDA [*pushing his shoulders*]: Sit down.

TOM: You want me to punch in red at the warehouse, Mother?

AMANDA: You have five minutes. I want to talk about Laura.

[*Screen legend*: "Plans and Provisions."]

TOM: All right! What about Laura?

AMANDA: We have to be making some plans and provisions for her. She's older than you, two years, and nothing has happened. She just drifts along doing nothing. It frightens me terribly how she just drifts along.

TOM: I guess she's the type that people call home girls.

AMANDA: There's no such type, and if there is, it's a pity! That is unless the home is hers, with a husband!

TOM: What?

AMANDA: Oh, I can see the handwriting on the wall as plain as I see the nose in front of my face! It's terrifying! More and more you remind me of your father! He was out all hours without explanation!—Then *left! Goodbye!* And me with the bag to hold. I saw that letter you got from the Merchant Marine. I know what you're dreaming of. I'm not standing here blindfolded. [*She pauses.*] Very well, then. Then *do* it! But not till there's somebody to take your place.

TOM: What do you mean?

AMANDA: I mean that as soon as Laura has got somebody to take care of her, married, a home of her own, independent —why, then you'll be free to go wherever you please, on land, on sea, whichever way the wind blows you! But until that time you've got to look out for your sister. I don't say me because I'm old and don't matter! I say for your sister because she's young and dependent.

I put her in business college—a dismal failure! Frightened her so it made her sick at the stomach. I took her over to the Young People's League at the church. Another fiasco. She spoke to nobody, nobody spoke to her. Now all she does is fool with those pieces of glass and play those worn-out records. What kind of a life is that for a girl to lead?

TOM: What can I do about it?

AMANDA: Overcome selfishness! Self, self, self is all that you ever think of!

[*Tom springs up and crosses to get his coat. It is ugly and bulky. He pulls on a cap with earmuffs.*]

33

Where is your muffler? Put your wool muffler on!

[*He snatches it angrily from the closet, tosses it around his neck and pulls both ends tight.*]

Tom! I haven't said what I had in mind to ask you.

TOM: I'm too late to—

AMANDA [*catching his arm—very importunately; then shyly*]: Down at the warehouse, aren't there some—nice young men?

TOM: No!

AMANDA: There *must* be—*some* . . .

TOM: Mother—[*He gestures.*]

AMANDA: Find out one that's clean-living—doesn't drink and ask him out for sister!

TOM: What?

AMANDA: For *sister!* To *meet!* Get *acquainted!*

TOM [*stamping to the door*]: Oh, my *go-osh!*

AMANDA: Will you?

[*He opens the door. She says, imploringly:*]

Will you?

[*He starts down the fire escape.*]

Will you? *Will* you, dear?

TOM [*calling back*]: Yes!

[*Amanda closes the door hesitantly and with a troubled but faintly hopeful expression.*]

[*Screen image*: The cover of a glamor magazine.]

[*The spotlight picks up Amanda at the phone.*]

AMANDA: Ella Cartwright? This is Amanda Wingfield!
How are you, honey?
How is that kidney condition?

[*There is a five-second pause.*]

Horrors!

[*There is another pause.*]

You're a Christian martyr, yes, honey, that's what you are, a
Christian martyr! Well, I just now happened to notice in
my little red book that your subscription to the *Companion*
has just run out! I knew that you wouldn't want to miss out
on the wonderful serial starting in this new issue. It's by Bessie
Mae Hopper, the first thing she's written since *Honeymoon for
Three.* Wasn't that a strange and interesting story? Well, this
one is even lovelier, I believe. It has a sophisticated, society
background. It's all about the horsey set on Long Island!

[*The light fades out.*]

SCENE FIVE

Legend on the screen: "Annunciation."

Music is heard as the light slowly comes on.

It is early dusk of a spring evening. Supper has just been finished in the Wingfield apartment. Amanda and Laura, in light-colored dresses, are removing dishes from the table in the dining room, which is shadowy, their movements formalized almost as a dance or ritual, their moving forms as pale and silent as moths. Tom, in white shirt and trousers, rises from the table and crosses toward the fire escape.

AMANDA [*as he passes her*]: Son, will you do me a favor?

TOM: What?

AMANDA: Comb your hair! You look so pretty when your hair is combed!

[*Tom slouches on the sofa with the evening paper. Its enormous headline reads: "Franco Triumphs."*]

There is only one respect in which I would like you to emulate your father.

TOM: What respect is that?

AMANDA: The care he always took of his appearance. He never allowed himself to look untidy.

[*He throws down the paper and crosses to the fire escape.*]

Where are you going?

TOM: I'm going out to smoke.

AMANDA: You smoke too much. A pack a day at fifteen cents a pack. How much would that amount to in a month?

36

Thirty times fifteen is how much, Tom? Figure it out and you will be astounded at what you could save. Enough to give you a night-school course in accounting at Washington U.! Just think what a wonderful thing that would be for you, son!

[*Tom is unmoved by the thought.*]

TOM: I'd rather smoke. [*He steps out on the landing, letting the screen door slam.*]

AMANDA [*sharply*]: I know! That's the tragedy of it. . . . [*Alone, she turns to look at her husband's picture.*]

[*Dance music: "The World Is Waiting for the Sunrise!"*]

TOM [*to the audience*]: Across the alley from us was the Paradise Dance Hall. On evenings in spring the windows and doors were open and the music came outdoors. Sometimes the lights were turned out except for a large glass sphere that hung from the ceiling. It would turn slowly about and filter the dusk with delicate rainbow colors. Then the orchestra played a waltz or a tango, something that had a slow and sensuous rhythm. Couples would come outside, to the relative privacy of the alley. You could see them kissing behind ash pits and telephone poles. This was the compensation for lives that passed like mine, without any change or adventure. Adventure and change were imminent in this year. They were waiting around the corner for all these kids. Suspended in the mist over Berchtesgaden, caught in the folds of Chamberlain's umbrella. In Spain there was Guernica! But here there was only hot swing music and liquor, dance halls, bars, and movies, and sex that hung in the gloom like a chandelier and flooded the world with brief, deceptive rainbows. . . . All the world was waiting for bombardments!

[*Amanda turns from the picture and comes outside.*]

37

AMANDA [*sighing*]: A fire escape landing's a poor excuse for a porch. [*She spreads a newspaper on a step and sits down, gracefully and demurely as if she were settling into a swing on a Mississippi veranda.*] What are you looking at?

TOM: The moon.

AMANDA: Is there a moon this evening?

TOM: It's rising over Garfinkel's Delicatessen.

AMANDA: So it is! A little silver slipper of a moon. Have you made a wish on it yet?

TOM: Um-hum.

AMANDA: What did you wish for?

TOM: That's a secret.

AMANDA: A secret, huh? Well, I won't tell mine either. I will be just as mysterious as you.

TOM: I bet I can guess what yours is.

AMANDA: Is my head so transparent?

TOM: You're not a sphinx.

AMANDA: No, I don't have secrets. I'll tell you what I wished for on the moon. Success and happiness for my precious children! I wish for that whenever there's a moon, and when there isn't a moon, I wish for it, too.

TOM: I thought perhaps you wished for a gentleman caller.

AMANDA: Why do you say that?

TOM: Don't you remember asking me to fetch one?

AMANDA: I remember suggesting that it would be nice for your sister if you brought home some nice young man from the warehouse. I think that I've made that suggestion more than once.

TOM: Yes, you have made it repeatedly.

AMANDA: Well?

TOM: We are going to have one.

AMANDA: *What?*

TOM: A gentleman caller!

[*The annunciation is celebrated with music.*]

[*Amanda rises.*]

[*Image on screen*: A caller with a bouquet.]

AMANDA: You mean you have asked some nice young man to come over?

TOM: Yep. I've asked him to dinner.

AMANDA: You really did?

TOM: I did!

AMANDA: You did, and did he—*accept?*

TOM: He did!

AMANDA: Well, well—well, well! That's—lovely!

TOM: I thought that you would be pleased.

AMANDA: It's definite then?

TOM: Very definite.

AMANDA: Soon?

TOM: Very soon.

39

AMANDA: For heaven's sake, stop putting on and tell me some things, will you?

TOM: What things do you want me to tell you?

AMANDA: *Naturally* I would like to know when he's *coming!*

TOM: He's coming tomorrow.

AMANDA: *Tomorrow?*

TOM: Yep. Tomorrow.

AMANDA: But, Tom!

TOM: Yes, Mother?

AMANDA: Tomorrow gives me no time!

TOM: Time for what?

AMANDA: Preparations! Why didn't you phone me at once, as soon as you asked him, the minute that he accepted? Then, don't you see, I could have been getting ready!

TOM: You don't have to make any fuss.

AMANDA: Oh, Tom, Tom, Tom, of course I have to make a fuss! I want things nice, not sloppy! Not thrown together. I'll certainly have to do some fast thinking, won't I?

TOM: I don't see why you have to think at all.

AMANDA: You just don't know. We can't have a gentleman caller in a pigsty! All my wedding silver has to be polished, the monogrammed table linen ought to be laundered! The windows have to be washed and fresh curtains put up. And how about clothes? We have to *wear* something, don't we?

TOM: Mother, this boy is no one to make a fuss over!

AMANDA: Do you realize he's the first young man we've introduced to your sister? It's terrible, dreadful, disgraceful that poor little sister has never received a single gentleman caller! Tom, come inside! [*She opens the screen door.*]

TOM: What for?

AMANDA: I want to ask you some things.

TOM: If you're going to make such a fuss, I'll call it off, I'll tell him not to come!

AMANDA: You certainly won't do anything of the kind. Nothing offends people worse than broken engagements. It simply means I'll have to work like a Turk! We won't be brilliant, but we will pass inspection. Come on inside.

[*Tom follows her inside, groaning.*]

Sit down.

TOM: Any particular place you would like me to sit?

AMANDA: Thank heavens I've got that new sofa! I'm also making payments on a floor lamp I'll have sent out! And put the chintz covers on, they'll brighten things up! Of course I'd hoped to have these walls re-papered. . . . What is the young man's name?

TOM: His name is O'Connor.

AMANDA: That, of course, means fish—tomorrow is Friday! I'll have that salmon loaf—with Durkee's dressing! What does he do? He works at the warehouse?

TOM: Of course! How else would I—

AMANDA: Tom, he—doesn't drink?

TOM: Why do you ask me that?

41

AMANDA: Your father *did!*

TOM: Don't get started on that!

AMANDA: He *does* drink, then?

TOM: Not that I know of!

AMANDA: Make sure, be certain! The last thing I want for my daughter's a boy who drinks!

TOM: Aren't you being a little bit premature? Mr. O'Connor has not yet appeared on the scene!

AMANDA: But will tomorrow. To meet your sister, and what do I know about his character? Nothing! Old maids are better off than wives of drunkards!

TOM: Oh, my God!

AMANDA: Be still!

TOM [*leaning forward to whisper*]: Lots of fellows meet girls whom they don't marry!

AMANDA: Oh, talk sensibly, Tom—and don't be sarcastic! [*She has gotten a hairbrush.*]

TOM: What are you doing?

AMANDA: I'm brushing that cowlick down! [*She attacks his hair with the brush.*] What is this young man's position at the warehouse?

TOM [*submitting grimly to the brush and the interrogation*]: This young man's position is that of a shipping clerk, Mother.

AMANDA: Sounds to me like a fairly responsible job, the sort of a job *you* would be in if you just had more *get-up*. What is his salary? Have you any idea?

TOM: I would judge it to be approximately eighty-five dollars a month.

AMANDA: Well—not princely, but—

TOM: Twenty more than I make.

AMANDA: Yes, how well I know! But for a family man, eighty-five dollars a month is not much more than you can just get by on. . . .

TOM: Yes, but Mr. O'Connor is not a family man.

AMANDA: He might be, mightn't he? Some time in the future?

TOM: I see. Plans and provisions.

AMANDA: You are the only young man that I know of who ignores the fact that the future becomes the present, the present the past, and the past turns into everlasting regret if you don't plan for it!

TOM: I will think that over and see what I can make of it.

AMANDA: Don't be supercilious with your mother! Tell me some more about this—what do you call him?

TOM: James D. O'Connor. The D. is for Delaney.

AMANDA: Irish on *both* sides! *Gracious!* And doesn't drink?

TOM: Shall I call him up and ask him right this minute?

AMANDA: The only way to find out about those things is to make discreet inquiries at the proper moment. When I was a girl in Blue Mountain and it was suspected that a young man drank, the girl whose attentions he had been receiving, if any girl *was,* would sometimes speak to the minister of his

43

church, or rather her father would if her father was living, and sort of feel him out on the young man's character. That is the way such things are discreetly handled to keep a young woman from making a tragic mistake!

TOM: Then how did you happen to make a tragic mistake?

AMANDA: That innocent look of your father's had everyone fooled! He *smiled*—the world was *enchanted!* No girl can do worse than put herself at the mercy of a handsome appearance! I hope that Mr. O'Connor is not too good-looking.

TOM: No, he's not too good-looking. He's covered with freckles and hasn't too much of a nose.

AMANDA: He's not right-down homely, though?

TOM: Not right-down homely. Just medium homely, I'd say.

AMANDA: Character's what to look for in a man.

TOM: That's what I've always said, Mother.

AMANDA: You've never said anything of the kind and I suspect you would never give it a thought.

TOM: Don't be so suspicious of me.

AMANDA: At least I hope he's the type that's up and coming.

TOM: I think he really goes in for self-improvement.

AMANDA: What reason have you to think so?

TOM: He goes to night school.

AMANDA [*beaming*]: Splendid! What does he do, I mean study?

TOM: Radio engineering and public speaking!

44

AMANDA: Then he has visions of being advanced in the world! Any young man who studies public speaking is aiming to have an executive job some day! And radio engineering? A thing for the future! Both of these facts are very illuminating. Those are the sort of things that a mother should know concerning any young man who comes to call on her daughter. Seriously or—not.

TOM: One little warning. He doesn't know about Laura. I didn't let on that we had dark ulterior motives. I just said, why don't you come and have dinner with us? He said okay and that was the whole conversation.

AMANDA: I bet it was! You're eloquent as an oyster. However, he'll know about Laura when he gets here. When he sees how lovely and sweet and pretty she is, he'll thank his lucky stars he was asked to dinner.

TOM: Mother, you mustn't expect too much of Laura.

AMANDA: What do you mean?

TOM: Laura seems all those things to you and me because she's ours and we love her. We don't even notice she's crippled any more.

AMANDA: Don't say crippled! You know that I never allow that word to be used!

TOM: But face facts, Mother. She is and—that's not all—

AMANDA: What do you mean "not all"?

TOM: Laura is very different from other girls.

AMANDA: I think the difference is all to her advantage.

TOM: Not quite all—in the eyes of others—strangers— she's terribly shy and lives in a world of her own and those

45

things make her seem a little peculiar to people outside the house.

AMANDA: Don't say peculiar.

TOM: Face the facts. She is.

[*The dance hall music changes to a tango that has a minor and somewhat ominous tone.*]

AMANDA: In what way is she peculiar—may I ask?

TOM [*gently*]: She lives in a world of her own—a world of little glass ornaments, Mother. . . .

[*He gets up. Amanda remains holding the brush, looking at him, troubled.*]

She plays old phonograph records and—that's about all— [*He glances at himself in the mirror and crosses to the door.*]

AMANDA [*sharply*]: Where are you going?

TOM: I'm going to the movies. [*He goes out the screen door.*]

AMANDA: Not to the movies, every night to the movies! [*She follows quickly to the screen door.*] I don't believe you always go to the movies!

[*He is gone. Amanda looks worriedly after him for a moment. Then vitality and optimism return and she turns from the door, crossing to the portieres.*]

Laura! Laura!

[*Laura answers from the kitchenette.*]

LAURA: Yes, Mother.

AMANDA: Let those dishes go and come in front!

46

[*Laura appears with a dish towel. Amanda speaks to her gaily.*]

Laura, come here and make a wish on the moon!

[*Screen image*: The Moon.]

LAURA [*entering*]: Moon—moon?

AMANDA: A little silver slipper of a moon. Look over your left shoulder, Laura, and make a wish!

[*Laura looks faintly puzzled as if called out of sleep. Amanda seizes her shoulders and turns her at an angle by the door.*]

Now! Now, darling, *wish!*

LAURA: What shall I wish for, Mother?

AMANDA [*her voice trembling and her eyes suddenly filling with tears*]: Happiness! Good fortune!

[*The sound of the violin rises and the stage dims out.*]

SCENE SIX

The light comes up on the fire escape landing. Tom is leaning against the grill, smoking.

[*Screen image*: The high school hero.]

TOM: And so the following evening I brought Jim home to dinner. I had known Jim slightly in high school. In high school Jim was a hero. He had tremendous Irish good nature and vitality with the scrubbed and polished look of white chinaware. He seemed to move in a continual spotlight. He was a star in basketball, captain of the debating club, president of the senior class and the glee club and he sang the male lead in the annual light operas. He was always running or bounding, never just walking. He seemed always at the point of defeating the law of gravity. He was shooting with such velocity through his adolescence that you would logically expect him to arrive at nothing short of the White House by the time he was thirty. But Jim apparently ran into more interference after his graduation from Soldan. His speed had definitely slowed. Six years after he left high school he was holding a job that wasn't much better than mine.

[*Screen image*: The Clerk.]

He was the only one at the warehouse with whom I was on friendly terms. I was valuable to him as someone who could remember his former glory, who had seen him win basketball games and the silver cup in debating. He knew of my secret practice of retiring to a cabinet of the washroom to work on poems when business was slack in the warehouse. He called me Shakespeare. And while the other boys in the warehouse regarded me with suspicious hostility, Jim took a humorous attitude toward me. Gradually his attitude affected the others, their hostility wore off and they also began to smile at me as

48

people smile at an oddly fashioned dog who trots across their path at some distance.

I knew that Jim and Laura had known each other at Soldan, and I had heard Laura speak admiringly of his voice. I didn't know if Jim remembered her or not. In high school Laura had been as unobtrusive as Jim had been astonishing. If he did remember Laura, it was not as my sister, for when I asked him to dinner, he grinned and said, "You know, Shakespeare, I never thought of you as having folks!"

He was about to discover that I did. . . .

[*Legend on screen*: "The accent of a coming foot."]

[*The light dims out on Tom and comes up in the Wingfield living room—a delicate lemony light. It is about five on a Friday evening of late spring which comes "scattering poems in the sky."*]

[*Amanda has worked like a Turk in preparation for the gentleman caller. The results are astonishing. The new floor lamp with its rose silk shade is in place, a colored paper lantern conceals the broken light fixture in the ceiling, new billowing white curtains are at the windows, chintz covers are on the chairs and sofa, a pair of new sofa pillows make their initial appearance. Open boxes and tissue paper are scattered on the floor.*]

[*Laura stands in the middle of the room with lifted arms while Amanda crouches before her, adjusting the hem of a new dress, devout and ritualistic. The dress is colored and designed by memory. The arrangement of Laura's hair is changed; it is softer and more becoming. A fragile, unearthly prettiness has come out in Laura: she is like a piece of translucent glass touched by light, given a momentary radiance, not actual, not lasting.*]

AMANDA [*impatiently*]: Why are you trembling?

49

LAURA: Mother, you've made me so nervous!

AMANDA: How have I made you nervous?

LAURA: By all this fuss! You make it seem so important!

AMANDA: I don't understand you, Laura. You couldn't be satisfied with just sitting home, and yet whenever I try to arrange something for you, you seem to resist it. [*She gets up.*] Now take a look at yourself. No, wait! Wait just a moment—I have an idea!

LAURA: What is it now?

[*Amanda produces two powder puffs which she wraps in handkerchiefs and stuffs in Laura's bosom.*]

LAURA: Mother, what are you doing?

AMANDA: They call them "Gay Deceivers"!

LAURA: I won't wear them!

AMANDA: You will!

LAURA: Why should I?

AMANDA: Because, to be painfully honest, your chest is flat.

LAURA: You make it seem like we were setting a trap.

AMANDA: All pretty girls are a trap, a pretty trap, and men expect them to be.

[*Legend on screen*: "A pretty trap."]

Now look at yourself, young lady. This is the prettiest you will ever be! [*She stands back to admire Laura.*] I've got to fix myself now! You're going to be surprised by your mother's appearance!

[*Amanda crosses through the portieres, humming gaily. Laura moves slowly to the long mirror and stares solemnly at herself. A wind blows the white curtains inward in a slow, graceful motion and with a faint, sorrowful sighing.*]

AMANDA [*from somewhere behind the portieres*]: It isn't dark enough yet.

[*Laura turns slowly before the mirror with a troubled look.*]

[*Legend on screen*: "This is my sister: Celebrate her with strings!" *Music plays.*]

AMANDA [*laughing, still not visible*]: I'm going to show you something. I'm going to make a spectacular appearance!

LAURA: What is it, Mother?

AMANDA: Possess your soul in patience—you will see! Something I've resurrected from that old trunk! Styles haven't changed so terribly much after all. . . . [*She parts the portieres.*] Now just look at your mother! [*She wears a girlish frock of yellowed voile with a blue silk sash. She carries a bunch of jonquils—the legend of her youth is nearly revived. Now she speaks feverishly:*] This is the dress in which I led the cotillion. Won the cakewalk twice at Sunset Hill, wore one Spring to the Governor's Ball in Jackson! See how I sashayed around the ballroom, Laura? [*She raises her skirt and does a mincing step around the room.*] I wore it on Sundays for my gentlemen callers! I had it on the day I met your father. . . . I had malaria fever all that Spring. The change of climate from East Tennessee to the Delta—weakened resistance. I had a little temperature all the time—not enough to be serious—just enough to make me restless and giddy! Invitations poured in—parties all over the Delta! "Stay in bed," said Mother, "you have a fever!"—but I just wouldn't. I took quinine but kept on going, going! Evenings, dances!

51

Afternoons, long, long rides! Picnics—lovely! So lovely, that country in May—all lacy with dogwood, literally flooded with jonquils! That was the spring I had the craze for jonquils. Jonquils became an absolute obsession. Mother said, "Honey, there's no more room for jonquils." And still I kept on bringing in more jonquils. Whenever, wherever I saw them, I'd say, "Stop! Stop! I see jonquils!" I made the young men help me gather the jonquils! It was a joke, Amanda and her jonquils. Finally there were no more vases to hold them, every available space was filled with jonquils. No vases to hold them? All right, I'll hold them myself! And then I—[*She stops in front of the picture. Music plays.*] met your father! Malaria fever and jonquils and then—this—boy. . . . [*She switches on the rose-colored lamp.*] I hope they get here before it starts to rain. [*She crosses the room and places the jonquils in a bowl on the table.*] I gave your brother a little extra change so he and Mr. O'Connor could take the service car home.

LAURA [*with an altered look*]: What did you say his name was?

AMANDA: O'Connor.

LAURA: What is his first name?

AMANDA: I don't remember. Oh, yes, I do. It was—Jim!

[*Laura sways slightly and catches hold of a chair.*]

[*Legend on screen*: "Not Jim!"]

LAURA [*faintly*]: Not—Jim!

AMANDA: Yes, that was it, it was Jim! I've never known a Jim that wasn't nice!

[*The music becomes ominous.*]

52

LAURA: Are you sure his name is Jim O'Connor?

AMANDA: Yes. Why?

LAURA: Is he the one that Tom used to know in high school?

AMANDA: He didn't say so. I think he just got to know him at the warehouse.

LAURA: There was a Jim O'Connor we both knew in high school—[*then, with effort*] If that is the one that Tom is bringing to dinner—you'll have to excuse me, I won't come to the table.

AMANDA: What sort of nonsense is this?

LAURA: You asked me once if I'd ever liked a boy. Don't you remember I showed you this boy's picture?

AMANDA: You mean the boy you showed me in the year-book?

LAURA: Yes, that boy.

AMANDA: Laura, Laura, were you in love with that boy?

LAURA: I don't know, Mother. All I know is I couldn't sit at the table if it was him!

AMANDA: It won't be him! It isn't the least bit likely. But whether it is or not, you will come to the table. You will not be excused.

LAURA: I'll have to be, Mother.

AMANDA: I don't intend to humor your silliness, Laura. I've had too much from you and your brother, both! So just sit down and compose yourself till they come. Tom has forgotten his key so you'll have to let them in, when they arrive.

LAURA [*panicky*]: Oh, Mother—*you* answer the door!

AMANDA [*lightly*]: I'll be in the kitchen—busy!

LAURA: Oh, Mother, please answer the door, don't make me do it!

AMANDA [*crossing into the kitchenette*]: I've got to fix the dressing for the salmon. Fuss, fuss—silliness!—over a gentleman caller!

[*The door swings shut. Laura is left alone.*]

[*Legend on screen: "Terror!"*]

[*She utters a low moan and turns off the lamp—sits stiffly on the edge of the sofa, knotting her fingers together.*]

[*Legend on screen: "The Opening of a Door!"*]

[*Tom and Jim appear on the fire escape steps and climb to the landing. Hearing their approach, Laura rises with a panicky gesture. She retreats to the portieres. The doorbell rings. Laura catches her breath and touches her throat. Low drums sound.*]

AMANDA [*calling*]: Laura, sweetheart! The door!

[*Laura stares at it without moving.*]

JIM: I think we just beat the rain.

TOM: Uh-huh. [*He rings again, nervously. Jim whistles and fishes for a cigarette.*]

AMANDA [*very, very gaily*]: Laura, that is your brother and Mr. O'Connor! Will you let them in, darling?

[*Laura crosses toward the kitchenette door.*]

LAURA [*breathlessly*]: Mother—you go to the door!

54

Amanda steps out of the kitchenette and stares furiously at Laura. She points imperiously at the door.]

LAURA: Please, please!

AMANDA [*in a fierce whisper*]: What is the matter with you, you silly thing?

LAURA [*desperately*]: Please, you answer it, *please!*

AMANDA: I told you I wasn't going to humor you, Laura. Why have you chosen this moment to lose your mind?

LAURA: Please, please, please, you go!

AMANDA: You'll have to go to the door because I can't!

LAURA [*despairingly*]: I can't either!

AMANDA: *Why?*

LAURA: I'm *sick!*

AMANDA: I'm sick, too—of your nonsense! Why can't you and your brother be normal people? Fantastic whims and behavior!

[*Tom gives a long ring.*]

Preposterous goings on! Can you give me one reason— [*She calls out lyrically.*] Coming! Just one second!—why you should be afraid to open a door? Now you answer it, Laura!

LAURA: Oh, oh, oh . . . [*She returns through the portieres, darts to the Victrola, winds it frantically and turns it on.*]

AMANDA: Laura Wingfield, you march right to that door!

LAURA: *Yes—yes, Mother!*

[*A faraway, scratchy rendition of "Dardanella" softens the air and gives her strength to move through it. She slips to*

55

the door and draws it cautiously open. Tom enters with the caller, Jim O'Connor.]

TOM: Laura, this is Jim. Jim, this is my sister, Laura.

JIM [*stepping inside*]: I didn't know that Shakespeare had a sister!

LAURA [*retreating, stiff and trembling, from the door*]: How—how do you do?

JIM [*heartily, extending his hand*]: Okay!

[*Laura touches it hesitantly with hers.*]

JIM: Your hand's *cold*, Laura!

LAURA: Yes, well—I've been playing the Victrola. . . .

JIM: Must have been playing classical music on it! You ought to play a little hot swing music to warm you up!

LAURA: Excuse me—I haven't finished playing the Victrola. . . . [*She turns awkwardly and hurries into the front room. She pauses a second by the Victrola. Then she catches her breath and darts through the portieres like a frightened deer.*]

JIM [*grinning*]: What was the matter?

TOM: Oh—with Laura? Laura is—terribly shy.

JIM: Shy, huh? It's unusual to meet a shy girl nowadays. I don't believe you ever mentioned you had a sister.

TOM: Well, now you know. I have one. Here is the *Post Dispatch*. You want a piece of it?

JIM: Uh-huh.

TOM: What piece? The comics?

JIM: Sports! [*He glances at it.*] Ole Dizzy Dean is on his bad behavior.

TOM [*uninterested*]: Yeah? [*He lights a cigarette and goes over to the fire-escape door.*]

JIM: Where are *you* going?

TOM: I'm going out on the terrace.

JIM [*going after him*]: You know, Shakespeare—I'm going to sell you a bill of goods!

TOM: What goods?

JIM: A course I'm taking.

TOM: Huh?

JIM: In public speaking! You and me, we're not the warehouse type.

TOM: Thanks—that's good news. But what has public speaking got to do with it?

JIM: It fits you for—executive positions!

TOM: Awww.

JIM: I tell you it's done a helluva lot for me.

[*Image on screen*: Executive at his desk.]

TOM: In what respect?

JIM: In every! Ask yourself what is the difference between you an' me and men in the office down front? Brains?—No! —Ability?—No! Then what? Just one little thing—

TOM: What is that one little thing?

JIM: Primarily it amounts to—social poise! Being able to square up to people and hold your own on any social level!

AMANDA [*from the kitchenette*]:Tom?

TOM: Yes, Mother?

AMANDA: Is that you and Mr. O'Connor?

TOM: Yes, Mother.

AMANDA: Well, you just make yourselves comfortable in there.

TOM: Yes, Mother.

AMANDA: Ask Mr. O'Connor if he would like to wash his hands.

JIM: Aw, no—no—thank you—I took care of that at the warehouse. Tom—

TOM: Yes?

JIM: Mr. Mendoza was speaking to me about you.

TOM: Favorably?

JIM: What do you think?

TOM: Well—

JIM: You're going to be out of a job if you don't wake up.

TOM: I am waking up—

JIM: You show no signs.

TOM: The signs are interior.

[*Image on screen*: The sailing vessel with the Jolly Roger again.]

TOM: I'm planning to change. [*He leans over the fire-escape rail, speaking with quiet exhilaration. The incandescent marquees and signs of the first-run movie houses light his face from across the alley. He looks like a voyager.*] I'm right at the point of committing myself to a future that doesn't include the warehou ᵽ and Mr. Mendoza or even a night-school course in public speaking.

JIM: What are you gassing about?

TOM: I'm tired of the movies.

JIM: Movies!

TOM: Yes, movies! Look at them— [*a wave toward the marvels of Grand Avenue*] All of those glamorous people— having adventures—hogging it all, gobbling the whole thing up! You know what happens? People go to the *movies* instead of *moving!* Hollywood characters are supposed to have all the adventures for everybody in America, while everybody in America sits in a dark room and watches them have them! Yes, until there's a war. That's when adventure becomes available to the masses! *Everyone's* dish, not only Gable's! Then the people in the dark room come out of the dark room to have some adventures themselves—goody, goody! It's our turn now, to go to the South Sea Island—to make a safari— to be exotic, far-off! But I'm not patient. I don't want to wait till then. I'm tired of the *movies* and I am *about* to *move!*

JIM [*incredulously*]: Move?

TOM: Yes.

JIM: When?

TOM: Soon!

JIM: Where? Where?

[*The music seems to answer the question, while Tom thinks it over. He searches in his pockets.*]

TOM: I'm starting to boil inside. I know I seem dreamy, but inside—well, I'm boiling! Whenever I pick up a shoe, I shudder a little thinking how short life is and what I am doing! Whatever that means, I know it doesn't mean shoes —except as something to wear on a traveler's feet! [*He finds what he has been searching for in his pockets and holds out a paper to Jim.*] Look—

JIM: What?

TOM: I'm a member.

JIM [*reading*]: The Union of Merchant Seamen.

TOM: I paid my dues this month, instead of the light bill.

JIM: You will regret it when they turn the lights off.

TOM: I won't be here.

JIM: How about your mother?

TOM: I'm like my father. The bastard son of a bastard! Did you notice how he's grinning in his picture in there? And he's been absent going on sixteen years!

JIM: You're just talking, you drip. How does your mother feel about it?

TOM: Shhh! Here comes Mother! Mother is not acquainted with my plans!

AMANDA [*coming through the portieres*]: Where are you all?

TOM: On the terrace, Mother.

[*They start inside. She advances to them. Tom is distinctly shocked at her appearance. Even Jim blinks a little. He is making his first contact with girlish Southern vivacity and in spite of the night-school course in public speaking is*

60

*somewhat thrown off the beam by the unexpected outlay of
social charm. Certain responses are attempted by Jim but
are swept aside by Amanda's gay laughter and chatter. Tom
is embarrassed but after the first shock Jim reacts very
warmly. He grins and chuckles, is altogether won over.*]

[*Image on screen*: Amanda as a girl.]

AMANDA [*coyly smiling, shaking her girlish ringlets*]:
Well, well, well, so this is Mr. O'Connor. Introductions entirely unnecessary. I've heard so much about you from my
boy. I finally said to him, Tom—good gracious!—why don't
you bring this paragon to supper? I'd like to meet this nice
young man at the warehouse!—instead of just hearing him
sing your praises so much! I don't know why my son is so
stand-offish—that's not Southern behavior!

Let's sit down and—I think we could stand a little more
air in here! Tom, leave the door open. I felt a nice fresh
breeze a moment ago. Where has it gone to? Mmm, so warm
already! And not quite summer, even. We're going to burn
up when summer really gets started. However, we're having—
we're having a very light supper. I think light things are
better fo' this time of year. The same as light clothes are. Light
clothes an' light food are what warm weather calls fo'. You
know our blood gets so thick during th' winter—it takes a
while fo' us to *adjust* ou'selves!—when the season changes . . .
It's come so quick this year. I wasn't prepared. All of a sudden
—heavens! Already summer! I ran to the trunk an' pulled
out this light dress—terribly old! Historical almost! But feels
so good—so good an' co-ol, y' know. . . .

TOM: Mother—

AMANDA: Yes, honey?

TOM: How about—supper?

AMANDA: Honey, you go ask Sister if supper is ready! You know that Sister is in full charge of supper! Tell her you hungry boys are waiting for it. [*to Jim*] Have you met Laura?

JIM: She—

AMANDA: Let you in? Oh, good, you've met already! It's rare for a girl as sweet an' pretty as Laura to be domestic! But Laura is, thank heavens, not only pretty but also very domestic. I'm not at all. I never was a bit. I never could make a thing but angel-food cake. Well, in the South we had so many servants. Gone, gone, gone. All vestige of gracious living! Gone completely! I wasn't prepared for what the future brought me. All of my gentlemen callers were sons of planters and so of course I assumed that I would be married to one and raise my family on a large piece of land with plenty of servants. But man proposes—and woman accepts the proposal! To vary that old, old saying a little bit—I married no planter! I married a man who worked for the telephone company! That gallantly smiling gentleman over there! [*She points to the picture.*] A telephone man who—fell in love with long-distance! Now he travels and I don't even know where! But what am I going on for about my—tribulations? Tell me yours—I hope you don't have any! Tom?

TOM [*returning*]: Yes, Mother?

AMANDA: Is supper nearly ready?

TOM: It looks to me like supper is on the table.

AMANDA: Let me look— [*She rises prettily and looks through the portieres.*] Oh, lovely! But where is Sister?

TOM: Laura is not feeling well and she says that she thinks she'd better not come to the table.

AMANDA: What? Nonsense! Laura? Oh, Laura!

LAURA [*from the kitchenette, faintly*]: Yes, Mother.

AMANDA: You really must come to the table. We won't be seated until you come to the table! Come in, Mr. O'Connor. You sit over there, and I'll. . . . Laura? Laura Wingfield! You're keeping us waiting, honey! We can't say grace until you come to the table!

[*The kitchenette door is pushed weakly open and Laura comes in. She is obviously quite faint, her lips trembling, her eyes wide and staring. She moves unsteadily toward the table.*]

[*Screen legend*: "Terror!"]

[*Outside a summer storm is coming on abruptly. The white curtains billow inward at the windows and there is a sorrowful murmur from the deep blue dusk.*]

[*Laura suddenly stumbles; she catches at a chair with a faint moan.*]

TOM: Laura!

AMANDA: Laura!

[*There is a clap of thunder.*]

[*Screen legend*: "Ah!"]

[*despairingly*] Why, Laura, you *are* ill, darling! Tom, help your sister into the living room, dear! Sit in the living room, Laura—rest on the sofa. Well! [*to Jim as Tom helps his sister to the sofa in the living room*] Standing over the hot stove made her ill! I told her that it was just too warm this evening, but—

[*Tom comes back to the table.*]

63

Is Laura all right now?

TOM: Yes.

AMANDA: What *is* that? Rain? A nice cool rain has come up! [*She gives Jim a frightened look.*] I think we may—have grace—now . . .

[*Tom looks at her stupidly.*] Tom, honey—you say grace!

TOM: Oh . . . "For these and all thy mercies—"

[*They bow their heads, Amanda stealing a nervous glance at Jim. In the living room Laura, stretched on the sofa, clenches her hand to her lips, to hold back a shuddering sob.*]

God's Holy Name be praised—

[*The scene dims out.*]

SCENE SEVEN

It is half an hour later. Dinner is just being finished in the dining room, Laura is still huddled upon the sofa, her feet drawn under her, her head resting on a pale blue pillow, her eyes wide and mysteriously watchful. The new floor lamp with its shade of rose-colored silk gives a soft, becoming light to her face, bringing out the fragile, unearthly prettiness which usually escapes attention. From outside there is a steady murmur of rain, but it is slackening and soon stops; the air outside becomes pale and luminous as the moon breaks through the clouds. A moment after the curtain rises, the lights in both rooms flicker and go out.

JIM: Hey, there, Mr. Light Bulb!

[*Amanda laughs nervously.*]

[*Legend on screen*: "Suspension of a public service."]

AMANDA: Where was Moses when the lights went out? Ha-ha. Do you know the answer to that one, Mr. O'Connor?

JIM: No, Ma'am, what's the answer?

AMANDA: In the dark!

[*Jim laughs appreciatively.*]

Everybody sit still. I'll light the candles. Isn't it lucky we have them on the table? Where's a match? Which of you gentlemen can provide a match?

JIM: Here.

AMANDA: Thank you, Sir.

JIM: Not at all, Ma'am!

AMANDA [*as she lights the candles*]: I guess the fuse has burnt out. Mr. O'Connor, can you tell a burnt-out fuse? I know I can't and Tom is a total loss when it comes to mechanics.

[*They rise from the table and go into the kitchenette, from where their voices are heard.*]

Oh, be careful you don't bump into something. We don't want our gentleman caller to break his neck. Now wouldn't that be a fine howdy-do?

JIM: Ha-ha! Where is the fuse-box?

AMANDA: Right here next to the stove. Can you see anything?

JIM: Just a minute.

AMANDA: Isn't electricity a mysterious thing? Wasn't it Benjamin Franklin who tied a key to a kite? We live in such a mysterious universe, don't we? Some people say that science clears up all the mysteries for us. In my opinion it only creates more! Have you found it yet?

JIM: No, Ma'am. All these fuses look okay to me.

AMANDA: Tom!

TOM: Yes, Mother?

AMANDA: That light bill I gave you several days ago. The one I told you we got the notices about?

[*Legend on screen*: "Ha!"]

TOM: Oh—yeah.

AMANDA: You didn't neglect to pay it by any chance?

TOM: Why, I—

AMANDA: Didn't! I might have known it!

JIM: Shakespeare probably wrote a poem on that light bill, Mrs. Wingfield.

AMANDA: I might have known better than to trust him with it! There's such a high price for negligence in this world!

JIM: Maybe the poem will win a ten-dollar prize.

AMANDA: We'll just have to spend the remainder of the evening in the nineteenth century, before Mr. Edison made the Mazda lamp!

JIM: Candlelight is my favorite kind of light.

AMANDA: That shows you're romantic! But that's no excuse for Tom. Well, we got through dinner. Very considerate of them to let us get through dinner before they plunged us into everlasting darkness, wasn't it, Mr. O'Connor?

JIM: Ha-ha!

AMANDA: Tom, as a penalty for your carelessness you can help me with the dishes.

JIM: Let me give you a hand.

AMANDA: Indeed you will not!

JIM: I ought to be good for something.

AMANDA: Good for something? [*Her tone is rhapsodic.*] *You?* Why, Mr. O'Connor, nobody, *nobody's* given me this much entertainment in years—as you have!

JIM: Aw, now, Mrs. Wingfield!

AMANDA: I'm not exaggerating, not one bit! But Sister is all by her lonesome. You go keep her company in the parlor! I'll give you this lovely old candelabrum that used to be on the altar at the Church of the Heavenly Rest. It was melted a little out of shape when the church burnt down. Lightning struck it one spring. Gypsy Jones was holding a revival at the time and he intimated that the church was destroyed because the Episcopalians gave card parties.

JIM: Ha-ha.

AMANDA: And how about you coaxing Sister to drink a little wine? I think it would be good for her! Can you carry both at once?

JIM: Sure. I'm Superman!

AMANDA: Now, Thomas, get into this apron!

[*Jim comes into the dining room, carrying the candela-brum, its candles lighted, in one hand and a glass of wine in the other. The door of the kitchenette swings closed on Amanda's gay laughter; the flickering light approaches the portieres. Laura sits up nervously as Jim enters. She can hardly speak from the almost intolerable strain of being alone with a stranger.*]

[*Screen legend*: "I don't suppose you remember me at all!"]

[*At first, before Jim's warmth overcomes her paralyzing shyness, Laura's voice is thin and breathless, as though she had just run up a steep flight of stairs. Jim's attitude is gently humorous. While the incident is apparently unimportant, it is to Laura the climax of her secret life.*]

JIM: Hello there, Laura.

LAURA [*faintly*]: Hello.

[*She clears her throat.*]

JIM: How are you feeling now? Better?

68

LAURA: Yes. Yes, thank you.

JIM: This is for you. A little dandelion wine. [*He extends the glass toward her with extravagant gallantry.*]

LAURA: Thank you.

JIM: Drink it—but don't get drunk!

[*He laughs heartily. Laura takes the glass uncertainly; she laughs shyly.*]

Where shall I set the candles?

LAURA: Oh—oh, anywhere . . .

JIM: How about here on the floor? Any objections?

LAURA: No.

JIM: I'll spread a newspaper under to catch the drippings. I like to sit on the floor. Mind if I do?

LAURA: Oh, no.

JIM: Give me a pillow?

LAURA: What?

JIM: A pillow!

LAURA: Oh . . . [*She hands him one quickly.*]

JIM: How about you? Don't you like to sit on the floor?

LAURA: Oh—yes.

JIM: Why don't you, then?

LAURA: I—will.

JIM: Take a pillow!

69

[*Laura does. She sits on the floor on the other side of the candelabrum. Jim crosses his legs and smiles engagingly at her.*] I can't hardly see you sitting way over there.

LAURA: I can—see you.

JIM: I know, but that's not fair, I'm in the limelight.

[*Laura moves her pillow closer.*]

Good! Now I can see you! Comfortable?

LAURA: Yes.

JIM: So am I. Comfortable as a cow! Will you have some gum?

LAURA: No, thank you.

JIM: I think that I will indulge, with your permission. [*He musingly unwraps a stick of gum and holds it up.*] Think of the fortune made by the guy that invented the first piece of chewing gum. Amazing, huh? The Wrigley Building is one of the sights of Chicago—I saw it when I went up to the Century of Progress. Did you take in the Century of Progress?

LAURA: No, I didn't.

JIM: Well, it was quite a wonderful exposition. What impressed me most was the Hall of Science. Gives you an idea of what the future will be in America, even more wonderful than the present time is! [*There is a pause. Jim smiles at her.*] Your brother tells me you're shy. Is that right, Laura?

LAURA: I—don't know.

JIM: I judge you to be an old-fashioned type of girl. Well, I think that's a pretty good type to be. Hope you don't think I'm being too personal—do you?

LAURA [*hastily, out of embarrassment*]: I believe I *will* take a piece of gum, if you—don't mind. [*clearing her throat*] Mr. O'Connor, have you—kept up with your singing?

JIM: Singing? Me?

LAURA: Yes. I remember what a beautiful voice you had.

JIM: When did you hear me sing?

[*Laura does not answer, and in the long pause which follows a man's voice is heard singing offstage.*]

VOICE:
O blow, ye winds, heigh-ho,
A-roving I will go!
I'm off to my love
With a boxing glove—
Ten thousand miles away!

JIM: You say you've heard me sing?

LAURA: Oh, yes! Yes, very often . . . I—don't suppose— you remember me—at all?

JIM [*smiling doubtfully*]: You know I have an idea I've seen you before. I had that idea soon as you opened the door. It seemed almost like I was about to remember your name. But the name that I started to call you—wasn't a name! And so I stopped myself before I said it.

LAURA: Wasn't it—Blue Roses?

JIM [*springing up, grinning*]: Blue Roses! My gosh, yes— Blue Roses! That's what I had on my tongue when you opened the door! Isn't it funny what tricks your memory plays? I didn't connect you with high school somehow or other. But that's where it was; it was high school. I didn't even know you were Shakespeare's sister! Gosh, I'm sorry.

71

LAURA: I didn't expect you to. You—barely knew me!

JIM: But we did have a speaking acquaintance, huh?

LAURA: Yes, we—spoke to each other.

JIM: When did you recognize me?

LAURA: Oh, right away!

JIM: Soon as I came in the door?

LAURA: When I heard your name I thought it was probably you. I knew that Tom used to know you a little in high school. So when you came in the door—well, then I was—sure.

JIM: Why didn't you *say* something, then?

LAURA [*breathlessly*]: I didn't know what to say, I was —too surprised!

JIM: For goodness' sakes! You know, this sure is funny!

LAURA: Yes! Yes, isn't it, though . . .

JIM: Didn't we have a class in something together?

LAURA: Yes, we did.

JIM: What class was that?

LAURA: It was—singing—chorus!

JIM: Aw!

LAURA: I sat across the aisle from you in the Aud.

JIM: Aw.

LAURA: Mondays, Wednesdays, and Fridays.

JIM: Now I remember—you always came in late.

LAURA: Yes, it was so hard for me, getting upstairs. I had that brace on my leg—it clumped so loud!

JIM: I never heard any clumping.

LAURA [*wincing at the recollection*]: To me it sounded like—thunder!

JIM: Well, well, well, I never even noticed.

LAURA: And everybody was seated before I came in. I had to walk in front of all those people. My seat was in the back row. I had to go clumping all the way up the aisle with everyone watching!

JIM: You shouldn't have been self-conscious.

LAURA: I know, but I was. It was always such a relief when the singing started.

JIM: Aw, yes, I've placed you now! I used to call you Blue Roses. How was it that I got started calling you that?

LAURA: I was out of school a little while with pleurosis. When I came back you asked me what was the matter. I said I had pleurosis—you thought I said *Blue Roses*. That's what you always called me after that!

JIM: I hope you didn't mind.

LAURA: Oh, no—I liked it. You see, I wasn't acquainted with many—people. . . .

JIM: As I remember you sort of stuck by yourself.

LAURA: I—I—never have had much luck at—making friends.

JIM: I don't see why you wouldn't.

LAURA: Well, I—started out badly.

JIM: You mean being—

LAURA: Yes, it sort of—stood between me—

JIM: You shouldn't have let it!

LAURA: I know, but it did, and—

JIM: You were shy with people!

LAURA: I tried not to be but never could—

JIM: Overcome it?

LAURA: No, I—I never could!

JIM: I guess being shy is something you have to work out of kind of gradually.

LAURA [*sorrowfully*]: Yes—I guess it—

JIM: Takes time!

LAURA: Yes—

JIM: People are not so dreadful when you know them. That's what you have to remember! And everybody has problems, not just you, but practically everybody has got some problems. You think of yourself as having the only problems, as being the only one who is disappointed. But just look around you and you will see lots of people as disappointed as you are. For instance, I hoped when I was going to high school that I would be further along at this time, six years later, than I am now. You remember that wonderful write-up I had in *The Torch?*

LAURA: Yes! [*She rises and crosses to the table.*]

JIM: It said I was bound to succeed in anything I went into!

[*Laura returns with the high school yearbook.*]

Holy Jeez! *The Torch!*

[*He accepts it reverently. They smile across the book with mutual wonder. Laura crouches beside him and they begin to turn the pages. Laura's shyness is dissolving in his warmth.*]

LAURA: Here you are in *The Pirates of Penzance!*

JIM [*wistfully*]: I sang the baritone lead in that operetta.

LAURA [*raptly*]: So—*beautifully!*

JIM [*protesting*]: Aw—

LAURA: Yes, yes—beautifully—beautifully!

JIM: You heard me?

LAURA: All three times!

JIM: No!

LAURA: Yes!

JIM: All three performances?

LAURA [*looking down*]: Yes.

JIM: Why?

LAURA: I—wanted to ask you to—autograph my program. [*She takes the program from the back of the yearbook and shows it to him.*]

JIM: Why didn't you ask me to?

LAURA: You were always surrounded by your own friends so much that I never had a chance to.

JIM: You should have just—

75

LAURA: Well, I—thought you might think I was—

JIM: Thought I might think you was—what?

LAURA: Oh—

JIM [*with reflective relish*]: I was beleaguered by females in those days.

LAURA: You were terribly popular!

JIM: Yeah—

LAURA: You had such a—friendly way—

JIM: I was spoiled in high school.

LAURA: Everybody—liked you!

JIM: Including you?

LAURA: I—yes, I—did, too— [*She gently closes the book in her lap.*]

JIM: Well, well, well! Give me that program, Laura.

[*She hands it to him. He signs it with a flourish.*]

There you are—better late than never!

LAURA: Oh, I—what a—surprise!

JIM: My signature isn't worth very much right now. But some day—maybe—it will increase in value! Being disappointed is one thing and being discouraged is something else. I am disappointed but I am not discouraged. I'm twenty-three years old. How old are you?

LAURA: I'll be twenty-four in June.

JIM: That's not old age!

LAURA: No, but—

JIM: You finished high school?

LAURA [*with difficulty*]: I didn't go back.

JIM: You mean you dropped out?

LAURA: I made bad grades in my final examinations. [*She rises and replaces the book and the program on the table. Her voice is strained.*] How is—Emily Meisenbach getting along?

JIM: Oh, that kraut-head!

LAURA: Why do you call her that?

JIM: That's what she was.

LAURA: You're not still—going with her?

JIM: I never see her.

LAURA: It said in the "Personal" section that you were— engaged!

JIM: I know, but I wasn't impressed by that—propaganda!

LAURA: It wasn't—the truth?

JIM: Only in Emily's optimistic opinion!

LAURA: Oh—

[*Legend*: "What have you done since high school?"]

[*Jim lights a cigarette and leans indolently back on his elbows smiling at Laura with a warmth and charm which lights her inwardly with altar candles. She remains by the table, picks up a piece from the glass menagerie collection, and turns it in her hands to cover her tumult.*]

JIM [*after several reflective puffs on his cigarette*]: What have you done since high school?

77

[*She seems not to hear him.*]

Huh?

[*Laura looks up.*]

I said what have you done since high school, Laura?

LAURA: Nothing much.

JIM: You must have been doing something these six long years.

LAURA: Yes.

JIM: Well, then, such as what?

LAURA: I took a business course at business college—

JIM: How did that work out?

LAURA: Well, not very—well—I had to drop out, it gave me—indigestion—

[*Jim laughs gently.*]

JIM: What are you doing now?

LAURA: I don't do anything—much. Oh, please don't think I sit around doing nothing! My glass collection takes up a good deal of time. Glass is something you have to take good care of.

JIM: What did you say—about glass?

LAURA: Collection I said—I have one— [*She clears her throat and turns away again, acutely shy.*]

JIM [*abruptly*]: You know what I judge to be the trouble with you? Inferiority complex! Know what that is? That's what they call it when someone low-rates himself! I understand it because I had it, too. Although my case was not so aggravated as yours seems to be. I had it until I took up public speaking, developed my voice, and learned that I had an aptitude for science. Before that time I never thought of myself as being outstanding in any way whatsoever! Now I've never made a regular study of it, but I have a friend who says I can analyze people better than doctors that make a profession of it. I don't claim that to be necessarily true, but I can sure guess a person's psychology, Laura! [*He takes out his gum.*] Excuse me, Laura. I always take it out when the flavor is gone. I'll use this scrap of paper to wrap it in. I know how it is to get it stuck on a shoe. [*He wraps the gum in paper and puts it in his pocket.*] Yep—that's what I judge to be your principal trouble. A lack of confidence in yourself as a person. You don't have the proper amount of faith in yourself. I'm basing that fact on a number of your remarks and also on certain observations I've made. For instance that clumping you thought was so awful in high school. You say that you even dreaded to walk into class. You see what you did? You dropped out of school, you gave up an education because of a clump, which as far as I know was practically non-existent! A little physical defect is what you have. Hardly noticeable even! Magnified thousands of times by imagination! You know what my strong advice to you is? Think of yourself as *superior* in some way!

LAURA: In what way would I think?

JIM: Why, man alive, Laura! Just look about you a little. What do you see? A world full of common people! All of 'em born and all of 'em going to die! Which of them has one-tenth of your good points! Or mine! Or anyone else's, as far as that goes—gosh! Everybody excels in some one thing. Some in many! [*He unconsciously glances at himself in the mirror.*] All you've got to do is discover in *what!* Take me, for instance. [*He adjusts his tie at the mirror.*] My interest happens to lie

79

in electro-dynamics. I'm taking a course in radio engineering at night school, Laura, on top of a fairly responsible job at the warehouse. I'm taking that course and studying public speaking.

LAURA: Ohhhh.

JIM: Because I believe in the future of television! [*turning his back to her.*] I wish to be ready to go up right along with it. Therefore I'm planning to get in on the ground floor. In fact I've already made the right connections and all that remains is for the industry itself to get under way! Full steam —[*His eyes are starry.*] *Knowledge—Zzzzzp! Money—Zzzzzzp!—Power!* That's the cycle democracy is built on!

[*His attitude is convincingly dynamic. Laura stares at him, even her shyness eclipsed in her absolute wonder. He suddenly grins.*]

I guess you think I think a lot of myself!

LAURA: No—o-o-o, I—

JIM: Now how about you? Isn't there something you take more interest in than anything else?

LAURA: Well, I do—as I said—have my—glass collection—

[*A peal of girlish laughter rings from the kitchenette.*]

JIM: I'm not right sure I know what you're talking about. What kind of glass is it?

LAURA: Little articles of it, they're ornaments mostly! Most of them are little animals made out of glass, the tiniest little animals in the world. Mother calls them a glass menagerie! Here's an example of one, if you'd like to see it! This one is one of the oldest. It's nearly thirteen.

[*Music:* "The Glass Menagerie."]

[*He stretches out his hand.*]

Oh, be careful—if you breathe, it breaks!

JIM: I'd better not take it. I'm pretty clumsy with things.

LAURA: Go on, I trust you with him! [*She places the piece in his palm.*] There now—you're holding him gently! Hold him over the light, he loves the light! You see how the light shines through him?

JIM: It sure does shine!

LAURA: I shouldn't be partial, but he is my favorite one.

JIM: What kind of a thing is this one supposed to be?

LAURA: Haven't you noticed the single horn on his forehead?

JIM: A unicorn, huh?

LAURA: Mmmm-hmmm!

JIM: Unicorns—aren't they extinct in the modern world?

LAURA: I know!

JIM: Poor little fellow, he must feel sort of lonesome.

LAURA [*smiling*]: Well, if he does, he doesn't complain about it. He stays on a shelf with some horses that don't have horns and all of them seem to get along nicely together.

JIM: How do you know?

LAURA [*lightly*]: I haven't heard any arguments among them!

JIM [*grinning*]: No arguments, huh? Well, that's a pretty good sign! Where shall I set him?

81

LAURA: Put him on the table. They all like a change of scenery once in a while!

JIM: Well, well, well, well—[*He places the glass piece on the table, then raises his arms and stretches.*] Look how big my shadow is when I stretch!

LAURA: Oh, oh, yes—it stretches across the ceiling!

JIM [*crossing to the door*]: I think it's stopped raining. [*He opens the fire-escape door and the background music changes to a dance tune.*] Where does the music come from?

LAURA: From the Paradise Dance Hall across the alley.

JIM: How about cutting the rug a little, Miss Wingfield?

LAURA: Oh, I—

JIM: Or is your program filled up? Let me have a look at it. [*He grasps an imaginary card.*] Why, every dance is taken! I'll just have to scratch some out.

[*Waltz music*: "La Golondrina."]

Ahhh, a waltz! [*He executes some sweeping turns by himself, then holds his arms toward Laura.*]

LAURA [*breathlessly*]: I—can't dance!

JIM: There you go, that inferiority stuff!

LAURA: I've never danced in my life!

JIM: Come on, try!

LAURA: Oh, but I'd step on you!

JIM: I'm not made out of glass.

LAURA: How—how—how do we start?

JIM: Just leave it to me. You hold your arms out a little.

LAURA: Like this?

JIM [*taking her in his arms*]: A little bit higher. Right. Now don't tighten up, that's the main thing about it—relax.

LAURA [*laughing breathlessly*]: It's hard not to.

JIM: Okay.

LAURA: I'm afraid you can't budge me.

JIM: What do you bet I can't? [*He swings her into motion.*]

LAURA: Goodness, yes, you can!

JIM: Let yourself go, now, Laura, just let yourself go.

LAURA: I'm—

JIM: Come on!

LAURA:—trying!

JIM: Not so stiff—easy does it!

LAURA: I know but I'm—

JIM: Loosen th' backbone! There now, that's a lot better.

LAURA: Am I?

JIM: Lots, lots better! [*He moves her about the room in a clumsy waltz.*]

LAURA: Oh, my!

JIM: Ha-ha!

LAURA: Oh, my goodness!

JIM: Ha-ha-ha!

[*They suddenly bump into the table, and the glass piece on it falls to the floor. Jim stops the dance.*]

83

What did we hit on?

LAURA: Table.

JIM: Did something fall off it? I think—

LAURA: Yes.

JIM: I hope that it wasn't the little glass horse with the horn!

LAURA: Yes. [*She stoops to pick it up.*]

JIM: Aw, aw, aw. Is it broken?

LAURA: Now it is just like all the other horses.

JIM: It's lost its—

LAURA: Horn! It doesn't matter. Maybe it's a blessing in disguise.

JIM: You'll never forgive me. I bet that that was your favorite piece of glass.

LAURA: I don't have favorites much. It's no tragedy, Freckles. Glass breaks so easily. No matter how careful you are. The traffic jars the shelves and things fall off them.

JIM: Still I'm awfully sorry that I was the cause.

LAURA [*smiling*]: I'll just imagine he had an operation. The horn was removed to make him feel less—freakish!

[*They both laugh.*]

Now he will feel more at home with the other horses, the ones that don't have horns. . . .

JIM: Ha-ha, that's very funny! [*Suddenly he is serious.*] I'm glad to see that you have a sense of humor. You know

—you're—well—very different! Surprisingly different from anyone else I know! [*His voice becomes soft and hesitant with a genuine feeling.*] Do you mind me telling you that?

[*Laura is abashed beyond speech.*]

I mean it in a nice way—

[*Laura nods shyly, looking away.*]

You make me feel sort of—I don't know how to put it! I'm usually pretty good at expressing things, but—this is something that I don't know how to say!

[*Laura touches her throat and clears it—turns the broken unicorn in her hands. His voice becomes softer.*]

Has anyone ever told you that you were pretty?

[*There is a pause, and the music rises slightly. Laura looks up slowly, with wonder, and shakes her head.*]

Well, you are! In a very different way from anyone else. And all the nicer because of the difference, too.

[*His voice becomes low and husky. Laura turns away, nearly faint with the novelty of her emotions.*]

I wish that you were my sister. I'd teach you to have some confidence in yourself. The different people are not like other people, but being different is nothing to be ashamed of. Because other people are not such wonderful people. They're one hundred times one thousand. You're one times one! They walk all over the earth. You just stay here. They're common as—weeds, but—you—well, you're—*Blue Roses!*

[*Image on screen*: Blue Roses.]

[*The music changes.*]

LAURA: But blue is wrong for—roses. . . .

JIM: It's right for you! You're—pretty!

LAURA: In what respect am I pretty?

JIM: In all respects—believe me! Your eyes—your hair—are pretty! [*He catches hold of her hand.*] You think I'm making this up because I'm invited to dinner and have to be nice. Oh, I could do that! I could put on an act for you, Laura, and say lots of things without being very sincere. But this time I am. I'm talking to you sincerely. I happened to notice you had this inferiority complex that keeps you from feeling comfortable with people. Somebody needs to build your confidence up and make you proud instead of shy and turning away and—blushing. Somebody—ought to—*kiss* you, Laura!

[*His hand slips slowly up her arm to her shoulder as the music swells tumultuously. He suddenly turns her about and kisses her on the lips. When he releases her, Laura sinks on the sofa with a bright, dazed look. Jim backs away and fishes in his pocket for a cigarette.*]

[*Legend on screen*: "A souvenir."]

Stumblejohn!

[*He lights the cigarette, avoiding her look. There is a peal of girlish laughter from Amanda in the kitchenette. Laura slowly raises and opens her hand. It still contains the little broken glass animal. She looks at it with a tender, bewildered expression.*]

Stumblejohn! I shouldn't have done that—that was way off the beam. You don't smoke, do you?

[*She looks up, smiling, not hearing the question. He sits beside her rather gingerly. She looks at him speechlessly—*

waiting. He coughs decorously and moves a little farther aside as he considers the situation and senses her feelings, dimly, with perturbation. He speaks gently.]

Would you—care for a—mint?

[She doesn't seem to hear him but her look grows brighter even.]

Peppermint? Life Saver? My pocket's a regular drugstore —wherever I go . . . . [He pops a mint in his mouth. Then he gulps and decides to make a clean breast of it. He speaks slowly and gingerly.] Laura, you know, if I had a sister like you, I'd do the same thing as Tom. I'd bring out fellows and —introduce her to them. The right type of boys—of a type to —appreciate her. Only—well—he made a mistake about me. Maybe I've got no call to be saying this. That may not have been the idea in having me over. But what if it was? There's nothing wrong about that. The only trouble is that in my case—I'm not in a situation to—do the right thing. I can't take down your number and say I'll phone. I can't call up next week and—ask for a date. I thought I had better explain the situation in case you—misunderstood it and—I hurt your feelings. . . .

[There is a pause. Slowly, very slowly, Laura's look changes, her eyes returning slowly from his to the glass figure in her palm. Amanda utters another gay laugh in the kitchenette.]

LAURA [*faintly*]: You—won't—call again?

JIM: No, Laura, I can't. [*He rises from the sofa.*] As I was just explaining, I've—got strings on me. Laura, I've—been going steady! I go out all the time with a girl named Betty. She's a home-girl like you, and Catholic, and Irish, and in a great many ways we—get along fine. I met her last summer on a moonlight boat trip up the river to Alton, on the *Majestic*. Well—right away from the start it was—love!

[*Legend*: Love!]

[*Laura sways slightly forward and grips the arm of the sofa. He fails to notice, now enrapt in his own comfortable being.*]

Being in love has made a new man of me!

[*Leaning stiffly forward, clutching the arm of the sofa, Laura struggles visibly with her storm. But Jim is oblivious; she is a long way off.*]

The power of love is really pretty tremendous! Love is something that—changes the whole world, Laura!

[*The storm abates a little and Laura leans back. He notices her again.*]

It happened that Betty's aunt took sick, she got a wire and had to go to Centralia. So Tom—when he asked me to din- ner—I naturally just accepted the invitation, not knowing that you—that he—that I— [*He stops awkwardly.*] Huh—I'm a stumblejohn!

[*He flops back on the sofa. The holy candles on the altar of Laura's face have been snuffed out. There is a look of almost infinite desolation. Jim glances at her uneasily.*]

I wish that you would—say something.

[*She bites her lip which was trembling and then bravely smiles. She opens her hand again on the broken glass figure. Then she gently takes his hand and raises it level with her own. She carefully places the unicorn in the palm of his hand, then pushes his fingers closed upon it.*]

What are you—doing that for? You want me to have him?
Laura?

[*She nods.*]

What for?

LAURA: A—souvenir . . . .

[*She rises unsteadily and crouches beside the Victrola to
wind it up.*]

[*Legend on screen*: "Things have a way of turning out
so badly!" *Or image*: "Gentleman caller waving goodbye—
gaily."]

[*At this moment Amanda rushes brightly back into the
living room. She bears a pitcher of fruit punch in an old-
fashioned cut-glass pitcher, and a plate of macaroons. The
plate has a gold border and poppies painted on it.*]

AMANDA: Well, well, well! Isn't the air delightful after the
shower? I've made you children a little liquid refreshment.

[*She turns gaily to Jim.*] Jim, do you know that song about
lemonade?

"Lemonade, lemonade
Made in the shade and stirred with a spade—
Good enough for any old maid!"

JIM [*uneasily*]: Ha-ha! No—I never heard it.

AMANDA: Why, Laura! You look so serious!

JIM: We were having a serious conversation.

AMANDA: Good! Now you're better acquainted!

JIM [*uncertainly*]: Ha-ha! Yes.

AMANDA: You modern young people are much more serious-minded than my generation. I was so gay as a girl!

JIM: You haven't changed, Mrs. Wingfield.

AMANDA: Tonight I'm rejuvenated! The gaiety of the occasion, Mr. O'Connor! [*She tosses her head with a peal of laughter, spilling some lemonade.*] Oooo! I'm baptizing myself!

JIM: Here—let me—

AMANDA [*setting the pitcher down*]: There now. I discovered we had some maraschino cherries. I dumped them in, juice and all!

JIM: You shouldn't have gone to that trouble, Mrs. Wingfield.

AMANDA: Trouble, trouble? Why, it was loads of fun! Didn't you hear me cutting up in the kitchen? I bet your ears were burning! I told Tom how outdone with him I was for keeping you to himself so long a time! He should have brought you over much, much sooner! Well, now that you've found your way, I want you to be a very frequent caller! Not just occasional but all the time. Oh, we're going to have a lot of gay times together! I see them coming! Mmm, just breathe that air! So fresh, and the moon's so pretty! I'll skip back out—I know where my place is when young folks are having a—serious conversation!

JIM: Oh, don t go out, Mrs. Wingfield. The fact of the matter is I've got to be going.

AMANDA: Going, now? You're joking! Why, it's only the shank of the evening, Mr. O'Connor!

JIM: Well, you know how it is.

AMANDA: You mean you're a young workingman and have to keep workingmen's hours. We'll let you off early tonight. But only on the condition that next time you stay later. What's the best night for you? Isn't Saturday night the best night for you workingmen?

JIM: I have a couple of time-clocks to punch, Mrs. Wingfield. One at morning, another one at night!

AMANDA: My, but you *are* ambitious! You work at night, too?

JIM: No, Ma'am, not work but—Betty!

[*He crosses deliberately to pick up his hat. The band at the Paradise Dance Hall goes into a tender waltz.*]

AMANDA: Betty? Betty? Who's—Betty!

[*There is an ominous cracking sound in the sky.*]

JIM: Oh, just a girl. The girl I go steady with!

[*He smiles charmingly. The sky falls.*]

[*Legend*: "The Sky Falls."]

AMANDA [*a long-drawn exhalation*]: Ohhhh . . . Is it a serious romance, Mr. O'Connor?

JIM: We're going to be married the second Sunday in June.

AMANDA: Ohhhh—how nice! Tom didn't mention that you were engaged to be married.

JIM: The cat's not out of the bag at the warehouse yet. You know how they are. They call you Romeo and stuff like that. [*He stops at the oval mirror to put on his hat. He carefully shapes the brim and the crown to give a discreetly dashing effect.*] It's been a wonderful evening, Mrs. Wingfield. I guess this is what they mean by Southern hospitality.

91

AMANDA: It really wasn't anything at all.

JIM: I hope it don't seem like I'm rushing off. But I promised Betty I'd pick her up at the Wabash depot, an' by the time I get my jalopy down there her train'll be in. Some women are pretty upset if you keep 'em waiting.

AMANDA: Yes, I know—the tyranny of women! [*She extends her hand.*] Goodbye, Mr. O'Connor. I wish you luck—and happiness—and success! All three of them, and so does Laura! Don't you, Laura?

LAURA: Yes!

JIM [*taking Laura's hand*]: Goodbye, Laura. I'm certainly going to treasure that souvenir. And don't you forget the good advice I gave you. [*He raises his voice to a cheery shout.*] So long, Shakespeare! Thanks again, ladies. Good night!

[*He grins and ducks jauntily out. Still bravely grimacing, Amanda closes the door on the gentleman caller. Then she turns back to the room with a puzzled expression. She and Laura don't dare to face each other. Laura crouches beside the Victrola to wind it.*]

AMANDA [*faintly*]: Things have a way of turning out so badly. I don't believe that I would play the Victrola. Well, well—well! Our gentleman caller was engaged to be married! [*She raises her voice.*] Tom!

TOM [*from the kitchenette*]: Yes, Mother?

AMANDA: Come in here a minute. I want to tell you something awfully funny.

TOM [*entering with a macaroon and a glass of the lemonade*]: Has the gentleman caller gotten away already?

AMANDA: The gentleman caller has made an early departure. What a wonderful joke you played on us!

TOM: How do you mean?

AMANDA: You didn't mention that he was engaged to be married.

TOM: Jim? Engaged?

AMANDA: That's what he just informed us.

TOM: I'll be jiggered! I didn't know about that.

AMANDA: That seems very peculiar.

TOM: What's peculiar about it?

AMANDA: Didn't you call him your best friend down at the warehouse?

TOM: He is, but how did I know?

AMANDA: It seems extremely peculiar that you wouldn't know your best friend was going to be married!

TOM: The warehouse is where I work, not where I know things about people!

AMANDA: You don't know things anywhere! You live in a dream; you manufacture illusions!

[*He crosses to the door.*]

Where are you going?

TOM: I'm going to the movies.

AMANDA: That's right, now that you've had us make such fools of ourselves. The effort, the preparations, all the expense! The new floor lamp, the rug, the clothes for Laura! All for what? To entertain some other girl's fiancé! Go to the

93

movies, go! Don't think about us, a mother deserted, an unmarried sister who's crippled and has no job! Don't let anything interfere with your selfish pleasure! Just go, go, go—to the movies!

TOM: All right, I will! The more you shout about my selfishness to me the quicker I'll go, and I won't go to the movies!

AMANDA: Go, then! Go to the moon—you selfish dreamer!

[*Tom smashes his glass on the floor. He plunges out on the fire escape, slamming the door. Laura screams in fright. The dance-hall music becomes louder. Tom stands on the fire escape, gripping the rail. The moon breaks through the storm clouds, illuminating his face.*]

[*Legend on screen:* "And so goodbye . . ."]

[*Tom's closing speech is timed with what is happening inside the house. We see, as though through soundproof glass, that Amanda appears to be making a comforting speech to Laura, who is huddled upon the sofa. Now that we cannot hear the mother's speech, her silliness is gone and she has dignity and tragic beauty. Laura's hair hides her face until, at the end of the speech, she lifts her head to smile at her mother. Amanda's gestures are slow and graceful, almost dancelike, as she comforts her daughter. At the end of her speech she glances a moment at the father's picture—then withdraws through the portieres. At the close of Tom's speech, Laura blows out the candles, ending the play.*]

TOM: I didn't go to the moon, I went much further—for time is the longest distance between two places. Not long after that I was fired for writing a poem on the lid of a shoe-box. I left Saint Louis. I descended the steps of this fire escape for a last time and followed, from then on, in my father's footsteps, attempting to find in motion what was lost in space. I traveled around a great deal. The cities swept about me like dead leaves, leaves that were brightly colored but torn away from the branches. I would have stopped, but I was pursued by something. It always came upon me unawares, taking me altogether by surprise. Perhaps it was a familiar bit of music. Perhaps it was only a piece of transparent glass. Perhaps I am walking along a street at night, in some strange city, before I have found companions. I pass the lighted window of a shop where perfume is sold. The window is filled with pieces of colored glass, tiny transparent bottles in delicate colors, like bits of a shattered rainbow. Then all at once my sister touches my shoulder. I turn around and look into her eyes. Oh, Laura, Laura, I tried to leave you behind me, but I am more faithful than I intended to be! I reach for a cigarette, I cross the street, I run into the movies or a bar, I buy a drink, I speak to the nearest stranger—anything that can blow your candles out!

[*Laura bends over the candles.*]

For nowadays the world is lit by lightning! Blow out your candles, Laura—and so goodbye. . . .

[*She blows the candles out.*]

A STREETCAR NAMED DESIRE

And so it was I entered the broken world
To trace the visionary company of love, its voice
An instant in the wind (I know not whither hurled)
But not for long to hold each desperate choice.

"The Broken Tower" *by* HART CRANE

A Streetcar Named Desire was presented at the Barrymore Theatre in New York on December 3, 1947, by Irene Selznick. It was directed by Elia Kazan, with the following cast:

Negro Woman	Gee Gee James
Eunice Hubbell	Peg Hillias
Stanley Kowalski	Marlon Brando
Stella Kowalski	Kim Hunter
Steve Hubbell	Rudy Bond
Harold Mitchell (Mitch)	Karl Malden
Mexican Woman	Edna Thomas
Blanche DuBois	Jessica Tandy
Pablo Gonzales	Nick Dennis
A Young Collector	Vito Christi
Nurse	Ann Dere
Doctor	Richard Garrick

Scenery and lighting by Jo Meilziner, costumes by Lucinda Ballard. The action of the play takes place in the spring, summer, and early fall in New Orleans. It was performed with intermissions after Scene Four and Scene Six.

Assistant to the producer	Irving Schneider
Musical Advisor	Lehman Engel

THE CHARACTERS

BLANCHE

STELLA

STANLEY

MITCH

EUNICE

STEVE

PABLO

A NEGRO WOMAN

A DOCTOR

A NURSE

A YOUNG COLLECTOR

A MEXICAN WOMAN

SCENE ONE

The exterior of a two-story corner building on a street in New Orleans which is named Elysian Fields and runs between the L & N tracks and the river. The section is poor but, unlike corresponding sections in other American cities, it has a raffish charm. The houses are mostly white frame, weathered grey, with rickety outside stairs and galleries and quaintly ornamented gables. This building contains two flats, upstairs and down. Faded white stairs ascend to the entrances of both.

It is first dark of an evening early in May. The sky that shows around the dim white building is a peculiarly tender blue, almost a turquoise, which invests the scene with a kind of lyricism and gracefully attenuates the atmosphere of decay. You can almost feel the warm breath of the brown river beyond the river warehouses with their faint redolences of bananas and coffee. A corresponding air is evoked by the music of Negro entertainers at a barroom around the corner. In this part of New Orleans you are practically always just around the corner, or a few doors down the street, from a tinny piano being played with the infatuated fluency of brown fingers. This "blue piano" expresses the spirit of the life which goes on here.

Two women, one white and one colored, are taking the air on the steps of the building. The white woman is Eunice, who occupies the upstairs flat; the colored woman a neighbor, for New Orleans is a cosmopolitan city where there is a relatively warm and easy intermingling of races in the old part of town.

Above the music of the "blue piano" the voices of people on the street can be heard overlapping.

101

[*Two men come around the corner, Stanley Kowalski and Mitch. They are about twenty-eight or thirty years old, roughly dressed in blue denim work clothes. Stanley carries his bowling jacket and a red-stained package from a butcher's. They stop at the foot of the steps.*]

STANLEY [*bellowing*]:
Hey, there! Stella, baby!

[*Stella comes out on the first floor landing, a gentle young woman, about twenty-five, and of a background obviously quite different from her husband's.*]

STELLA [*mildly*]:
Don't holler at me like that. Hi, Mitch.

STANLEY:
Catch!

STELLA:
What?

STANLEY:
Meat!

[*He heaves the package at her. She cries out in protest but manages to catch it: then she laughs breathlessly. Her husband and his companion have already started back around the corner.*]

STELLA [*calling after him*]:
Stanley! Where are you going?

STANLEY:
Bowling!

STELLA:
Can I come watch?

STANLEY:

Come on. [*He goes out.*]

STELLA:

Be over soon. [*to the white woman*] Hello, Eunice. How are you?

EUNICE:

I'm all right. Tell Steve to get him a poor boy's sandwich 'cause nothing's left here.

[*They all laugh; the colored woman does not stop. Stella goes out.*]

COLORED WOMAN:

What was that package he th'ew at 'er? [*She rises from steps, laughing louder.*]

EUNICE:

You hush, now!

NEGRO WOMAN:

Catch *what!*

[*She continues to laugh. Blanche comes around the corner, carrying a valise. She looks at a slip of paper, then at the building, then again at the slip and again at the building. Her expression is one of shocked disbelief. Her appearace is incongruous to this setting. She is daintily dressed in a white suit with a fluffy bodice, necklace and earrings of pearl, white gloves and hat, looking as if she were arriving at a summer tea or cocktail party in the garden district. She is about five years older than Stella. Her delicate beauty must avoid a strong light. There is something about her uncertain manner, as well as her white clothes, that suggests a moth.*]

103

EUNICE [*finally*]:
What's the matter, honey? Are you lost?

BLANCHE [*with faintly hysterical humor*]:
They told me to take a street-car named Desire, and then transfer to one called Cemeteries and ride six blocks and get off at—Elysian Fields!

EUNICE:
That's where you are now.

BLANCHE:
At Elysian Fields?

EUNICE:
This here is Elysian Fields.

BLANCHE:
They mustn't have—understood—what number I wanted ...

EUNICE:
What number you lookin' for?

[*Blanche wearily refers to the slip of paper.*]

BLANCHE:
Six thirty-two.

EUNICE:
You don't have to look no further.

BLANCHE [*uncomprehendingly*]:
I'm looking for my sister, Stella DuBois. I mean—Mrs. Stanley Kowalski.

EUNICE:
That's the party.—You just did miss her, though.

BLANCHE:
This—can this be—her home?

EUNICE:
She's got the downstairs here and I got the up.

BLANCHE:
Oh. She's—out?

EUNICE:
You noticed that bowling alley around the corner?

BLANCHE:
I'm—not sure I did.

EUNICE:
Well, that's where she's at, watchin' her husband bowl. [*There is a pause*] You want to leave your suitcase here an' go find her?

BLANCHE:
No.

NEGRO WOMAN:
I'll go tell her you come.

BLANCHE:
Thanks.

NEGRO WOMAN:
You welcome. [*She goes out.*]

EUNICE:
She wasn't expecting you?

BLANCHE:
No. No, not tonight.

EUNICE:
Well, why don't you just go in and make yourself at home till they get back.

105

BLANCHE:

How could I—do that?

EUNICE:

We own this place so I can let you in.

[*She gets up and opens the downstairs door. A light goes on behind the blind, turning it light blue. Blanche slowly follows her into the downstairs flat. The surrounding areas dim out as the interior is lighted.*]

[*Two rooms can be seen, not too clearly defined. The one first entered is primarily a kitchen but contains a folding bed to be used by Blanche. The room beyond this is a bedroom. Off this room is a narrow door to a bathroom.*]

EUNICE [*defensively, noticing Blanche's look*]:

It's sort of messed up right now but when it's clean it's real sweet.

BLANCHE:

Is it?

EUNICE:

Uh-huh, I think so. So you're Stella's sister?

BLANCHE:

Yes. [*wanting to get rid of her*] Thanks for letting me in.

EUNICE:

Por nada, as the Mexicans say, *por nada!* Stella spoke of you.

BLANCHE:

Yes?

EUNICE:

I think she said you taught school.

BLANCHE:

Yes.

EUNICE:

And you're from Mississippi, huh?

BLANCHE:

Yes.

EUNICE:

She showed me a picture of your home-place, the plantation.

BLANCHE:

Belle Reve?

EUNICE:

A great big place with white columns.

BLANCHE:

Yes...

EUNICE:

A place like that must be awful hard to keep up.

BLANCHE:

If you will excuse me, I'm just about to drop.

EUNICE:

Sure, honey. Why don't you set down?

BLANCHE:

What I meant was I'd like to be left alone.

EUNICE [*offended*]:

Aw. I'll make myself scarce, in that case.

107

BLANCHE:

I didn't mean to be rude, but—

EUNICE:

I'll drop by the bowling alley an' hustle her up. [*She goes out the door.*]

[*Blanche sits in a chair very stiffly with her shoulders slightly hunched and her legs pressed close together and her hands tightly clutching her purse as if she were quite cold. After a while the blind look goes out of her eyes and she begins to look slowly around. A cat screeches. She catches her breath with a startled gesture. Suddenly she notices something in a half opened closet. She springs up and crosses to it, and removes a whiskey bottle. She pours a half tumbler of whiskey and tosses it down. She carefully replaces the bottle and washes out the tumbler at the sink. Then she resumes her seat in front of the table.*]

BLANCHE [*faintly to herself*]:
I've got to keep hold of myself!

[*Stella comes quickly around the corner of the building and runs to the door of the downstairs flat.*]

STELLA [*calling out joyfully*]:
Blanche!

[*For a moment they stare at each other. Then Blanche springs up and runs to her with a wild cry.*]

BLANCHE:

Stella, oh, Stella, Stella! Stella for Star!

[*She begins to speak with feverish vivacity as if she feared for either of them to stop and think. They catch each other in a spasmodic embrace.*]

BLANCHE:

Now, then, let me look at you. But don't you look at me, Stella, no, no, no, not till later, not till I've bathed and rested! And turn that over-light off! Turn that off! I won't be looked at in this merciless glare! [*Stella laughs and complies*] Come back here now! Oh, my baby! Stella! Stella for Star! [*She embraces her again*] I thought you would never come back to this horrible place! What am I saying? I didn't mean to say that. I meant to be nice about it and say—Oh, what a convenient location and such—Ha-a-ha! Precious lamb! You haven't said a *word* to me.

STELLA:

You haven't given me a chance to, honey! [*She laughs, but her glance at Blanche is a little anxious.*]

BLANCHE:

Well, now you talk. Open your pretty mouth and talk while I look around for some liquor! I know you must have some liquor on the place! Where could it be, I wonder? Oh, I spy, I spy!

[*She rushes to the closet and removes the bottle; she is shaking all over and panting for breath as she tries to laugh. The bottle nearly slips from her grasp.*]

STELLA [*noticing*]:

Blanche, you sit down and let me pour the drinks. I don't know what we've got to mix with. Maybe a coke's in the icebox. Look'n see, honey, while I'm—

BLANCHE:

No coke, honey, not with my nerves tonight! Where— where—where is—?

STELLA:

Stanley? Bowling! He loves it. They're having a—found some soda!—tournament...

BLANCHE:

Just water, baby, to chase it! Now don't get worried, your sister hasn't turned into a drunkard, she's just all shaken up and hot and tired and dirty! You sit down, now, and explain this place to me! What are you doing in a place like this?

STELLA:

Now, Blanche—

BLANCHE:

Oh, I'm not going to be hypocritical, I'm going to be honestly critical about it! Never, never, never in my worst dreams could I picture— Only Poe! Only Mr. Edgar Allan Poe!—could do it justice! Out there I suppose is the ghoul-haunted woodland of Weir! [*She laughs.*]

STELLA:

No, honey, those are the L & N tracks.

BLANCHE:

No, now seriously, putting joking aside. Why didn't you tell me, why didn't you write me, honey, why didn't you let me know?

STELLA [*carefully, pouring herself a drink*]:
Tell you what, Blanche?

BLANCHE:

Why, that you had to live in these conditions!

STELLA:

Aren't you being a little intense about it? It's not that bad at all! New Orleans isn't like other cities.

BLANCHE:

This has got nothing to do with New Orleans. You might as well say—forgive me, blessed baby! [*She suddenly stops short*] The subject is closed!

STELLA [*a little drily*]:

Thanks.

[*During the pause, Blanche stares at her. She smiles at Blanche.*]

BLANCHE [*looking down at her glass, which shakes in her hand*]:

You're all I've got in the world, and you're not glad to see me!

STELLA [*sincerely*]:

Why, Blanche, you know that's not true.

BLANCHE:

No?—I'd forgotten how quiet you were.

STELLA:

You never did give me a chance to say much, Blanche. So I just got in the habit of being quiet around you.

BLANCHE [*vaguely*]:

A good habit to get into . . . [*then, abruptly*] You haven't asked me how I happened to get away from the school before the spring term ended.

STELLA:

Well, I thought you'd volunteer that information—if you wanted to tell me.

BLANCHE:

You thought I'd been fired?

STELLA:

No, I—thought you might have—resigned ...

BLANCHE:

I was so exhausted by all I'd been through my—nerves
broke. [*nervously tamping cigarette*] I was on the verge
of—lunacy, almost! So Mr. Graves—Mr. Graves is the
high school superintendent—he suggested I take a leave
of absence. I couldn't put all of those details into the
wire ... [*She drinks quickly*] Oh, this buzzes right
through me and feels so *good!*

STELLA:

Won't you have another?

BLANCHE:

No, one's my limit.

STELLA:

Sure?

BLANCHE:

You haven't said a word about my appearance.

STELLA:

You look just fine.

BLANCHE:

God love you for a liar! Daylight never exposed so total
a ruin! But you—you've put on some weight, yes, you're
just as plump as a little partridge! And it's so becoming
to you!

STELLA:

Now, Blanche—

BLANCHE:

Yes, it is, it is or I wouldn't say it! You just have to watch around the hips a little. Stand up.

STELLA:

Not now.

BLANCHE:

You hear me? I said stand up! [*Stella complies reluctantly*] You messy child, you, you've spilt something on that pretty white lace collar! About your hair—you ought to have it cut in a feather bob with your dainty features. Stella, you have a maid, don't you?

STELLA:

No. With only two rooms it's—

BLANCHE:

What? *Two* rooms, did you say?

STELLA:

This one and—[*She is embarrassed.*]

BLANCHE:

The other one? [*She laughs sharply. There is an embarrassed silence.*]

BLANCHE:

The other one? [*She laughs sharply. There is an embarrassed silence.*] I am going to take just one little tiny nip more, sort of to put the stopper on, so to speak.... Then put the bottle away so I won't be tempted. [*She rises*] I want you to look at *my* figure! [*She turns around*] You know I haven't put on one ounce in ten years, Stella? I weigh what I weighed the summer you left Belle Reve. The summer Dad died and you left us ...

STELLA [*a little wearily*]:

It's just incredible, Blanche, how well you're looking.

113

BLANCHE [*They both laugh uncomfortably*.]:
But, Stella, there's only two rooms, I don't see where
you're going to put me!

STELLA:
We're going to put you in here.

BLANCHE:
What kind of bed's this—one of those collapsible things?
[*She sits on it.*]

STELLA:
Does it feel all right?

BLANCHE [*dubiously*]:
Wonderful, honey. I don't like a bed that gives much.
But there's no door between the two rooms, and Stanley
—will it be decent?

STELLA:
Stanley is Polish, you know.

BLANCHE:
Oh, yes. They're something like Irish, aren't they?

STELLA:
Well—

BLANCHE:
Only not so—highbrow? [*They both laugh again in the
same way*] I brought some nice clothes to meet all your
lovely friends in.

STELLA:
I'm afraid you won't think they are lovely.

BLANCHE:
What are they like?

114

STELLA:

They're Stanley's friends.

BLANCHE:

Polacks?

STELLA:

They're a mixed lot, Blanche.

BLANCHE:

Heterogeneous—types?

STELLA:

Oh, yes. Yes, types is right!

BLANCHE:

Well—anyhow—I brought nice clothes and I'll wear them. I guess you're hoping I'll say I'll put up at a hotel, but I'm not going to put up at a hotel. I want to be *near* you, got to be *with* somebody, I *can't* be *alone!* Because— as you must have noticed—I'm—*not* very *well* ... [*Her voice drops and her look is frightened.*]

STELLA:

You seem a little bit nervous or overwrought or something.

BLANCHE:

Will Stanley like me, or will I be just a visiting in-law, Stella? I couldn't stand that.

STELLA:

You'll get along fine together, if you'll just try not to— well—compare him with men that we went out with at home.

BLANCHE:

Is he so—different?

115

STELLA:

Yes. A different species.

BLANCHE:

In what way; what's he like?

STELLA:

Oh, you can't describe someone you're in love with! Here's a picture of him! [*She hands a photograph to Blanche.*]

BLANCHE:

An officer?

STELLA:

A Master Sergeant in the Engineers' Corps. Those are decorations!

BLANCHE:

He had those on when you met him?

STELLA:

I assure you I wasn't just blinded by all the brass.

BLANCHE:

That's not what I—

STELLA:

But of course there were things to adjust myself to later on.

BLANCHE:

Such as his civilian background! [*Stella laughs uncertainly*] How did he take it when you said I was coming?

STELLA:

Oh, Stanley doesn't know yet.

116

BLANCHE [*frightened*]:
You—haven't told him?

STELLA:
He's on the road a good deal.

BLANCHE:
Oh. Travels?

STELLA:
Yes.

BLANCHE:
Good. I mean—isn't it?

STELLA [*half to herself*]:
I can hardly stand it when he is away for a night...

BLANCHE:
Why, Stella!

STELLA:
When he's away for a week I nearly go wild!

BLANCHE:
Gracious!

STELLA:
And when he comes back I cry on his lap like a baby...
[*She smiles to herself.*]

BLANCHE:
I guess that is what is meant by being in love... [*Stella
looks up with a radiant smile.*] Stella—

STELLA:
What?

BLANCHE [*in an uneasy rush*]:
I haven't asked you the things you probably thought I

117

was going to ask. And so I'll expect you to be understanding about what *I* have to tell *you*.

STELLA:

What, Blanche? [*Her face turns anxious.*]

BLANCHE:

Well, Stella—you're going to reproach me, I know that you're bound to reproach me—but before you do—take into consideration—you left! I stayed and struggled! You came to New Orleans and looked out for yourself! *I* stayed at *Belle Reve* and tried to hold it together! I'm not meaning this in any reproachful way, but *all* the burden descended on *my* shoulders.

STELLA:

The best I could do was make my own living, Blanche. [*Blanche begins to shake again with intensity.*]

BLANCHE:

I know, I know. But you are the one that abandoned Belle Reve, not I! I stayed and fought for it, bled for it, almost died for it!

STELLA:

Stop this hysterical outburst and tell me what's happened? What do you mean fought and bled? What kind of—

BLANCHE:

I knew you would, Stella. I knew you would take this attitude about it!

STELLA:

About—what?—please!

BLANCHE [*slowly*]:
The loss—the loss . . .

STELLA:

Belle Reve? Lost, is it? No!

BLANCHE:

Yes, Stella.

[*They stare at each other across the yellow-checked linoleum of the table. Blanche slowly nods her head and Stella looks slowly down at her hands folded on the table. The music of the "blue piano" grows louder. Blanche touches her handkerchief to her forehead.*]

STELLA:

But how did it go? What happened?

BLANCHE [*springing up*]:

You're a fine one to ask me how it went!

STELLA:

Blanche!

BLANCHE:

You're a fine one to sit there *accusing me* of it!

STELLA:

Blanche!

BLANCHE:

I, I, *I* took the blows in my face and my body! All of those deaths! The long parade to the graveyard! Father, mother! Margaret, that dreadful way! So big with it, it couldn't be put in a coffin! But had to be burned like rubbish! You just came home in time for the funerals, Stella. And funerals are pretty compared to deaths. Funerals are quiet, but deaths—not always. Sometimes their breathing is hoarse, and sometimes it rattles, and sometimes they even cry out to you, "Don't let me go!"

119

Even the old, sometimes, say, "Don't let me go." As if you were able to stop them! But funerals are quiet, with pretty flowers. And, oh, what gorgeous boxes they pack them away in! Unless you were there at the bed when they cried out, "Hold me!" you'd never suspect there was the struggle for breath and bleeding. You didn't dream, but I saw! *Saw! Saw!* And now you sit there telling me with your eyes that I let the place go! How in hell do you think all that sickness and dying was paid for? Death is expensive, Miss Stella! And old Cousin Jessie's right after Margaret's, hers! Why, the Grim Reaper had put up his tent on our doorstep! . . . Stella. Belle Reve was his headquarters! Honey—that's how it slipped through my fingers! Which of them left us a fortune? Which of them left a cent of insurance even? Only poor Jessie—one hundred to pay for her coffin. That was all, Stella! And I with my pitiful salary at the school. Yes, accuse me! Sit there and stare at me, thinking I let the place go! *I* let the place go? Where were *you!* In bed with your—Polack!

STELLA [*springing*]:
Blanche! You be still! That's enough! [*She starts out.*]

BLANCHE:
Where are you going?

STELLA:
I'm going into the bathroom to wash my face.

BLANCHE:
Oh, Stella, Stella, you're crying!

STELLA:
Does that surprise you?

120

BLANCHE:

Forgive me—I didn't mean to—

[*The sound of men's voices is heard. Stella goes into the bathroom, closing the door behind her. When the men appear, and Blanche realizes it must be Stanley return- ing, she moves uncertainly from the bathroom door to the dressing table, looking apprehensively toward the front door. Stanley enters, followed by Steve and Mitch. Stanley pauses near his door, Steve by the foot of the spiral stair, and Mitch is slightly above and to the right of them, about to go out. As the men enter, we hear some of the following dialogue.*]

STANLEY:

Is that how he got it?

STEVE:

Sure that's how he got it. He hit the old weather-bird for 300 bucks on a six-number-ticket.

MITCH:

Don't tell him those things; he'll believe it.

[*Mitch starts out.*]

STANLEY [*restraining Mitch*]:

Hey, Mitch—come back here.

[*Blanche, at the sound of voices, retires in the bed- room. She picks up Stanley's photo from dressing table, looks at it, puts it down. When Stanley enters the apartment, she darts and hides behind the screen at the head of bed.*]

STEVE [*to Stanley and Mitch*]:

Hey, are we playin' poker tomorrow?

121

STANLEY:

Sure—at Mitch's.

MITCH [*hearing this, returns quickly to the stair rail*]:

No—not at my place. My mother's still sick!

STANLEY:

Okay, at my place ... [*Mitch starts out again*] But you bring the beer!

[*Mitch pretends not to hear—calls out "Goodnight, all," and goes out, singing.*]

EUNICE [*heard from above*]:

Break it up down there! I made the spaghetti dish and ate it myself.

STEVE [*going upstairs*]:

I told you and phoned you we was playing. [*to the men*] Jax beer!

EUNICE:

You never phoned me once.

STEVE:

I told you at breakfast—and phoned you at lunch ...

EUNICE:

Well, never mind about that. You just get yourself home here once in a while.

STEVE:

You want it in the papers?

[*More laughter and shouts of parting come from the men. Stanley throws the screen door of the kitchen open and comes in. He is of medium height, about five feet eight or nine, and strongly, compactly built. Animal joy in his being is implicit in all his movements and attitudes. Since earliest manhood the center of his*

*life has been pleasure with women, the giving and
taking of it, not with weak indulgence, dependently,
but with the power and pride of a richly feathered
male bird among hens. Branching out from this complete and satisfying center are all the auxiliary chan-
nels of his life, such as his heartiness with men, his
appreciation of rough humor, his love of good drink
and food and games, his car, his radio, everything that
is his, that bears his emblem of the gaudy seed-bearer.
He sizes women up at a glance, with sexual classifica-
tions, crude images flashing into his mind and deter-
mining the way he smiles at them.]*

BLANCHE [*drawing involuntarily back from his stare*]:
You must be Stanley. I'm Blanche.

STANLEY:
Stella's sister?

BLANCHE:
Yes.

STANLEY:
H'lo. Where's the little woman?

BLANCHE:
In the bathroom.

STANLEY:
Oh. Didn't know you were coming in town

BLANCHE:
I—uh—

STANLEY:
Where you from, Blanche?

BLANCHE:
Why, I—live in Laurel.

[*He has crossed to the closet and removed the whiskey bottle.*]

STANLEY:

In Laurel, huh? Oh, yeah. Yeah, in Laurel, that's right. Not in my territory. Liquor goes fast in hot weather.

[*He holds the bottle to the light to observe its depletion.*]

Have a shot?

BLANCHE:

No, I—rarely touch it.

STANLEY:

Some people rarely touch it, but it touches them often.

BLANCHE [*faintly*]:

Ha-ha.

STANLEY:

My clothes're stickin' to me. Do you mind if I make myself comfortable? [*He starts to remove his shirt.*]

BLANCHE:

Please, please do.

STANLEY:

Be comfortable is my motto.

BLANCHE:

It's mine, too. It's hard to stay looking fresh. I haven't washed or even powdered my face and—here you are!

STANLEY:

You know you can catch cold sitting around in damp things, especially when you been exercising hard like bowling is. You're a teacher, aren't you?

124

BLANCHE:
Yes.

STANLEY:
What do you teach, Blanche?

BLANCHE:
English.

STANLEY:
I never was a very good English student. How long you here for, Blanche?

BLANCHE:
I—don't know yet.

STANLEY:
You going to shack up here?

BLANCHE:
I thought I would if it's not inconvenient for you all.

STANLEY:
Good.

BLANCHE:
Traveling wears me out.

STANLEY:
Well, take it easy.

[*A cat screeches near the window. Blanche springs up.*]

BLANCHE:
What's that?

STANLEY:
Cats . . . Hey, Stella!

125

STELLA [*faintly, from the bathroom*]:
Yes, Stanley.

STANLEY:

Haven't fallen in, have you? [*He grins at Blanche. She tries unsuccessfully to smile back. There is a silence*] I'm afraid I'll strike you as being the unrefined type. Stella's spoke of you a good deal. You were married once, weren't you?

[*The music of the polka rises up, faint in the distance.*]

BLANCHE:

Yes. When I was quite young.

STANLEY:

What happened?

BLANCHE:

The boy—the boy died. [*She sinks back down*] I'm afraid I'm—going to be sick!

[*Her head falls on her arms.*]

SCENE TWO

It is six o'clock the following evening. Blanche is bath-
ing. Stella is completing her toilette. Blanche's dress, a
flowered print, is laid out on Stella's bed.
Stanley enters the kitchen from outside, leaving the door
open on the perpetual "blue piano" around the corner.

STANLEY:

What's all this monkey doings?

STELLA:

Oh, Stan! [*She jumps up and kisses him, which he ac-*
cepts with lordly composure] I'm taking Blanche to
Galatoire's for supper and then to a show, because it's
your poker night.

STANLEY:

How about my supper, huh? I'm not going to no Galatoire's for supper!

STELLA:

I put you a cold plate on ice.

STANLEY:

Well, isn't that just dandy!

STELLA:

I'm going to try to keep Blanche out till the party breaks
up because I don't know how she would take it. So we'll
go to one of the little places in the Quarter afterward
and you'd better give me some money.

STANLEY:

Where is she?

STELLA:

She's soaking in a hot tub to quiet her nerves. She's terribly upset.

STANLEY:

Over what?

STELLA:

She's been through such an ordeal.

STANLEY:

Yeah?

STELLA:

Stan, we've—lost Belle Reve!

STANLEY:

The place in the country?

STELLA:

Yes.

STANLEY:

How?

STELLA [*vaguely*]:

Oh, it had to be—sacrificed or something. [*There is a pause while Stanley considers. Stella is changing into her dress*] When she comes in be sure to say something nice about her appearance. And, oh! Don't mention the baby. I haven't said anything yet, I'm waiting until she gets in a quieter condition.

STANLEY [*ominously*]:

So?

STELLA:

And try to understand her and be nice to her, Stan.

BLANCHE [*singing in the bathroom*]:

"From the land of the sky blue water,
  They brought a captive maid!"

STELLA:

She wasn't expecting to find us in such a small place. You see I'd tried to gloss things over a little in my letters.

STANLEY:

So?

STELLA:

And admire her dress and tell her she's looking wonderful. That's important with Blanche. Her little weakness!

STANLEY:

Yeah. I get the idea. Now let's skip back a little to where you said the country place was disposed of.

STELLA:

Oh!—yes . . .

STANLEY:

How about that? Let's have a few more details on that subjeck.

STELLA:

It's best not to talk much about it until she's calmed down.

STANLEY:

So that's the deal, huh? Sister Blanche cannot be annoyed with business details right now!

STELLA:

You saw how she was last night.

STANLEY:

Uh-hum, I saw how she was. Now let's have a gander at the bill of sale.

STELLA:

I haven't seen any.

129

STANLEY:

She didn't show you no papers, no deed of sale or nothing like that, huh?

STELLA:

It seems like it wasn't sold.

STANLEY:

Well, what in hell was it then, give away? To charity?

STELLA:

Shhh! She'll hear you.

STANLEY:

I don't care if she hears me. Let's see the papers!

STELLA:

There weren't any papers, she didn't show any papers, I don't care about papers.

STANLEY:

Have you ever heard of the Napoleonic code?

STELLA:

No, Stanley, I haven't heard of the Napoleonic code and if I have, I don't see what it—

STANLEY:

Let me enlighten you on a point or two, baby.

STELLA:

Yes?

STANLEY:

In the state of Louisiana we have the Napoleonic code according to which what belongs to the wife belongs to the husband and vice versa. For instance if I had a piece of property, or you had a piece of property—

STELLA:

My head is swimming!

STANLEY:

All right. I'll wait till she gets through soaking in a hot
tub and then I'll inquire if *she* is acquainted with the
Napoleonic code. It looks to me like you have been swindled, baby, and when you're swindled under the Napoleonic code I'm swindled *too*. And I don't like to be
swindled.

STELLA:

There's plenty of time to ask her questions later but if
you do now she'll go to pieces again. I don't understand
what happened to Belle Reve but you don't know how
ridiculous you are being when you suggest that my sister
or I or anyone of our family could have perpetrated a
swindle on anyone else.

STANLEY:

Then where's the money if the place was sold?

STELLA:

Not sold—*lost, lost!*

[*He stalks into bedroom, and she follows him.*]

Stanley!

[*He pulls open the wardrobe trunk standing in middle of room and jerks out an armful of dresses.*]

STANLEY:

Open your eyes to this stuff! You think she got them out
of a teacher's pay?

STELLA:

Hush!

131

STANLEY:

Look at these feathers and furs that she come here to preen herself in! What's this here? A solid-gold dress, I believe! And this one! What is these here? Fox-pieces! [*He blows on them*] Genuine fox fur-pieces, a half a mile long! Where are your fox-pieces, Stella? Bushy snow-white ones, no less! Where are your white fox-pieces?

STELLA:

Those are inexpensive summer furs that Blanche has had a long time.

STANLEY:

I got an acquaintance who deals in this sort of merchandise. I'll have him in here to appraise it. I'm willing to bet you there's thousands of dollars invested in this stuff here!

STELLA:

Don't be such an idiot, Stanley!

[*He hurls the furs to the day bed. Then he jerks open small drawer in the trunk and pulls up a fistful of costume jewelry.*]

STANLEY:

And what have we here? The treasure chest of a pirate!

STELLA:

Oh, Stanley!

STANLEY:

Pearls! Ropes of them! What is this sister of yours, a deep-sea diver? Bracelets of solid gold, too! Where are your pearls and gold bracelets?

STELLA:

Shhh! Be still, Stanley!

132

STANLEY:

And diamonds! A crown for an empress!

STELLA:

A rhinestone tiara she wore to a costume ball.

STANLEY:

What's rhinestone?

STELLA:

Next door to glass.

STANLEY:

Are you kidding? I have an acquaintance that works in a jewelry store. I'll have him in here to make an appraisal of this. Here's your plantation, or what was left of it, here!

STELLA:

You have no idea how stupid and horrid you're being! Now close that trunk before she comes out of the bathroom!

[*He kicks the trunk partly closed and sits on the kitchen table.*]

STANLEY:

The Kowalskis and the DuBoises have different notions.

STELLA [*angrily*]:

Indeed they have, thank heavens!—*I'm* going outside.

[*She snatches up her white hat and gloves and crosses to the outside door*] You come out with me while Blanche is getting dressed.

STANLEY:

Since when do you give me orders?

STELLA:

Are you going to stay here and insult her?

STANLEY:

You're damn tootin' I'm going to stay here.

[*Stella goes out to the porch. Blanche comes out of the bathroom in a red satin robe.*]

BLANCHE [*airily*]:

Hello, Stanley! Here I am, all freshly bathed and scented, and feeling like a brand new human being!

[*He lights a cigarette.*]

STANLEY:

That's good.

BLANCHE [*drawing the curtains at the windows*]:

Excuse me while I slip on my pretty new dress!

STANLEY:

Go right ahead, Blanche.

[*She closes the drapes between the rooms.*]

BLANCHE:

I understand there's to be a little card party to which we ladies are cordially *not* invited!

STANLEY [*ominously*]:

Yeah?

[*Blanche throws off her robe and slips into a flowered print dress.*]

BLANCHE:

Where's Stella?

STANLEY:

Out on the porch.

BLANCHE:

I'm going to ask a favor of you in a moment.

STANLEY:

What could that be, I wonder?

BLANCHE:

Some buttons in back! You may enter!

[*He crosses through drapes with a smoldering look.*]

How do I look?

STANLEY:

You look all right.

BLANCHE:

Many thanks! Now the buttons!

STANLEY:

I can't do nothing with them.

BLANCHE:

You men with your big clumsy fingers. May I have a drag on your cig?

STANLEY:

Have one for yourself.

BLANCHE:

Why, thanks! . . . It looks like my trunk has exploded.

STANLEY:

Me an' Stella were helping you unpack.

BLANCHE:

Well, you certainly did a fast and thorough job of it!

STANLEY:

It looks like you raided some stylish shops in Paris.

135

BLANCHE:

Ha-ha! Yes—clothes are my passion!

STANLEY:

What does it cost for a string of fur-pieces like that?

BLANCHE:

Why, those were a tribute from an admirer of mine!

STANLEY:

He must have had a lot of—admiration!

BLANCHE:

Oh, in my youth I excited some admiration. But look at me now! [*She smiles at him radiantly*] Would you think it possible that I was once considered to be—attractive?

STANLEY:

Your looks are okay.

BLANCHE:

I was fishing for a compliment, Stanley.

STANLEY:

I don't go in for that stuff.

BLANCHE:

What—stuff?

STANLEY:

Compliments to women about their looks. I never met a woman that didn't know if she was good-looking or not without being told, and some of them give themselves credit for more than they've got. I once went out with a doll who said to me, "I am the glamorous type, I am the glamorous type!" I said, "So what?"

BLANCHE:
And what did she say then?

STANLEY:
She didn't say nothing. That shut her up like a clam.

BLANCHE:
Did it end the romance?

STANLEY:
It ended the conversation—that was all. Some men are took in by this Hollywood glamor stuff and some men are not.

BLANCHE:
I'm sure you belong in the second category.

STANLEY:
That's right.

BLANCHE:
I cannot imagine any witch of a woman casting a spell over you.

STANLEY:
That's—right.

BLANCHE:
You're simple, straightforward and honest, a little bit on the primitive side I should think. To interest you a woman would have to— [*She pauses with an indefinite gesture.*]

STANLEY [*slowly*]:
Lay . . . her cards on the table.

BLANCHE [*smiling*]:
Well, I never cared for wishy-washy people. That was

137

why, when you walked in here last night, I said to my-self—"My sister has married a man!"—Of course that was all that I could tell about you.

STANLEY [*booming*]:

Now let's cut the re-bop!

BLANCHE [*pressing hands to her ears*]:

Ouuuuu!

STELLA [*calling from the steps*]:

Stanley! You come out here and let Blanche finish dressing!

BLANCHE:

I'm through dressing, honey.

STELLA:

Well, you come out, then.

STANLEY:

Your sister and I are having a little talk.

BLANCHE [*lightly*]:

Honey, do me a favor. Run to the drugstore and get me a lemon Coke with plenty of chipped ice in it!—Will you do that for me, sweetie?

STELLA [*uncertainly*]:

Yes. [*She goes around the corner of the building.*]

BLANCHE:

The poor little thing was out there listening to us, and I have an idea she doesn't understand you as well as I do. ... All right; now, Mr. Kowalski, let us proceed without any more double-talk. I'm ready to answer all questions. I've nothing to hide. What is it?

STANLEY:

There is such a thing in this state of Louisiana as the

Napoleonic code, according to which whatever belongs
to my wife is also mine—and vice versa.

BLANCHE:

My, but you have an impressive judicial air!

[*She sprays herself with her atomizer; then playfully
sprays him with it. He seizes the atomizer and slams it
down on the dresser. She throws back her head and
laughs.*]

STANLEY:

If I didn't know that you was my wife's sister I'd get
ideas about you!

BLANCHE:

Such as what!

STANLEY:

Don't play so dumb. You know what!

BLANCHE [*she puts the atomizer on the table*]:

All right. Cards on the table. That suits me. [*She turns
to Stanley.*] I know I fib a good deal. After all, a woman's
charm is fifty per cent illusion, but when a thing is important I tell the truth, and this is the truth: I haven't
cheated my sister or you or anyone else as long as I have
lived.

STANLEY:

Where's the papers? In the trunk?

BLANCHE:

Everything that I own is in that trunk.

[*Stanley crosses to the trunk, shoves it roughly open
and begins to open compartments.*]

BLANCHE:

What in the name of heaven are you thinking of! What's

139

in the back of that little boy's mind of yours? That I am absconding with something, attempting some kind of treachery on my sister?—Let me do that! It will be faster and simpler ...[*She crosses to the trunk and takes out a box*] I keep my papers mostly in this tin box. [*She opens it.*]

STANLEY:

What's them underneath? [*He indicates another sheaf of paper.*]

BLANCHE

These are love-letters, yellowing with antiquity, all from one boy. [*He snatches them up. She speaks fiercely*] Give those back to me!

STANLEY:

I'll have a look at them first!

BLANCHE:

The touch of your hands insults them!

STANLEY:

Don't pull that stuff!

[*He rips off the ribbon and starts to examine them. Blanche snatches them from him, and they cascade to the floor.*]

BLANCHE:

Now that you've touched them I'll burn them!

STANLEY [*staring, baffled*]:

What in hell are they?

BLANCHE [*on the floor gathering them up*]:

Poems a dead boy wrote. I hurt him the way that you would like to hurt me, but you can't! I'm not young and

vulnerable any more. But my young husband was and I
—never mind about that! Just give them back to me!

STANLEY:

What do you mean by saying you'll have to burn them?

BLANCHE:

I'm sorry, I must have lost my head for a moment. Everyone has something he won't let others touch because of
their—intimate nature . . .

[*She now seems faint with exhaustion and she sits
down with the strong box and puts on a pair of glasses
and goes methodically through a large stack of
papers.*]

Ambler & Ambler. Hmmmmm. . . . Crabtree. . . . More
Ambler & Ambler.

STANLEY:

What is Ambler & Ambler?

BLANCHE:

A firm that made loans on the place.

STANLEY:

Then it *was* lost on a mortgage?

BLANCHE [*touching her forehead*]:
That must've been what happened.

STANLEY:

I don't want no ifs, ands or buts! What's all the rest of
them papers?

[*She hands him the entire box. He carries it to the
table and starts to examine the papers.*]

BLANCHE [*picking up a large envelope containing more
papers*]:

There are thousands of papers, stretching back over hundreds of years, affecting Belle Reve as, piece by piece, our improvident grandfathers and father and uncles and brothers exchanged the land for their epic fornications—to put it plainly! [*She removes her glasses with an exhausted laugh*] The four-letter word deprived us of our plantation, till finally all that was left—and Stella can verify that!—was the house itself and about twenty acres of ground, including a graveyard, to which now all but Stella and I have retreated. [*She pours the contents of the envelope on the table*] Here all of them are, all papers! I hereby endow you with them! Take them, peruse them—commit them to memory, even! I think it's wonderfully fitting that Belle Reve should finally be this bunch of old papers in your big, capable hands! . . . I wonder if Stella's come back with my lemon Coke . . . [*She leans back and closes her eyes.*]

STANLEY:

I have a lawyer acquaintance who will study these out.

BLANCHE:

Present them to him with a box of aspirin tablets.

STANLEY [*becoming somewhat sheepish*]:

You see, under the Napoleonic code—a man has to take an interest in his wife's affairs—especially now that she's going to have a baby.

[*Blanche opens her eyes. The "blue piano" sounds louder.*]

BLANCHE:

Stella? Stella going to have a baby? [*dreamily*] I didn't know she was going to have a baby!

[*She gets up and crosses to the outside door. Stella*

142

*appears around the corner with a carton from the drug-
store.*

[*Stanley goes into the bedroom with the envelope and
the box.*

[*The inner rooms fade to darkness and the outside
wall of the house is visible. Blanche meets Stella at the
foot of the steps to the sidewalk.*]

BLANCHE:

Stella, Stella for star! How lovely to have a baby! It's all
right. Everything's all right.

STELLA:

I'm sorry he did that to you.

BLANCHE:

Oh, I guess he's just not the type that goes for jasmine
perfume, but maybe he's what we need to mix with our
blood now that we've lost Belle Reve. We thrashed it out.
I feel a bit shaky, but I think I handled it nicely, I laughed
and treated it all as a joke. [*Steve and Pablo appear, carrying a case of beer.*] I called him a little boy and laughed
and flirted. Yes, I was flirting with your husband! [*as the
men approach*] The guests are gathering for the poker
party. [*The two men pass between them, and enter the
house.*] Which way do we go now, Stella—this way? '

STELLA:

No, this way. [*She leads Blanche away.*]

BLANCHE [*laughing*]:

The blind are leading the blind!

[*A tamale Vendor is heard calling.*]

VENDOR'S VOICE:

Red-hot!

SCENE THREE

THE POKER NIGHT

There is a picture of Van Gogh's of a billiard-parlor at night. The kitchen now suggests that sort of lurid nocturnal brilliance, the raw colors of childhood's spectrum. Over the yellow linoleum of the kitchen table hangs an electric bulb with a vivid green glass shade. The poker players—Stanley, Steve, Mitch and Pablo—wear colored shirts, solid blues, a purple, a red-and-white check, a light green, and they are men at the peak of their physical manhood, as coarse and direct and powerful as the primary colors. There are vivid slices of watermelon on the table, whiskey bottles and glasses. The bedroom is relatively dim with only the light that spills between the portieres and through the wide window on the street.

For a moment, there is absorbed silence as a hand is dealt.

STEVE:
Anything wild this deal?

PABLO:
One-eyed jacks are wild.

STEVE:
Give me two cards.

PABLO:
You, Mitch?

MITCH:
I'm out.

PABLO:
One.

MITCH:

Anyone want a shot?

STANLEY:

Yeah. Me.

PABLO:

Why don't somebody go to the Chinaman's and bring back a load of chop suey?

STANLEY:

When I'm losing you want to eat! Ante up! Openers? Openers! Get y'r ass off the table, Mitch. Nothing belongs on a poker table but cards, chips and whiskey.

[*He lurches up and tosses some watermelon rinds to the floor.*]

MITCH:

Kind of on your high horse, ain't you?

STANLEY:

How many?

STEVE:

Give me three.

STANLEY:

One.

MITCH:

I'm out again. I oughta go home pretty soon.

STANLEY:

Shut up.

MITCH:

I gotta sick mother. She don't go to sleep until I come in at night.

145

STANLEY:

Then why don't you stay home with her?

MITCH:

She says to go out, so I go, but I don't enjoy it. All the while I keep wondering how she is.

STANLEY:

Aw, for the sake of Jesus, go home, then!

PABLO:

What've you got?

STEVE:

Spade flush.

MITCH:

You all are married. But I'll be alone when she goes.— I'm going to the bathroom.

STANLEY:

Hurry back and we'll fix you a sugar-tit.

MITCH:

Aw, go rut. [*He crosses through the bedroom into the bathroom.*]

STEVE [*dealing a hand*]:

Seven card stud. [*telling his joke as he deals*] This ole farmer is out in back of his house sittin' down th'owing corn to the chickens when all at once he hears a loud cackle and this young hen comes lickety split around the side of the house with the rooster right behind her and gaining on her fast.

STANLEY [*impatient with the story*]:
Deal!

146

STEVE:

But when the rooster catches sight of the farmer th'owing the corn he puts on the brakes and lets the hen get away and starts pecking corn. And the old farmer says, "Lord God, I hopes I never gits *that* hongry!"

[*Steve and Pablo laugh. The sisters appear around the corner of the building.*]

STELLA:

The game is still going on.

BLANCHE:

How do I look?

STELLA:

Lovely, Blanche.

BLANCHE:

I feel so hot and frazzled. Wait till I powder before you open the door. Do I look done in?

STELLA:

Why no. You are as fresh as a daisy.

BLANCHE:

One that's been picked a few days.

[*Stella opens the door and they enter.*]

STELLA:

Well, well, well. I see you boys are still at it!

STANLEY:

Where you been?

STELLA:

Blanche and I took in a show. Blanche, this is Mr. Gonzales and Mr. Hubbell.

147

BLANCHE:
Please don't get up.

STANLEY:
Nobody's going to get up, so don't be worried.

STELLA:
How much longer is this game going to continue?

STANLEY:
Till we get ready to quit.

BLANCHE:
Poker is so fascinating. Could I kibitz?

STANLEY:
You could not. Why don't you women go up and sit with
Eunice?

STELLA:
Because it is nearly two-thirty. [*Blanche crosses into the
bedroom and partially closes the portieres*] Couldn't you
call it quits after one more hand?

[*A chair scrapes. Stanley gives a loud whack of his
hand on her thigh.*]

STELLA [*sharply*]:
That's not fun, Stanley.

[*The men laugh. Stella goes into the bedroom.*]

STELLA:
It makes me so mad when he does that in front of people.

BLANCHE:
I think I will bathe.

STELLA:

Again?

BLANCHE:

My nerves are in knots. Is the bathroom occupied?

STELLA:

I don't know.

[*Blanche knocks. Mitch opens the door and comes out, still wiping his hands on a towel.*]

BLANCHE:

Oh!—good evening.

MITCH:

Hello. [*He stares at her.*]

STELLA:

Blanche, this is Harold Mitchell. My sister, Blanche DuBois.

MITCH [*with awkward courtesy*]:

How do you do, Miss DuBois.

STELLA:

How is your mother now, Mitch?

MITCH:

About the same, thanks. She appreciated your sending over that custard.—Excuse me, please.

[*He crosses slowly back into the kitchen, glancing back at Blanche and coughing a little shyly. He realizes he still has the towel in his hands and with an embarrassed laugh hands it to Stella. Blanche looks after him with a certain interest.*]

149

BLANCHE:

That one seems—superior to the others.

STELLA:

Yes, he is.

BLANCHE:

I thought he had a sort of sensitive look.

STELLA:

His mother is sick.

BLANCHE:

Is he married?

STELLA:

No.

BLANCHE:

Is he a wolf?

STELLA:

Why, Blanche! [*Blanche laughs.*] I don't think he would be.

BLANCHE:

What does—what does he do?

[*She is unbuttoning her blouse.*]

STELLA:

He's on the precision bench in the spare parts department. At the plant Stanley travels for.

BLANCHE:

Is that something much?

STELLA:

No. Stanley's the only one of his crowd that's likely to get anywhere.

150

SCENE THREE

BLANCHE:
What makes you think Stanley will?

STELLA:
Look at him.

BLANCHE:
I've looked at him.

STELLA:
Then you should know.

BLANCHE:
I'm sorry, but I haven't noticed the stamp of genius even on Stanley's forehead.

[*She takes off the blouse and stands in her pink silk brassiere and white skirt in the light through the portieres. The game has continued in undertones.*]

STELLA:
It isn't on his forehead and it isn't genius.

BLANCHE:
Oh. Well, what is it, and where? I would like to know.

STELLA:
It's a drive that he has. You're standing in the light, Blanche!

BLANCHE:
Oh, am I!

[*She moves out of the yellow streak of light. Stella has removed her dress and put on a light blue satin kimona.*]

STELLA [*with girlish laughter*]:
You ought to see their wives.

151

BLANCHE [*laughingly*]:
I can imagine. Big, beefy things, I suppose.

STELLA:
You know that one upstairs? [*more laughter*] One time
[*laughing*] the plaster—[*laughing*] cracked—

STANLEY:
You hens cut out that conversation in there!

STELLA:
You can't hear us.

STANLEY:
Well, you can hear me and I said to hush up!

STELLA:
This is my house and I'll talk as much as I want to!

BLANCHE:
Stella, don't start a row.

STELLA:
He's half drunk!—I'll be out in a minute.

[*She goes into the bathroom. Blanche rises and crosses
leisurely to a small white radio and turns it on.*]

STANLEY:
Awright, Mitch, you in?

MITCH:
What? Oh!—No, I'm out!

[*Blanche moves back into the streak of light. She raises
her arms and stretches, as she moves indolently back
to the chair.*

[*Rhumba music comes over the radio. Mitch rises at the table.*]

STANLEY:
Who turned that on in there?

BLANCHE:
I did. Do you mind?

STANLEY:
Turn it off!

STEVE:
Aw, let the girls have their music.

PABLO:
Sure, that's good, leave it on!

STEVE:
Sounds like Xavier Cugat!

[*Stanley jumps up and, crossing to the radio, turns it off. He stops short at the sight of Blanche in the chair. She returns his look without flinching. Then he sits again at the poker table.*]

[*Two of the men have started arguing hotly.*]

STEVE:
I didn't hear you name it.

PABLO:
Didn't I name it, Mitch?

MITCH:
I wasn't listenin'.

PABLO:
What were you doing, then?

STANLEY:

He was looking through them drapes. [*He jumps up and jerks roughly at curtains to close them*] Now deal the hand over again and let's play cards or quit. Some people get ants when they win.

[*Mitch rises as Stanley returns to his seat.*]

STANLEY [*yelling*]:
Sit down!

MITCH:
I'm going to the "head." Deal me out.

PABLO:
Sure he's got ants now. Seven five-dollar bills in his pants pocket folded up tight as spitballs.

STEVE:
Tomorrow you'll see him at the cashier's window getting them changed into quarters.

STANLEY:
And when he goes home he'll deposit them one by one in a piggy bank his mother give him for Christmas. [*dealing*] This game is Spit in the Ocean.

[*Mitch laughs uncomfortably and continues through the portieres. He stops just inside.*]

BLANCHE [*softly*]:
Hello! The Little Boys' Room is busy right now.

MITCH:
We've—been drinking beer.

BLANCHE:
I hate beer.

MITCH:

It's—a hot weather drink.

BLANCHE:

Oh, I don't think so; it always makes me warmer. Have you got any cigs? [*She has slipped on the dark red satin wrapper.*]

MITCH:

Sure.

BLANCHE:

What kind are they?

MITCH:

Luckies.

BLANCHE:

Oh, good. What a pretty case. Silver?

MITCH:

Yes. Yes; read the inscription.

BLANCHE:

Oh, is there an inscription? I can't make it out. [*He strikes a match and moves closer*] Oh! [*reading with feigned difficulty*]:

"And if God choose,
I shall but love thee better—after—death!"

Why, that's from my favorite sonnet by Mrs. Browning!

MITCH:

You know it?

BLANCHE:

Certainly I do!

MITCH:

There's a story connected with that inscription.

BLANCHE:
It sounds like a romance.

MITCH:
A pretty sad one.

BLANCHE:
Oh?

MITCH:
The girl's dead now.

BLANCHE [*in a tone of deep sympathy*]:
Oh!

MITCH:
She knew she was dying when she give me this. A very strange girl, very sweet—very!

BLANCHE:
She must have been fond of you. Sick people have such deep, sincere attachments.

MITCH:
That's right, they certainly do.

BLANCHE:
Sorrow makes for sincerity, I think.

MITCH:
It sure brings it out in people.

BLANCHE:
The little there is belongs to people who have experienced some sorrow.

MITCH:
I believe you are right about that.

BLANCHE:

I'm positive that I am. Show me a person who hasn't known any sorrow and I'll show you a shuperficial— Listen to me! My tongue is a little—thick! You boys are responsible for it. The show let out at eleven and we couldn't come home on account of the poker game so we had to go somewhere and drink. I'm not accustomed to having more than one drink. Two is the limit—and *three!* [*She laughs*] Tonight I had three.

STANLEY:

Mitch!

MITCH:

Deal me out. I'm talking to Miss—

BLANCHE:

DuBois.

MITCH:

Miss DuBois?

BLANCHE:

It's a French name. It means woods and Blanche means white, so the two together mean white woods. Like an orchard in spring! You can remember it by that.

MITCH:

You're French?

BLANCHE:

We are French by extraction. Our first American ancestors were French Huguenots.

MITCH:

You are Stella's sister, are you not?

157

BLANCHE:

Yes, Stella is my precious little sister. I call her little in spite of the fact she's somewhat older than I. Just slightly. Less than a year. Will you do something for me?

MITCH:

Sure. What?

BLANCHE:

I bought this adorable little colored paper lantern at a Chinese shop on Bourbon. Put it over the light bulb! Will you, please?

MITCH:

Be glad to.

BLANCHE:

I can't stand a naked light bulb, any more than I can a rude remark or a vulgar action.

MITCH [*adjusting the lantern*]:

I guess we strike you as being a pretty rough bunch.

BLANCHE:

I'm very adaptable—to circumstances.

MITCH:

Well, that's a good thing to be. You are visiting Stanley and Stella?

BLANCHE:

Stella hasn't been so well lately, and I came down to help her for a while. She's very run down.

MITCH:

You're not—?

BLANCHE:

Married? No, no. I'm an old maid schoolteacher!

MITCH:

You may teach school but you're certainly not an old maid.

BLANCHE:

Thank you, sir! I appreciate your gallantry!

MITCH:

So you are in the teaching profession?

BLANCHE:

Yes. Ah, yes...

MITCH:

Grade school or high school or—

STANLEY [*bellowing*]:

Mitch!

MITCH:

Coming!

BLANCHE:

Gracious, what lung-power! ... I teach high school. In Laurel.

MITCH:

What do you teach? What subject?

BLANCHE:

Guess!

MITCH:

I bet you teach art or music? [*Blanche laughs delicately*] Of course I could be wrong. You might teach arithmetic.

BLANCHE:

Never arithmetic, sir; never arithmetic! [*with a laugh*] I don't even know my multiplication tables! No, I have the misfortune of being an English instructor. I attempt

159

to instill a bunch of bobby-soxers and drugstore Romeos with reverence for Hawthorne and Whitman and Poe!

MITCH:

I guess that some of them are more interested in other things.

BLANCHE:

How very right you are! Their literary heritage is not what most of them treasure above all else! But they're sweet things! And in the spring, it's touching to notice them making their first discovery of love! As if nobody had ever known it before!

[*The bathroom door opens and Stella comes out. Blanche continues talking to Mitch.*]

Oh! Have you finished? Wait—I'll turn on the radio.

[*She turns the knobs on the radio and it begins to play "Wien, Wien, nur du allein." Blanche waltzes to the music with romantic gestures. Mitch is delighted and moves in awkward imitation like a dancing bear.*

[*Stanley stalks fiercely through the portieres into the bedroom. He crosses to the small white radio and snatches it off the table. With a shouted oath, he tosses the instrument out the window.*]

STELLA:

Drunk — drunk — animal thing, you! [*She rushes through to the poker table*] All of you—please go home! If any of you have one spark of decency in you—

BLANCHE [*wildly*]:
Stella, watch out, he's—

[*Stanley charges after Stella.*]

MEN [*feebly*]:
Take it easy, Stanley. Easy, fellow.—Let's all—

STELLA:
You lay your hands on me and I'll—

[*She backs out of sight. He advances and disappears. There is the sound of a blow. Stella cries out. Blanche screams and runs into the kitchen. The men rush forward and there is grappling and cursing. Something is overturned with a crash.*]

BLANCHE [*shrilly*]:
My sister is going to have a baby!

MITCH:
This is terrible.

BLANCHE:
Lunacy, absolute lunacy!

MITCH:
Get him in here, men.

[*Stanley is forced, pinioned by the two men, into the bedroom. He nearly throws them off. Then all at once he subsides and is limp in their grasp.*

[*They speak quietly and lovingly to him and he leans his face on one of their shoulders.*]

STELLA [*in a high, unnatural voice, out of sight*]:
I want to go away, I want to go away!

MITCH:
Poker shouldn't be played in a house with women.

161

[*Blanche rushes into the bedroom*]

BLANCHE:
I want my sister's clothes! We'll go to that woman's upstairs!

MITCH:
Where is the clothes?

BLANCHE [*opening the closet*]:
I've got them! [*She rushes through to Stella*] Stella, Stella, precious! Dear, dear little sister, don't be afraid!

[*With her arms around Stella, Blanche guides her to the outside door and upstairs.*]

STANLEY [*dully*]:
What's the matter; what's happened?

MITCH:
You just blew your top, Stan.

PABLO:
He's okay, now.

STEVE:
Sure, my boy's okay!

MITCH:
Put him on the bed and get a wet towel.

PABLO:
I think coffee would do him a world of good, now.

STANLEY [*thickly*]:
I want water.

162

MITCH.

Put him under the shower!

[*The men talk quietly as they lead him to the bathroom.*]

STANLEY:

Let the rut go of me, you sons of bitches!

[*Sounds of blows are heard. The water goes on full tilt.*]

STEVE:

Let's get quick out of here!

[*They rush to the poker table and sweep up their winings on their way out.*]

MITCH [*sadly but firmly*]:

Poker should not be played in a house with women.

[*The door closes on them and the place is still. The Negro entertainers in the bar around the corner play "Paper Doll" slow and blue. After a moment Stanley comes out of the bathroom dripping water and still in his clinging wet polka dot drawers.*]

STANLEY:

Stella! [*There is a pause*] My baby doll's left me!

[*He breaks into sobs. Then he goes to the phone and dials, still shuddering with sobs.*]

Eunice? I want my baby! [*He waits a moment; then he hangs up and dials again*] Eunice! I'll keep on ringin' until I talk with my baby!

[*An indistinguishable shrill voice is heard. He hurls phone to floor. Dissonant brass and piano sounds as the*

163

*rooms dim out to darkness and the outer walls appear
in the night light. The "blue piano" plays for a brief
interval.*

[*Finally, Stanley stumbles half-dressed out to the
porch and down the wooden steps to the pavement
before the building. There he throws back his head
like a baying hound and bellows his wife's name:
"Stella! Stella, sweetheart! Stella!"*]

STANLEY:

Stell-*lahhhhh!*

EUNICE [*calling down from the door of her upper
apartment*]:

Quit that howling out there an' go back to bed!

STANLEY:

I want my baby down here. Stella, Stella!

EUNICE:

She ain't comin' down so you quit! Or you'll git th' law
on you!

STANLEY:

Stella!

EUNICE:

You can't beat on a woman an' then call 'er back! She
won't come! And her goin' t' have a baby! . . . You
stinker! You whelp of a Polack, you! I hope they do haul
you in and turn the fire hose on you, same as the last
time!

STANLEY [*humbly*]:

Eunice, I want my girl to come down with me!

EUNICE:

Hah! [*She slams her door.*]

STANLEY [*with heaven-splitting violence*]:
STELL-LAHHHHH!

[*The low-tone clarinet moans. The door upstairs opens
again. Stella slips down the rickety stairs in her robe.
Her eyes are glistening with tears and her hair loose
about her throat and shoulders. They stare at each other.
Then they come together with low, animal moans. He
falls to his knees on the steps and presses his face to her
belly, curving a little with maternity. Her eyes go
blind with tenderness as she catches his head and
raises him level with her. He snatches the screen door
open and lifts her off her feet and bears her into the
dark flat.*

[*Blanche comes out on the upper landing in her robe
and slips fearfully down the steps.*]

BLANCHE:

Where is my little sister? Stella? Stella?

[*She stops before the dark entrance of her sister's flat.
Then catches her breath as if struck. She rushes down
to the walk before the house. She looks right and left
as if for a sanctuary.*

[*The music fades away. Mitch appears from around the
corner.*]

MITCH:

Miss DuBois?

BLANCHE:

Oh!

165

MITCH:

All quiet on the Potomac now?

BLANCHE:

She ran downstairs and went back in there with him.

MITCH:

Sure she did.

BLANCHE:

I'm terrified!

MITCH:

Ho-ho! There's nothing to be scared of. They're crazy about each other.

BLANCHE:

I'm not used to such—

MITCH:

Naw, it's a shame this had to happen when you just got here. But don't take it serious.

BLANCHE:

Violence! Is so—

MITCH:

Set down on the steps and have a cigarette with me.

BLANCHE:

I'm not properly dressed.

MITCH:

That don't make no difference in the Quarter.

BLANCHE:

Such a pretty silver case.

MITCH:

I showed you the inscription, didn't I?

BLANCHE:

Yes. [*During the pause, she looks up at the sky*] There's so much—so much confusion in the world . . . [*He coughs diffidently*] Thank you for being so kind! I need kindness now.

SCENE FOUR

It is early the following morning. There is a confusion of street cries like a choral chant.

Stella is lying down in the bedroom. Her face is serene in the early morning sunlight. One hand rests on her belly, rounding slightly with new maternity. From the other dangles a book of colored comics. Her eyes and lips have that almost narcotized tranquility that is in the faces of Eastern idols.

The table is sloppy with remains of breakfast and the debris of the preceding night, and Stanley's gaudy pyjamas lie across the threshold of the bathroom. The outside door is slightly ajar on a sky of summer brilliance.

Blanche appears at this door. She has spent a sleepless night and her appearance entirely contrasts with Stella's. She presses her knuckles nervously to her lips as she looks through the door, before entering.

BLANCHE:
Stella?

STELLA [*stirring lazily*]:
Hmmh?

[*Blanche utters a moaning cry and runs into the bedroom, throwing herself down beside Stella in a rush of hysterical tenderness.*]

BLANCHE:
Baby, my baby sister!

STELLA [*drawing away from her*]:
Blanche, what is the matter with you?

[*Blanche straightens up slowly and stands beside the bed looking down at her sister with knuckles pressed to her lips.*]

BLANCHE:
He's left?

STELLA:
Stan? Yes.

BLANCHE:
Will he be back?

STELLA:
He's gone to get the car greased. Why?

BLANCHE:
Why! I've been half crazy, Stella! When I found out you'd been insane enough to come back in here after what happened—I started to rush in after you!

STELLA:
I'm glad you didn't.

BLANCHE:
What were you thinking of? [*Stella makes an indefinite gesture*] Answer me! What? What?

STELLA:
Please, Blanche! Sit down and stop yelling.

BLANCHE:
All right, Stella. I will repeat the question quietly now. How could you come back in this place last night? Why, you must have slept with him!

169

[*Stella gets up in a calm and leisurely way.*]

STELLA:

Blanche, I'd forgotten how excitable you are. You're making much too much fuss about this.

BLANCHE:

Am I?

STELLA:

Yes, you are, Blanche. I know how it must have seemed to you and I'm awful sorry it had to happen, but it wasn't anything as serious as you seem to take it. In the first place, when men are drinking and playing poker anything can happen. It's always a powder-keg. He didn't know what he was doing. . . . He was as good as a lamb when I came back and he's really very, very ashamed of himself.

BLANCHE:

And that—that makes it all right?

STELLA:

No, it isn't all right for anybody to make such a terrible row, but — people do sometimes. Stanley's always smashed things. Why, on our wedding night—soon as we came in here—he snatched off one of my slippers and rushed about the place smashing light bulbs with it.

BLANCHE:

He did—*what?*

STELLA:

He smashed all the light bulbs with the heel of my slipper! [*She laughs.*]

BLANCHE:

And you—you *let* him? Didn't *run*, didn't *scream?*

STELLA:

I was—sort of—thrilled by it. [*She waits for a moment*] Eunice and you had breakfast?

BLANCHE:

Do you suppose I wanted any breakfast?

STELLA:

There's some coffee left on the stove.

BLANCHE:

You're so—matter of fact about it, Stella.

STELLA:

What other can I be? He's taken the radio to get it fixed. It didn't land on the pavement so only one tube was smashed.

BLANCHE:

And you are standing there smiling!

STELLA:

What do you want me to do?

BLANCHE:

Pull yourself together and face the facts.

STELLA:

What are they, in your opinion?

BLANCHE:

In my opinion? You're married to a madman!

STELLA:

No!

BLANCHE:

Yes, you are, your fix is worse than mine is! Only you're not being sensible about it. I'm going to *do* something. Get hold of myself and make myself a new life!

171

STELLA:

Yes?

BLANCHE:

But you've given in. And that isn't right, you're not old! You can get out.

STELLA [*slowly and emphatically*]:
I'm not in anything I want to get out of.

BLANCHE [*incredulously*]:
What—Stella?

STELLA:

I said I am not in anything that I have a desire to get out of. Look at the mess in this room! And those empty bottles! They went through two cases last night! He promised this morning that he was going to quit having these poker parties, but you know how long such a promise is going to keep. Oh, well, it's his pleasure, like mine is movies and bridge. People have got to tolerate each other's habits, I guess.

BLANCHE:

I don't understand you. [*Stella turns toward her*] I don't understand your indifference. Is this a Chinese philosophy you've—cultivated?

STELLA:

Is what—what?

BLANCHE:

This — shuffling about and mumbling — 'One tube smashed—beer bottles—mess in the kitchen!'—as if nothing out of the ordinary has happened! [*Stella laughs uncertainly and picking up the broom, twirls it in her hands.*]

BLANCHE:

Are you deliberately shaking that thing in my face?

STELLA:

No.

BLANCHE:

Stop it. Let go of that broom. I won't have you cleaning up for him!

STELLA:

Then who's going to do it? Are you?

BLANCHE:

I? I!

STELLA:

No, I didn't think so.

BLANCHE:

Oh, let me think, if only my mind would function! We've got to get hold of some money, that's the way out!

STELLA:

I guess that money is always nice to get hold of.

BLANCHE:

Listen to me. I have an idea of some kind. [*Shakily she twists a cigarette into her holder*] Do you remember Shep Huntleigh? [*Stella shakes her head*] Of course you remember Shep Huntleigh. I went out with him at college and wore his pin for a while. Well—

STELLA:

Well?

BLANCHE:

I ran into him last winter. You know I went to Miami during the Christmas holidays?

173

STELLA:

No.

BLANCHE:

Well, I did. I took the trip as an investment, thinking I'd meet someone with a million dollars.

STELLA:

Did you?

BLANCHE:

Yes. I ran into Shep Huntleigh—I ran into him on Biscayne Boulevard, on Christmas Eve, about dusk . . . getting into his car—Cadillac convertible; must have been a block long!

STELLA:

I should think it would have been—inconvenient in traffic!

BLANCHE:

You've heard of oil wells?

STELLA:

Yes—remotely.

BLANCHE:

He has them, all over Texas. Texas is literally spouting gold in his pockets.

STELLA:

My, my.

BLANCHE:

Y'know how indifferent I am to money. I think of money in terms of what it does for you. But he could do it, he could certainly do it!

STELLA:

Do what, Blanche?

BLANCHE:

Why—set us up in a—shop!

STELLA:

What kind of a shop?

BLANCHE:

Oh, a—shop of some kind! He could do it with half what his wife throws away at the races.

STELLA:

He's married?

BLANCHE:

Honey, would I be here if the man weren't married? [*Stella laughs a little. Blanche suddenly springs up and crosses to phone. She speaks shrilly*] How do I get Western Union?—Operator! Western Union!

STELLA:

That's a dial phone, honey.

BLANCHE:

I can't dial, I'm too—

STELLA:

Just dial O.

BLANCHE:

O?

STELLA:

Yes, "O" for Operator! [*Blanche considers a moment; then she puts the phone down.*]

BLANCHE:

Give me a pencil. Where is a slip of paper? I've got to write it down first—the message, I mean . . .

175

[*She goes to the dressing table, and grabs up a sheet of Kleenex and an eyebrow pencil for writing equipment.*]

Let me see now ... [*She bites the pencil*] 'Darling Shep. Sister and I in desperate situation.'

STELLA:
I beg your pardon!

BLANCHE:
'Sister and I in desperate situation. Will explain details later. Would you be interested in—?' [*She bites the pencil again*] 'Would you be—interested—in . . .' [*She smashes the pencil on the table and springs up*] You never get anywhere with direct appeals!

STELLA [*with a laugh*]:
Don't be so ridiculous, darling!

BLANCHE:
But I'll think of something, I've *got* to think of—something! Don't, don't laugh at me, Stella! Please, please don't—I—I want you to look at the contents of my purse! Here's what's in it! [*She snatches her purse open*] Sixty-five measly cents in coin of the realm!

STELLA [*crossing to bureau*]:
Stanley doesn't give me a regular allowance, he likes to pay bills himself, but—this morning he gave me ten dollars to smooth things over. You take five of it, Blanche, and I'll keep the rest.

BLANCHE:
Oh, no. No, Stella.

STELLA [*insisting*]:

I know how it helps your morale just having a little pocket-money on you.

BLANCHE:

No, thank you—I'll take to the streets!

STELLA:

Talk sense! How did you happen to get so low on funds?

BLANCHE:

Money just goes—it goes places. [*She rubs her forehead*] Sometime today I've got to get hold of a Bromo!

STELLA:

I'll fix you one now.

BLANCHE:

Not yet—I've got to keep thinking!

STELLA:

I wish you'd just let things go, at least for a—while . . .

BLANCHE:

Stella, I can't live with him! You can, he's your husband. But how could I stay here with him, after last night, with just those curtains between us?

STELLA:

Blanche, you saw him at his worst last night.

BLANCHE:

On the contrary, I saw him at his best! What such a man has to offer is animal force and he gave a wonderful exhibition of that! But the only way to live with such a man is to—go to bed with him! And that's your job—not mine!

177

STELLA:

After you've rested a little, you'll see it's going to work out. You don't have to worry about anything while you're here. I mean—expenses...

BLANCHE:

I have to plan for us both, to get us both—out!

STELLA:

You take it for granted that I am in something that I want to get out of.

BLANCHE:

I take it for granted that you still have sufficient memory of Belle Reve to find this place and these poker players impossible to live with.

STELLA:

Well, you're taking entirely too much for granted.

BLANCHE:

I can't believe you're in earnest.

STELLA:

No?

BLANCHE:

I understand how it happened—a little. You saw him in uniform, an officer, not here but—

STELLA:

I'm not sure it would have made any difference where I saw him.

BLANCHE:

Now don't say it was one of those mysterious electric things between people! If you do I'll laugh in your face.

STELLA:

I am not going to say anything more at all about it!

BLANCHE:

All right, then, don't!

STELLA:

But there are things that happen between a man and a woman in the dark—that sort of make everything else seem—unimportant. [*pause*]

BLANCHE:

What you are talking about is brutal desire—just— Desire!—the name of that rattle-trap streetcar that bangs through the Quarter, up one old narrow street and down another ...

STELLA:

Haven't you ever ridden on that streetcar?

BLANCHE:

It brought me here.—Where I'm not wanted and where I'm ashamed to be ...

STELLA:

Then don't you think your superior attitude is a bit out of place?

BLANCHE:

I am not being or feeling at all superior, Stella. Believe me I'm not! It's just this. This is how I look at it. A man like that is someone to go out with—once—twice—three times when the devil is in you. But live with? Have a child by?

STELLA:

I have told you I love him.

179

BLANCHE:

Then I *tremble* for you! I just—*tremble* for you....

STELLA:

I can't help your trembling if you insist on trembling!

[*There is a pause.*]

BLANCHE:

May I—speak—*plainly?*

STELLA:

Yes, do. Go ahead. As plainly as you want to.

[*Outside, a train approaches. They are silent till the noise subsides. They are both in the bedroom.*

[*Under cover of the train's noise Stanley enters from outside. He stands unseen by the women, holding some packages in his arms, and overhears their following conversation. He wears an undershirt and grease-stained seersucker pants.*]

BLANCHE:

Well—if you'll forgive me—he's *common!*

STELLA:

Why, yes, I suppose he is.

BLANCHE:

Suppose! You can't have forgotten that much of our bringing up, Stella, that you just *suppose* that any part of a gentleman's in his nature! *Not one particle, no!* Oh, if he was just—*ordinary!* Just *plain*—but good and wholesome, but—*no.* There's something downright—*bestial*—about him! You're hating me saying this, aren't you?

STELLA [*coldly*]:

Go on and say it all, Blanche.

BLANCHE:

He acts like an animal, has an animal's habits! Eats like one, moves like one, talks like one! There's even something—sub-human—something not quite to the stage of humanity yet! Yes, something—ape-like about him, like one of those pictures I've seen in—anthropological studies! Thousands and thousands of years have passed him right by, and there he is—Stanley Kowalski—survivor of the Stone Age! Bearing the raw meat home from the kill in the jungle! And you—*you* here—*waiting* for him! Maybe he'll strike you or maybe grunt and kiss you! That is, if kisses have been discovered yet! Night falls and the other apes gather! There in the front of the cave, all grunting like him, and swilling and gnawing and hulking! His poker night!—you call it—this party of apes! Somebody growls—some creature snatches at something—the fight is on! *God!* Maybe we are a long way from being made in God's image, but Stella—my sister—there has been *some* progress since then! Such things as art—as poetry and music—such kinds of new light have come into the world since then! In some kinds of people some tenderer feelings have had some little beginning! That we have got to make *grow!* And *cling* to, and hold as our flag! In this dark march toward whatever it is we're approaching. . . . *Don't—don't hang back with the brutes!*

[*Another train passes outside. Stanley hesitates, licking his lips. Then suddenly he turns stealthily about and withdraws through front door. The women are still unaware of his presence. When the train has passed he calls through the closed front door.*]

181

STANLEY:
Hey! Hey, Stella!

STELLA [*who has listened gravely to Blanche*]:
Stanley!

BLANCHE:
Stell, I—

[*But Stella has gone to the front door. Stanley enters casually with his packages.*]

STANLEY:
Hiyuh, Stella. Blanche back?

STELLA:
Yes, she's back.

STANLEY:
Hiyuh, Blanche. [*He grins at her.*]

STELLA:
You must've got under the car.

STANLEY:
Them darn mechanics at Fritz's don't know their ass fr'm— *Hey!*

[*Stella has embraced him with both arms, fiercely, and full in the view of Blanche. He laughs and clasps her head to him. Over her head he grins through the curtains at Blanche.*

[*As the lights fade away, with a lingering brightness on their embrace, the music of the "blue piano" and trumpet and drums is heard.*]

SCENE FIVE

Blanche is seated in the bedroom fanning herself with a palm leaf as she reads over a just-completed letter. Suddenly she bursts into a peal of laughter. Stella is dressing in the bedroom.

STELLA:

What are you laughing at, honey?

BLANCHE:

Myself, myself, for being such a liar! I'm writing a letter to Shep. [*She picks up the letter*] "Darling Shep. I am spending the summer on the wing, making flying visits here and there. And who knows, perhaps I shall take a sudden notion to *swoop* down on *Dallas!* How would you feel about that? Ha-ha! [*She laughs nervously and brightly, touching her throat as if actually talking to Shep*] Forewarned is forearmed, as they say!"—How does that sound?

STELLA:

Uh-huh . . .

BLANCHE [*going on nervously*]:

"Most of my sister's friends go north in the summer but some have homes on the Gulf and there has been a continued round of entertainments, teas, cocktails, and luncheons—"

[*A disturbance is heard upstairs at the Hubbell's apartment.*]

STELLA:

Eunice seems to be having some trouble with Steve.

183

[*Eunice's voice shouts in terrible wrath.*]

EUNICE:

I heard about you and that blonde!

STEVE:

That's a damn lie!

EUNICE:

You ain't pulling the wool over my eyes! I wouldn't mind if you'd stay down at the Four Deuces, but you always going up.

STEVE:

Who ever seen me up?

EUNICE:

I seen you chasing her 'round the balcony—I'm gonna call the vice squad!

STEVE:

Don't you throw that at me!

EUNICE [*shrieking*]:

You hit me! I'm gonna call the police!

[*A clatter of aluminum striking a wall is heard, followed by a man's angry roar, shouts and overturned furniture. There is a crash; then a relative hush.*]

BLANCHE [*brightly*]:

Did he *kill* her?

[*Eunice appears on the steps in daemonic disorder.*]

STELLA:

No! She's coming downstairs.

184

EUNICE:

Call the police, I'm going to call the police! [*She rushes around the corner.*]

[*They laugh lightly. Stanley comes around the corner in his green and scarlet silk bowling shirt. He trots up the steps and bangs into the kitchen. Blanche registers his entrance with nervous gestures.*]

STANLEY:

What's a matter with Eun-uss?

STELLA:

She and Steve had a row. Has she got the police?

STANLEY:

Naw. She's gettin' a drink.

STELLA:

That's much more practical!

[*Steve comes down nursing a bruise on his forehead and looks in the door.*]

STEVE:
She here?

STANLEY:

Naw, naw. At the Four Deuces.

STEVE:

That rutting hunk! [*He looks around the corner a bit timidly, then turns with affected boldness and runs after her.*]

BLANCHE:

I must jot that down in my notebook. Ha-ha! I'm com-

185

piling a notebook of quaint little words and phrases I've picked up here.

STANLEY:

You won't pick up nothing here you ain't heard before.

BLANCHE:

Can I count on that?

STANLEY:

You can count on it up to five hundred.

BLANCHE:

That's a mighty high number. [*He jerks open the bureau drawer, slams it shut and throws shoes in a corner. At each noise Blanche winces slightly. Finally she speaks*] What sign were you born under?

STANLEY [*while he is dressing*]:

Sign?

BLANCHE:

Astrological sign. I bet you were born under Aries. Aries people are forceful and dynamic. They dote on noise! They love to bang things around! You must have had lots of banging around in the army and now that you're out, you make up for it by treating inanimate objects with such a fury!

[*Stella has been going in and out of closet during this scene. Now she pops her head out of the closet.*]

STELLA:

Stanley was born just five minutes after Christmas.

BLANCHE:

Capricorn—the Goat!

STANLEY:

What sign were *you* born under?

BLANCHE:

Oh, my birthday's next month, the fifteenth of September; that's under Virgo.

STANLEY:

What's Virgo?

BLANCHE:

Virgo is the Virgin.

STANLEY [*contemptuously*]:

Hah! [*He advances a little as he knots his tie*] Say, do you happen to know somebody named Shaw?

[*Her face expresses a faint shock. She reaches for the cologne bottle and dampens her handkerchief as she answers carefully.*]

BLANCHE:

Why, everybody knows somebody named Shaw!

STANLEY:

Well, this somebody named Shaw is under the impression he met you in Laurel, but I figure he must have got you mixed up with some other party because this other party is someone he met at a hotel called the Flamingo.

[*Blanche laughs breathlessly as she touches the cologne-dampened handkerchief to her temples.*]

BLANCHE:

I'm afraid he does have me mixed up with this "other party." The Hotel Flamingo is not the sort of establishment I would dare to be seen in!

187

STANLEY:

You know of it?

BLANCHE:

Yes, I've seen it and smelled it.

STANLEY:

You must've got pretty close if you could smell it.

BLANCHE:

The odor of cheap perfume is penetrating.

STANLEY:

That stuff you use is expensive?

BLANCHE:

Twenty-five dollars an ounce! I'm nearly out. That's just a hint if you want to remember my birthday! [*She speaks lightly but her voice has a note of fear.*]

STANLEY:

Shaw must've got you mixed up. He goes in and out of Laurel all the time so he can check on it and clear up any mistake.

[*He turns away and crosses to the portieres. Blanche closes her eyes as if faint. Her hand trembles as she lifts the handkerchief again to her forehead.*

[*Steve and Eunice come around corner. Steve's arm is around Eunice's shoulder and she is sobbing luxuriously and he is cooing love-words. There is a murmur of thunder as they go slowly upstairs in a tight embrace.*]

STANLEY [*to Stella*]:

I'll wait for you at the Four Deuces!

STELLA:

Hey! Don't I rate one kiss?

STANLEY:

Not in front of your sister.

[*He goes out. Blanche rises from her chair. She seems faint; looks about her with an expression of almost panic.*]

BLANCHE:

Stella! What have you heard about me?

STELLA:

Huh?

BLANCHE:

What have people been telling you about me?

STELLA:

Telling?

BLANCHE:

You haven't heard any—unkind—gossip about me?

STELLA:

Why, no, Blanche, of course not!

BLANCHE:

Honey, there was—a good deal of talk in Laurel.

STELLA:

About *you*, Blanche?

BLANCHE:

I wasn't so good the last two years or so, after Belle Reve had started to slip through my fingers.

189

STELLA:

All of us do things we—

BLANCHE:

I never was hard or self-sufficient enough. When people are soft—soft people have got to shimmer and glow—they've got to put on soft colors, the colors of butterfly wings, and put a—paper lantern over the light.... It isn't enough to be soft. You've got to be soft *and attractive*. And I—I'm fading now! I don't know how much longer I can turn the trick.

[*The afternoon has faded to dusk. Stella goes into the bedroom and turns on the light under the paper lantern. She holds a bottled soft drink in her hand.*]

BLANCHE:

Have you been listening to me?

STELLA:

I don't listen to you when you are being morbid! [*She advances with the bottled Coke.*]

BLANCHE [*with abrupt change to gaiety*]:

Is that Coke for me?

STELLA:

Not for anyone else!

BLANCHE:

Why, you precious thing, you! Is it just Coke?

STELLA [*turning*]:

You mean you want a shot in it!

BLANCHE:

Well, honey, a shot never does a Coke any harm! Let me! You mustn't wait on me!

STELLA:

I like to wait on you, Blanche. It makes it seem more like home. [*She goes into the kitchen, finds a glass and pours a shot of whiskey into it.*]

BLANCHE:

I have to admit I love to be waited on ...

[*She rushes into the bedroom. Stella goes to her with the glass. Blanche suddenly clutches Stella's free hand with a moaning sound and presses the hand to her lips. Stella is embarrassed by her show of emotion. Blanche speaks in a choked voice.*]

You're—you're—so *good* to me! And I—

STELLA:

Blanche.

BLANCHE:

I know, I won't! You hate me to talk sentimental! But honey, *believe* I feel things more than I *tell* you! I *won't* stay long! I won't, I *promise* I—

STELLA:

Blanche!

BLANCHE [*hysterically*]:

I won't, I promise, *I'll* go! Go *soon!* I will *really!* I *won't* hang around until he—throws me out ...

STELLA:

Now will you stop talking foolish?

BLANCHE:

Yes, honey. Watch how you pour—that fizzy stuff foams over!

191

[*Blanche laughs shrilly and grabs the glass, but her hand shakes so it almost slips from her grasp. Stella pours the Coke into the glass. It foams over and spills. Blanche gives a piercing cry.*]

STELLA [*shocked by the cry*]:
Heavens!

BLANCHE:
Right on my pretty white skirt!

STELLA:
Oh ... Use my hanky. Blot gently.

BLANCHE [*slowly recovering*]:
I know—gently—gently...

STELLA:
Did it stain?

BLANCHE:
Not a bit. Ha-ha! Isn't that lucky? [*She sits down shakily, taking a grateful drink. She holds the glass in both hands and continues to laugh a little.*]

STELLA:
Why did you scream like that?

BLANCHE:
I don't know why I screamed! [*continuing nervously*] Mitch—Mitch is coming at seven. I guess I am just feeling nervous about our relations. [*She begins to talk rapidly and breathlessly*] He hasn't gotten a thing but a good-night kiss, that's all I have given him, Stella. I want his respect. And men don't want anything they get too easy. But on the other hand men lose interest quickly. Especially when the girl is over—thirty. They think a

girl over thirty ought to—the vulgar term is—"put out."
. . . And I—I'm not "putting out." Of course he—he
doesn't know—I mean I haven't informed him—of my
real age!

STELLA:
Why are you sensitive about your age?

BLANCHE:
Because of hard knocks my vanity's been given. What I
mean is—he thinks I'm sort of—prim and proper, you
know! [*She laughs out sharply*] I want to *deceive* him
enough to make him—want me . . .

STELLA:
Blanche, do you want *him?*

BLANCHE:
I want to *rest!* I want to breathe quietly again! Yes—I
want Mitch . . . *very badly!* Just think! If it happens! I
can leave here and not be anyone's problem . . .

[*Stanley comes around the corner with a drink under
his belt.*]

STANLEY [*bawling*]:
Hey, Steve! Hey, Eunice! Hey, Stella!

[*There are joyous calls from above. Trumpet and
drums are heard from around the corner.*]

STELLA [*kissing Blanche impulsively*]:
It *will* happen!

BLANCHE [*doubtfully*]:
It will?

STELLA:
It *will!* [*She goes across into the kitchen, looking back*

193

at Blanche.] It will, honey, *it will.* . . . But don't take another drink! [*Her voice catches as she goes out the door to meet her husband.*

[*Blanche sinks faintly back in her chair with her drink. Eunice shrieks with laughter and runs down the steps. Steve bounds after her with goat-like screeches and chases her around corner. Stanley and Stella twine arms as they follow, laughing.*

[*Dusk settles deeper. The music from the Four Deuces is slow and blue.*]

BLANCHE:

Ah, me, ah, me, ah, me . . .

[*Her eyes fall shut and the palm leaf fan drops from her fingers. She slaps her hand on the chair arm a couple of times. There is a little glimmer of lightning about the building.*

[*A Young Man comes along the street and rings the bell.*]

BLANCHE:

Come in.

[*The Young Man appears through the portieres. She regards him with interest.*]

BLANCHE:

Well, well! What can I do for *you?*

YOUNG MAN:

I'm collecting for *The Evening Star.*

BLANCHE:

I didn't know that stars took up collections.

194

YOUNG MAN:

It's the paper.

BLANCHE:

I know, I was joking—feebly! Will you—have a drink?

YOUNG MAN:

No, ma'am. No, thank you. I can't drink on the job.

BLANCHE:

Oh, well, now, let's see. . . . No, I don't have a dime! I'm not the lady of the house. I'm her sister from Mississippi. I'm one of those poor relations you've heard about.

YOUNG MAN:

That's all right. I'll drop by later. [*He starts to go out. She approaches a little.*]

BLANCHE:

Hey! [*He turns back shyly. She puts a cigarette in a long holder*] Could you give me a light? [*She crosses toward him. They meet at the door between the two rooms.*]

YOUNG MAN:

Sure. [*He takes out a lighter*] This doesn't always work.

BLANCHE:

It's temperamental? [*It flares*] Ah!—thank you. [*He starts away again*] Hey! [*He turns again, still more uncertainly. She goes close to him*] Uh—what time is it?

YOUNG MAN:

Fifteen of seven, ma'am.

BLANCHE:

So late? Don't you just love these long rainy afternoons in New Orleans when an hour isn't just an hour—but a

195

little piece of eternity dropped into your hands—and who knows what to do with it? [*She touches his shoulders.*] You—uh—didn't get wet in the rain?

YOUNG MAN:

No, ma'am. I stepped inside.

BLANCHE:

In a drugstore? And had a soda?

YOUNG MAN:

Uh-huh.

BLANCHE:

Chocolate?

YOUNG MAN:

No, ma'am. Cherry.

BLANCHE [*laughing*]:

Cherry!

YOUNG MAN:

A cherry soda.

BLANCHE:

You make my mouth water. [*She touches his cheek lightly, and smiles. Then she goes to the trunk.*]

YOUNG MAN:

Well, I'd better be going—

BLANCHE [*stopping him*]:

Young man!

[*He turns. She takes a large, gossamer scarf from the trunk and drapes it about her shoulders.*]

[*In the ensuing pause, the "blue piano" is heard. It continues through the rest of this scene and the opening of the next. The young man clears his throat and looks yearningly at the door.*]

Young man! Young, young, young man! Has anyone ever told you that you look like a young Prince out of the Arabian Nights?

[*The Young Man laughs uncomfortably and stands like a bashful kid. Blanche speaks softly to him.*]

Well, you do, honey lamb! Come here. I want to kiss you, just once, softly and sweetly on your mouth!

[*Without waiting for him to accept, she crosses quickly to him and presses her lips to his.*]

Now run along, now, quickly! It would be nice to keep you, but I've got to be good—and keep my hands off children.

[*He stares at her a moment. She opens the door for him and blows a kiss at him as he goes down the steps with a dazed look. She stands there a little dreamily after he has disappeared. Then Mitch appears around the corner with a bunch of roses.*]

BLANCHE [*gaily*]:
Look who's coming! My Rosenkavalier! Bow to me first . . . now present them! *Ahhhh—Merciiii!*

[*She looks at him over them, coquettishly pressing them to her lips. He beams at her self-consciously.*]

SCENE SIX

*It is about two A.M. on the same evening. The outer wall
of the building is visible. Blanche and Mitch come in.
The utter exhaustion which only a neurasthenic personality can know is evident in Blanche's voice and manner.
Mitch is stolid but depressed. They have probably been
out to the amusement park on Lake Pontchartrain, for
Mitch is bearing, upside down, a plaster statuette of Mae
West, the sort of prize won at shooting galleries and carnival games of chance.*

BLANCHE [*stopping lifelessly at the steps*]:
Well—
[*Mitch laughs uneasily.*]
Well...

MITCH:
I guess it must be pretty late—and you're tired.

BLANCHE:
Even the hot tamale man has deserted the street, and he
hangs on till the end. [*Mitch laughs uneasily again*]
How will you get home?

MITCH:
I'll walk over to Bourbon and catch an owl-car.

BLANCHE [*laughing grimly*]:
Is that streetcar named Desire still grinding along the
tracks at this hour?

MITCH [*heavily*]:
I'm afraid you haven't gotten much fun out of this evening, Blanche.

198

BLANCHE:

I spoiled it for *you*.

MITCH:

No, you didn't, but I felt all the time that I wasn't giving you much—entertainment.

BLANCHE:

I simply couldn't rise to the occasion. That was all. I don't think I've ever tried so hard to be gay and made such a dismal mess of it. I get ten points for trying!—I *did* try.

MITCH:

Why did you try if you didn't feel like it, Blanche?

BLANCHE:

I was just obeying the law of nature.

MITCH:

Which law is that?

BLANCHE:

The one that says the lady must entertain the gentleman —or no dice! See if you can locate my door key in this purse. When I'm so tired my fingers are all thumbs!

MITCH [*rooting in her purse*]:
This it?

BLANCHE:

No, honey, that's the key to my trunk which I must soon be packing.

MITCH:

You mean you are leaving here soon?

BLANCHE:

I've outstayed my welcome.

199

MITCH:

This it?

[*The music fades away.*]

BLANCHE:

Eureka! Honey, you open the door while I take a last look at the sky. [*She leans on the porch rail. He opens the door and stands awkwardly behind her.*] I'm looking for the Pleiades, the Seven Sisters, but these girls are not out tonight. Oh, yes they are, there they are! God bless them! All in a bunch going home from their little bridge party.... Y' get the door open? Good boy! I guess you— want to go now ...

[*He shuffles and coughs a little.*]

MITCH:

Can I—uh—kiss you—good night?

BLANCHE:

Why do you always ask me if you may?

MITCH:

I don't know whether you want me to or not.

BLANCHE:

Why should you be so doubtful?

MITCH:

That night when we parked by the lake and I kissed you, you—

BLANCHE:

Honey, it wasn't the kiss I objected to. I liked the kiss very much. It was the other little—familiarity—that I— felt obliged to—discourage.... I didn't resent it! Not a bit in the world! In fact, I was somewhat flattered that you—desired me! But, honey, you know as well as I do that a single girl, a girl alone in the world, has got to keep a firm hold on her emotions or she'll be lost!

MITCH [*solemnly*]:

Lost?

BLANCHE:

I guess you are used to girls that like to be lost. The kind that get lost immediately, on the first date!

MITCH:

I like you to be exactly the way that you are, because in all my—experience—I have never known anyone like you.

[*Blanche looks at him gravely; then she bursts into laughter and then claps a hand to her mouth.*]

MITCH:

Are you laughing at me?

BLANCHE:

No, honey. The lord and lady of the house have not yet returned, so come in. We'll have a nightcap. Let's leave the lights off. Shall we?

MITCH:

You just—do what you want to.

[*Blanche precedes him into the kitchen. The outer wall of the building disappears and the interiors of the two rooms can be dimly seen.*]

BLANCHE [*remaining in the first room*]:

The other room's more comfortable—go on in. This crashing around in the dark is my search for some liquor.

MITCH:

You want a drink?

201

BLANCHE:

I want *you* to have a drink! You have been so anxious and solemn all evening, and so have I; we have both been anxious and solemn and now for these few last remaining moments of our lives together—I want to create—*joie de vivre!* I'm lighting a candle.

MITCH:

That's good.

BLANCHE:

We are going to be very Bohemian. We are going to pretend that we are sitting in a little artists' cafe on the Left Bank in Paris! [*She lights a candle stub and puts it in a bottle.*] *Je suis la Dame aux Camellias! Vous êtes— Armand!* Understand French?

MITCH [*heavily*]:

Naw. Naw, I—

BLANCHE:

Voulez-vous couchez avec moi ce soir? Vous ne comprenez pas? Ah, quelle dommage!—I mean it's a damned good thing. . . . I've found some liquor! Just enough for two shots without any dividends, honey . . .

MITCH [*heavily*]:

That's—good.

[*She enters the bedroom with the drinks and the candle.*]

BLANCHE:

Sit down! Why don't you take off your coat and loosen your collar?

MITCH:

I better leave it on.

BLANCHE:

No. I want you to be comfortable.

MITCH:

I am ashamed of the way I perspire. My shirt is sticking to me.

BLANCHE:

Perspiration is healthy. If people didn't perspire they would die in five minutes. [*She takes his coat from him*] This is a nice coat. What kind of material is it?

MITCH:

They call that stuff alpaca.

BLANCHE:

Oh. Alpaca.

MITCH:

It's very light-weight alpaca.

BLANCHE:

Oh. Light weight alpaca.

MITCH:

I don't like to wear a wash-coat even in summer because I sweat through it.

BLANCHE:

Oh.

MITCH:

And it don't look neat on me. A man with a heavy build has got to be careful of what he puts on him so he don't look too clumsy.

BLANCHE:

You are not too heavy.

203

MITCH:

You don't think I am?

BLANCHE:

You are not the delicate type. You have a massive bone-structure and a very imposing physique.

MITCH:

Thank you. Last Christmas I was given a membership to the New Orleans Athletic Club.

BLANCHE:

Oh, good.

MITCH:

It was the finest present I ever was given. I work out there with the weights and I swim and I keep myself fit. When I started there, I was getting soft in the belly but now my belly is hard. It is so hard now that a man can punch me in the belly and it don't hurt me. Punch me! Go on! See? [*She pokes lightly at him.*]

BLANCHE:

Gracious. [*Her hand touches her chest.*]

MITCH:

Guess how much I weigh, Blanche?

BLANCHE:

Oh, I'd say in the vicinity of—one hundred and eighty?

MITCH:

Guess again.

BLANCHE:

Not that much?

MITCH:

No. More.

BLANCHE:

Well, you're a tall man and you can carry a good deal of weight without looking awkward.

MITCH:

I weigh two hundred and seven pounds and I'm six feet one and one half inches tall in my bare feet—without shoes on. And that is what I weigh stripped.

BLANCHE:

Oh, my goodness, me! It's awe-inspiring.

MITCH [*embarrassed*]:

My weight is not a very interesting subject to talk about. [*He hesitates for a moment*] What's yours?

BLANCHE:

My weight?

MITCH:

Yes.

BLANCHE:

Guess!

MITCH:

Let me lift you.

BLANCHE:

Samson! Go on, lift me. [*He comes behind her and puts his hands on her waist and raises her lightly off the ground*] Well?

MITCH:

You are light as a feather.

BLANCHE:

Ha-ha! [*He lowers her but keeps his hands on her waist. Blanche speaks with an affectation of demureness*] You may release me now.

MITCH:

Huh?

BLANCHE [*gaily*]:

I said unhand me, sir. [*He fumblingly embraces her. Her voice sounds gently reproving*] Now, Mitch. Just because Stanley and Stella aren't at home is no reason why you shouldn't behave like a gentleman.

MITCH:

Just give me a slap whenever I step out of bounds.

BLANCHE:

That won't be necessary. You're a natural gentleman, one of the very few that are left in the world. I don't want you to think that I am severe and old maid school-teacherish or anything like that. It's just—well—

MITCH:

Huh?

BLANCHE:

I guess it is just that I have—old-fashioned ideals! [*She rolls her eyes, knowing he cannot see her face. Mitch goes to the front door. There is a considerable silence between them. Blanche sighs and Mitch coughs self-consciously.*]

MITCH [*finally*]:

Where's Stanley and Stella tonight?

206

BLANCHE:

They have gone out. With Mr. and Mrs. Hubbell upstairs.

MITCH:

Where did they go?

BLANCHE:

I think they were planning to go to a midnight prevue at Loew's State.

MITCH:

We should all go out together some night.

BLANCHE:

No. That wouldn't be a good plan.

MITCH:

Why not?

BLANCHE:

You are an old friend of Stanley's?

MITCH:

We was together in the Two-forty-first.

BLANCHE:

I guess he talks to you frankly?

MITCH:

Sure.

BLANCHE:

Has he talked to you about me?

MITCH:

Oh—not very much.

BLANCHE:

The way you say that, I suspect that he has.

MITCH:

No, he hasn't said much.

BLANCHE:

But what he *has* said. What would you say his attitude toward me was?

MITCH:

Why do you want to ask that?

BLANCHE:

Well—

MITCH:

Don't you get along with him?

BLANCHE:

What do you think?

MITCH:

I don't think he understands you.

BLANCHE:

That is putting it mildly. If it weren't for Stella about to have a baby, I wouldn't be able to endure things here.

MITCH:

He isn't—nice to you?

BLANCHE:

He is insufferably rude. Goes out of his way to offend me.

MITCH:

In what way, Blanche?

BLANCHE:

Why, in every conceivable way.

208

MITCH:

I'm surprised to hear that.

BLANCHE:

Are you?

MITCH:

Well, I—don't see how anybody could be rude to you.

BLANCHE:

It's really a pretty frightful situation. You see, there's no privacy here. There's just these portieres between the two rooms at night. He stalks through the rooms in his underwear at night. And I have to ask him to close the bathroom door. That sort of commonness isn't necessary. You probably wonder why I don't move out. Well, I'll tell you frankly. A teacher's salary is barely sufficient for her living expenses. I didn't save a penny last year and so I had to come here for the summer. That's why I have to put up with my sister's husband. And he has to put up with me, apparently so much against his wishes. . . . Surely he must have told you how much he hates me!

MITCH:

I don't think he hates you.

BLANCHE:

He hates me. Or why would he insult me? The first time I laid eyes on him I thought to myself, that man is my executioner! That man will destroy me, unless ——

MITCH:

Blanche—

BLANCHE:

Yes, honey?

209

MITCH:

Can I ask you a question?

BLANCHE:

Yes. What?

MITCH:

How old are you?

[*She makes a nervous gesture.*]

BLANCHE:

Why do you want to know?

MITCH:

I talked to my mother about you and she said, "How old is Blanche?" And I wasn't able to tell her. [*There is another pause.*]

BLANCHE:

You talked to your mother about me?

MITCH:

Yes.

BLANCHE:

Why?

MITCH:

.I told my mother how nice you were, and I liked you.

BLANCHE:

Were you sincere about that?

MITCH:

You know I was.

BLANCHE:

Why did your mother want to know my age?

MITCH:

Mother is sick.

BLANCHE:

I'm sorry to hear it. Badly?

MITCH:

She won't live long. Maybe just a few months.

BLANCHE:

Oh.

MITCH:

She worries because I'm not settled.

BLANCHE:

Oh.

MITCH:

She wants me to be settled down before she— [*His voice is hoarse and he clears his throat twice, shuffling nervously around with his hands in and out of his pockets.*]

BLANCHE:

You love her very much, don't you?

MITCH:

Yes.

BLANCHE:

I think you have a great capacity for devotion. You will be lonely when she passes on, won't you? [*Mitch clears his throat and nods.*] I understand what that is.

MITCH:

To be lonely?

BLANCHE:

I loved someone, too, and the person I loved I lost.

MITCH:

Dead? [*She crosses to the window and sits on the sill, looking out. She pours herself another drink.*] A man?

BLANCHE:

He was a boy, just a boy, when I was a very young girl. When I was sixteen, I made the discovery—love. All at once and much, much too completely. It was like you suddenly turned a blinding light on something that had always been half in shadow, that's how it struck the world for me. But I was unlucky. Deluded. There was something different about the boy, a nervousness, a softness and tenderness which wasn't like a man's, although he wasn't the least bit effeminate looking—still —that thing was there. . . . He came to me for help. I didn't know that. I didn't find out anything till after our marriage when we'd run away and come back and all I knew was I'd failed him in some mysterious way and wasn't able to give the help he needed but couldn't speak of! He was in the quicksands and clutching at me—but I wasn't holding him out, I was slipping in with him! I didn't know that. I didn't know anything except I loved him unendurably but without being able to help him or help myself. Then I found out. In the worst of all possible ways. By coming suddenly into a room that I thought was empty—which wasn't empty, but had two people in it . . . the boy I had married and an older man who had been his friend for years . . .

[*A locomotive is heard approaching outside. She claps her hands to her ears and crouches over. The headlight of the locomotive glares into the room as it thunders past. As the noise recedes she straightens slowly and continues speaking.*]

212

Afterward we pretended that nothing had been discovered. Yes, the three of us drove out to Moon Lake Casino, very drunk and laughing all the way.

[*Polka music sounds, in a minor key faint with distance.*]

We danced the Varsouviana! Suddenly in the middle of the dance the boy I had married broke away from me and ran out of the casino. A few moments later—a shot!

[*The polka stops abruptly.*

[*Blanche rises stiffly. Then, the polka resumes in a major key.*]

I ran out—all did!—all ran and gathered about the terrible thing at the edge of the lake! I couldn't get near for the crowding. Then somebody caught my arm. "Don't go any closer! Come back! You don't want to see!" See? See what! Then I heard voices say—Allan! Allan! The Grey boy! He'd stuck the revolver into his mouth, and fired—so that the back of his head had been—blown away!

[*She sways and covers her face.*]

It was because—on the dance floor—unable to stop myself—I'd suddenly said—"I saw! I know! You disgust me..." And then the searchlight which had been turned on the world was turned off again and never for one moment since has there been any light that's stronger than this—kitchen—candle...

[*Mitch gets up awkwardly and moves toward her a little. The polka music increases. Mitch stands beside her.*]

213

MITCH [*drawing her slowly into his arms*]:
You need somebody. And I need somebody, too. Could it be—you and me, Blanche?

[*She stares at him vacantly for a moment. Then with a soft cry huddles in his embrace. She makes a sobbing effort to speak but the words won't come. He kisses her forehead and her eyes and finally her lips. The Polka tune fades out. Her breath is drawn and released in long, grateful sobs.*]

BLANCHE:
Sometimes—there's God—so quickly!

SCENE SEVEN

It is late afternoon in mid-September.

The portieres are open and a table is set for a birthday supper, with cake and flowers.

Stella is completing the decorations as Stanley comes in.

STANLEY:
What's all this stuff for?

STELLA:
Honey, it's Blanche's birthday.

STANLEY:
She here?

STELLA:
In the bathroom.

STANLEY [*mimicking*]:
"Washing out some things"?

STELLA:
I reckon so.

STANLEY:
How long she been in there?

STELLA:
All afternoon.

STANLEY [*mimicking*]:
"Soaking in a hot tub"?

STELLA:
Yes.

215

STANLEY:

Temperature 100 on the nose, and she soaks herself in a hot tub.

STELLA:

She says it cools her off for the evening.

STANLEY:

And you run out an' get her cokes, I suppose? And serve 'em to Her Majesty in the tub? [*Stella shrugs*] Set down here a minute.

STELLA:

Stanley, I've got things to do.

STANLEY:

Set down! I've got th' dope on your big sister, Stella.

STELLA:

Stanley, stop picking on Blanche.

STANLEY:

That girl calls *me* common!

STELLA:

Lately you been doing all you can think of to rub her the wrong way, Stanley, and Blanche is sensitive and you've got to realize that Blanche and I grew up under very different circumstances than you did.

STANLEY:

So I been told. And told and told and told! You know she's been feeding us a pack of lies here?

STELLA:

No, I don't, and—

STANLEY:

Well, she has, however. But now the cat's out of the bag! I found out some things!

STELLA:

What—things?

STANLEY:

Things I already suspected. But now I got proof from the most reliable sources—which I have checked on!

[*Blanche is singing in the bathroom a saccharine popular ballad which is used contrapuntally with Stanley's speech.*]

STELLA [*to Stanley*]:

Lower your voice!

STANLEY:

Some canary bird, huh!

STELLA:

Now please tell me quietly what you think you've found out about my sister.

STANLEY:

Lie Number One: All this squeamishness she puts on! You should just know the line she's been feeding to Mitch. He thought she had never been more than kissed by a fellow! But Sister Blanche is no lily! Ha-ha! Some lily she is!

STELLA:

What have you heard and who from?

STANLEY:

Our supply-man down at the plant has been going through Laurel for years and he knows all about her and everybody else in the town of Laurel knows all about her. She is as famous in Laurel as if she was the President of the United States, only she is not respected by any party! This supply-man stops at a hotel called the Flamingo.

BLANCHE [*singing blithely*]:

"Say, it's only a paper moon, Sailing over a cardboard sea
—But it wouldn't be make-believe If you believed in
me!"

STELLA:

What about the—Flamingo?

STANLEY:

She stayed there, too.

STELLA:

My sister lived at Belle Reve.

STANLEY:

This is after the home-place had slipped through her lily-
white fingers! She moved to the Flamingo! A second-
class hotel which has the advantage of not interfering in
the private social life of the personalities there! The
Flamingo is used to all kinds of goings-on. But even the
management of the Flamingo was impressed by Dame
Blanche! In fact they was so impressed by Dame Blanche
that they requested her to turn in her room key—for
permanently! This happened a couple of weeks before
she showed here.

BLANCHE [*singing*]:

"It's a Barnum and Bailey world, Just as phony as it
can be—
But it wouldn't be make-believe If you believed in me!"

STELLA:

What—contemptible—lies!

STANLEY:

Sure, I can see how you would be upset by this. She pulled
the wool over your eyes as much as Mitch's!

218

STELLA:

It's pure invention! There's not a word of truth in it and if I were a man and this creature had dared to invent such things in my presence—

BLANCHE [*singing*]:

"Without your love,
  It's a honky-tonk parade!
Without your love,
  It's a melody played In a penny arcade..."

STANLEY:

Honey, I told you I thoroughly checked on these stories! Now wait till I finished. The trouble with Dame Blanche was that she couldn't put on her act any more in Laurel! They got wised up after two or three dates with her and then they quit, and she goes on to another, the same old line, same old act, same old hooey! But the town was too small for this to go on forever! And as time went by she became a town character. Regarded as not just different but downright loco—nuts.

[*Stella draws back.*]

And for the last year or two she has been washed up like poison. That's why she's here this summer, visiting royalty, putting on all this act—because she's practically told by the mayor to get out of town! Yes, did you know there was an army camp near Laurel and your sister's was one of the places called "Out-of-Bounds"?

BLANCHE:

"It's only a paper moon, Just as phony as it can be—
  But it wouldn't be make-believe If you believed in me!"

219

STANLEY:

Well, so much for her being such a refined and particular type of girl. Which brings us to Lie Number Two.

STELLA:

I don't want to hear any more!

STANLEY:

She's not going back to teach school! In fact I am willing to bet you that she never had no idea of returning to Laurel! She didn't resign temporarily from the high school because of her nerves! No, siree, Bob! She didn't. They kicked her out of that high school before the spring term ended—and I hate to tell you the reason that step was taken! A seventeen-year-old boy—she'd gotten mixed up with!

BLANCHE:

"It's a Barnum and Bailey world, Just as phony as it can be—"

[*In the bathroom the water goes on loud; little breathless cries and peals of laughter are heard as if a child were frolicking in the tub.*]

STELLA:

This is making me—sick!

STANLEY:

The boy's dad learned about it and got in touch with the high school superintendent. Boy, oh, boy, I'd like to have been in that office when Dame Blanche was called on the carpet! I'd like to have seen her trying to squirm out of that one! But they had her on the hook good and proper

220

that time and she knew that the jig was all up! They told her she better move on to some fresh territory. Yep, it was practickly a town ordinance passed against her!

[*The bathroom door is opened and Blanche thrusts her head out, holding a towel about her hair.*]

BLANCHE:

Stella!

STELLA [*faintly*]:

Yes, Blanche?

BLANCHE:

Give me another bath-towel to dry my hair with. I've just washed it.

STELLA:

Yes, Blanche. [*She crosses in a dazed way from the kitchen to the bathroom door with a towel.*]

BLANCHE:

What's the matter, honey?

STELLA:

Matter? Why?

BLANCHE:

You have such a strange expression on your face!

STELLA:

Oh— [*She tries to laugh*] I guess I'm a little tired!

BLANCHE:

Why don't you bathe, too, soon as I get out?

STANLEY [*calling from the kitchen*]:

How soon is that going to be?

BLANCHE:

Not so terribly long! Possess your soul in patience!

221

STANLEY:

It's not my soul, it's my kidneys I'm worried about!

[*Blanche slams the door. Stanley laughs harshly. Stella comes slowly back into the kitchen.*]

STANLEY:

Well, what do you think of it?

STELLA:

I don't believe all of those stories and I think your supply-man was mean and rotten to tell them. It's possible that some of the things he said are partly true. There are things about my sister I don't approve of—things that caused sorrow at home. She was always—flighty!

STANLEY:

Flighty!

STELLA:

But when she was young, very young, she married a boy who wrote poetry. . . . He was extremely good-looking. I think Blanche didn't just love him but worshipped the ground he walked on! Adored him and thought him almost too fine to be human! But then she found out—

STANLEY:

What?

STELLA:

This beautiful and talented young man was a degenerate. Didn't your supply-man give you that information?

STANLEY:

All we discussed was recent history. That must have been a pretty long time ago.

STELLA:

Yes, it was—a pretty long time ago ...

[*Stanley comes up and takes her by the shoulders rather gently. She gently withdraws from him. Automatically she starts sticking little pink candles in the birthday cake.*]

STANLEY:

How many candles you putting in that cake?

STELLA:

I'll stop at twenty-five.

STANLEY:

Is company expected?

STELLA:

We asked Mitch to come over for cake and ice-cream.

[*Stanley looks a little uncomfortable. He lights a cigarette from the one he has just finished.*]

STANLEY:

I wouldn't be expecting Mitch over tonight.

[*Stella pauses in her occupation with candles and looks slowly around at Stanley.*]

STELLA:

Why?

STANLEY:

Mitch is a buddy of mine. We were in the same outfit together—Two-forty-first Engineers. We work in the same plant and now on the same bowling team. You think I could face him if—

STELLA:

Stanley Kowalski, did you—did you repeat what that—?

223

STANLEY:

You're goddam right I told him! I'd have that on my conscience the rest of my life if I knew all that stuff and let my best friend get caught!

STELLA:

Is Mitch through with her?

STANLEY:

Wouldn't you be if—?

STELLA:

I said, *Is Mitch through with her?*

[*Blanche's voice is lifted again, serenely as a bell. She sings "But it wouldn't be make-believe If you believed in me."*]

STANLEY:

No, I don't think he's necessarily through with her—just wised up!

STELLA:

Stanley, she thought Mitch was—going to—going to marry her. I was hoping so, too.

STANLEY:

Well, he's not going to marry her. Maybe he *was,* but he's not going to jump in a tank with a school of sharks— now! [*He rises*] Blanche! Oh, Blanche! Can I please get in my bathroom? [*There is a pause.*]

BLANCHE:

Yes, indeed, sir! Can you wait one second while I dry?

STANLEY:

Having waited one hour I guess one second ought to pass in a hurry.

224

STELLA:

And she hasn't got her job? Well, what will she do!

STANLEY:

She's not stayin' here after Tuesday. You know that, don't you? Just to make sure I bought her ticket myself. A bus ticket?

STELLA:

In the first place, Blanche wouldn't go on a bus.

STANLEY:

She'll go on a bus and like it.

STELLA:

No, she won't, no, she won't, Stanley!

STANLEY:

She'll go! Period. P.S. She'll go *Tuesday!*

STELLA [*slowly*]:

What'll—she—do? What on earth will she—*do!*

STANLEY:

Her future is mapped out for her.

STELLA:

What do you mean?

[*Blanche sings.*]

STANLEY:

Hey, canary bird! Toots! Get *OUT* of the *BATH-ROOM!*

[*The bathroom door flies open and Blanche emerges with a gay peal of laughter, but as Stanley crosses past her, a frightened look appears in her face, almost a look of panic. He doesn't look at her but slams the bathroom door shut as he goes in.*]

225

BLANCHE [*snatching up a hair-brush*]:

Oh, I feel so good after my long, hot bath, I feel so good and cool and—rested!

STELLA [*sadly and doubtfully from the kitchen*]:

Do you, Blanche?

BLANCHE [*snatching up a hairbrush*]:

Yes, I do, so refreshed! [*She tinkles her highball glass.*] A hot bath and a long, cold drink always give me a brand new outlook on life! [*She looks through the portieres at Stella, standing between them, and slowly stops brushing*] Something has happened!—What is it?

STELLA [*turning away quickly*]:

Why, nothing has happened, Blanche.

BLANCHE:

You're lying! Something has!

[*She stares fearfully at Stella, who pretends to be busy at the table. The distant piano goes into a hectic breakdown.*]

SCENE EIGHT

Three quarters of an hour later.

The view through the big windows is fading gradually into a still-golden dusk. A torch of sunlight blazes on the side of a big water-tank or oil-drum across the empty lot toward the business district which is now pierced by pin-points of lighted windows or windows reflecting the sunset.

The three people are completing a dismal birthday supper. Stanley looks sullen. Stella is embarrassed and sad.

Blanche has a tight, artificial smile on her drawn face. There is a fourth place at the table which is left vacant.

BLANCHE [*suddenly*]:
Stanley, tell us a joke, tell us a funny story to make us all laugh. I don't know what's the matter, we're all so solemn. Is it because I've been stood up by my beau?

[*Stella laughs feebly.*]

It's the first time in my entire experience with men, and I've had a good deal of all sorts, that I've actually been stood up by anybody! Ha-ha! I don't know how to take it.... Tell us a funny little story, Stanley! Something to help us out.

STANLEY:
I didn't think you liked my stories, Blanche.

BLANCHE:
I like them when they're amusing but not indecent.

STANLEY:
I don't know any refined enough for your taste.

227

BLANCHE:

Then let me tell one.

STELLA:

Yes, you tell one, Blanche. You used to know lots of good stories.

[*The music fades.*]

BLANCHE:

Let me see, now. . . . I must run through my repertoire! Oh, yes—I love parrot stories! Do you all like parrot stories? Well, this one's about the old maid and the parrot. This old maid, she had a parrot that cursed a blue streak and knew more vulgar expressions than Mr. Kowalski!

STANLEY:

Huh.

BLANCHE:

And the only way to hush the parrot up was to put the cover back on its cage so it would think it was night and go back to sleep. Well, one morning the old maid had just uncovered the parrot for the day—when who should she see coming up the front walk but the preacher! Well, she rushed back to the parrot and slipped the cover back on the cage and then she let in the preacher. And the parrot was perfectly still, just as quiet as a mouse, but just as she was asking the preacher how much sugar he wanted in his coffee—the parrot broke the silence with a loud—[*She whistles*]—and said—"God *damn,* but that was a short day!"

[*She throws back her head and laughs. Stella also makes an ineffectual effort to seem amused. Stanley pays no attention to the story but reaches way over the table to spear his fork into the remaining chop which he eats with his fingers.*]

BLANCHE:

Apparently Mr. Kowalski was not amused.

STELLA:

Mr. Kowalski is too busy making a pig of himself to think of anything else!

STANLEY:

That's right, baby.

STELLA:

Your face and your fingers are disgustingly greasy. Go and wash up and then help me clear the table.

[*He hurls a plate to the floor.*]

STANLEY:

That's how I'll clear the table! [*He seizes her arm*] Don't ever talk that way to me! "Pig—Polack—disgusting—vulgar—greasy!"—them kind of words have been on your tongue and your sister's too much around here! What do you two think you are? A pair of queens? Remember what Huey Long said—"Every Man is a King!" And I am the king around here, so don't forget it! [*He hurls a cup and saucer to the floor*] My place is cleared! You want me to clear your places?

[*Stella begins to cry weakly. Stanley stalks out on the porch and lights a cigarette.*

[*The Negro entertainers around the corner are heard.*]

BLANCHE:

What happened while I was bathing? What did he tell you, Stella?

STELLA:

Nothing, nothing, nothing!

BLANCHE:

I think he told you something about Mitch and me! You know why Mitch didn't come but you won't tell me! [*Stella shakes her head helplessly*] I'm going to call him!

STELLA:

I wouldn't call him, Blanche.

BLANCHE:

I am, I'm going to call him on the phone.

STELLA [*miserably*]:

I wish you wouldn't.

BLANCHE:

I intend to be given some explanation from someone!

[*She rushes to the phone in the bedroom. Stella goes out on the porch and stares reproachfully at her husband. He grunts and turns away from her.*]

STELLA:

I hope you're pleased with your doings. I never had so much trouble swallowing food in my life, looking at that girl's face and the empty chair! [*She cries quietly.*]

BLANCHE [*at the phone*]:

Hello. Mr. Mitchell, please. . . . Oh. . . . I would like to leave a number if I may. Magnolia 9047. And say it's important to call. . . . Yes, very important. . . . Thank you. [*She remains by the phone with a lost, frightened look.*]

[*Stanley turns slowly back toward his wife and takes her clumsily in his arms.*]

STANLEY:

Stell, it's gonna be all right after she goes and after you've had the baby. It's gonna be all right again between you and me the way that it was. You remember that way that it was? Them nights we had together? God, honey, it's gonna be sweet when we can make noise in the night the way that we used to and get the colored lights going with nobody's sister behind the curtains to hear us!

[*Their upstairs neighbors are heard in bellowing laughter at something. Stanley chuckles.*]

Steve an' Eunice...

STELLA:

Come on back in. [*She returns to the kitchen and starts lighting the candles on the white cake.*] Blanche?

BLANCHE:

Yes. [*She returns from the bedroom to the table in the kitchen.*] Oh, those pretty, pretty little candles! Oh, don't burn them, Stella.

STELLA:

I certainly will.

[*Stanley comes back in.*]

BLANCHE:

You ought to save them for baby's birthdays. Oh, I hope candles are going to glow in his life and I hope that his

231

eyes are going to be like candles, like two blue candles lighted in a white cake!

STANLEY [*sitting down*]:
What poetry!

BLANCHE [*she pauses reflectively for a moment*]:
I shouldn't have called him.

STELLA:
There's lots of things could have happened.

BLANCHE:
There's no excuse for it, Stella. I don't have to put up with insults. I won't be taken for granted.

STANLEY:
Goddamn, it's hot in here with the steam from the bathroom.

BLANCHE:
I've said I was sorry three times. [*The piano fades out.*] I take hot baths for my nerves. Hydrotherapy, they call it. You healthy Polack, without a nerve in your body, of course you don't know what anxiety feels like!

STANLEY:
I am not a Polack. People from Poland are Poles, not Polacks. But what I am is a one-hundred-per-cent American, born and raised in the greatest country on earth and proud as hell of it, so don't ever call me a Polack.

[*The phone rings. Blanche rises expectantly.*]

BLANCHE:
Oh, that's for me, I'm sure.

STANLEY:

I'm not sure. Keep your seat. [*He crosses leisurely to phone.*] H'lo. Aw, yeh, hello, Mac.

[*He leans against wall, staring insultingly in at Blanche. She sinks back in her chair with a frightened look. Stella leans over and touches her shoulder.*]

BLANCHE:

Oh, keep your hands off me, Stella. What is the matter with you? Why do you look at me with that pitying look?

STANLEY [*bawling*]:

QUIET IN THERE!—We've got a noisy woman on the place.—Go on, Mac. At Riley's? No, I don't wanta bowl at Riley's. I had a little trouble with Riley last week. I'm the team captain, ain't I? All right, then, we're not gonna bowl at Riley's, we're gonna bowl at the West Side or the Gala! All right, Mac. See you!

[*He hangs up and returns to the table. Blanche fiercely controls herself, drinking quickly from her tumbler of water. He doesn't look at her but reaches in a pocket. Then he speaks slowly and with false amiability.*]

Sister Blanche, I've got a little birthday remembrance for you.

BLANCHE:

Oh, have you, Stanley? I wasn't expecting any, I—I don't know why Stella wants to observe my birthday! I'd much rather forget it—when you—reach twenty-seven! Well—age is a subject that you'd prefer to—ignore!

STANLEY:

Twenty-seven?

233

BLANCHE [*quickly*]:
What is it? Is it for *me*?

[*He is holding a little envelope toward her.*]

STANLEY:
Yes, I hope you like it!

BLANCHE:
Why, why—Why, it's a—

STANLEY:
Ticket! Back to Laurel! On the Greyhound! Tuesday!

[*The Varsouviana music steals in softly and continues playing. Stella rises abruptly and turns her back. Blanches tries to smile. Then she tries to laugh. Then she gives both up and springs from the table and runs into the next room. She clutches her throat and then runs into the bathroom. Coughing, gagging sounds are heard.*]

Well!

STELLA:
You didn't need to do that.

STANLEY:
Don't forget all that I took off her.

STELLA:
You needn't have been so cruel to someone alone as she is.

STANLEY:
Delicate piece she is.

STELLA:
She is. She was. You didn't know Blanche as a girl. Nobody, nobody, was tender and trusting as she was. But people like you abused her, and forced her to change.

234

[*He crosses into the bedroom, ripping off his shirt, and changes into a brilliant silk bowling shirt. She follows him.*]

Do you think you're going bowling now?

STANLEY:

Sure.

STELLA:

You're not going bowling. [*She catches hold of his shirt*] Why did you do this to her?

STANLEY:

I done nothing to no one. Let go of my shirt. You've torn it.

STELLA:

I want to know why. Tell me why.

STANLEY:

When we first met, me and you, you thought I was common. How right you was, baby. I was common as dirt. You showed me the snapshot of the place with the columns. I pulled you down off them columns and how you loved it, having them colored lights going! And wasn't we happy together, wasn't it all okay till she showed here?

[*Stella makes a slight movement. Her look goes suddenly inward as if some interior voice had called her name. She begins a slow, shuffling progress from the bedroom to the kitchen, leaning and resting on the back of the chair and then on the edge of a table with a blind look and listening expression. Stanley, finishing with his shirt, is unaware of her reaction.*]

And wasn't we happy together? Wasn't it all okay? Till

235

she showed here. Hoity-toity, describing me as an ape. [*He suddenly notices the change in Stella*] Hey, what is it, Stell? [*He crosses to her.*]

STELLA [*quietly*]:

Take me to the hospital.

[*He is with her now, supporting her with his arm, murmuring indistinguishably as they go outside.*]

SCENE NINE

A while later that evening. Blanche is seated in a tense hunched position in a bedroom chair that she has re-covered with diagonal green and white stripes. She has on her scarlet satin robe. On the table beside chair is a bottle of liquor and a glass. The rapid, feverish polka tune, the "Varsouviana," is heard. The music is in her mind; she is drinking to escape it and the sense of disaster closing in on her, and she seems to whisper the words of the song. An electric fan is turning back and forth across her.

Mitch comes around the corner in work clothes: blue denim shirt and pants. He is unshaven. He climbs the steps to the door and rings. Blanche is startled.

BLANCHE:

Who is it, please?

MITCH [*hoarsely*]:

Me. Mitch.

[*The polka tune stops.*]

BLANCHE:

Mitch!—Just a minute.

[*She rushes about frantically, hiding the bottle in a closet, crouching at the mirror and dabbing her face with cologne and powder. She is so excited that her breath is audible as she dashes about. At last she rushes to the door in the kitchen and lets him in.*]

Mitch!—Y'know, I really shouldn't let you in after the treatment I have received from you this evening! So utterly uncavalier! But hello, beautiful!

237

[*She offers him her lips. He ignores it and pushes past her into the flat. She looks fearfully after him as he stalks into the bedroom.*]

My, my, what a cold shoulder! And such uncouth apparel! Why, you haven't even shaved! The unforgivable insult to a lady! But I forgive you. I forgive you because it's such a relief to see you. You've stopped that polka tune that I had caught in my head. Have you ever had anything caught in your head? No, of course you haven't, you dumb angel-puss, you'd never get anything awful caught in your head!

[*He stares at her while she follows him while she talks. It is obvious that he has had a few drinks on the way over.*]

MITCH:

Do we have to have that fan on?

BLANCHE:

No!

MITCH:

I don't like fans.

BLANCHE:

Then let's turn it off, honey. I'm not partial to them!

[*She presses the switch and the fan nods slowly off. She clears her throat uneasily as Mitch plumps himself down on the bed in the bedroom and lights a cigarette.*]

I don't know what there is to drink. I—haven't investigated.

MITCH:

I don't want Stan's liquor.

BLANCHE:

It isn't Stan's. Everything here isn't Stan's. Some things on the premises are actually mine! How is your mother? Isn't your mother well?

MITCH:

Why?

BLANCHE:

Something's the matter tonight, but never mind. I won't cross-examine the witness. I'll just— [*She touches her forehead vaguely. The polka tune starts up again.*] —pretend I don't notice anything different about you! That—music again . . .

MITCH:

What music?

BLANCHE:

The "Varsouviana"! The polka tune they were playing when Allan— Wait!

[*A distant revolver shot is heard. Blanche seems relieved.*]

There now, the shot! It always stops after that.

[*The polka music dies out again.*]

Yes, now it's stopped.

MITCH:

Are you boxed out of your mind?

BLANCHE:

I'll go and see what I can find in the way of— [*She crosses into the closet, pretending to search for the bottle.*]

239

Oh, by the way, excuse me for not being dressed. But I'd practically given you up! Had you forgotten your invitation to supper?

MITCH:

I wasn't going to see you any more.

BLANCHE:

Wait a minute. I can't hear what you're saying and you talk so little that when you do say something, I don't want to miss a single syllable of it.... What am I looking around here for? Oh, yes—liquor! We've had so much excitement around here this evening that I *am* boxed out of my mind! [*She pretends suddenly to find the bottle. He draws his foot up on the bed and stares at her contemptuously.*] Here's something. Southern Comfort! What is that, I wonder?

MITCH:

If you don't know, it must belong to Stan.

BLANCHE:

Take your foot off the bed. It has a light cover on it. Of course you boys don't notice things like that. I've done so much with this place since I've been here.

MITCH:

I bet you have.

BLANCHE:

You saw it before I came. Well, look at it now! This room is almost—dainty! I want to keep it that way. I wonder if this stuff ought to be mixed with something? Ummm, it's sweet, so sweet! It's terribly, terribly sweet!

Why, it's a *liqueur,* I believe! Yes, that's what it *is,* a liqueur! [*Mitch grunts.*] I'm afraid you won't like it, but try it, and maybe you will.

MITCH:

I told you already I don't want none of his liquor and I mean it. You ought to lay off his liquor. He says you been lapping it up all summer like a wild cat!

BLANCHE:

What a fantastic statement! Fantastic of him to say it, fantastic of you to repeat it! I won't descend to the level of such cheap accusations to answer them, even!

MITCH:
Huh.

BLANCHE:

What's in your mind? I see something in your eyes!

MITCH [*getting up*]:
It's dark in here.

BLANCHE:

I like it dark. The dark is comforting to me.

MITCH:

I don't think I ever seen you in the light. [*Blanche laughs breathlessly*] That's a fact!

BLANCHE:
Is it?

MITCH:
I've never seen you in the afternoon.

BLANCHE:
Whose fault is that?

MITCH:

You never want to go out in the afternoon.

BLANCHE:

Why, Mitch, you're at the plant in the afternoon!

MITCH:

Not Sunday afternoon. I've asked you to go out with me sometimes on Sundays but you always make an excuse. You never want to go out till after six and then it's always some place that's not lighted much.

BLANCHE:

There is some obscure meaning in this but I fail to catch it.

MITCH:

What it means is I've never had a real good look at you, Blanche. Let's turn the light on here.

BLANCHE [*fearfully*]:
Light? Which light? What for?

MITCH:

This one with the paper thing on it. [*He tears the paper lantern off the light bulb. She utters a frightened gasp.*]

BLANCHE:

What did you do that for?

MITCH:

So I can take a look at you good and plain!

BLANCHE:

Of course you don't really mean to be insulting!

MITCH:

No, just realistic.

242

BLANCHE:

I don't want realism. I want magic! [*Mitch laughs*] Yes, yes, magic! I try to give that to people. I misrepresent things to them. I don't tell truth, I tell what *ought* to be truth. And if that is sinful, then let me be damned for it!—*Don't turn the light on!*

[*Mitch crosses to the switch. He turns the light on and stares at her. She cries out and covers her face. He turns the light off again.*]

MITCH [*slowly and bitterly*]:

I don't mind you being older than what I thought. But all the rest of it—Christ! That pitch about your ideals being so old-fashioned and all the malarkey that you've dished out all summer. Oh, I knew you weren't sixteen any more. But I was a fool enough to believe you was straight.

BLANCHE:

Who told you I wasn't—"straight"? My loving brother-in-law. And you believed him.

MITCH:

I called him a liar at first. And then I checked on the story. First I asked our supply-man who travels through Laurel. And then I talked directly over long-distance to this merchant.

BLANCHE:

Who is this merchant?

MITCH:

Kiefaber.

243

BLANCHE:

The merchant Kiefaber of Laurel! I know the man. He whistled at me. I put him in his place. So now for revenge he makes up stories about me.

MITCH:

Three people, Kiefaber, Stanley and Shaw, swore to them!

BLANCHE:

Rub-a-dub-dub, three men in a tub! And such a filthy tub!

MITCH:

Didn't you stay at a hotel called The Flamingo?

BLANCHE:

Flamingo? No! Tarantula was the name of it! I stayed at a hotel called The Tarantula Arms!

MITCH [*stupidly*]:
Tarantula?

BLANCHE:

Yes, a big spider! That's where I brought my victims. [*She pours herself another drink*] Yes, I had many intimacies with strangers. After the death of Allan—intimacies with strangers was all I seemed able to fill my empty heart with. . . . I think it was panic, just panic, that drove me from one to another, hunting for some protection—here and there, in the most—unlikely places—even, at last, in a seventeen-year-old boy but—somebody wrote the superintendent about it—"This woman is morally unfit for her position!"

[*She throws back her head with convulsive, sobbing laughter. Then she repeats the statement, gasps, and drinks.*]

True? Yes, I suppose—unfit somehow—anyway. . . . So I came here. There was nowhere else I could go. I was played out. You know what played out is? My youth was suddenly gone up the water-spout, and—I met you. You said you needed somebody. Well, I needed somebody, too. I thanked God for you, because you seemed to be gentle—a cleft in the rock of the world that I could hide in! But I guess I was asking, hoping—too much! Kiefaber, Stanley and Shaw have tied an old tin can to the tail of the kite.

[*There is a pause. Mitch stares at her dumbly.*]

MITCH:
You lied to me, Blanche.

BLANCHE:
Don't say I lied to you.

MITCH:
Lies, lies, inside and out, all lies.

BLANCHE:
Never inside, I didn't lie in my heart . . .

[*A Vendor comes around the corner. She is a blind Mexican woman in a dark shawl, carrying bunches of those gaudy tin flowers that lower-class Mexicans display at funerals and other festive occasions. She is calling barely audibly. Her figure is only faintly visible outside the building.*]

MEXICAN WOMAN:
Flores. Flores. Flores para los muertos. Flores. Flores.

245

BLANCHE:

What? Oh! Somebody outside ... [*She goes to the door, opens it and stares at the Mexican Woman.*]

MEXICAN WOMAN [*she is at the door and offers Blanche some of her flowers*]:

Flores? Flores para los muertos?

BLANCHE [*frightened*]:

No, no! Not now! Not now!

[*She darts back into the apartment, slamming the door.*]

MEXICAN WOMAN [*she turns away and starts to move down the street*]:

Flores para los muertos.

[*The polka tune fades in.*]

BLANCHE [*as if to herself*]:

Crumble and fade and—regrets—recriminations. . . "If you'd done this, it wouldn't've cost me that!"

MEXICAN WOMAN:

Corones para los muertos. Corones ...

BLANCHE:

Legacies! Huh.... And other things such as bloodstained pillow-slips—"Her linen needs changing"—"Yes, Mother. But couldn't we get a colored girl to do it?" No, we couldn't of course. Everything gone but the—

MEXICAN WOMAN:

Flores.

BLANCHE:

Death—I used to sit here and she used to sit over there

and death was as close as you are. . . . We didn't dare even admit we had ever heard of it!

MEXICAN WOMAN:

Flores para los muertos, flores—flores . . .

BLANCHE:

The opposite is desire. So do you wonder? How could you possibly wonder! Not far from Belle Reve, before we had lost Belle Reve, was a camp where they trained young soldiers. On Saturday nights they would go in town to get drunk—

MEXICAN WOMAN [softly]:

Corones . . .

BLANCHE:

—and on the way back they would stagger onto my lawn and call—"Blanche! Blanche!"—the deaf old lady remaining suspected nothing. But sometimes I slipped outside to answer their calls. . . . Later the paddy-wagon would gather them up like daisies . . . the long way home . . .

[The Mexican Woman turns slowly and drifts back off with her soft mournful cries. Blanche goes to the dresser and leans forward on it. After a moment, Mitch rises and follows her purposefully. The polka music fades away. He places his hands on her waist and tries to turn her about.]

BLANCHE:

What do you want?

MITCH [fumbling to embrace her]:

What I been missing all summer.

BLANCHE:

Then marry me, Mitch!

MITCH:

I don't think I want to marry you any more.

BLANCHE:

No?

MITCH [*dropping his hands from her waist*]:

You're not clean enough to bring in the house with my mother.

BLANCHE:

Go away, then. [*He stares at her*] Get out of here quick before I start screaming fire! [*Her throat is tightening with hysteria*] Get out of here quick before I start screaming fire.

[*He still remains staring. She suddenly rushes to the big window with its pale blue square of the soft summer light and cries wildly.*]

Fire! Fire! Fire!

[*With a startled gasp, Mitch turns and goes out the outer door, clatters awkwardly down the steps and around the corner of the building. Blanche staggers back from the window and falls to her knees. The distant piano is slow and blue.*]

SCENE TEN

It is a few hours later that night.

Blanche has been drinking fairly steadily since Mitch left. She has dragged her wardrobe trunk into the center of the bedroom. It hangs open with flowery dresses thrown across it. As the drinking and packing went on, a mood of hysterical exhilaration came into her and she has decked herself out in a somewhat soiled and crumpled white satin evening gown and a pair of scuffed silver slippers with brilliants set in their heels.

Now she is placing the rhinestone tiara on her head before the mirror of the dressing-table and murmuring excitedly as if to a group of spectral admirers.

BLANCHE:

How about taking a swim, a moonlight swim at the old rock-quarry? If anyone's sober enough to drive a car! Ha-ha! Best way in the world to stop your head buzzing! Only you've got to be careful to dive where the deep pool is—if you hit a rock you don't come up till tomorrow . . .

[*Tremblingly she lifts the hand mirror for a closer inspection. She catches her breath and slams the mirror face down with such violence that the glass cracks. She moans a little and attempts to rise.*

[*Stanley appears around the corner of the building. He still has on the vivid green silk bowling shirt. As he rounds the corner the honky-tonk music is heard. It continues softly throughout the scene.*

[*He enters the kitchen, slamming the door. As he peers in at Blanche, he gives a low whistle. He has had a few drinks on the way and has brought some quart beer bottles home with him.*]

BLANCHE:

How is my sister?

STANLEY:

She is doing okay.

BLANCHE:

And how is the baby?

STANLEY [*grinning amiably*]:

The baby won't come before morning so they told me to go home and get a little shut-eye.

BLANCHE:

Does that mean we are to be alone in here?

STANLEY:

Yep. Just me and you, Blanche. Unless you got somebody hid under the bed. What've you got on those fine feathers for?

BLANCHE:

Oh, that's right. You left before my wire came.

STANLEY:

You got a wire?

BLANCHE:

I received a telegram from an old admirer of mine

STANLEY:

Anything good?

BLANCHE:

I think so. An invitation.

STANLEY:

What to? A fireman's ball?

BLANCHE [*throwing back her head*]:
A cruise of the Caribbean on a yacht!

STANLEY:
Well, well. What do you know?

BLANCHE:
I have never been so surprised in my life.

STANLEY:
I guess not.

BLANCHE:
It came like a bolt from the blue!

STANLEY:
Who did you say it was from?

BLANCHE:
An old beau of mine.

STANLEY:
The one that give you the white fox-pieces?

BLANCHE:
Mr. Shep Huntleigh. I wore his ATO pin my last year at college. I hadn't seen him again until last Christmas. I ran in to him on Biscayne Boulevard. Then—just now —this wire—inviting me on a cruise of the Caribbean! The problem is clothes. I tore into my trunk to see what I have that's suitable for the tropics!

STANLEY:
And come up with that—gorgeous—diamond—tiara?

BLANCHE:
This old relic? Ha-ha! It's only rhinestones.

251

STANLEY:

Gosh. I thought it was Tiffany diamonds. [*He unbuttons his shirt.*]

BLANCHE:

Well, anyhow, I shall be entertained in style.

STANLEY:

Uh-huh. It goes to show, you never know what is coming.

BLANCHE:

Just when I thought my luck had begun to fail me—

STANLEY:

Into the picture pops this Miami millionaire.

BLANCHE:

This man is not from Miami. This man is from Dallas.

STANLEY:

This man is from Dallas?

BLANCHE:

Yes, this man is from Dallas where gold spouts out of the ground!

STANLEY:

Well, just so he's from somewhere! [*He starts removing his shirt.*]

BLANCHE:

Close the curtains before you undress any further.

STANLEY [*amiably*]:

This is all I'm going to undress right now. ⌈*He rips the sack off a quart beer bottle*⌉ Seen a bottle-opener?

[*She moves slowly toward the dresser, where she stands with her hands knotted together.*]

I used to have a cousin who could open a beer bottle with his teeth. [*Pounding the bottle cap on the corner of table*] That was his only accomplishment, all he could do—he was just a human bottle-opener. And then one time, at a wedding party, he broke his front teeth off! After that he was so ashamed of himself he used t' sneak out of the house when company came . . .

[*The bottle cap pops off and a geyser of foam shoots up. Stanley laughs happily, holding up the bottle over his head.*]

Ha-ha! Rain from heaven! [*He extends the bottle toward her*] Shall we bury the hatchet and make it a loving-cup? Huh?

BLANCHE:

No, thank you.

STANLEY:

Well, it's a red-letter night for us both. You having an oil millionaire and me having a baby.

[*He goes to the bureau in the bedroom and crouches to remove something from the bottom drawer.*]

BLANCHE [*drawing back*]:

What are you doing in here?

STANLEY:

Here's something I always break out on special occasions like this. The silk pyjamas I wore on my wedding night!

BLANCHE:

Oh.

STANLEY:

When the telephone rings and they say, "You've got a son!" I'll tear this off and wave it like a flag! [*He shakes out a brilliant pyjama coat*] I guess we are both entitled to put on the dog. [*He goes back to the kitchen with the coat over his arm.*]

BLANCHE:

When I think of how divine it is going to be to have such a thing as privacy once more—I could weep with joy!

STANLEY:

This millionaire from Dallas is not going to interfere with your privacy any?

BLANCHE:

It won't be the sort of thing you have in mind. This man is a gentleman and he respects me. [*improvising fever- ishly*] What he wants is my companionship. Having great wealth sometimes makes people lonely! A culti- vated woman, a woman of intelligence and breeding, can enrich a man's life—immeasurably! I have those things to offer, and this doesn't take them away. Physical beauty is passing. A transitory possession. But beauty of the mind and richness of the spirit and tenderness of the heart—and I have all of those things—aren't taken away, but grow! Increase with the years! How strange that I should be called a destitute woman! When I have all of these treasures locked in my heart. [*A choked sob comes from her*] I think of myself as a very, very rich woman! But I have been foolish—casting my pearls before swine!

STANLEY:

Swine, huh?

BLANCHE:

Yes, swine! Swine! And I'm thinking not only of you but of your friend, Mr. Mitchell. He came to see me tonight. He dared to come here in his work clothes! And to repeat slander to me, vicious stories that he had gotten from you! I gave him his walking papers . . .

STANLEY:

You did, huh?

BLANCHE:

But then he came back. He returned with a box of roses to beg my forgiveness! He implored my forgiveness. But some things are not forgivable. Deliberate cruelty is not forgivable. It is the one unforgivable thing in my opinion and it is the one thing of which I have never, never been guilty. And so I told him, I said to him, "Thank you," but it was foolish of me to think that we could ever adapt ourselves to each other. Our ways of life are too different. Our attitudes and our backgrounds are incompatible. We have to be realistic about such things. So farewell, my friend! And let there be no hard feelings . . .

STANLEY:

Was this before or after the telegram came from the Texas oil millionaire?

BLANCHE:

What telegram? No! No, after! As a matter of fact, the wire came just as—

STANLEY:

As a matter of fact there wasn't no wire at all!

BLANCHE:

Oh, oh!

STANLEY:

There isn't no millionaire! And Mitch didn't come back with roses 'cause I know where he is—

255

BLANCHE:

Oh!

STANLEY:

There isn't a goddam thing but imagination!

BLANCHE:

Oh!

STANLEY:

And lies and conceit and tricks!

BLANCHE:

Oh!

STANLEY:

And look at yourself! Take a look at yourself in that worn-out Mardi Gras outfit, rented for fifty cents from some rag-picker! And with the crazy crown on! What queen do you think you are?

BLANCHE:

Oh—God . . .

STANLEY:

I've been on to you from the start! Not once did you pull any wool over this boy's eyes! You come in here and sprinkle the place with powder and spray perfume and cover the light-bulb with a paper lantern, and lo and behold the place has turned into Egypt and you are the Queen of the Nile! Sitting on your throne and swilling down my liquor! I say—*Ha!—Ha!* Do you hear me? *Ha—ha—ha!* [*He walks into the bedroom.*]

BLANCHE:

Don't come in here!

[*Lurid reflections appear on the walls around Blanche.*

*The shadows are of a grotesque and menacing form.
She catches her breath, crosses to the phone and jig-
gles the hook. Stanley goes into the bathroom and
closes the door.*]

Operator, operator! Give me long-distance, please. . . . I
want to get in touch with Mr. Shep Huntleigh of Dallas.
He's so well known he doesn't require any address. Just
ask anybody who—Wait!!—No, I couldn't find it right
now. . . . Please understand, I—No! No, wait! . . . One
moment! Someone is—Nothing! Hold on, please!

[*She sets the phone down and crosses warily into the
kitchen. The night is filled with inhuman voices like
cries in a jungle.*

[*The shadows and lurid reflections move sinuously as
flames along the wall spaces.*

[*Through the back wall of the rooms, which have become transparent, can be seen the sidewalk. A prostitute has rolled a drunkard. He pursues her along the
walk, overtakes her and there is a struggle. A police-
man's whistle breaks it up. The figures disappear.*

[*Some moments later the Negro Woman appears
around the corner with a sequined bag which the
prostitute had dropped on the walk. She is rooting
excitedly through it.*

[*Blanche presses her knuckles to her lips and returns
slowly to the phone. She speaks in a hoarse whisper.*]

BLANCHE:

Operator! Operator! Never mind long-distance. Get
Western Union. There isn't time to be—Western—Western Union!

[*She waits anxiously.*]

Western Union? Yes! I—want to—Take down this message! "In desperate, desperate circumstances! Help me! Caught in a trap. Caught in—" *Oh!*

[*The bathroom door is thrown open and Stanley comes out in the brilliant silk pyjamas. He grins at her as he knots the tasseled sash about his waist. She gasps and backs away from the phone. He stares at her for a count of ten. Then a clicking becomes audible from the telephone, steady and rasping.*]

STANLEY:

You left th' phone off th' hook.

[*He crosses to it deliberately and sets it back on the hook. After he has replaced it, he stares at her again, his mouth slowly curving into a grin, as he weaves between Blanche and the outer door.*]

[*The barely audible "blue piano" begins to drum up louder. The sound of it turns into the roar of an approaching locomotive. Blanche crouches, pressing her fists to her ears until it has gone by.*]

BLANCHE [*finally straightening*]:

Let me—let me get by you!

STANLEY:

Get by me? Sure. Go ahead. [*He moves back a pace in the doorway.*]

BLANCHE:

You—you stand over there! [*She indicates a further position.*]

258

STANLEY [*grinning*]:

You got plenty of room to walk by me now.

BLANCHE:

Not with you there! But I've got to get out somehow!

STANLEY:

You think I'll interfere with you? Ha-ha!

[*The "blue piano" goes softly. She turns confusedly and makes a faint gesture. The inhuman jungle voices rise up. He takes a step toward her, biting his tongue which protrudes between his lips.*]

STANLEY [*softly*]:

Come to think of it—maybe you wouldn't be bad to— interfere with . . .

[*Blanche moves backward through the door into the bedroom.*]

BLANCHE:

Stay back! Don't you come toward me another step or I'll—

STANLEY:

What?

BLANCHE:

Some awful thing will happen! It will!

STANLEY:

What are you putting on now?

[*They are now both inside the bedroom.*]

BLANCHE:

I warn you, don't, I'm in danger!

[*He takes another step. She smashes a bottle on the table and faces him, clutching the broken top.*]

STANLEY:

What did you do that for?

BLANCHE:

So I could twist the broken end in your face!

STANLEY:

I bet you would do that!

BLANCHE:

I would! I will if you—

STANLEY:

Oh! So you want some roughhouse! All right, let's have some roughhouse!

[*He springs toward her, overturning the table. She cries out and strikes at him with the bottle top but he catches her wrist.*]

Tiger—tiger! Drop the bottle-top! Drop it! We've had this date with each other from the beginning!

[*She moans. The bottle-top falls. She sinks to her knees: He picks up her inert figure and carries her to the bed. The hot trumpet and drums from the Four Deuces sound loudly.*]

SCENE ELEVEN

It is some weeks later. Stella is packing Blanche's things. Sound of water can be heard running in the bathroom.

The portieres are partly open on the poker players— Stanley, Steve, Mitch and Pablo—who sit around the table in the kitchen. The atmosphere of the kitchen is now the same raw, lurid one of the disastrous poker night.

The building is framed by the sky of turquoise. Stella has been crying as she arranges the flowery dresses in the open trunk.

Eunice comes down the steps from her flat above and enters the kitchen. There is an outburst from the poker table.

STANLEY:

Drew to an inside straight and made it, by God.

PABLO:

Maldita sea tu suerto!

STANLEY:

Put it in English, greaseball.

PABLO:

I am cursing your rutting luck.

STANLEY [*prodigiously elated*]:

You know what luck is? Luck is believing you're lucky. Take at Salerno. I believed I was lucky. I figured that 4 out of 5 would not come through but I would . . . and I did. I put that down as a rule. To hold front position in this rat-race you've got to believe you are lucky.

MITCH:

You ... you ... you.... Brag ... brag ... bull ... bull.

[*Stella goes into the bedroom and starts folding a dress.*]

STANLEY:

What's the matter with him?

EUNICE [*walking past the table*]:

I always did say that men are callous things with no feelings, but this does beat anything. Making pigs of yourselves. [*She comes through the portieres into the bedroom.*]

STANLEY:

What's the matter with her?

STELLA:

How is my baby?

EUNICE:

Sleeping like a little angel. Brought you some grapes. [*She puts them on a stool and lowers her voice.*] Blanche?

STELLA:

Bathing.

EUNICE:

How is she?

STELLA:

She wouldn't eat anything but asked for a drink.

EUNICE:

What did you tell her?

STELLA:

I—just told her that—we'd made arrangements for her

to rest in the country. She's got it mixed in her mind with
Shep Huntleigh.

[*Blanche opens the bathroom door slightly.*]

BLANCHE:
Stella.

STELLA:
Yes, Blanche?

BLANCHE:
If anyone calls while I'm bathing take the number and
tell them I'll call right back.

STELLA:
Yes.

BLANCHE:
That cool yellow silk—the bouclé. See if it's crushed. If
it's not too crushed I'll wear it and on the lapel that silver
and turquoise pin in the shape of a seahorse. You will
find them in the heart-shaped box I keep my accessories
in. And Stella . . . Try and locate a bunch of artificial
violets in that box, too, to pin with the seahorse on the
lapel of the jacket.

[*She closes the door. Stella turns to Eunice.*]

STELLA:
I don't know if I did the right thing.

EUNICE:
What else could you do?

STELLA:
I couldn't believe her story and go on living with Stanley.

263

EUNICE:

Don't ever believe it. Life has got to go on. No matter what happens, you've got to keep on going.

[*The bathroom door opens a little.*]

BLANCHE [*looking out*]:

Is the coast clear?

STELLA:

Yes, Blanche. [*to Eunice*] Tell her how well she's looking.

BLANCHE:

Please close the curtains before I come out.

STELLA:

They're closed.

STANLEY:

—How many for you?

PABLO:

—Two.

STEVE:

—Three.

[*Blanche appears in the amber light of the door. She has a tragic radiance in her red satin robe following the sculptural lines of her body. The "Varsouviana" rises audibly as Blanche enters the bedroom.*]

BLANCHE [*with faintly hysterical vivacity*]:

I have just washed my hair.

STELLA:

Did you?

BLANCHE:

I'm not sure I got the soap out.

EUNICE:

Such fine hair!

BLANCHE: [*accepting the compliment*]:
It's a problem. Didn't I get a call?

STELLA:

Who from, Blanche?

BLANCHE:

Shep Huntleigh ...

STELLA:

Why, not yet, honey!

BLANCHE:

How strange! I—

[*At the sound of Blanche's voice Mitch's arm supporting his cards has sagged and his gaze is dissolved into space. Stanley slaps him on the shoulder.*]

STANLEY:

Hey, Mitch, come to!

[*The sound of this new voice shocks Blanche. She makes a shocked gesture, forming his name with her lips. Stella nods and looks quickly away. Blanche stands quite still for some moments—the silver-backed mirror in her hand and a look of sorrowful perplexity as though all human experience shows on her face. Blanche finally speaks but with sudden hysteria.*]

BLANCHE:

What's going on here?

265

[*She turns from Stella to Eunice and back to Stella. Her rising voice penetrates the concentration of the game. Mitch ducks his head lower but Stanley shoves back his chair as if about to rise. Steve places a restraining hand on his arm.*]

BLANCHE [*continuing*]:

What's happened here? I want an explanation of what's happened here.

STELLA [*agonizingly*]:

Hush! Hush!

EUNICE:

Hush! Hush! Honey.

STELLA:

Please, Blanche.

BLANCHE:

Why are you looking at me like that? Is something wrong with me?

EUNICE:

You look wonderful, Blanche. Don't she look wonderful?

STELLA:

Yes.

EUNICE:

I understand you are going on a trip.

STELLA:

Yes, Blanche *is*. She's going on a vacation.

EUNICE:

I'm green with envy.

BLANCHE:

Help me, help me get dressed!

STELLA [*handing her dress*]:

Is this what you—

BLANCHE:

Yes, it will do! I'm anxious to get out of here—this place is a trap!

EUNICE:

What a pretty blue jacket.

STELLA:

It's lilac colored.

BLANCHE:

You're both mistaken. It's Della Robbia blue. The blue of the robe in the old Madonna pictures. Are these grapes washed?

[*She fingers the bunch of grapes which Eunice had brought in.*]

EUNICE:

Huh?

BLANCHE:

Washed, I said. Are they washed?

EUNICE:

They're from the French Market.

BLANCHE:

That doesn't mean they've been washed. [*The cathedral*

267

bells chime] Those cathedral bells—they're the only clean thing in the Quarter. Well, I'm going now. I'm ready to go.

EUNICE [*whispering*]:
She's going to walk out before they get here.

STELLA:
Wait, Blanche.

BLANCHE:
I don't want to pass in front of those men.

EUNICE:
Then wait'll the game breaks up.

STELLA:
Sit down and . . .

[*Blanche turns weakly, hesitantly about. She lets them push her into a chair.*]

BLANCHE:
I can smell the sea air. The rest of my time I'm going to spend on the sea. And when I die, I'm going to die on the sea. You know what I shall die of? [*She plucks a grape*] I shall die of eating an unwashed grape one day out on the ocean. I will die—with my hand in the hand of some nice-looking ship's doctor, a very young one with a small blond mustache and a big silver watch. "Poor lady," they'll say, "the quinine did her no good. That unwashed grape has transported her soul to heaven." [*The cathedral chimes are heard*] And I'll be buried at sea sewn up in a clean white sack and dropped overboard—at noon—in the blaze of summer—and into an ocean as blue as [*chimes again*] my first lover's eyes!

[*A Doctor and a Matron have appeared around the corner of the building and climbed the steps to the porch. The gravity of their profession is exaggerated— the unmistakable aura of the state institution with its cynical detachment. The Doctor rings the doorbell. The murmur of the game is interrupted.*]

EUNICE [*whispering to Stella*]:
That must be them.

[*Stella presses her fists to her lips.*]

BLANCHE [*rising slowly*]:
What is it?

EUNICE [*affectedly casual*]:
Excuse me while I see who's at the door.

STELLA:
Yes.

[*Eunice goes into the kitchen.*]

BLANCHE [*tensely*]:
I wonder if it's for me.

[*A whispered colloquy takes place at the door.*]

EUNICE [*returning, brightly*]:
Someone is calling for Blanche.

BLANCHE:
It *is* for me, then! [*She looks fearfully from one to the other and then to the portieres. The"Varsouviana" faintly plays*] Is it the gentleman I was expecting from Dallas?

EUNICE:
I think it is, Blanche.

BLANCHE:

I'm not quite ready.

STELLA:

Ask him to wait outside.

BLANCHE:

I . . .

[*Eunice goes back to the portieres. Drums sound very softly.*]

STELLA:

Everything packed?

BLANCHE:

My silver toilet articles are still out.

STELLA:

Ah!

EUNICE [*returning*]:

They're waiting in front of the house.

BLANCHE:

They! Who's "they"?

EUNICE:

There's a lady with him.

BLANCHE:

I cannot imagine who this "lady" could be! How is she dressed?

EUNICE:

Just—just a sort of a—plain-tailored outfit.

BLANCHE:

Possibly she's—[*Her voice dies out nervously.*]

STELLA:

Shall we go, Blanche?

BLANCHE:

Must we go through that room?

STELLA:

I will go with you.

BLANCHE:

How do I look?

STELLA:

Lovely.

EUNICE [*echoing*]:

Lovely.

[*Blanche moves fearfully to the portieres. Eunice draws them open for her. Blanche goes into the kitchen.*]

BLANCHE [*to the men*]:

Please don't get up. I'm only passing through.

[*She crosses quickly to outside door. Stella and Eunice follow. The poker players stand awkwardly at the table—all except Mitch, who remains seated, looking down at the table. Blanche steps out on a small porch at the side of the door. She stops short and catches her breath.*]

DOCTOR:

How do you do?

BLANCHE:

You are not the gentleman I was expecting. [*She suddenly gasps and starts back up the steps. She stops by*

271

Stella, who stands just outside the door, and speaks in a
frightening whisper] That man isn't Shep Huntleigh.

[*The "Varsouviana" is playing distantly.*

[*Stella stares back at Blanche. Eunice is holding
Stella's arm. There is a moment of silence—no sound
but that of Stanley steadily shuffling the cards.*

[*Blanche catches her breath again and slips back into
the flat. She enters the flat with a peculiar smile, her
eyes wide and brilliant. As soon as her sister goes past
her, Stella closes her eyes and clenches her hands.
Eunice throws her arms comfortingly about her. Then
she starts up to her flat. Blanche stops just inside the
door. Mitch keeps staring down at his hands on the
table, but the other men look at her curiously. At last
she starts around the table toward the bedroom. As
she does, Stanley suddenly pushes back his chair and
rises as if to block her way. The Matron follows her
into the flat.*]

STANLEY:
Did you forget something?

BLANCHE [*shrilly*]:
Yes! Yes, I forgot something!

[*She rushes past him into the bedroom. Lurid reflections appear on the walls in odd, sinuous shapes. The
"Varsouviana" is filtered into a weird distortion, accompanied by the cries and noises of the jungle. Blanche
seizes the back of a chair as if to defend herself.*]

STANLEY [*sotto voce*]:
Doc, you better go in.

272

DOCTOR [*sotto voce, motioning to the Matron*]:
Nurse, bring her out.

[*The Matron advances on one side, Stanley on the other. Divested of all the softer properties of womanhood, the Matron is a peculiarly sinister figure in her severe dress. Her voice is bold and toneless as a firebell.*]

MATRON:
Hello, Blanche.

[*The greeting is echoed and re-echoed by other mysterious voices behind the walls, as if reverberated through a canyon of rock.*]

STANLEY:
She says that she forgot something.

[*The echo sounds in threatening whispers.*]

MATRON:
That's all right.

STANLEY:
What did you forget, Blanche?

BLANCHE:
I— I—

MATRON:
It don't matter. We can pick it up later.

STANLEY:
Sure. We can send it along with the trunk.

BLANCHE [*retreating in panic*]:
I don't know you—I don't know you. I want to be—left alone—please!

273

MATRON:

Now, Blanche!

ECHOES [*rising and falling*]:

Now, Blanche—now, Blanche—now, Blanche!

STANLEY:

You left nothing here but spilt talcum and old empty perfume bottles—unless it's the paper lantern you want to take with you. You want the lantern?

[*He crosses to dressing table and seizes the paper lantern, tearing it off the light bulb, and extends it toward her. She cries out as if the lantern was herself. The Matron steps boldly toward her. She screams and tries to break past the Matron. All the men spring to their feet. Stella runs out to the porch, with Eunice following to comfort her, simultaneously with the confused voices of the men in the kitchen. Stella rushes into Eunice's embrace on the porch.*]

STELLA:

Oh, my God, Eunice help me! Don't let them do that to her, don't let them hurt her! Oh, God, oh, please God, don't hurt her! What are they doing to her? What are they doing? [*She tries to break from Eunice's arms.*]

EUNICE:

No, honey, no, no, honey. Stay here. Don't go back in there. Stay with me and don't look.

STELLA:

What have I done to my sister? Oh, God, what have I done to my sister?

EUNICE:

You done the right thing, the only thing you could do.

She couldn't stay here; there wasn't no other place for her to go.

[*While Stella and Eunice are speaking on the porch the voices of the men in the kitchen overlap them. Mitch has started toward the bedroom. Stanley crosses to block him. Stanley pushes him aside. Mitch lunges and strikes at Stanley. Stanley pushes Mitch back. Mitch collapses at the table, sobbing.*

[*During the preceding scenes, the Matron catches hold of Blanche's arm and prevents her flight. Blanche turns wildly and scratches at the Matron. The heavy woman pinions her arms. Blanche cries out hoarsely and slips to her knees.*]

MATRON:

These fingernails have to be trimmed. [*The Doctor comes into the room and she looks at him.*] Jacket, Doctor?

DOCTOR:

Not unless necessary.

[*He takes off his hat and now he becomes personalized. The unhuman quality goes. His voice is gentle and reassuring as he crosses to Blanche and crouches in front of her. As he speaks her name, her terror subsides a little. The lurid reflections fade from the walls, the inhuman cries and noises die out and her own hoarse crying is calmed.*]

DOCTOR:

Miss DuBois.

[*She turns her face to him and stares at him with des-*

275

perate pleading. He smiles; then he speaks to the Matron.]
It won't be necessary.

BLANCHE [*faintly*]:
Ask her to let go of me.

DOCTOR [*to the Matron*]:
Let go.

[*The Matron releases her. Blanche extends her hands toward the Doctor. He draws her up gently and supports her with his arm and leads her through the portieres.*]

BLANCHE [*holding tight to his arm*]:
Whoever you are—I have always depended on the kindness of strangers.

[*The poker players stand back as Blanche and the Doctor cross the kitchen to the front door. She allows him to lead her as if she were blind. As they go out on the porch, Stella cries out her sister's name from where she is crouched a few steps up on the stairs.*]

STELLA:
Blanche! Blanche, Blanche!

[*Blanche walks on without turning, followed by the Doctor and the Matron. They go around the corner of the building.*

[*Eunice descends to Stella and places the child in her arms. It is wrapped in a pale blue blanket. Stella accepts the child, sobbingly. Eunice continues downstairs and enters the kitchen where the men, except for*

276

Stanley, are returning silently to their places about the table. Stanley has gone out on the porch and stands at the foot of the steps looking at Stella.]

STANLEY [*a bit uncertainly*]:
Stella?

[*She sobs with inhuman abandon. There is something luxurious in her complete surrender to crying now that her sister is gone.*]

STANLEY [*voluptuously, soothingly*]:
Now, honey. Now, love. Now, now, love. [*He kneels beside her and his fingers find the opening of her blouse*] Now, now, love. Now, love....

[*The luxurious sobbing, the sensual murmur fade away under the swelling music of the "blue piano" and the muted trumpet.*]

STEVE:
This game is seven-card stud.

CURTAIN

CAT ON A HOT TIN ROOF

And you, my father, there on the sad height,
Curse, bless, me now with your fierce tears, I pray.
Do not go gentle into that good night.
Rage, rage against the dying of the light!

DYLAN THOMAS

TO AUDREY WOOD

PERSON—TO—PERSON

Of course it is a pity that so much of all creative work is so closely related to the personality of the one who does it.

It is sad and embarrassing and unattractive that those emotions that stir him deeply enough to demand expression, and to charge their expression with some measure of light and power, are nearly all rooted, however changed in their surface, in the particular and sometimes peculiar concerns of the artist himself, that special world, the passions and images of it that each of us weaves about him from birth to death, a web of monstrous complexity, spun forth at a speed that is incalculable to a length beyond measure, from the spider mouth of his own singular perceptions.

It is a lonely idea, a lonely condition, so terrifying to think of that we usually don't. And so we talk to each other, write and wire each other, call each other short and long distance across land and sea, clasp hands with each other at meeting and at parting, fight each other and even destroy each other because of this always somewhat thwarted effort to break through walls to each other. As a character in a play once said, "We're all of us sentenced to solitary confinement inside our own skins."

Personal lyricism is the outcry of prisoner to prisoner from the cell in solitary where each is confined for the duration of his life.

I once saw a group of little girls on a Mississippi sidewalk, all dolled up in their mothers' and sisters' castoff finery, old raggedy ball gowns and plumed hats and high-heeled slippers, enacting a meeting of ladies in a parlor with a perfect mimicry of polite Southern gush and simper. But one child was not satisfied with the attention paid her enraptured performance by the others, they were too involved in their own perform- ances to suit her, so she stretched out her skinny arms and threw back her skinny neck and shrieked to the deaf heavens and her equally oblivious playmates, "Look at me, look at me, look at me!"

And then her mother's high-heeled slippers threw her off balance and she fell to the sidewalk in a great howling tangle of soiled white satin and torn pink net, and still nobody looked at her.

I wonder if she is not, now, a Southern writer.

Of course it is not only Southern writers, of lyrical bent, who engage in such histrionics and shout, "Look at me!" Perhaps it is a parable of all artists. And not always do we topple over and land in a tangle of trappings that don't fit us. However, it is well to be aware of that peril, and not to content yourself with a demand for attention, to know that out of your personal lyricism, your sidewalk histrionics, something has to be created that will not only attract observers but participants in the performance.

I try very hard to do that.

The fact that I want you to observe what I do for your possible pleasure and to give you knowledge of things that I feel I may know better than you, because my world is different from yours, as different as every man's world is from the world of others, is not enough excuse for a personal lyricism that has not yet mastered its necessary trick of rising above the singular to the plural concern, from personal to general import. But for years and years now, which may have passed like a dream because of this obsession, I have been trying to learn how to perform this trick and make it truthful, and sometimes I feel that I am able to do it. Sometimes, when the enraptured street-corner performer in me cries out "Look at me!," I feel that my hazardous footwear and fantastic regalia may not quite throw me off balance. Then, suddenly, you fellow performers in the sidewalk show may turn to give me your attention and allow me to hold it, at least for the interval between 8:40 and 11 something P.M.

Eleven years ago this month of March, when I was far closer than I knew, only nine months away from that long-delayed, but always expected, something that I lived for, the time when I would first catch and hold an audience's attention, I wrote my first preface to a long play. The final paragraph went like this:

"There is too much to say and not enough time to say it. Nor is there power enough. I am not a good writer. Sometimes I am a very bad writer indeed. There is hardly a successful writer in the field who cannot write circles around me . . . but I think of writing as something more organic than words, something closer to being and action. I want to work more and more with a more plastic theatre than the one I have (worked with) before. I have never for one moment doubted that there are people—millions!—to say things to. We come to each other, gradually, but with love. It is the short reach of my arms that hinders, not the length and multiplicity of theirs. With love and with honesty, the embrace is inevitable."

This characteristically emotional, if not rhetorical, statement of mine at that time seems to suggest that I thought of myself as having a highly personal, even intimate relationship with people who go to see plays. I did and I still do. A morbid shyness once prevented me from having much direct communication with people, and possibly that is why I began to write

283

to them plays and stories. But even now when that tongue-locking, face-flushing, silent and crouching timidity has worn off with the passage of the troublesome youth that it sprang from, I still find it somehow easier to "level with" crowds of strangers in the hushed twilight of orchestra and balcony sections of theatres than with individuals across a table from me. Their being strangers somehow makes them more familiar and more approachable, easier to talk to.

Of course I know that I have sometimes presumed too much upon corresponding sympathies and interest in those to whom I talk boldly, and this has led to rejections that were painful and costly enough to inspire more prudence. But when I weigh one thing against another, an easy liking against a hard respect, the balance always tips the same way, and whatever the risk of being turned a cold shoulder, I still don't want to talk to people only about the surface aspects of their lives, the sort of things that acquaintances laugh and chatter about on ordinary social occasions.

I feel that they get plenty of that, and heaven knows so do I, before and after the little interval of time in which I have their attention and say what I have to say to them. The discretion of social conversation, even among friends, is exceeded only by the discretion of "the deep six," that grave wherein nothing is mentioned at all. Emily Dickinson, that lyrical spinster of Amherst, Massachusetts, who wore a strict and savage heart on a taffeta sleeve, commented wryly on that kind of posthumous discourse among friends in these lines:

> *I died for beauty, but was scarce*
> *Adjusted in the tomb,*
> *When one who died for truth was lain*
> *In an adjoining room.*

He questioned softly why I failed?
"For beauty," I replied.
"And I for truth,—the two are one;
We brethren are," he said.

And so, as kinsmen met a night,
We talked between the rooms,
Until the moss had reached our lips,
And covered up our names.

Meanwhile!—I want to go on talking to you as freely and intimately about what we live and die for as if I knew you better than anyone else whom you know.

Tennessee Williams
1955

CHARACTERS OF THE PLAY

MARGARET

BRICK

MAE, sometimes called Sister Woman

BIG MAMA

DIXIE, a little girl

BIG DADDY

REVEREND TOOKER

GOOPER, sometimes called Brother Man

DOCTOR BAUGH, pronounced "Baw"

LACEY, a Negro servant

SOOKEY, another

Another little girl and two small boys

(The playing script of Act III also includes TRIXIE, another little girl, also DAISY, BRIGHTIE and SMALL, servants.)

Cat on a Hot Tin Roof was presented at the Morosco Theatre in New York on March 24, 1955, by The Playwrights' Company. It was directed by Elia Kazan; the stage sets were designed by Jo Mielziner, and the costumes by Lucinda Ballard. The cast was as follows:

LACEY	MAXWELL GLANVILLE
SOOKEY	MUSA WILLIAMS
MARGARET	BARBARA BEL GEDDES
BRICK	BEN GAZZARA
MAE	MADELEINE SHERWOOD
GOOPER	PAT HINGLE
BIG MAMA	MILDRED DUNNOCK
DIXIE	PAULINE HAHN
BUSTER	DARRYL RICHARD
SONNY	SETH EDWARDS
TRIXIE	JANICE DUNN
BIG DADDY	BURL IVES
REVEREND TOOKER	FRED STEWART
DOCTOR BAUGH	R. G. ARMSTRONG
DAISY	EVA VAUGHAN SMITH
BRIGHTIE	BROWNIE MCGHEE
SMALL	SONNY TERRY

SKETCH OF STAGE SETTING FOR THE NEW YORK PRODUCTION BY JO MIELZINER

NOTES FOR THE DESIGNER

The set is the bed-sitting-room of a plantation home in the Mississippi Delta. It is along an upstairs gallery which probably runs around the entire house; it has two pairs of very wide doors opening onto the gallery, showing white balustrades against a fair summer sky that fades into dusk and night during the course of the play, which occupies precisely the time of its performance, excepting, of course, the fifteen minutes of intermission.

Perhaps the style of the room is not what you would expect in the home of the Delta's biggest cotton-planter. It is Victorian with a touch of the Far East. It hasn't changed much since it was occupied by the original owners of the place, Jack Straw and Peter Ochello, a pair of old bachelors who shared this room all their lives together. In other words, the room must evoke some ghosts; it is gently and poetically haunted by a relationship that must have involved a tenderness which was uncommon. This may be irrelevant or unnecessary, but I once saw a reproduction of a faded photograph of the verandah of Robert Louis Stevenson's home on that Samoan Island where he spent his last years, and there was a quality of tender light on weathered wood, such as porch furniture made of bamboo and wicker, exposed to tropical suns and tropical rains, which came to mind when I thought about the set for this play, bringing also to mind the grace and comfort of light, the reassurance it gives, on a late and fair afternoon in summer, the way that no matter what, even dread of death, is gently touched and soothed by it. For the set is the background for a play that deals with human extremities of emotion, and it needs that softness behind it.

The bathroom door, showing only pale-blue tile and silver towel racks, is in one side wall; the hall door in the opposite wall. Two articles of furniture need mention: a big double bed which staging should make a functional part of the set as often as suitable, the surface of which should be slightly raked to make figures on it seen more easily; and against the wall space between the two huge double doors upstage: a monumental monstrosity peculiar to our times, a *huge* console combination of radio-phonograph (hi-fi with three speakers) TV set *and* liquor cabinet, bearing and containing many glasses and bottles, all in one piece, which is a composition of muted silver tones, and the opalescent tones of reflecting glass, a chromatic link, this thing, between the sepia (tawny gold) tones of the interior and the cool (white and blue) tones of the gallery and sky. This piece of furniture (?!), this monument, is a very complete and compact little shrine to virtually all the comforts and illusions behind which we hide from such things as the characters in the play are faced with. . . .

The set should be far less realistic than I have so far implied in this description of it. I think the walls below the ceiling should dissolve mysteriously into air; the set should be roofed by the sky; stars and moon suggested by traces of milky pallor, as if they were observed through a telescope lens out of focus.

Anything else I can think of? Oh, yes, fanlights (transoms shaped like an open glass fan) above all the doors in the set, with panes of blue and amber, and above all, the designer should take as many pains to give the actors room to move about freely (to show their restlessness, their passion for breaking out) as if it were a set for a ballet.

An evening in summer. The action is continuous, with two intermissions.

ACT ONE

At the rise of the curtain someone is taking a shower in the bathroom, the door of which is half open. A pretty young woman, with anxious lines in her face, enters the bedroom and crosses to the bathroom door.

MARGARET [*shouting above roar of water*]:
One of those no-neck monsters hit me with a hot buttered biscuit so I have t' change!

[*Margaret's voice is both rapid and drawling. In her long speeches she has the vocal tricks of a priest delivering a liturgical chant, the lines are almost sung, always continuing a little beyond her breath so she has to gasp for another. Sometimes she intersperses the lines with a little wordless singing, such as "Da-da-daaaa!"*]

[*Water turns off and Brick calls out to her, but is still unseen. A tone of politely feigned interest, masking indifference, or worse, is characteristic of his speech with Margaret.*]

BRICK:
Wha'd you say, Maggie? Water was on s' loud I couldn't hearya. . . .

MARGARET:
Well, I!—just remarked that!—one of th' no-neck monsters messed up m' lovely lace dress so I got t'—cha-a-ange. . . .

[*She opens and kicks shut drawers of the dresser.*]

BRICK:
Why d'ya call Gooper's kiddies no-neck monsters?

MARGARET:
Because they've got no necks! Isn't that a good enough reason?

295

BRICK:
Don't they have any necks?

MARGARET:
None visible. Their fat little heads are set on their fat little bodies without a bit of connection.

BRICK:
That's too bad.

MARGARET:
Yes, it's too bad because you can't wring their necks if they've got no necks to wring! Isn't that right, honey?

[*She steps out of her dress, stands in a slip of ivory satin and lace.*]

Yep, they're no-neck monsters, all no-neck people are monsters . . .

[*Children shriek downstairs.*]

Hear them? Hear them screaming? I don't know where their voice boxes are located since they don't have necks. I tell you I got so nervous at that table tonight I thought I would throw back my head and utter a scream you could hear across the Arkansas border an' parts of Louisiana an' Tennessee. I said to your charming sister-in-law, Mae, honey, couldn't you feed those precious little things at a separate table with an oilcloth cover? They make such a mess an' the lace cloth looks *so* pretty! She made enormous eyes at me and said, "Ohhh, noooooo! On Big Daddy's birthday? Why, he would never forgive me!" Well, I want you to know, Big Daddy hadn't been at the table two minutes with those five no-neck monsters slobbering and drooling over their food before he threw down his fork an' shouted, "Fo' God's sake, Gooper, why

don't you put them pigs at a trough in th' kitchen?"—Well,
I swear, I simply could have di-ieed!

Think of it, Brick, they've got five of them and number six
is coming. They've brought the whole bunch down here like
animals to display at a county fair. Why, they have those
children doin' tricks all the time! "Junior, show Big Daddy
how you do this, show Big Daddy how you do that, say your
little piece fo' Big Daddy, Sister. Show your dimples, Sugar.
Brother, show Big Daddy how you stand on your head!"—It
goes on all the time, along with constant little remarks and
innuendos about the fact that you and I have not produced
any children, are totally childless and therefore totally useless!
—Of course it's comical but it's also disgusting since it's so
obvious what they're up to!

BRICK [*without interest*]:
What are they up to, Maggie?

MARGARET:
Why, you know what they're up to!

BRICK [*appearing*]:
No, I don't know what they're up to.

[*He stands there in the bathroom doorway drying his hair
with a towel and hanging onto the towel rack because one
ankle is broken, plastered and bound. He is still slim and
firm as a boy. His liquor hasn't started tearing him down
outside. He has the additional charm of that cool air of
detachment that people have who have given up the
struggle. But now and then, when disturbed, something
flashes behind it, like lightning in a fair sky, which shows
that at some deeper level he is far from peaceful. Perhaps
in a stronger light he would show some signs of deliques-*

297

cence, but the fading, still warm, light from the gallery treats him gently.]

MARGARET:
I'll tell you what they're up to, boy of mine!—They're up to cutting you out of your father's estate, and—

[*She freezes momentarily before her next remark. Her voice drops as if it were somehow a personally embarassing admission.*]

—Now we know that Big Daddy's dyin' of—*cancer.* . . .

[*There are voices on the lawn below: long-drawn calls across distance. Margaret raises her lovely bare arms and powders her armpits with a light sigh.*

[*She adjusts the angle of a magnifying mirror to straighten an eyelash, then rises fretfully saying:*]

There's so much light in the room it—

BRICK [*softly but sharply*]:
Do we?

MARGARET:
Do we what?

BRICK:
Know Big Daddy's dyin' of cancer?

MARGARET:
Got the report today.

BRICK:
Oh . . .

MARGARET [*letting down bamboo blinds which cast long, gold-fretted shadows over the room*]:

Yep, got th' report just now . . . it didn't surprise me, Baby.
. . .

[*Her voice has range, and music; sometimes it drops low
as a boy's and you have a sudden image of her playing
boy's games as a child.*]

I recognized the symptoms soon's we got here last spring and
I'm willin' to bet you that Brother Man and his wife were
pretty sure of it, too. That more than likely explains why
their usual summer migration to the coolness of the Great
Smokies was passed up this summer in favor of—hustlin'
down here ev'ry whipstitch with their whole screamin' tribe!
And why so many allusions have been made to Rainbow Hill
lately. You know what Rainbow Hill is? Place that's famous
for treatin' alcoholics an dope fiends in the movies!

BRICK:
I'm not in the movies.

MARGARET:
No, and you don't take dope. Otherwise you're a perfect
candidate for Rainbow Hill, Baby, and that's where they aim
to ship you—over my dead body! Yep, over my dead body
they'll ship you there, but nothing would please them better.
Then Brother Man could get a-hold of the purse strings and
dole out remittances to us, maybe get power of attorney and
sign checks for us and cut off our credit wherever, whenever
he wanted! Son-of-a-bitch!—How'd you like that, Baby?—
Well, you've been doin' just about ev'rything in your power
to bring it about, you've just been doin' ev'rything you can
think of to aid and abet them in this scheme of theirs! Quit-
tin' work, devoting yourself to the occupation of drinkin'!
—Breakin' your ankle last night on the high school athletic
field: doin' what? Jumpin' hurdles? At two or three in the

299

morning? Just fantastic! Got in the paper. *Clarksdale Register* carried a nice little item about it, human interest story about a well-known former athlete stagin' a one-man track meet on the Glorious Hill High School athletic field last night, but was slightly out of condition and didn't clear the first hurdle! Brother Man Gooper claims he exercised his influence t' keep it from goin' out over AP or UP or every goddam "P."

But, Brick? You still have one big advantage!

[*During the above swift flood of words, Brick has reclined with contrapuntal leisure on the snowy surface of the bed and has rolled over carefully on his side or belly.*]

BRICK [*wryly*]:
Did you *say* something, Maggie?

MARGARET:
Big Daddy dotes on you, honey. And he can't stand Brother Man and Brother Man's wife, that monster of fertility, Mae; she's downright odious to him! Know how I know? By little expressions that flicker over his face when that woman is holding fo'th on one of her choice topics such as—how she refused twilight sleep!—when the twins were delivered! Because she feels motherhood's an experience that a woman ought to experience fully!—in order to fully appreciate the wonder and beauty of it! HAH!

[*This loud "HAH!" is accompanied by a violent action such as slamming a drawer shut.*]

—and how she made Brother Man come in an' stand beside her in the delivery room so he would not miss out on the "wonder and beauty" of it either!—producin' those no-neck monsters. . . .

[*A speech of this kind would be antipathetic from almost anybody but Margaret; she makes it oddly funny, because*

300

*her eyes constantly twinkle and her voice shakes with
laughter which is basically indulgent.*]

—Big Daddy shares my attitude toward those two! As for
me, well—I give him a laugh now and then and he tolerates
me. In fact!—I sometimes suspect that Big Daddy harbors a
little unconscious "lech" fo' me. . . .

BRICK:
What makes you think that Big Daddy has a lech for you,
Maggie?

MARGARET:
Way he always drops his eyes down my body when I'm talkin'
to him, drops his eyes to my boobs an' licks his old chops!
Ha ha!

BRICK:
That kind of talk is disgusting.

MARGARET:
Did anyone ever tell you that you're an ass-aching Puritan,
Brick?

I think it's mighty fine that that ole fellow, on the doorstep
of death, still takes in my shape with what I think is deserved
appreciation!

And you wanta know something else? Big Daddy didn't
know how many little Maes and Goopers had been produced! "How many kids have you got?" he asked at the
table, just like Brother Man and his wife were new acquaintances to him! Big Mama said he was jokin', but that ole boy
wasn't jokin', Lord, no!

And when they infawmed him that they had five already and
were turning out number six!—the news seemed to come as
a sort of unpleasant surprise . . .

301

[*Children yell below.*]

Scream, monsters!

[*Turns to Brick with a sudden, gay, charming smile which fades as she notices that he is not looking at her but into fading gold space with a troubled expression.*

[*It is constant rejection that makes her humor "bitchy."*]

Yes, you should of been at that supper-table, Baby.

[*Whenever she calls him "baby" the word is a soft caress.*]

Y'know, Big Daddy, bless his ole sweet soul, he's the dearest ole thing in the world, but he does hunch over his food as if he preferred not to notice anything else. Well, Mae an' Gooper were side by side at the table, direckly across from Big Daddy, watchin' his face like hawks while they jawed an' jabbered about the cuteness an' brillance of th' no-neck monsters!

[*She giggles with a hand fluttering at her throat and her breast and her long throat arched.*

[*She comes downstage and recreates the scene with voice and gesture.*]

And the no-neck monsters were ranged around the table, some in high chairs and some on th' *Books of Knowledge,* all in fancy little paper caps in honor of Big Daddy's birthday, and all through dinner, well, I want you to know that Brother Man an' his partner never once, for one moment, stopped exchanging pokes an' pinches an' kicks an' signs an' signals! —Why, they were like a couple of cardsharps fleecing a sucker.—Even Big Mama, bless her ole sweet soul, she isn't th' quickest an' brightest thing in the world, she finally noticed, at last, an' said to Gooper, "Gooper, what are you an'

302

Mae makin' all these signs at each other about?"—I swear t' goodness, I nearly choked on my chicken!

[Margaret, back at the dressing table, still doesn't see Brick. He is watching her with a look that is not quite definable—Amused? shocked? contemptuous?—part of those and part of something else.]

Y'know—your brother Gooper still cherishes the illusion he took a giant step up on the social ladder when he married Miss Mae Flynn of the Memphis Flynns.

[Margaret moves about the room as she talks, stops before the mirror, moves on.]

But I have a piece of Spanish news for Gooper. The Flynns never had a thing in this world but money and they lost that, they were nothing at all but fairly successful climbers. Of course, Mae Flynn came out in Memphis eight years before I made my debut in Nashville, but I had friends at Ward-Belmont who came from Memphis and they used to come to see me and I used to go to see them for Christmas and spring vacations, and so I know who rates an' who doesn't rate in Memphis society. Why, y'know ole Papa Flynn, he barely escaped doing time in the Federal pen for shady manipulations on th' stock market when his chain stores crashed, and as for Mae having been a cotton carnival queen, as they remind us so often, lest we forget, well, that's one honor that I don't envy her for!—Sit on a brass throne on a tacky float an' ride down Main Street, smilin', bowin', and blowin' kisses to all the trash on the street—

[She picks out a pair of .jeweled sandals and rushes to the dressing table.]

Why, year before last, when Susan McPheeters was singled

303

out fo' that honor, y' know what happened to her? Y'know what happened to poor little Susie McPheeters?

BRICK [*absently*]:
No. What happened to little Susie McPheeters?

MARGARET:
Somebody spit tobacco juice in her face.

BRICK [*dreamily*]:
Somebody spit tobacco juice in her face?

MARGARET:
That's right, some old drunk leaned out of a window in the Hotel Gayoso and yelled, "Hey, Queen, hey, hey, there, Queenie!" Poor Susie looked up and flashed him a radiant smile and he shot out a squirt of tobacco juice right in poor Susie's face.

BRICK:
Well, what d'you know about that.

MARGARET [*gaily*]:
What do I know about it? I was there, I saw it!

BRICK [*absently*]:
Must have been kind of funny.

MARGARET:
Susie didn't think so. Had hysterics. Screamed like a banshee. They had to stop th' parade an' remove her from her throne an' go on with—

[*She catches sight of him in the mirror, gasps slightly, wheels about to face him. Count ten.*]

—Why are you looking at me like that?

BRICK [*whistling softly, now*]:
Like what, Maggie?

MARGARET [*intensely, fearfully*]:
The way y' were lookin' at me just now, befo' I caught your
eye in the mirror and you started t' whistle! I don't know how
t' describe it but it froze my blood!—I've caught you lookin'
at me like that so often lately. What are you thinkin' of
when you look at me like that?

BRICK:
I wasn't conscious of lookin' at you, Maggie.

MARGARET:
Well, I was conscious of it! What were you thinkin'?

BRICK:
I don't remember thinking of anything, Maggie.

MARGARET:
Don't you think I know that—? Don't you—?—Think I
know that—?

BRICK [*coolly*]:
Know *what*, Maggie?

MARGARET [*struggling for expression*]:
That I've gone through this—*hideous!*—*transformation*, become—*hard! Frantic!*

[*Then she adds, almost tenderly:*]

—*cruel!!*

That's what you've been observing in me lately. How could
y' help but observe it? That's all right. I'm not—thin-skinned
any more, can't afford t' be thin-skinned any more.

[*She is now recovering her power.*]

—But Brick? Brick?

BRICK:
Did you say something?

305

MARGARET:

I was *goin' t'* say something: that I get—lonely. Very!

BRICK:

Ev'rybody gets that . . .

MARGARET:

Living with someone you love can be lonelier—than living entirely *alone*!—if the one that y' love doesn't love you. . . .

[*There is a pause. Brick hobbles downstage and asks, without looking at her:*]

BRICK:

Would you like to live alone, Maggie?

[*Another pause: then—after she has caught a quick, hurt breath:*]

MARGARET:

No!—God!—I wouldn't!

[*Another gasping breath. She forcibly controls what must have been an impulse to cry out. We see her deliberately, very forcibly, going all the way back to the world in which you can talk about ordinary matters.*]

Did you have a nice shower?

BRICK:

Uh-huh.

MARGARET:

Was the water cool?

BRICK:

No.

MARGARET:

But it made y' feel fresh, huh?

BRICK:
Fresher. . . .

MARGARET:
I know something would make y' feel *much* fresher!

BRICK:
What?

MARGARET:
An alcohol rub. Or cologne, a rub with cologne!

BRICK:
That's good after a workout but I haven't been workin' out, Maggie.

MARGARET:
You've kept in good shape, though.

BRICK [*indifferently*]:
You think so, Maggie?

MARGARET:
I always thought drinkin' men lost their looks, but I was plainly mistaken.

BRICK [*wryly*]:
Why, thanks, Maggie.

MARGARET:
You're the only drinkin' man I know that it never seems t' put fat on.

BRICK:
I'm gettin' softer, Maggie.

MARGARET:
Well, sooner or later it's bound to soften you up. It was just beginning to soften up Skipper when—

[*She stops short.*]

I'm sorry. I never could keep my fingers off a sore—I wish you *would* lose your looks. If you did it would make the martyrdom of Saint Maggie a little more bearable. But no such goddam luck. I actually believe you've gotten better looking since you've gone on the bottle. Yeah, a person who didn't know you would think you'd never had a tense nerve in your body or a strained muscle.

[*There are sounds of croquet on the lawn below: the click of mallets, light voices, near and distant.*]

Of course, you always had that detached quality as if you were playing a game without much concern over whether you won or lost, and now that you've lost the game, not lost but just quit playing, you have that rare sort of charm that usually only happens in very old or hopelessly sick people, the charm of the defeated.—You look so cool, so cool, so enviably cool.

[*Music is heard.*]

They're playing croquet. The moon has appeared and it's white, just beginning to turn a little bit yellow. . . .

You were a wonderful lover. . . .

Such a wonderful person to go to bed with, and I think mostly because you were really indifferent to it. Isn't that right? Never had any anxiety about it, did it naturally, easily, slowly, with absolute confidence and perfect calm, more like opening a door for a lady or seating her at a table than giving expression to any longing for her. Your indifference made you wonderful at lovemaking—*strange?*—but true. . . .

You know, if I thought you would never, never, *never* make love to me again—I would go downstairs to the kitchen and pick out the longest and sharpest knife I could find and stick it straight into my heart, I swear that I would!

But one thing I don't have is the charm of the defeated, my hat is still in the ring, and I am determined to win!

[*There is the sound of croquet mallets hitting croquet balls.*]

—What is the victory of a cat on a hot tin roof?—I wish I knew....

Just staying on it, I guess, as long as she can....

[*More croquet sounds.*]

Later tonight I'm going to tell you I love you an' maybe by that time you'll be drunk enough to believe me. Yes, they're playing croquet....

Big Daddy is dying of cancer....

What were you thinking of when I caught you looking at me like that? Were you thinking of Skipper?

[*Brick takes up his crutch, rises.*]

Oh, excuse me, forgive me, but laws of silence don't work! No, laws of silence don't work....

[*Brick crosses to the bar, takes a quick drink, and rubs his head with a towel.*]

Laws of silence don't work....

When something is festering in your memory or your imagination, laws of silence don't work, it's just like shutting a door and locking it on a house on fire in hope of forgetting that the house is burning. But not facing a fire doesn't put it out. Silence about a thing just magnifies it. It grows and festers in silence, becomes malignant....

309

Get dressed, Brick.

[*He drops his crutch.*]

BRICK:
I've dropped my crutch.

[*He has stopped rubbing his hair dry but still stands hanging onto the towel rack in a white towel-cloth robe.*]

MARGARET:
Lean on me.

BRICK:
No, just give me my crutch.

MARGARET:
Lean on my shoulder.

BRICK:
I don't want to lean on your shoulder, I want my crutch!

[*This is spoken like sudden lightning.*]

Are you going to give me my crutch or do I have to get down on my knees on the floor and—

MARGARET:
Here, here, take it, take it!

[*She has thrust the crutch at him.*]

BRICK [*hobbling out*]:
Thanks . . .

MARGARET:
We mustn't scream at each other, the walls in this house have ears. . . .

[*He hobbles directly to liquor cabinet to get a new drink.*]

—but that's the first time I've heard you raise your voice in a long time, Brick. A crack in the wall?—Of composure?

—I think that's a good sign. . . .

A sign of nerves in a player on the defensive!

[*Brick turns and smiles at her coolly over his fresh drink.*]

BRICK:
It just hasn't happened yet, Maggie.

MARGARET:
What?

BRICK:
The click I get in my head when I've had enough of this stuff to make me peaceful. . . .

Will you do me a favor?

MARGARET:
Maybe I will. What favor?

BRICK:
Just, just keep your voice down!

MARGARET [*in a hoarse whisper*]:
I'll do you that favor, I'll speak in a whisper, if not shut up completely, if *you* will do *me* a favor and make that drink your last one till after the party.

BRICK:
What party?

MARGARET:
Big Daddy's birthday party.

BRICK:
Is this Big Daddy's birthday?

311

MARGARET:
You know this is Big Daddy's birthday!

BRICK:
No, I don't, I forgot it.

MARGARET:
Well, I remembered it for you. . . .

[*They are both speaking as breathlessly as a pair of kids after a fight, drawing deep exhausted breaths and looking at each other with faraway eyes, shaking and panting together as if they had broken apart from a violent struggle.*]

BRICK:
Good for you, Maggie.

MARGARET:
You just have to scribble a few lines on this card.

BRICK:
You scribble something, Maggie.

MARGARET:
It's got to be your handwriting; it's your present, I've given him my present; it's got to be your handwriting!

[*The tension between them is building again, the voices becoming shrill once more.*]

BRICK:
I didn't get him a present.

MARGARET:
I got one for you.

BRICK:
All right. You write the card, then.

MARGARET:
And have him know you didn't remember his birthday?

BRICK:
I didn't remember his birthday.

MARGARET:
You don't have to prove you didn't!

BRICK:
I don't want to fool him about it.

MARGARET:
Just write "Love, Brick!" for God's—

BRICK:
No.

MARGARET:
You've *got* to!

BRICK:
I don't have to do anything I don't want to do. You keep forgetting the conditions on which I agreed to stay on living with you.

MARGARET [*out before she knows it*]:
I'm not living with you. We occupy the same cage.

BRICK:
You've got to remember the conditions agreed on.

MARGARET:
They're impossible conditions!

BRICK:
Then why don't you—?

MARGARET:
HUSH! Who is out there? Is somebody at the door?

[*There are footsteps in hall.*]

MAE [*outside*]:
May I enter a moment?

MARGARET:
Oh, *you!* Sure. Come in, Mae.

[*Mae enters bearing aloft the bow of a young lady's archery set.*]

MAE:
Brick, is this thing yours?

MARGARET:
Why, Sister Woman—that's my Diana Trophy. Won it at the intercollegiate archery contest on the Ole Miss campus.

MAE:
It's a mighty dangerous thing to leave exposed round a house full of nawmal rid-blooded children attracted t'weapons.

MARGARET:
"Nawmal rid-blooded children attracted t'weapons" ought t'be taught to keep their hands off things that don't belong to them.

MAE:
Maggie, honey, if you had children of your own you'd know how funny that is. Will you please lock this up and put the key out of reach?

MARGARET:
Sister Woman, nobody is plotting the destruction of your kiddies. —Brick and I still have our special archers' license. We're goin' deer-huntin' on Moon Lake as soon as the season starts. I love to run with dogs through chilly woods, run, run leap over obstructions—

314

[*She goes into the closet carrying the bow.*]

MAE:
How's the injured ankle, Brick?

BRICK:
Doesn't hurt. Just itches.

MAE:
Oh, my! Brick—Brick, you should've been downstairs after supper! Kiddies put on a show. Polly played the piano, Buster an' Sonny drums, an' then they turned out the lights an' Dixie an' Trixie puhfawmed a toe dance in fairy costume with *spahkluhs!* Big Daddy just beamed! He just beamed!

MARGARET [*from the closet with a sharp laugh*]:
Oh, I bet. It breaks my heart that we missed it!

[*She reenters.*]

But Mae? Why did y'give dawgs' names to all your kiddies?

MAE:
Dogs' names?

[*Margaret has made this observation as she goes to raise the bamboo blinds, since the sunset glare has diminished. In crossing she winks at Brick.*]

MARGARET [*sweetly*]:
Dixie, Trixie, Buster, Sonny, Polly!—Sounds like four dogs and a parrot ... animal act in a circus!

MAE:
Maggie?

[*Margaret turns with a smile.*]

Why are you so catty?

315

MARGARET:
Cause I'm a cat! But why can't *you* take a joke, Sister Woman?

MAE:
Nothin' pleases me more than a joke that's funny. You know the real names of our kiddies. Buster's real name is Robert. Sonny's real name is Saunders. Trixie's real name is Marlene and Dixie's—

[*Someone downstairs calls for her. "Hey, Mae!"—She rushes to door, saying:*]

Intermission is over!

MARGARET [*as Mae closes door*]:
I wonder what Dixie's real name is?

BRICK:
Maggie, being catty doesn't help things any . . .

MARGARET:
I know! *WHY!*—Am I so catty?—Cause I'm consumed with envy an' eaten up with longing?—Brick, I've laid out your beautiful Shantung silk suit from Rome and one of your monogrammed silk shirts. I'll put your cuff links in it, those lovely star sapphires I get you to wear so rarely. . . .

BRICK:
I can't get trousers on over this plaster cast.

MARGARET:
Yes, you can, I'll help you.

BRICK:
I'm not going to get dressed, Maggie.

MARGARET:
Will you just put on a pair of white silk pajamas?

316

BRICK:
Yes, I'll do that, Maggie.

MARGARET:
Thank you, thank you so *much!*

BRICK:
Don't mention it.

MARGARET:
Oh, Brick! How long does it have t' go on? This punishment? Haven't I done time enough, haven't I served my term, can't I apply for a—pardon?

BRICK:
Maggie, you're spoiling my liquor. Lately your voice always sounds like you'd been running upstairs to warn somebody that the house was on fire!

MARGARET:
Well, no wonder, no wonder. Y'know what I feel like, Brick?

[*Children's and grownups' voices are blended, below, in a loud but uncertain rendition of "My Wild Irish Rose."*]

I feel all the time like a cat on a hot tin roof!

BRICK:
Then jump off the roof, jump off it, cats can jump off roofs and land on their four feet uninjured!

MARGARET:
Oh, yes!

BRICK:
Do it!—fo' God's sake, do it ...

MARGARET:
Do what?

317

BRICK:
Take a lover!

MARGARET:
I can't see a man but you! Even with my eyes closed, I just see you! Why don't you get ugly, Brick, why don't you please get fat or ugly or something so I could stand it?

[*She rushes to hall door, opens it, listens.*]

The concert is still going on! Bravo, no-necks, bravo!

[*She slams and locks door fiercely.*]

BRICK:
What did you lock the door for?

MARGARET:
To give us a little privacy for a while.

BRICK:
You know better, Maggie.

MARGARET:
No, I don't know better. . . .

[*She rushes to gallery doors, draws the rose-silk drapes across them.*]

BRICK:
Don't make a fool of yourself.

MARGARET:
I don't mind makin' a fool of myself over you!

BRICK:
I mind, Maggie. I feel embarrassed for you.

MARGARET:
Feel embarrassed! But don't continue my torture. I can't live on and on under these circumstances.

318

BRICK:
You agreed to—

MARGARET:
I know but—

BRICK:
—Accept that condition!

MARGARET:
I CAN'T! CAN'T! CAN'T!

[*She seizes his shoulder.*]

BRICK:
Let go!

[*He breaks away from her and seizes the small boudoir chair and raises it like a lion-tamer facing a big circus cat.*

[*Count five. She stares at him with her fist pressed to her mouth, then bursts into shrill, almost hysterical laughter. He remains grave for a moment, then grins and puts the chair down.*

[*Big Mama calls through closed door.*]

BIG MAMA:
Son? Son? Son?

BRICK:
What is it, Big Mama?

BIG MAMA [*outside*]:
Oh, son! We got the most wonderful news about Big Daddy. I just had t' run up an' tell you right this—

[*She rattles the knob.*]

—What's this door doin', locked, faw? You all think there's robbers in the house?

319

MARGARET:
Big Mama, Brick is dressin', he's not dressed yet.

BIG MAMA:
That's all right, it won't be the first time I've seen Brick not dressed. Come on, open this door!

[*Margaret, with a grimace, goes to unlock and open the hall door, as Brick hobbles rapidly to the bathroom and kicks the door shut. Big Mama has disappeared from the hall.*]

MARGARET:
Big Mama?

[*Big Mama appears through the opposite gallery doors behind Margaret, huffing and puffing like an old bulldog. She is a short, stout woman; her sixty years and 170 pounds have left her somewhat breathless most of the time; she's always tensed like a boxer, or rather, a Japanese wrestler. Her "family" was maybe a little superior to Big Daddy's, but not much. She wears a black or silver lace dress and at least half a million in flashy gems. She is very sincere.*]

BIG MAMA [*loudly, startling Margaret*]:
Here—I come through Gooper's and Mae's gall'ry door. Where's Brick? *Brick*—Hurry on out of there, son, I just have a second and want to give you the news about Big Daddy.— I hate locked doors in a house. . . .

MARGARET [*with affected lightness*]:
I've noticed you do, Big Mama, but people have got to have *some* moments of privacy, don't they?

BIG MAMA:
No, ma'am, not in *my* house. [*without pause*] Whacha took off you' dress faw? I thought that little lace dress was so sweet on yuh, honey.

320

MARGARET:
I thought it looked sweet on me, too, but one of m' cute little table-partners used it for a napkin so—!

BIG MAMA [*picking up stockings on floor*]:
What?

MARGARET:
You know, Big Mama, Mae and Gooper's so touchy about those children—thanks, Big Mama . . .

[*Big Mama has thrust the picked-up stockings in Margaret's hand with a grunt.*]

—that you just don't dare to suggest there's any room for improvement in their—

BIG MAMA:
Brick, hurry out!—Shoot, Maggie, you just don't like children.

MARGARET:
I do SO like children! Adore them!—well brought up!

BIG MAMA [*gentle—loving*]:
Well, why don't you have some and bring them up well, then, instead of all the time pickin' on Gooper's an' Mae's?

GOOPER [*shouting up the stairs*]:
Hey, hey, Big Mama, Betsy an' Hugh got to go, waitin' t' tell yuh g'by!

BIG MAMA:
Tell 'em to hold their hawses, I'll be right down in a jiffy!

[*She turns to the bathroom door and calls out.*]

Son? Can you hear me in there?

[*There is a muffled answer.*]

321

We just got the full report from the laboratory at the Ochsner Clinic, completely negative, son, ev'rything negative, right on down the line! Nothin' a-tall's wrong with him but some little functional thing called a spastic colon. Can you hear me, son?

MARGARET:
He can hear you, Big Mama.

BIG MAMA:
Then why don't he say something? God Almighty, a piece of news like that should make him shout. It made *me* shout, I can tell you. I shouted and sobbed and fell right down on my knees!—Look!

[*She pulls up her skirt.*]

See the bruises where I hit my kneecaps? Took both doctors to haul me back on my feet!

[*She laughs—she always laughs like hell at herself.*]

Big Daddy was furious with me! But ain't that wonderful news?

[*Facing bathroom again, she continues:*]

After all the anxiety we been through to git a report like that on Big Daddy's birthday? Big Daddy tried to hide how much of a load that news took off his mind, but didn't fool *me*. He was mighty close to crying about it *himself!*

[*Goodbyes are shouted downstairs, and she rushes to door.*]

Hold those people down there, don't let them go!—Now, git dressed, we're all comin' up to this room fo' Big Daddy's birthday party because of your ankle.—How's his ankle, Maggie?

MARGARET:
Well, he broke it, Big Mama.

BIG MAMA:
I know he broke it.

[*A phone is ringing in hall. A Negro voice answers: "Mistuh Polly's res'dence."*]

I mean does it hurt him much still.

MARGARET:
I'm afraid I can't give you that information, Big Mama. You'll have to ask Brick if it hurts much still or not.

SOOKEY [*in the hall*]:
It's Memphis, Mizz Polly, it's Miss Sally in Memphis.

BIG MAMA:
Awright, Sookey.

[*Big Mama rushes into the hall and is heard shouting on the phone:*]

Hello, Miss Sally. How are you, Miss Sally?—Yes, well, I was just gonna call you about it. *Shoot!*—

[*She raises her voice to a bellow.*]

Miss Sally? Don't ever call me from the Gayoso Lobby, too much talk goes on in that hotel lobby, no wonder you can't hear me! Now listen, Miss Sally. They's nothin' serious wrong with Big Daddy. We got the report just now, they's nothin' wrong but a thing called a—spastic! *SPASTIC!*—colon . . .

[*She appears at the hall door and calls to Margaret.*]

—Maggie, come out here and talk to that fool on the phone. I'm shouted breathless!

323

MARGARET [*goes out and is heard sweetly at phone*]:
Miss Sally? This is Brick's wife, Maggie. So nice to hear your
voice. Can you hear *mine?* Well, *good!*—Big Mama just
wanted you to know that they've got the report from the
Ochsner Clinic and what Big Daddy has is a spastic colon.
Yes. Spastic colon, Miss Sally. That's right, spastic colon.
G'bye, Miss Sally, hope I'll see you real soon!

[*Hangs up a little before Miss Sally was probably ready to
terminate the talk. She returns through the hall door.*]

She heard me perfectly. I've discovered with deaf people the
thing to do is not shout at them but just enunciate clearly. My
rich old Aunt Cornelia was deaf as the dead but I could make
her hear me just by sayin' each word slowly, distinctly, close
to her ear. I read her the *Commercial Appeal* ev'ry night, read
her the classified ads in it, even, she never missed a word of it.
But was she a mean ole thing! Know what I got when she
died? Her unexpired subscriptions to five magazines and the
Book-of-the-Month Club and a LIBRARY full of ev'ry dull
book ever written! All else went to her hellcat of a sister . . .
meaner than she was, even!

[*Big Mama has been straightening things up in the room
during this speech.*]

BIG MAMA [*closing closet door on discarded clothes*]:
Miss Sally sure is a case! Big Daddy says she's always got her
hand out fo' something. He's not mistaken. That poor ole
thing always has her hand out fo' somethin'. I don't think
Big Daddy gives her as much as he should.

[*Somebody shouts for her downstairs and she shouts:*]

I'm comin'!

[*She starts out. At the hall door, turns and jerks a fore-
finger, first toward the bathroom door, then toward the*

liquor cabinet, meaning: "Has Brick been drinking?" Margaret pretends not to understand, cocks her head and raises her brows as if the pantomimic performance was completely mystifying to her.

[*Big Mama rushes back to Margaret:*]

Shoot! Stop playin' so dumb!—I mean has he been drinkin' that stuff much yet?

MARGARET [*with a little laugh*]:
Oh! I think he had a highball after supper.

BIG MAMA:
Don't laugh about it!—Some single men stop drinkin' when they git married and others start! Brick never touched liquor before he—!

MARGARET [*crying out*]:
THAT'S NOT FAIR!

BIG MAMA:
Fair or not fair I want to ask you a question, one question: D'you make Brick happy in bed?

MARGARET:
Why don't you ask if he makes *me* happy in bed?

BIG MAMA:
Because I know that—

MARGARET:
It works both ways!

BIG MAMA:
Something's not right! You're childless and my son drinks!

[*Someone has called her downstairs and she has rushed to the door on the line above. She turns at the door and points at the bed.*]

325

—When a marriage goes on the rocks, the rocks are *there*, right *there!*

MARGARET:
That's—

[*Big Mama has swept out of the room and slammed the door.*]

—not—*fair . . .*

[*Margaret is alone, completely alone, and she feels it. She draws in, hunches her shoulders, raises her arms with fists clenched, shuts her eyes tight as a child about to be stabbed with a vaccination needle. When she opens her eyes again, what she sees is the long oval mirror and she rushes straight to it, stares into it with a grimace and says: "Who are you?"—Then she crouches a little and answers herself in a different voice which is high, thin, mocking: "I am Maggie the Cat!"—Straightens quickly as bathroom door opens a little and Bricks calls out to her.*]

BRICK:
Has Big Mama gone?

MARGARET:
She's gone.

[*He opens the bathroom door and hobbles out, with his liquor glass now empty, straight to the liquor cabinet. He is whistling softly. Margaret's head pivots on her long, slender throat to watch him.*

[*She raises a hand uncertainly to the base of her throat, as if it was difficult for her to swallow, before she speaks:*]

You know, our sex life didn't just peter out in the usual way, it was cut off short, long before the natural time for it to, and

326

it's going to revive again, just as sudden as that. I'm confident of it. That's what I'm keeping myself attractive for. For the time when you'll see me again like other men see me. Yes, like other men see me. They still see me, Brick, and they like what they see. Uh-huh. Some of them would give their—

Look, Brick!

[*She stands before the long oval mirror, touches her breast and then her hips with her two hands.*]

How high my body stays on me!—Nothing has fallen on me —not a fraction. . . .

[*Her voice is soft and trembling: a pleading child's. At this moment as he turns to glance at her—a look which is like a player passing a ball to another player, third down and goal to go—she has to capture the audience in a grip so tight that she can hold it till the first intermission without any lapse of attention.*]

Other men still want me. My face looks strained, sometimes, but I've kept my figure as well as you've kept yours, and men admire it. I still turn heads on the street. Why, last week in Memphis everywhere that I went men's eyes burned holes in my clothes, at the country club and in restaurants and department stores, there wasn't a man I met or walked by that didn't just eat me up with his eyes and turn around when I passed him and look back at me. Why, at Alice's party for her New York cousins, the best-lookin' man in the crowd—followed me upstairs and tried to force his way in the powder room with me, followed me to the door and tried to force his way in!

BRICK:
Why didn't you let him, Maggie?

MARGARET:

Because I'm not that common, for one thing. Not that I wasn't almost tempted to. You like to know who it was? It was Sonny Boy Maxwell, that's who!

BRICK:

Oh, yeah, Sonny Boy Maxwell, he was a good end-runner but had a little injury to his back and had to quit.

MARGARET:

He has no injury now and has no wife and still has a lech for me!

BRICK:

I see no reason to lock him out of a powder room in that case.

MARGARET:

And have someone catch me at it? I'm not that stupid. Oh, I might sometime cheat on you with someone, since you're so insultingly eager to have me do it!—But if I do, you can be damned sure it will be in a place and a time where no one but me and the man could possibly know. Because I'm not going to give you any excuse to divorce me for being unfaithful or anything else. . . .

BRICK:

Maggie, I wouldn't divorce you for being unfaithful or anything else. Don't you know that? Hell. I'd be relieved to know that you'd found yourself a lover.

MARGARET:

Well, I'm taking no chances. No, I'd rather stay on this hot tin roof.

BRICK:

A hot tin roof's 'n uncomfo'table place t' stay on. . . .

[*He starts to whistle softly.*]

MARGARET [*through his whistle*]:
Yeah, but I can stay on it just as long as I have to.

BRICK:
You could leave me, Maggie.

[*He resumes whistle. She wheels about to glare at him.*]

MARGARET:
Don't want to and will not! Besides if I did, you don't have a cent to pay for it but what you get from Big Daddy and he's dying of cancer!

[*For the first time a realization of Big Daddy's doom seems to penetrate to Brick's consciousness, visibly, and he looks at Margaret.*]

BRICK:
Big Mama just said he *wasn't,* that the report was okay.

MARGARET:
That's what she thinks because she got the same story that they gave Big Daddy. And was just as taken in by it as he was, poor ole things. . . .

But tonight they're going to tell her the truth about it. When Big Daddy goes to bed, they're going to tell her that he is dying of cancer.

[*She slams the dresser drawer.*]

—It's malignant and it's terminal.

BRICK:
Does Big Daddy know it?

MARGARET:
Hell, do they *ever* know it? Nobody says, "You're dying." You have to fool them. They have to fool *themselves.*

329

BRICK:
Why?

MARGARET:
Why? Because human beings dream of life everlasting, that's the reason! But most of them want it on earth and not in heaven.

[*He gives a short, hard laugh at her touch of humor.*]

Well. . . . [*She touches up her mascara.*] That's how it is, anyhow. . . . [*She looks about.*] Where did I put down my cigarette? Don't want to burn up the home-place, at least not with Mae and Gooper and their five monsters in it!

[*She has found it and sucks at it greedily. Blows out smoke and continues:*]

So this is Big Daddy's last birthday. And Mae and Gooper, they know it, oh, *they* know it, all right. They got the first information from the Ochsner Clinic. That's why they rushed down here with their no-neck monsters. Because. Do you know something? Big Daddy's made no will? Big Daddy's never made out any will in his life, and so this campaign's afoot to impress him, forcibly as possible, with the fact that you drink and I've borne no children!

[*He continues to stare at her a moment, then mutters something sharp but not audible and hobbles rather rapidly out onto the long gallery in the fading, much faded, gold light.*]

MARGARET [*continuing her liturgical chant*]:
Y'know, I'm *fond* of Big Daddy, I am genuinely fond of that old man, I really *am,* you know. . . .

BRICK [*faintly, vaguely*]:
Yes, I know you are. . . .

MARGARET:

I've always sort of admired him in spite of his coarseness, his four-letter words and so forth. Because Big Daddy *is* what he *is,* and he makes no bones about it. He hasn't turned gentleman farmer, he's still a Mississippi redneck, as much of a redneck as he must have been when he was just overseer here on the old Jack Straw and Peter Ochello place. But he got hold of it an' built it into th' biggest an' finest plantation in the Delta.——I've always *liked* Big Daddy....

[*She crosses to the proscenium.*]

Well, this is Big Daddy's last birthday. I'm sorry about it. But I'm facing the facts. It takes money to take care of a drinker and that's the office that I've been elected to lately.

BRICK:

You don't have to take care of me.

MARGARET:

Yes, I do. Two people in the same boat have got to take care of each other. At least you want money to buy more Echo Spring when this supply is exhausted, or will you be satisfied with a ten-cent beer?

Mae an' Gooper are plannin' to freeze us out of Big Daddy's estate because you drink and I'm childless. But we can defeat that plan. We're *going* to defeat that plan!

Brick, y'know, I've been so God damn disgustingly poor all my life!——That's the *truth,* Brick!

BRICK:

I'm not sayin' it isn't.

MARGARET:

Always had to suck up to people I couldn't stand because they had money and I was poor as Job's turkey. You don't

331

know what that's like. Well, I'll tell you, it's like you would feel a thousand miles away from Echo Spring!—And had to get back to it on that broken ankle . . . without a crutch!

That's how it feels to be as poor as Job's turkey and have to suck up to relatives that you hated because they had money and all you had was a bunch of hand-me-down clothes and a few old moldly three-per-cent government bonds. My daddy loved his liquor, he fell in love with his liquor the way you've fallen in love with Echo Spring!—And my poor Mama, having to maintain some semblance of social position, to keep appearances up, on an income of one hundred and fifty dollars a month on those old government bonds!

When I came out, the year that I made my debut, I had just two evening dresses! One Mother made me from a pattern in *Vogue,* the other a hand-me-down from a snotty rich cousin I hated!

—The dress that I married you in was my grandmother's weddin' gown. . . .

So that's why I'm like a cat on a hot tin roof!

> [*Brick is still on the gallery. Someone below calls up to him in a warm Negro voice, "Hiya, Mistuh Brick, how yuh feelin'?" Brick raises his liquor glass as if that answered the question.*]

MARGARET:
You can be young without money, but you can't be old without it. You've got to be old *with* money because to be old without it is just too awful, you've got to be one or the other, either *young* or *with money,* you can't be old and *without* it.—That's the *truth,* Brick. . . .

> [*Brick whistles softly, vaguely.*]

Well, now I'm dressed, I'm all dressed, there's nothing else for me to do.

[*Forlornly, almost fearfully.*]

I'm dressed, all dressed, nothing else for me to do. . . .

[*She moves about restlessly, aimlessly, and speaks, as if to herself.*]

I know when I made my mistake.—What am I—? Oh!—my bracelets. . . .

[*She starts working a collection of bracelets over her hands onto her wrists, about six on each, as she talks.*]

I've thought a whole lot about it and now I know when I made my mistake. Yes, I made my mistake when I told you the truth about that thing with Skipper. Never should have confessed it, a fatal error, tellin' you about that thing with Skipper.

BRICK:
Maggie, shut up about Skipper. I mean it, Maggie; you got to shut up about Skipper.

MARGARET:
You ought to understand that Skipper and I—

BRICK:
You don't think I'm serious, Maggie? You're fooled by the fact that I am saying this quiet? Look, Maggie. What you're doing is a dangerous thing to do. You're—you're—you're—foolin' with something that—nobody ought to fool with.

MARGARET:
This time I'm going to finish what I have to say to you. Skipper and I made love, if love you could call it, because it made both of us feel a little bit closer to you. You see, you

333

son of a bitch, you asked too much of people, of me, of him, of all the unlucky poor damned sons of bitches that happen to love you, and there was a whole pack of them, yes, there was a pack of them besides me and Skipper, you asked too goddam much of people that loved you, you—superior creature!—you godlike being!—And so we made love to each other to dream it was you, both of us! Yes, yes, yes! Truth, truth! What's so awful about it? I like it, I think the truth is—yeah! I shouldn't have told you. . . .

BRICK [*holding his head unnaturally still and uptilted a bit*]:
It was Skipper that told me about it. Not you, Maggie.

MARGARET:
I told you!

BRICK:
After he told me!

MARGARET:
What does it matter who—?

[*Brick turns suddenly out upon the gallery and calls:*]

BRICK:
Little girl! Hey, little girl!

LITTLE GIRL [*at a distance*]:
What, Uncle Brick?

BRICK:
Tell the folks to come up!—Bring everybody upstairs!

MARGARET:
I can't stop myself! I'd go on telling you this in front of them all, if I had to!

334

BRICK:
Little girl! Go on, go on, will you? Do what I told you, call them!

MARGARET:
Because it's got to be told and you, you!—you never let me!

[*She sobs, then controls herself, and continues almost calmly.*]

It was one of those beautiful, ideal things they tell about in the Greek legends, it couldn't be anything else, you being you, and that's what made it so sad, that's what made it so awful, because it was love that never could be carried through to anything satisfying or even talked about plainly. Brick, I tell you, you got to believe me, Brick, I *do* understand all about it! I—I think it was—*noble!* Can't you tell I'm sincere when I say I respect it? My only point, the only point that I'm making, is life has got to be allowed to continue even after the *dream* of life is—all—over. . . .

[*Brick is without his crutch. Leaning on furniture, he crosses to pick it up as she continues as if possessed by a will outside herself:*]

Why I remember when we double-dated at college, Gladys Fitzgerald and I and you and Skipper, it was more like a date between you and Skipper. Gladys and I were just sort of tagging along as if it was necessary to chaperone you!—to make a good public impression—

BRICK [*turns to face her, half lifting his crutch*]:
Maggie, you want me to hit you with this crutch? Don't you know I could kill you with this crutch?

MARGARET:
Good Lord, man, d' you think I'd care if you did?

335

BRICK:

One man has one great good true thing in his life. One great good thing which is true!—I had friendship with Skipper.— You are naming it dirty!

MARGARET:

I'm not naming it dirty! I am naming it clean.

BRICK:

Not love with you, Maggie, but friendship with Skipper was that one great true thing, and you are naming it dirty!

MARGARET:

Then you haven't been listenin', not understood what I'm saying! I'm naming it so damn clean that it killed poor Skipper!—You two had something that had to be kept on ice, yes, incorruptible, yes!—and death was the only icebox where you could keep it. . . .

BRICK:

I married you, Maggie. Why would I marry you, Maggie, if I was—?

MARGARET:

Brick, don't brain me yet, let me finish!—I know, believe me I know, that it was only Skipper that harbored even any *unconscious* desire for anything not perfectly pure between you two!—Now let me skip a little. You married me early that summer we graduated out of Ole Miss, and we were happy, weren't we, we were blissful, yes, hit heaven together ev'ry time that we loved! But that fall you an' Skipper turned down wonderful offers of jobs in order to keep on bein' foot-ball heroes—pro-football heroes. You organized the Dixie Stars that fall, so you could keep on bein' teammates forever! But somethin' was not right with it!—*Me included!*—between you. Skipper began hittin' the bottle . . . you got a spinal injury—couldn't play the Thanksgivin' game in Chicago, watched it on TV from a traction bed in Toledo. I joined Skipper. The Dixie Stars lost because poor Skipper was drunk. We drank together that night all night in the bar of the Blackstone and when cold day was comin' up over the Lake an' we were comin' out drunk to take a dizzy look at it, I said, "SKIPPER! STOP LOVIN' MY HUSBAND OR TELL HIM HE'S GOT TO LET YOU ADMIT IT TO HIM!"—one way or another!

HE SLAPPED ME HARD ON THE MOUTH!—then turned and ran without stopping once, I am sure, all the way back into his room at the Blackstone. . . .

—When I came to his room that night, with a little scratch like a shy little mouse at his door, he made that pitiful, ineffectual little attempt to prove that what I had said wasn't true. . . .

[*Brick strikes at her with crutch, a blow that shatters the gemlike lamp on the table.*]

—In this way, I destroyed him, by telling him truth that he and his world which he was born and raised in, yours and his world, had told him could not be told?

—From then on Skipper was nothing at all but a receptacle for liquor and drugs. . . .

—*Who shot cock robin? I with my*—

[*She throws back her head with tight shut eyes.*]

—*merciful arrow!*

[*Brick strikes at her; misses.*]

Missed me!—Sorry,—I'm not tryin' to whitewash my behavior, Christ, no! Brick, I'm not good. I don't know why

337

people have to pretend to be good, nobody's good. The rich or the well-to-do can afford to respect moral patterns, conventional moral patterns, but I could never afford to, yeah, but—I'm honest! Give me credit for just that, will you *please?*—Born poor, raised poor, expect to die poor unless I manage to get us something out of what Big Daddy leaves when he dies of cancer! But Brick?!—*Skipper is dead! I'm alive!* Maggie the cat is—

[*Brick hops awkwardly forward and strikes at her again with his crutch.*]

—alive! I am alive, alive! I am ...

[*He hurls the crutch at her, across the bed she took refuge behind, and pitches forward on the floor as she completes her speech.*]

—alive!

[*A little girl, Dixie, bursts into the room, wearing an Indian war bonnet and firing a cap pistol at Margaret and shouting: "Bang, bang, bang!"*

[*Laughter downstairs floats through the open hall door. Margaret had crouched gasping to bed at child's entrance. She now rises and says with cool fury:*]

Little girl, your mother or someone should teach you—[*gasping*]—to knock at a door before you come into a room. Otherwise people might think that you—lack—good breeding. . . .

DIXIE:

Yanh, yanh, yanh, what is Uncle Brick doin' on th' floor?

BRICK:

I tried to kill your Aunt Maggie, but I failed—and I fell. Little girl, give me my crutch so I can get up off th' floor.

MARGARET:

Yes, give your uncle his crutch, he's a cripple, honey, he broke his ankle last night jumping hurdles on the high school athletic field!

DIXIE:

What were you jumping hurdles for, Uncle Brick?

BRICK:

Because I used to jump them, and people like to do what they used to do, even after they've stopped being able to do it. . . .

MARGARET:

That's right, that's your answer, now go away, little girl.

[*Dixie fires cap pistol at Margaret three times.*]

Stop, you stop that, monster! You little no-neck monster!

[*She seizes the cap pistol and hurls it through gallery doors.*]

DIXIE [*with a precocious instinct for the cruelest thing*]:
You're *jealous!*—You're just jealous because you can't have babies!

[*She sticks out her tongue at Margaret as she sashays past her with her stomach stuck out, to the gallery. Margaret slams the gallery doors and leans panting against them. There is a pause. Brick has replaced his spilt drink and sits, faraway, on the great four-poster bed.*]

MARGARET:

You see?—they gloat over us being childless, even in front of their five little no-neck monsters!

[*Pause. Voices approach on the stairs.*]

Brick?—I've been to a doctor in Memphis, a—a gynecologist. . . .

339

I've been completely examined, and there is no reason why we can't have a child whenever we want one. And this is my time by the calendar to conceive. Are you listening to me? Are you? Are you LISTENING TO ME!

BRICK:
Yes. I hear you, Maggie.

[*His attention returns to her inflamed face.*]

—But how in hell on earth do you imagine—that you're going to have a child by a man that can't stand you?

MARGARET:
That's a problem that I will have to work out.

[*She wheels about to face the hall door.*]

Here they come!

[*The lights dim.*]

CURTAIN

ACT TWO

There is no lapse of time. Margaret and Brick are in the same positions they held at the end of Act I.

MARGARET [*at door*]:
Here they come!

[*Big Daddy appears first, a tall man with a fierce, anxious look, moving carefully not to betray his weakness even, or especially, to himself.*]

BIG DADDY:
Well, Brick.

BRICK:
Hello, Big Daddy.—Congratulations!

BIG DADDY:
—Crap. . . .

[*Some of the people are approaching through the hall, others along the gallery: voices from both directions. Gooper and Reverend Tooker become visible outside gallery doors, and their voices come in clearly.*

[*They pause outside as Gooper lights a cigar.*]

REVEREND TOOKER [*vivaciously*]:
Oh, but St. Paul's in Grenada has three memorial windows, and the latest one is a Tiffany stained-glass window that cost twenty-five hundred dollars, a picture of Christ the Good Shepherd with a Lamb in His arms.

GOOPER:
Who give that window, Preach?

REVEREND TOOKER:

Clyde Fletcher's widow. Also presented St. Paul's with a baptismal font.

GOOPER:

Y'know what somebody ought t' give your church is a *coolin'* system, Preach.

REVEREND TOOKER:

Yes, siree, Bob! And y'know what Gus Hamma's family gave in his memory to the church at Two Rivers? A complete new stone parish-house with a basketball court in the basement and a—

BIG DADDY [*uttering a loud barking laugh which is far from truly mirthful*]:

Hey, Preach! What's all this talk about memorials, Preach? Y' think somebody's about t' kick off around here? 'S that it?

[*Startled by this interjection, Reverend Tooker decides to laugh at the question almost as loud as he can.*

[*How he would answer the question we'll never know, as he's spared that embarrassment by the voice of Gooper's wife, Mae, rising high and clear as she appears with "Doc" Baugh, the family doctor, through the hall door.*]

MAE [*almost religiously*]:

—Let's see now, they've had their *tyyy*-phoid shots, and their tetanus shots, their diphtheria shots and their hepatitis shots and their polio shots, they got *those* shots every month from May through September, and—Gooper? Hey! Gooper!— What all have the kiddies been shot faw?

MARGARET [*overlapping a bit*]:

Turn on the hi-fi, Brick! Let's have some music t' start off th' party with!

342

[*The talk becomes so general that the room sounds like a great aviary of chattering birds. Only Brick remains unengaged, leaning upon the liquor cabinet with his faraway smile, an ice cube in a paper napkin with which he now and then rubs his forehead. He doesn't respond to Margaret's command. She bounds forward and stoops over the instrument panel of the console.*]

GOOPER:

We gave 'em that thing for a third anniversary present, got three speakers in it.

[*The room is suddenly blasted by the climax of a Wagnerian opera or a Beethoven symphony.*]

BIG DADDY:
Turn that dam thing off!

[*Almost instant silence, almost instantly broken by the shouting charge of Big Mama, entering through hall door like a charging rhino.*]

BIG MAMA:
Wha's my Brick, wha's mah precious baby!!

BIG DADDY:
Sorry! Turn it back on!

[*Everyone laughs very loud. Big Daddy is famous for his jokes at Big Mama's expense, and nobody laughs louder at these jokes than Big Mama herself, though sometimes they're pretty cruel and Big Mama has to pick up or fuss with something to cover the hurt that the loud laugh doesn't quite cover.*

[*On this occasion, a happy occasion because the dread in her heart has also been lifted by the false report on Big Daddy's condition, she giggles, grotesquely, coyly, in Big*

343

*Daddy's direction and bears down upon Brick, all very
quick and alive.]*

BIG MAMA:

Here he is, here's my precious baby! What's that you've got
in your hand? You put that liquor down, son, your hand was
made fo' holdin' somethin' better than that!

GOOPER:

Look at Brick put it down!

*[Brick has obeyed Big Mama by draining the glass and
handing it to her. Again everyone laughs, some high, some
low.]*

BIG MAMA:

Oh, you bad boy, you, you're my bad little boy. Give Big
Mama a kiss, you bad boy, you!—Look at him shy away,
will you? Brick never liked bein' kissed or made a fuss over,
I guess because he's always had too much of it!

Son, you turn that thing off!

[Brick has switched on the TV set.]

I can't stand TV, radio was bad enough but TV has gone it
one better, I mean—*[plops wheezing in chair]*—one worse,
ha ha! Now what'm I sittin' down here faw? I want t' sit
next to my sweetheart on the sofa, hold hands with him and
love him up a little!

*[Big Mama has on a black and white figured chiffon. The
large irregular patterns, like the markings of some massive
animal, the luster of her great diamonds and many pearls,
the brilliants set in the silver frames of her glasses, her
riotous voice, booming laugh, have dominated the room
since she entered. Big Daddy has been regarding her with
a steady grimace of chronic annoyance.]*

BIG MAMA [*still louder*]:
Preacher, Preacher, hey, Preach! Give me you' hand an' help me up from this chair!

REVEREND TOOKER:
None of your tricks, Big Mama!

BIG MAMA:
What tricks? You give me you' hand so I can get up an'—

[*Reverend Tooker extends her his hand. She grabs it and pulls him into her lap with a shrill laugh that spans an octave in two notes.*]

Ever seen a preacher in a fat lady's lap? Hey, hey, folks! Ever seen a preacher in a fat lady's lap?

[*Big Mama is notorious throughout the Delta for this sort of inelegant horseplay. Margaret looks on with indulgent humor, sipping Dubonnet "on the rocks" and watching Brick, but Mae and Gooper exchange signs of humorless anxiety over these antics, the sort of behavior which Mae thinks may account for their failure to quite get in with the smartest young married set in Memphis, despite all. One of the Negroes, Lacy or Sookey, peeks in, cackling. They are waiting for a sign to bring in the cake and champagne. But Big Daddy's not amused. He doesn't understand why, in spite of the infinite mental relief he's received from the doctor's report, he still has these same old fox teeth in his guts. "This spastic thing sure is something," he says to himself, but aloud he roars at Big Mama:*]

BIG DADDY:
BIG MAMA, WILL YOU QUIT HORSIN'?—You're too old an' too fat fo' that sort of crazy kid stuff an' besides a woman with your blood pressure—she had two hundred last spring! —is riskin' a stroke when you mess around like that. . . .

BIG MAMA:
Here comes Big Daddy's birthday!

[*Negroes in white jackets enter with an enormous birthday cake ablaze with candles and carrying buckets of champagne with satin ribbons about the bottle necks.*

[*Mae and Gooper strike up song, and everybody, including the Negroes and Children, joins in. Only Brick remains aloof.*]

EVERYONE:
Happy birthday to you.
Happy birthday to you.
Happy birthday, Big Daddy—

[*Some sing: "Dear, Big Daddy!"*]

Happy birthday to you.

[*Some sing: "How old are you?"*]

[*Mae has come down center and is organizing her children like a chorus. She gives them a barely audible: "One, two, three!" and they are off in the new tune.*]

CHILDREN:
Skinamarinka—dinka—dink
Skinamarinka—do
We love you.
Skinamarinka—dinka—dink
Skinamarinka—do.

[*All together, they turn to Big Daddy.*]

Big Daddy, you!

[*They turn back front, like a musical comedy chorus.*]

We love you in the morning;

We love you in the night.
We love you when we're with you,
And we love you out of sight.
Skinamarinka—dinka—dink
Skinamarinka—do.

[*Mae turns to Big Mama.*]

Big Mama, too!

[*Big Mama bursts into tears. The Negroes leave.*]

BIG DADDY:
Now Ida, what the hell is the matter with you?

MAE:
She's just so happy.

BIG MAMA:
I'm just so happy, Big Daddy, I have to cry or something.

[*Sudden and loud in the hush:*]

Brick, do you know the wonderful news that Doc Baugh got from the clinic about Big Daddy? Big Daddy's one hundred per cent!

MARGARET:
Isn't that wonderful?

BIG MAMA:
He's just one hundred per cent. Passed the examination with flying colors. Now that we know there's nothing wrong with Big Daddy but a spastic colon, I can tell you something. I was worried sick, half out of my mind, for fear that Big Daddy might have a thing like—

[*Margaret cuts through this speech, jumping up and exclaiming shrilly:*]

347

MARGARET:
Brick, honey, aren't you going to give Big Daddy his birthday present?

[Passing by him, she snatches his liquor glass from him.

[She picks up a fancily wrapped package.]

Here it is, Big Daddy, this is from Brick!

BIG MAMA:
This is the biggest birthday Big Daddy's ever had, a hundred presents and bushels of telegrams from—

MAE [*at same time*]:
What is it, Brick?

GOOPER:
I bet 500 to 50 that Brick don't *know* what it is.

BIG MAMA:
The fun of presents is not knowing what they are till you open the package. Open your present, Big Daddy.

BIG DADDY:
Open it you'self. I want to ask Brick somethin! Come here, Brick.

MARGARET:
Big Daddy's callin' you, Brick.

[She is opening the package.]

BRICK:
Tell Big Daddy I'm crippled.

BIG DADDY:
I see you're crippled. I want to know how you got crippled.

MARGARET [*making diversionary tactics*]:
Oh, look, oh, look, why, it's a cashmere robe!

[*She holds the robe up for all to see.*]

MAE:
You sound surprised, Maggie.

MARGARET:
I never saw one before.

MAE:
That's funny.—*Hah!*

MARGARET [*turning on her fiercely, with a brilliant smile*]:
Why is it funny? All my family ever had was family—and luxuries such as cashmere robes still surprise me!

BIG DADDY [*ominously*]:
Quiet!

MAE [*heedless in her fury*]:
I don't see how you could be so surprised when you bought it yourself at Loewenstein's in Memphis last Saturday. You know how I know?

BIG DADDY:
I said, Quiet!

MAE:
—I know because the salesgirl that sold it to you waited on me and said, Oh, Mrs. Pollitt, your sister-in-law just bought a cashmere robe for your husband's father!

MARGARET:
Sister Woman! Your talents are wasted as a housewife and mother, you really ought to be with the FBI or—

BIG DADDY:
QUIET!

[*Reverend Tooker's reflexes are slower than the others'. He finishes a sentence after the bellow.*]

349

REVEREND TOOKER [*to Doc Baugh*]:
—the Stork and the Reaper are running neck and neck!

[*He starts to laugh gaily when he notices the silence and Big Daddy's glare. His laugh dies falsely.*]

BIG DADDY:
Preacher, I hope I'm not butting in on more talk about memorial stained-glass windows, am I, Preacher?

[*Reverend Tooker laughs feebly, then coughs dryly in the embarrassed silence.*]

Preacher?

BIG MAMA:
Now, Big Daddy, don't you pick on Preacher!

BIG DADDY [*raising his voice*]:
You ever hear that expression all hawk and no spit? You bring that expression to mind with that little dry cough of yours, all hawk an' no spit. . . .

[*The pause is broken only by a short startled laugh from Margaret, the only one there who is conscious of and amused by the grotesque.*]

MAE [*raising her arms and jangling her bracelets*]:
I wonder if the mosquitoes are active tonight?

BIG DADDY:
What's that, Little Mama? Did you make some remark?

MAE:
Yes, I said I wondered if the mosquitoes would eat us alive if we went out on the gallery for a while.

BIG DADDY:
Well, if they do, I'll have your bones pulverized for fertilizer!

350

BIG MAMA [*quickly*]:
Last week we had an airplane spraying the place and I think
it done some good, at least I haven't had a—

BIG DADDY [*cutting her speech*]:
Brick, they tell me, if what they tell me is true, that you done
some jumping last night on the high school athletic field?

BIG MAMA:
Brick, Big Daddy is talking to you, son.

BRICK [*smiling vaguely over his drink*]:
What was that, Big Daddy?

BIG DADDY:
They said you done some jumping on the high school track
field last night.

BRICK:
That's what they told me, too.

BIG DADDY:
Was it jumping or humping that you were doing out there?
What were doing out there at three A.M., layin' a woman
on that cinder track?

BIG MAMA:
Big Daddy, you are off the sick-list, now, and I'm not going
to excuse you for talkin' so—

BIG DADDY:
Quiet!

BIG MAMA:
—*nasty* in front of Preacher and—

BIG DADDY:
QUIET!—I ast you, Brick, if you was cuttin' you'self a piece
o' poon-tang last night on that cinder track? I thought maybe

351

you were chasin' poon-tang on that track an' tripped over something in the heat of the chase—'sthat it?

[*Gooper laughs, loud and false, others nervously following suit. Big Mama stamps her foot, and purses her lips, crossing to Mae and whispering something to her as Brick meets his father's hard, intent, grinning stare with a slow, vague smile that he offers all situations from behind the screen of his liquor.*]

BRICK:
No, sir, I don't think so....

MAE [*at the same time, sweetly*]:
Reverend Tooker, let's you and I take a stroll on the widow's walk.

[*She and the preacher go out on the gallery as Big Daddy says:*]

BIG DADDY:
Then what the hell were you doing out there at three o'clock in the morning?

BRICK:
Jumping the hurdles, Big Daddy, runnin' and jumpin' the hurdles, but those high hurdles have gotten too high for me, now.

BIG DADDY:
Cause you was drunk?

BRICK [*his vague smile fading a little*]:
Sober I wouldn't have tried to jump the *low* ones. . . .

BIG MAMA [*quickly*]:
Big Daddy, blow out the candles on your birthday cake!

MARGARET [*at the same time*]:
I want to propose a toast to Big Daddy Pollitt on his sixty-fifth birthday, the biggest cotton planter in—

BIG DADDY [*bellowing with fury and disgust*]:
I told you to stop it, now stop it, quit this—!

BIG MAMA [*coming in front of Big Daddy with the cake*]:
Big Daddy, I will not allow you to talk that way, not even on your birthday, I—

BIG DADDY:
I'll talk like I want to on my birthday, Ida, or any other goddam day of the year and anybody here that don't like it knows what they can do!

BIG MAMA:
You don't mean that!

BIG DADDY:
What makes you think I don't mean it?

[*Meanwhile various discreet signals have been exchanged and Gooper has also gone out on the gallery.*]

BIG MAMA:
I just know you don't mean it.

BIG DADDY:
You don't know a goddam thing and you never did!

BIG MAMA:
Big Daddy, you don't mean that.

BIG DADDY:
Oh, yes, I do, oh, yes, I do, I mean it! I put up with a whole

353

lot of crap around here because I thought I was dying. And you thought I was dying and you started taking over, well, you can stop taking over now, Ida, because I'm not gonna die, you can just stop now this business of taking over because you're not taking over because I'm not dying, I went through the laboratory and the goddam exploratory operation and there's nothing wrong with me but a spastic colon. And I'm not dying of cancer which you thought I was dying of. Ain't that so? Didn't you think that I was dying of cancer, Ida?

[*Almost everybody is out on the gallery but the two old people glaring at each other across the blazing cake.*

[*Big Mama's chest heaves and she presses a fat fist to her mouth.*

[*Big Daddy continues, hoarsely:*]

Ain't that so, Ida? Didn't you have an idea I was dying of cancer and now you could take control of this place and everything on it? I got that impression, I seemed to get that impression. Your loud voice everywhere, your fat old body butting in here and there!

BIG MAMA:
Hush! The Preacher!

BIG DADDY:
Rut the goddam preacher!

[*Big Mama gasps loudly and sits down on the sofa which is almost too small for her.*]

Did you hear what I said? I said rut the goddam preacher!

[*Somebody closes the gallery doors from outside just as there is a burst of fireworks and excited cries from the children.*]

BIG MAMA:

I never seen you act like this before and I can't think what's got in you!

BIG DADDY:

I went through all that laboratory and operation and all just so I would know if you or me was boss here! Well, now it turns out that I am and you ain't—and that's my birthday present—and my cake and champagne!—because for three years now you been gradually taking over. Bossing. Talking. Sashaying your fat old body around the place I made! I made this place! I was overseer on it! I was the overseer on the old Straw and Ochello plantation. I quit school at ten! I quit school at ten years old and went to work like a nigger in the fields. And I rose to be overseer of the Straw and Ochello plantation. And old Straw died and I was Ochello's partner and the place got bigger and bigger and bigger and bigger and bigger! I did all that myself with no goddam help from you, and now you think you're just about to take over. Well, I am just about to tell you that you are not just about to take over, you are not just about to take over a God damn thing. Is that clear to you, Ida? Is that very plain to you, now? Is that understood completely? I been through the laboratory from A to Z. I've had the goddam exploratory operation, and nothing is wrong with me but a spastic colon—made spastic, I guess, by *disgust!* By all the goddam lies and liars that I have had to put up with, and all the goddam hypocrisy that I lived with all these forty years that we been livin' together!

Hey! Ida!! Blow out the candles on the birthday cake! Purse up your lips and draw a deep breath and blow out the goddam candles on the cake!

BIG MAMA:
Oh, Big Daddy, oh, oh, oh, Big Daddy!

355

BIG DADDY:
What's the matter with you?

BIG MAMA:
In all these years you never believed that I loved you??

BIG DADDY:
Huh?

BIG MAMA:
And I did, I did so much, I did love you!—I even loved your hate and your hardness, Big Daddy!

[*She sobs and rushes awkwardly out onto the gallery.*]

BIG DADDY [*to himself*]:
Wouldn't it be funny if that was true....

[*A pause is followed by a burst of light in the sky from the fireworks.*]

BRICK! HEY, BRICK!

[*He stands over his blazing birthday cake.*

[*After some moments, Brick hobbles in on his crutch, holding his glass.*

[*Margaret follows him with a bright, anxious smile.*]

I didn't call you, Maggie. I called Brick.

MARGARET:
I'm just delivering him to you.

[*She kisses Brick on the mouth which he immediately wipes with the back of his hand. She flies girlishly back out. Brick and his father are alone.*]

BIG DADDY:
Why did you do that?

BRICK:
Do what, Big Daddy?

BIG DADDY:
Wipe her kiss off your mouth like she'd spit on you.

BRICK:
I don't know. I wasn't conscious of it.

BIG DADDY:
That woman of yours has a better shape on her than Gooper's but somehow or other they got the same look about them.

BRICK:
What sort of look is that, Big Daddy?

BIG DADDY:
I don't know how to describe it but it's the same look.

BRICK:
They don't look peaceful, do they?

BIG DADDY:
No, they sure in hell don't.

BRICK:
They look nervous as cats?

BIG DADDY:
That's right, they look nervous as cats.

BRICK:
Nervous as a couple of cats on a hot tin roof?

BIG DADDY:
That's right, boy, they look like a couple of cats on a hot tin roof. It's funny that you and Gooper being so different would pick out the same type of woman.

357

BRICK:
Both of us married into society, Big Daddy.

BIG DADDY:
Crap . . . I wonder what gives them both that look?

BRICK:
Well. They're sittin' in the middle of a big piece of land, Big Daddy, twenty-eight thousand acres is a pretty big piece of land and so they're squaring off on it, each determined to knock off a bigger piece of it than the other whenever you let it go.

BIG DADDY:
I got a surprise for those women. I'm not gonna let it go for a long time yet if that's what they're waiting for.

BRICK:
That's right, Big Daddy. You just sit tight and let them scratch each other's eyes out. . . .

BIG DADDY:
You bet your life I'm going to sit tight on it and let those sons of bitches scratch their eyes out, ha ha ha. . . .

But Gooper's wife's a good breeder, you got to admit she's fertile. Hell, at supper tonight she had them all at the table and they had to put a couple of extra leafs in the table to make room for them, she's got five head of them, now, and another one's comin'.

BRICK:
Yep, number six is comin'. . . .

BIG DADDY:
Brick, you know, I swear to God, I don't know the way it happens?

BRICK:

The way what happens, Big Daddy?

BIG DADDY:

You git you a piece of land, by hook or crook, an' things start growin' on it, things accumulate on it, and the first thing you know it's completely out of hand, completely out of hand!

BRICK:

Well, they say nature hates a vacuum, Big Daddy.

BIG DADDY:

That's what they say, but sometimes I think that a vacuum is a hell of a lot better than some of the stuff that nature replaces it with.

Is someone out there by that door?

BRICK:

Yep.

BIG DADDY:

Who?

[*He has lowered his voice.*]

BRICK:

Someone int'rested in what we say to each other.

BIG DADDY:

Gooper?——*GOOPER!*

[*After a discreet pause, Mae appears in the gallery door.*]

MAE:

Did you call Gooper, Big Daddy?

BIG DADDY:

Aw, it was you.

359

MAE:
Do you want Gooper, Big Daddy?

BIG DADDY:
No, and I don't want you. I want some privacy here, while I'm having a confidential talk with my son Brick. Now it's too hot in here to close them doors, but if I have to close those rutten doors in order to have a private talk with my son Brick, just let me know and I'll close 'em. Because I hate eavesdroppers, I don't like any kind of sneakin' an' spyin'.

MAE:
Why, Big Daddy—

BIG DADDY:
You stood on the wrong side of the moon, it threw your shadow!

MAE:
I was just—

BIG DADDY:
You was just nothing but *spyin'* an' you *know* it!

MAE [*begins to sniff and sob*]:
Oh, Big Daddy, you're so unkind for some reason to those that really love you!

BIG DADDY:
Shut up, shut up, shut up! I'm going to move you and Gooper out of that room next to this! It's none of your goddam business what goes on in here at night between Brick an' Maggie. You listen at night like a couple of rutten peekhole spies and go and give a report on what you hear to Big Mama an' she comes to me and says they say such and such and so and so about what they heard goin' on between Brick an' Maggie, and Jesus, it makes me sick. I'm goin' to move you an' Gooper

out of that room, I can't stand sneakin' an' spyin', it makes me sick. . . .

[*Mae throws back her head and rolls her eyes heavenward and extends her arms as if invoking God's pity for this unjust martyrdom; then she presses a handkerchief to her nose and flies from the room with a loud swish of skirts.*]

BRICK [*now at the liquor cabinet*]:
They listen, do they?

BIG DADDY:
Yeah. They listen and give reports to Big Mama on what goes on in here between you and Maggie. They say that—

[*He stops as if embarrassed.*]

—You won't sleep with her, that you sleep on the sofa. Is that true or not true? If you don't like Maggie, get rid of Maggie!—What are you doin' there now?

BRICK:
Fresh'nin' up my drink.

BIG DADDY:
Son, you know you got a real liquor problem?

BRICK:
Yes, sir, yes, I know.

BIG DADDY:
Is that why you quit sports-announcing, because of this liquor problem?

BRICK:
Yes, sir, yes, sir, I guess so.

[*He smiles vaguely and amiably at his father across his replenished drink.*]

361

BIG DADDY:
Son, don't guess about it, it's too important.

BRICK [*vaguely*]:
Yes, sir.

BIG DADDY:
And listen to me, don't look at the damn chandelier. . . .

[*Pause. Big Daddy's voice is husky.*]

—Somethin' else we picked up at th' big fire sale in Europe.

[*Another pause.*]

Life is important. There's nothing else to hold onto. A man that drinks is throwing his life away. Don't do it, hold onto your life. There's nothing else to hold onto. . . .

Sit down over here so we don't have to raise our voices, the walls have ears in this place.

BRICK [*hobbling over to sit on the sofa beside him*]:
All right, Big Daddy.

BIG DADDY:
Quit!—how'd that come about? Some disappointment?

BRICK:
I don't know. Do you?

BIG DADDY:
I'm askin' you, God damn it! How in hell would I know if you don't?

BRICK:
I just got out there and found that I had a mouth full of cotton. I was always two or three beats behind what was goin' on on the field and so I—

BIG DADDY:
Quit!

BRICK [*amiably*]:
Yes, quit.

BIG DADDY:
Son?

BRICK:
Huh?

BIG DADDY [*inhales loudly and deeply from his cigar; then bends suddenly a little forward, exhaling loudly and raising a hand to his forehead*]:

—Whew!—ha ha!—I took in too much smoke, it made me a little lightheaded. . . .

[*The mantel clock chimes.*]

Why is it so damn hard for people to talk?

BRICK:
Yeah. . . .

[*The clock goes on sweetly chiming till it has completed the stroke of ten.*]

—Nice peaceful-soundin' clock, I like to hear it all night. . . .

[*He slides low and comfortable on the sofa; Big Daddy sits up straight and rigid with some unspoken anxiety. All his gestures are tense and jerky as he talks. He wheezes and pants and sniffs through his nervous speech, glancing quickly, shyly, from time to time, at his son.*]

BIG DADDY:
We got that clock the summer we wint to Europe, me an' Big Mama on that damn Cook's Tour, never had such an awful

363

time in my life, I'm tellin' you, son, those gooks over there, they gouge your eyeballs out in their grand hotels. And Big Mama bought more stuff than you could haul in a couple of boxcars, that's no crap. Everywhere she wint on this whirl-wind tour, she bought, bought, bought. Why, half that stuff she bought is still crated up in the cellar, under water last spring!

[*He laughs.*]

That Europe is nothin' on earth but a great big auction, that's all it is, that bunch of old worn-out places, it's just a big fire-sale, the whole rutten thing, an' Big Mama wint wild in it, why, you couldn't hold that woman with a mule's harness! Bought, bought, bought!—lucky I'm a rich man, yes siree, Bob, an' half that stuff is mildewin' in th' basement. It's lucky I'm a rich man, it sure is lucky, well, I'm a rich man, Brick, yep, I'm a mighty rich man.

[*His eyes light up for a moment.*]

Y'know how much I'm worth? Guess, Brick! Guess how much I'm worth!

[*Brick smiles vaguely over his drink.*]

Close on ten million in cash an' blue-chip stocks, outside, mind you, of twenty-eight thousand acres of the richest land this side of the valley Nile!

[*A puff and crackle and the night sky blooms with an eerie greenish glow. Children shriek on the gallery.*]

But a man can't buy his life with it, he can't buy back his life with it when his life has been spent, that's one thing not offered in the Europe fire-sale or in the American markets or any markets on earth, a man can't buy his life with it, he can't buy back his life when his life is finished. . . .

That's a sobering thought, a very sobering thought, and that's a thought that I was turning over in my head, over and over and over—until today. . . .

I'm wiser and sadder, Brick, for this experience which I just gone through. They's one thing else that I remember in Europe.

BRICK:
What is that, Big Daddy?

BIG DADDY:
The hills around Barcelona in the country of Spain and the children running over those bare hills in their bare skins beggin' like starvin' dogs with howls and screeches, and how fat the priests are on the streets of Barcelona, so many of them and so fat and so pleasant, ha ha!—Y'know I could feed that country? I got money enough to feed that goddam country, but the human animal is a selfish beast and I don't reckon the money I passed out there to those howling children in the hills around Barcelona would more than upholster one of the chairs in this room, I mean pay to put a new cover on this chair!

Hell, I threw them money like you'd scatter feed corn for chickens, I threw money at them just to get rid of them long enough to climb back into th' car and—drive away. . . .

And then in Morocco, them Arabs, why, prostitution begins at four or five, that's no exaggeration, why, I remember one day in Marrakech, that old walled Arab city, I set on a broken-down wall to have a cigar, it was fearful hot there and this Arab woman stood in the road and looked at me till I was embarrassed, she stood stock still in the dusty hot road and looked at me till I was embarrassed. But listen to this. She had a naked child with her, a little naked girl with her, barely

365

able to toddle, and after a while she set this child on the ground and give her a push and whispered something to her.

This child come toward me, barely able t' walk, come toddling up to me and—

Jesus, it makes you sick t' remember a thing like this!
It stuck out its hand and tried to unbutton my trousers!

That child was not yet five! Can you believe me? Or do you think that I am making this up? I wint back to the hotel and said to Big Mama, Git packed! We're clearing out of this country. . . .

BRICK:
Big Daddy, you're on a talkin' jag tonight.

BIG DADDY [*ignoring this remark*]:
Yes, sir, that's how it is, the human animal is a beast that dies but the fact that he's dying don't give him pity for others, no, sir, it—

—Did you say something?

BRICK:
Yes.

BIG DADDY:
What?

BRICK:
Hand me over that crutch so I can get up.

BIG DADDY:
Where you goin'?

BRICK:
I'm takin' a little short trip to Echo Spring.

BIG DADDY:
To where?

BRICK:
Liquor cabinet. . . .

BIG DADDY:
Yes, sir, boy—

[*He hands Brick the crutch.*]

—the human animal is a beast that dies and if he's got money he buys and buys and buys and I think the reason he buys everything he can buy is that in the back of his mind he has the crazy hope that one of his purchases will be life ever-lasting!—Which it never can be. . . . The human animal is a beast that—

BRICK [*at the liquor cabinet*]:
Big Daddy, you sure are shootin' th' breeze here tonight.

[*There is a pause and voices are heard outside.*]

BIG DADDY:
I been quiet here lately, spoke not a word, just sat and stared into space. I had something heavy weighing on my mind but tonight that load was took off me. That's why I'm talking.— The sky looks diff'rent to me. . . .

BRICK:
You know what I like to hear most?

BIG DADDY:
What?

BRICK:
Solid quiet. Perfect unbroken quiet.

367

BIG DADDY:
Why?

BRICK:
Because it's more peaceful.

BIG DADDY:
Man, you'll hear a lot of that in the grave.

[*He chuckles agreeably.*]

BRICK:
Are you through talkin' to me?

BIG DADDY:
Why are you so anxious to shut me up?

BRICK:
Well, sir, ever so often you say to me, Brick, I want to have a
talk with you, but when we talk, it never materializes. Nothing is said. You sit in a chair and gas about this and that and
I look like I listen. I try to look like I listen, but I don't
listen, not much. Communication is—awful hard between
people an'—somehow between you and me, it just don't—

BIG DADDY:
Have you ever been scared? I mean have you ever felt downright terror of something?

[*He gets up.*]

Just one moment. I'm going to close these doors. . . .

[*He closes doors on gallery as if he were going to tell an
important secret.*]

BRICK:
What?

BIG DADDY:
Brick?

BRICK:
Huh?

BIG DADDY:
Son, I thought I had it!

BRICK:
Had what? Had what, Big Daddy?

BIG DADDY:
Cancer!

BRICK:
Oh . . .

BIG DADDY:
I thought the old man made out of bones had laid his cold and heavy hand on my shoulder!

BRICK:
Well, Big Daddy, you kept a tight mouth about it.

BIG DADDY:
A pig squeals. A man keeps a tight mouth about it, in spite of a man not having a pig's advantage.

BRICK:
What advantage is that?

BIG DADDY:
Ignorance—of mortality—is a comfort. A man don't have that comfort, he's the only living thing that conceives of death, that knows what it is. The others go without knowing which is the way that anything living should go, go without knowing, without any knowledge of it, and yet a pig squeals,

369

but a man sometimes, he can keep a tight mouth about it. Sometimes he—

[*There is a deep, smoldering ferocity in the old man.*]

—can keep a tight mouth about it. I wonder if—

BRICK:
What, Big Daddy?

BIG DADDY:
A whiskey highball would injure this spastic condition?

BRICK:
No, sir, it might do it good.

BIG DADDY [*grins suddenly, wolfishly*]:
Jesus, I can't tell you! The sky is open! Christ, it's open again! It's open, boy, it's open!

[*Brick looks down at his drink.*]

BRICK:
You feel better, Big Daddy?

BIG DADDY:
Better? Hell! I can breathe!—All of my life I been like a doubled up fist. . . .

[*He pours a drink.*]

—Poundin', smashin', drivin'!—now I'm going to loosen these doubled-up hands and touch things *easy* with them. . . .

[*He spreads his hands as if caressing the air.*]

You know what I'm contemplating?

BRICK [*vaguely*]:
No, sir. What are you contemplating?

BIG DADDY:

Ha ha!—*Pleasure!*—pleasure with *women!*

[*Brick's smile fades a little but lingers.*]

Brick, this stuff burns me!—

—Yes, boy. I'll tell you something that you might not guess. I still have desire for women and this is my sixty-fifth birthday.

BRICK:

I think that's mighty remarkable, Big Daddy.

BIG DADDY:

Remarkable?

BRICK:

Admirable, Big Daddy.

BIG DADDY:

You're damn right it is, remarkable and admirable both. I realize now that I never had me enough. I let many chances slip by because of scruples about it, scruples, convention—crap. . . . All that stuff is bull, bull, bull!—It took the shadow of death to make me see it. Now that shadow's lifted, I'm going to cut loose and have, what is it they call it, have me a—ball!

BRICK:

A ball, huh?

BIG DADDY:

That's right, a ball, a ball! Hell!—I slept with Big Mama till, let's see, five years ago, till I was sixty and she was fifty-eight, and never even liked her, never did!

[*The phone has been ringing down the hall. Big Mama enters, exclaiming:*]

371

BIG MAMA:

Don't you men hear that phone ring? I heard it way out on the gall'ry.

BIG DADDY:

There's five rooms off this front gall'ry that you could go through. Why do you go through this one?

[*Big Mama makes a playful face as she bustles out the hall door.*]

Hunh!—Why, when Big Mama goes out of a room, I can't remember what that woman looks like, but when Big Mama comes back into the room, boy, then I see what she looks like, and I wish I didn't!

[*Bends over laughing at this joke till it hurts his guts and he straightens with a grimace. The laugh subsides to a chuckle as he puts the liquor glass a little distrustfully down on the table.*

[*Brick has risen and hobbled to the gallery doors.*]

Hey! Where you goin'?

BRICK:

Out for a breather.

BIG DADDY:

Not yet you ain't. Stay here till this talk is finished, young fellow.

BRICK:

I thought it was finished, Big Daddy.

BIG DADDY:

It ain't even begun.

BRICK:

My mistake. Excuse me. I just wanted to feel that river breeze.

372

BIG DADDY:

Turn on the ceiling fan and set back down in that chair.

[*Big Mama's voice rises, carrying down the hall.*]

BIG MAMA:

Miss Sally, you're a case! You're a caution, Miss Sally. Why didn't you give me a chance to explain it to you?

BIG DADDY:

Jesus, she's talking to my old maid sister again.

BIG MAMA:

Well, goodbye, now, Miss Sally. You come down real soon, Big Daddy's dying to see you! Yaisss, goodbye, Miss Sally....

[*She hangs up and bellows with mirth. Big Daddy groans and covers his ears as she approaches.*

[*Bursting in:*]

Big Daddy, that was Miss Sally callin' from Memphis again! You know what she done, Big Daddy? She called her doctor in Memphis to git him to tell her what that spastic thing is! Ha-*HAAAA!*—And called back to tell me how relieved she was that—Hey! Let me in!

[*Big Daddy has been holding the door half closed against her.*]

BIG DADDY:

Naw I ain't. I told you not to come and go through this room. You just back out and go through those five other rooms.

BIG MAMA:

Big Daddy? Big Daddy? Oh, big Daddy!—You didn't mean those things you said to me, did you?

[*He shuts door firmly against her but she still calls.*]

Sweetheart? Sweetheart? Big Daddy? You didn't mean those awful things you said to me?—I know you didn't. I know you didn't mean those things in your heart. . . .

[*The childlike voice fades with a sob and her heavy footsteps retreat down the hall. Brick has risen once more on his crutches and starts for the gallery again.*]

BIG DADDY:

All I ask of that woman is that she leave me alone. But she can't admit to herself that she makes me sick. That comes of having slept with her too many years. Should of quit much sooner but that old woman she never got enough of it— and I was good in bed . . . I never should of wasted so much of it on her. . . . They say you got just so many and each one is numbered. Well, I got a few left in me, a few, and I'm going to pick me a good one to spend 'em on! I'm going to pick me a choice one, I don't care how much she costs, I'll smother her in—minks! Ha ha! I'll strip her naked and smother her in minks and choke her with diamonds! Ha ha! I'll strip her naked and choke her with diamonds and smother her with minks and hump her from hell to breakfast. *Ha aha ha ha ha!*

MAE [*gaily at door*]:
Who's that laughin' in there?

GOOPER:
Is Big Daddy laughin' in there?

BIG DADDY:
Crap!—them two—*drips.* . . .

[*He goes over and touches Brick's shoulder.*]

Yes, son. Brick, boy.—I'm—*happy!* I'm happy, son, I'm happy!

374

[*He chokes a little and bites his under lip, pressing his head quickly, shyly against his son's head and then, coughing with embarrassment, goes uncertainly back to the table where he set down the glass. He drinks and makes a grimace as it burns his guts. Brick sighs and rises with effort.*]

What makes you so restless? Have you got ants in your britches?

BRICK:
Yes, sir . . .

BIG DADDY:
Why?

BRICK:
—Something—hasn't—happened. . . .

BIG DADDY:
Yeah? What is that!

BRICK [*sadly*]:
—the click. . . .

BIG DADDY:
Did you say click?

BRICK:
Yes, click.

BIG DADDY:
What click?

BRICK:
A click that I get in my head that makes me peaceful.

BIG DADDY:
I sure in hell don't know what you're talking about, but it disturbs me.

375

BRICK:
It's just a mechanical thing.

BIG DADDY:
What is a mechanical thing?

BRICK:
This click that I get in my head that makes me peaceful. I got to drink till I get it. It's just a mechanical thing, something like a—like a—like a—

BIG DADDY:
Like a—

BRICK:
Switch clicking off in my head, turning the hot light off and the cool night on and—

[*He looks up, smiling sadly.*]

—all of a sudden there's—peace!

BIG DADDY [*whistles long and soft with astonishment; he goes back to Brick and clasps his son's two shoulders*]:

Jesus! I didn't know it had gotten that bad with you. Why, boy, you're—*alcoholic!*

BRICK:
That's the truth, Big Daddy. I'm alcoholic.

BIG DADDY:
This shows how I—let things go!

BRICK:
I have to hear that little click in my head that makes me peaceful. Usually I hear it sooner than this, sometimes as early as—noon, but—

—Today it's—dilatory. . . .

—I just haven't got the right level of alcohol in my bloodstream yet!

[*This last statement is made with energy as he freshens his drink.*]

BIG DADDY:
Uh—huh. Expecting death made me blind. I didn't have no idea that a son of mine was turning into a drunkard under my nose.

BRICK [*gently*]:
Well, now you do, Big Daddy, the news has penetrated.

BIG DADDY:
UH-huh, yes, now I do, the news has—penetrated. . . .

BRICK:
And so if you'll excuse me—

BIG DADDY:
No, I won't excuse you.

BRICK:
—I'd better sit by myself till I hear that click in my head, it's just a mechanical thing but it don't happen except when I'm alone or talking to no one. . . .

BIG DADDY:
You got a long, long time to sit still, boy, and talk to no one, but now you're talkin' to me. At least I'm talking to you. And you set there and listen until I tell you the conversation is over!

BRICK:
But this talk is like all the others we've ever had together in our lives! It's nowhere, nowhere!—it's—it's *painful*, Big Daddy. . . .

377

BIG DADDY:

All right, then let it be painful, but don't you move from that chair!—I'm going to remove that crutch. . . .

[*He seizes the crutch and tosses it across room.*]

BRICK:

I can hop on one foot, and if I fall, I can crawl!

BIG DADDY:

If you ain't careful you're gonna crawl off this plantation and then, by Jesus, you'll have to hustle your drinks along Skid Row!

BRICK:

That'll come, Big Daddy.

BIG DADDY:

Naw, it won't. You're my son and I'm going to straighten you out; now that *I'm* straightened out, I'm going to straighten out you!

BRICK:

Yeah?

BIG DADDY:

Today the report come in from Ochsner Clinic. Y'know what they told me?

[*His face glows with triumph.*]

The only thing that they could detect with all the instruments of science in that great hospital is a little spastic condition of the colon! And nerves torn to pieces by all that worry about it.

[*A little girl bursts into room with a sparkler clutched in each fist, hops and shrieks like a monkey gone mad and rushes back out again as Big Daddy strikes at her.*]

[*Silence. The two men stare at each other. A woman laughs gaily outside.*]

I want you to know I breathed a sigh of relief almost as powerful as the Vicksburg tornado!

BRICK:
You weren't ready to go?

BIG DADDY:
GO WHERE?—crap. . . .

—When you are gone from here, boy, you are long gone and no where! The human machine is not no different from the animal machine or the fish machine or the bird machine or the reptile machine or the insect machine! It's just a whole God damn lot more complicated and consequently more trouble to keep together. Yep. I thought I had it. The earth shook under my foot, the sky come down like the black lid of a kettle and I couldn't breathe!—Today!!—that lid was lifted, I drew my first free breath in—how many years?— *God!—three.* . . .

[*There is laughter outside, running footsteps, the soft, plushy sound and light of exploding rockets.*

[*Brick stares at him soberly for a long moment; then makes a sort of startled sound in his nostrils and springs up on one foot and hops across the room to grab his crutch, swinging on the furniture for support. He gets the crutch and flees as if in horror for the gallery. His father seizes him by the sleeve of his white silk pajamas.*]

Stay here, you son of a bitch!—till I say go!

BRICK:
I can't.

379

BIG DADDY:

You sure in hell will, God damn it.

BRICK:

No, I can't. We talk, you talk, in—circles! We get no where, no where! It's always the same, you say you want to talk to me and don't have a ruttin' thing to say to me!

BIG DADDY:

Nothin' to say when I'm tellin' you I'm going to live when I thought I was dying?!

BRICK:

Oh—*that!*—Is that what you have to say to me?

BIG DADDY:

Why, you son of a bitch! Ain't that, ain't that—*important?!*

BRICK:

Well, you said that, that's said, and now I—

BIG DADDY:

Now you set back down.

BRICK:

You're all balled up, you—

BIG DADDY:

I ain't balled up!

BRICK:

You are, you're all balled up!

BIG DADDY:

Don't tell me what I am, you drunken whelp! I'm going to tear this coat sleeve off if you don't set down!

BRICK:

Big Daddy—

BIG DADDY:
Do what I tell you! I'm the boss here, now! I want you to know I'm back in the driver's seat now!

[*Big Mama rushes in, clutching her great heaving bosom.*]

What in hell do you want in here, Big Mama?

BIG MAMA:
Oh, Big Daddy! Why are you shouting like that? I just cain't *stainnnnnnnd*—it. . . .

BIG DADDY [*raising the back of his hand above his head*]:
GIT!—outa here.

[*She rushes back out, sobbing.*]

BRICK [*softly, sadly*]:
Christ. . . .

BIG DADDY [*fiercely*]:
Yeah! Christ!—is right . . .

[*Brick breaks loose and hobbles toward the gallery.*]

[*Big Daddy jerks his crutch from under Brick so he steps with the injured ankle. He utters a hissing cry of anguish, clutches a chair and pulls it over on top of him on the floor.*]

Son of a—tub of—hog fat. . . .

BRICK:
Big Daddy! Give me my crutch.

[*Big Daddy throws the crutch out of reach.*]

Give me that crutch, Big Daddy.

BIG DADDY:
Why do you drink?

BRICK:
Don't know, give me my crutch!

BIG DADDY:
You better think why you drink or give up drinking!

BRICK:
Will you please give me my crutch so I can get up off this floor?

BIG DADDY:
First you answer my question. Why do you drink? Why are you throwing your life away, boy, like somethin' disgusting you picked up on the street?

BRICK [*getting onto his knees*]:
Big Daddy, I'm in pain, I stepped on that foot.

BIG DADDY:
Good! I'm glad you're not too numb with the liquor in you to feel some pain!

BRICK:
You—spilled my—drink . . .

BIG DADDY:
I'll make a bargain with you. You tell me why you drink and I'll hand you one. I'll pour you the liquor myself and hand it to you.

BRICK:
Why do I drink?

BIG DADDY:
Yea! Why?

BRICK:
Give me a drink and I'll tell you.

382

BIG DADDY:
Tell me first!

BRICK:
I'll tell you in one word.

BIG DADDY:
What word?

BRICK:
DISGUST!

[*The clock chimes softly, sweetly. Big Daddy gives it a short, outraged glance.*]

Now how about that drink?

BIG DADDY:
What are you disgusted with? You got to tell me that, first. Otherwise being disgusted don't make no sense!

BRICK:
Give me my crutch.

BIG DADDY:
You heard me, you got to tell me what I asked you first.

BRICK:
I told you, I said to kill my disgust!

BIG DADDY:
DISGUST WITH WHAT!

BRICK:
You strike a hard bargain.

BIG DADDY:
What are you disgusted with?—an' I'll pass you the liquor.

383

BRICK:
I can hop on one foot, and if I fall, I can crawl.

BIG DADDY:
You want liquor that bad?

BRICK [*dragging himself up, clinging to bedstead*]:
Yeah, I want it that bad.

BIG DADDY:
If I give you a drink, will you tell me what it is you're disgusted with, Brick?

BRICK:
Yes, sir, I will try to.

[*The old man pours him a drink and solemnly passes it to him.*

[*There is silence as Brick drinks.*]

Have you ever heard the word "mendacity"?

BIG DADDY:
Sure. Mendacity is one of them five dollar words that cheap politicians throw back and forth at each other.

BRICK:
You know what it means?

BIG DADDY:
Don't it mean lying and liars?

BRICK:
Yes, sir, lying and liars.

BIG DADDY:
Has someone been lying to you?

CHILDREN [*chanting in chorus offstage*]:
We want Big Dad-dee!
We want Big Dad-dee!

[*Gooper appears in the gallery door.*]

GOOPER:
Big Daddy, the kiddies are shouting for you out there.

BIG DADDY [*fiercely*]:
Keep out, Gooper!

GOOPER:
'Scuse *me!*

[*Big Daddy slams the doors after Gooper.*]

BIG DADDY:
Who's been lying to you, has Margaret been lying to you, has
your wife been lying to you about something, Brick?

BRICK:
Not her. That wouldn't matter.

BIG DADDY:
Then who's been lying to you, and what about?

BRICK:
No one single person and no one lie. . . .

BIG DADDY:
Then what, what then, for Christ's sake?

BRICK:
—The whole, the whole—thing. . . .

BIG DADDY:
Why are you rubbing your head? You got a headache?

385

BRICK:
No, I'm tryin' to—

BIG DADDY:
—Concentrate, but you can't because your brain's all soaked with liquor, is that the trouble? Wet brain!

[*He snatches the glass from Brick's hand.*]

What do you know about this mendacity thing? Hell! I could write a book on it! Don't you know that? I could write a book on it and still not cover the subject? Well, I could, I could write a goddam book on it and still not cover the subject anywhere near enough!!—Think of all the lies I got to put up with!—Pretenses! Ain't that mendacity? Having to pretend stuff you don't think or feel or have any idea of? Having for instance to act like I care for Big Mama!—I haven't been able to stand the sight, sound, or smell of that woman for forty years now!—even when I *laid* her!—regular as a piston. . . .

Pretend to love that son of a bitch of a Gooper and his wife Mae and those five same screechers out there like parrots in a jungle? Jesus! Can't stand to look at 'em!

Church!—it bores the bejesus out of me but I go!—I go an' sit there and listen to the fool preacher!

Clubs!—Elks! Masons! Rotary!—*crap!*

[*A spasm of pain makes him clutch his belly. He sinks into a chair and his voice is softer and hoarser.*]

You I *do* like for some reason, did always have some kind of real feeling for—affection—respect—yes, always. . . .

You and being a success as a planter is all I ever had any devotion to in my whole life!—and that's the truth. . . .

386

I don't know why, but it is!

I've lived with mendacity!—Why can't *you* live with it? Hell, you *got* to live with it, there's nothing *else* to *live* with except mendacity, is there?

BRICK:
Yes, sir. Yes, sir there is something else that you can live with!

BIG DADDY:
What?

BRICK [*lifting his glass*]:
This!—Liquor. . . .

BIG DADDY:
That's not living, that's dodging away from life.

BRICK:
I want to dodge away from it.

BIG DADDY:
Then why don't you kill yourself, man?

BRICK:
I like to drink. . . .

BIG DADDY:
Oh, God, I can't talk to you. . . .

BRICK:
I'm sorry, Big Daddy.

BIG DADDY:
Not as sorry as I am. I'll tell you something. A little while back when I thought my number was up—

[*This speech should have torrential pace and fury.*]

387

—before I found out it was just this—spastic—colon. I thought about you. Should I or should I not, if the jig was up, give you this place when I go—since I hate Gooper an' Mae an' know that they hate me, and since all five same monkeys are little Maes an' Goopers.—And I thought, No!—Then I thought, Yes!—I couldn't make up my mind. I hate Gooper and his five same monkeys and that bitch Mae! Why should I turn over twenty-eight thousand acres of the richest land this side of the valley Nile to not my kind?—But why in hell, on the other hand, Brick—should I subsidize a goddam fool on the bottle?—Liked or not liked, well, maybe even—*loved!* —Why should I do that?—Subsidize worthless behavior? Rot? Corruption?

BRICK [*smiling*]:
I understand.

BIG DADDY:
Well, if you do, you're smarter than I am, God damn it, because I don't understand. And this I will tell you frankly. I didn't make up my mind at all on that question and still to this day I ain't made out no will!—Well, now I don't *have* to. The pressure is gone. I can just wait and see if you pull yourself together or if you don't.

BRICK:
That's right, Big Daddy.

BIG DADDY:
You sound like you thought I was kidding.

BRICK [*rising*]:
No, sir, I know you're not kidding.

BIG DADDY:
But you don't care—?

BRICK [*hobbling toward the gallery door*]:
No, sir, I don't care. . . .

Now how about taking a look at your birthday fireworks and getting some of that cool breeze off the river?

[*He stands in the gallery doorway as the night sky turns pink and green and gold with successive flashes of light.*]

BIG DADDY:
WAIT!—Brick. . . .

[*His voice drops. Suddenly there is something shy, almost tender, in his restraining gesture.*]

Don't let's—leave it like this, like them other talks we've had, we've always—talked around things, we've—just talked around things for some rutten reason, I don't know what, it's always like something was left not spoken, something avoided because neither of us was honest enough with the—other. . . .

BRICK:
I never lied to you, Big Daddy.

BIG DADDY:
Did I ever to *you?*

BRICK:
No, sir. . . .

BIG DADDY:
Then there is at least two people that never lied to each other.

BRICK:
But we've never *talked* to each other.

BIG DADDY:
We can *now.*

389

BRICK:

Big Daddy, there don't seem to be anything much to say.

BIG DADDY:

You say that you drink to kill your disgust with lying.

BRICK:

You said to give you a reason.

BIG DADDY:

Is liquor the only thing that'll kill this disgust?

BRICK:

Now. Yes.

BIG DADDY:

But not once, huh?

BRICK:

Not when I was still young an' believing. A drinking man's someone who wants to forget he isn't still young an' believing.

BIG DADDY:

Believing what?

BRICK:

Believing. . . .

BIG DADDY:

Believing *what?*

BRICK [*stubbornly evasive*]:

Believing. . . .

BIG DADDY:

I don't know what the hell you mean by believing and I don't think you know what you mean by believing, but if you still got sports in your blood, go back to sports announcing and—

BRICK:
Sit in a glass box watching games I can't play? Describing what I can't do while players do it? Sweating out their disgust and confusion in contests I'm not fit for? Drinkin' a coke, half bourbon, so I can stand it? That's no goddam good any more, no help—time just outran me, Big Daddy—got there first . . .

BIG DADDY:
I think you're passing the buck.

BRICK:
You know many drinkin' men?

BIG DADDY [*with a slight, charming smile*]:
I have known a fair number of that species.

BRICK:
Could any of them tell you why he drank?

BIG DADDY:
Yep, you're passin' the buck to things like time and disgust with "mendacity" and—crap!—if you got to use that kind of language about a thing, it's ninety-proof bull, and I'm not buying any.

BRICK:
I had to give you a reason to get a drink!

BIG DADDY:
You started drinkin' when your friend Skipper died.

[*Silence for five beats. Then Brick makes a startled movement, reaching for his crutch.*]

BRICK:
What are you suggesting?

391

BIG DADDY:
I'm suggesting nothing.

[*The shuffle and clop of Brick's rapid hobble away from his father's steady, grave attention.*]

—But Gooper an' Mae suggested that there was something not right exactly in your—

BRICK [*stopping short downstage as if backed to a wall*]: "Not right"?

BIG DADDY:
Not, well, exactly *normal* in your friendship with—

BRICK:
They suggested that, too? I thought that was Maggie's suggestion.

[*Brick's detachment is at last broken through. His heart is accelerated; his forehead sweat-beaded; his breath becomes more rapid and his voice hoarse. The thing they're discussing, timidly and painfully on the side of Big Daddy, fiercely, violently on Brick's side, is the inadmissible thing that Skipper died to disavow between them. The fact that if it existed it had to be disavowed to "keep face" in the world they lived in, may be at the heart of the "mendacity" that Brick drinks to kill his disgust with. It may be the root of his collapse. Or maybe it is only a single manifestation of it, not even the most important. The bird that I hope to catch in the net of this play is not the solution of one man's psychological problem. I'm trying to catch the true quality of experience in a group of people, that cloudy, flickering, evanescent—fiercely charged!—interplay of live human beings in the thundercloud of a common crisis. Some mystery should be left in the revelation of character in a play, just as a great deal of mystery is always left in*]

the revelation of character in life, even in one's own char-
acter to himself. This does not absolve the playwright of his
duty to observe and probe as clearly and deeply as he legiti-
mately *can: but it should steer him away from "pat" con-*
clusions, facile definitions which make a play just a play,
not a snare for the truth of human experience.

[*The following scene should be played with great concen-*
tration, with most of the power leashed but palpable in
what is left unspoken.]

Who else's suggestion is it, is it *yours?* How many others
thought that Skipper and I were—

BIG DADDY [*gently*]:
Now, hold on, hold on a minute, son.—I knocked around in
my time.

BRICK:
What's that got to do with—

BIG DADDY:
I said "Hold on!"—I bummed, I bummed this country till I
was—

BRICK:
Whose suggestion, who else's suggestion is it?

BIG DADDY:
Slept in hobo jungles and railroad Y's and flophouses in all
cities before I—

BRICK:
Oh, *you* think so, too, you call me your son and a queer. Oh!
Maybe that's why you put Maggie and me in this room that
was Jack Straw's and Peter Ochello's, in which that pair of
old sisters slept in a double bed where both of 'em died!

393

BIG DADDY:

Now just don't go throwing rocks at—

[*Suddenly Reverend Tooker appears in the gallery doors, his head slightly, playfully, fatuously cocked, with a practised clergyman's smile, sincere as a bird call blown on a hunter's whistle, the living embodiment of the pious, conventional lie.*

[*Big Daddy gasps a little at this perfectly timed, but incongruous, apparition.*]

—What're you lookin' for, Preacher?

REVEREND TOOKER:

The gentleman's lavatory, ha ha!—heh, heh...

BIG DADDY [*with strained courtesy*]:

—Go back out and walk down to the other end of the gallery, Reverend Tooker, and use the bathroom connected with my bedroom, and if you can't find it, ask them where it is!

REVEREND TOOKER:

Ah, thanks.

[*He goes out with a deprecatory chuckle.*]

BIG DADDY:

It's hard to talk in this place...

BRICK:

Son of a—!

BIG DADDY [*leaving a lot unspoken*]:

—I seen all things and understood a lot of them, till 1910. Christ, the year that—I had worn my shoes through, hocked my—I hopped off a yellow dog freight car half a mile down the road, slept in a wagon of cotton outside the gin—Jack Straw an' Peter Ochello took me in. Hired me to manage this

394

place which grew into this one.—When Jack Straw died— why, old Peter Ochello quit eatin' like a dog does when its master's dead, and died, too!

BRICK:
Christ!

BIG DADDY:
I'm just saying I understand such—

BRICK [*violently*]:
Skipper is dead. I have not quit eating!

BIG DADDY:
No, but you started drinking.

[*Brick wheels on his crutch and hurls his glass across the room shouting.*]

BRICK:
YOU THINK SO, TOO?

BIG DADDY:
Shhh!

[*Footsteps run on the gallery. There are women's calls.*]

[*Big Daddy goes toward the door.*]

Go way!—Just broke a glass. . . .

[*Brick is transformed, as if a quiet mountain blew suddenly up in volcanic flame.*]

BRICK:
You think so, too? You think so, too? You think me an' Skipper did, did, did!—*sodomy!*—together?

BIG DADDY:
Hold—!

395

BRICK:
That what you—

BIG DADDY:
—*ON*—a minute!

BRICK:
You think we did dirty things between us, Skipper an'—

BIG DADDY:
Why are you shouting like that? Why are you—

BRICK:
—Me, is that what you think of Skipper, is that—

BIG DADDY:
—so excited? I don't think nothing. I don't know nothing. I'm simply telling you what—

BRICK:
You think that Skipper and me were a pair of dirty old men?

BIG DADDY:
Now that's—

BRICK:
Straw? Ochello? A couple of—

BIG DADDY:
Now just—

BRICK:
—ducking sissies? Queers? Is that what you—

BIG DADDY:
Shhh.

BRICK:
—think?

[*He loses his balance and pitches to his knees without noticing the pain. He grabs the bed and drags himself up.*]

BIG DADDY:
Jesus!—Whew.... Grab my hand!

BRICK:
Naw, I don't want your hand....

BIG DADDY:
Well, I want yours. Git up!

[*He draws him up, keeps an arm about him with concern and affection.*]

You broken out in a sweat! You're panting like you'd run a race with—

BRICK [*freeing himself from his father's hold*]:
Big Daddy, you shock me, Big Daddy, you, you—*shock* me! Talkin' so—

[*He turns away from his father.*]

—casually!—about a—thing like that ...

—Don't you know how people *feel* about things like that? How, how *disgusted* they are by things like that? Why, at Ole Miss when it was discovered a pledge to our fraternity, Skipper's and mine, did a, *attempted* to do a, unnatural thing with—

We not only dropped him like a hot rock!—We told him to git off the campus, and he did, he got!—All the way to—

[*He halts, breathless.*]

BIG DADDY:
—Where?

397

BRICK:
—North Africa, last I heard!

BIG DADDY:
Well, I have come back from further away than that, I have just now returned from the other side of the moon, death's country, son, and I'm not easy to shock by anything here.

[*He comes downstage and faces out.*]

Always, anyhow, lived with too much space around me to be infected by ideas of other people. One thing you can grow on a big place more important than cotton!—is *tolerance!*—I grown it.

[*He returns toward Brick.*]

BRICK:
Why can't exceptional friendship, *real, real, deep, deep friendship!* between two men be respected as something clean and decent without being thought of as—

BIG DADDY:
It can, it is, for God's sake.

BRICK:
—*Fairies. . . .*

[*In his utterance of this word, we gauge the wide and profound reach of the conventional mores he got from the world that crowned him with early laurel.*]

BIG DADDY:
I told Mae an' Gooper—

BRICK:
Frig Mae and Gooper, frig all dirty lies and liars!—Skipper and me had a clean, true thing between us!—had a clean friendship, practically all our lives, till Maggie got the idea

398

you're talking about. Normal? No!—It was too rare to be normal, any true thing between two people is too rare to be normal. Oh, once in a while he put his hand on my shoulder or I'd put mine on his, oh, maybe even, when we were touring the country in pro-football an' shared hotel-rooms we'd reach across the space between the two beds and shake hands to say goodnight, yeah, one or two times we—

BIG DADDY:
Brick, nobody thinks that that's not normal!

BRICK:
Well, they're mistaken, it was! It was a pure an' true thing an' that's not normal.

[*They both stare straight at each other for a long moment. The tension breaks and both turn away as if tired.*]

BIG DADDY:
Yeah, it's—hard t'—talk. . . .

BRICK:
All right, then, let's—let it go. . . .

BIG DADDY:
Why did Skipper crack up? Why have you?

[*Brick looks back at his father again. He has already decided, without knowing that he has made this decision, that he is going to tell his father that he is dying of cancer. Only this could even the score between them: one inadmissible thing in return for another.*]

BRICK [*ominously*]:
All right. You're asking for it, Big Daddy. We're finally going to have that real true talk you wanted. It's too late to stop it, now, we got to carry it through and cover every subject.

[*He hobbles back to the liquor cabinet.*]

Uh-huh.

[*He opens the ice bucket and picks up the silver tongs with slow admiration of their frosty brightness.*]

Maggie declares that Skipper and I went into pro-football after we left "Ole Miss" because we were scared to grow up ...

[*He moves downstage with the shuffle and clop of a cripple on a crutch. As Margaret did when her speech became "recitative," he looks out into the house, commanding its attention by his direct, concentrated gaze—a broken, "tragically elegant" figure telling simply as much as he knows of "the Truth":*]

—Wanted to—keep on tossing—those long, long!—high, high!—passes that—couldn't be intercepted except by time, the aerial attack that made us famous! And so we did, we did, we kept it up for one season, that aerial attack, we held it high!—Yeah, but—

—that summer, Maggie, she laid the law down to me, said, Now or never, and so I married Maggie. . . .

BIG DADDY:
How was Maggie in bed?

BRICK [*wryly*]:
Great! the greatest!

[*Big Daddy nods as if he thought so.*]

She went on the road that fall with the Dixie Stars. Oh, she made a great show of being the world's best sport. She wore a—wore a—tall bearskin cap! A shako, they call it, a dyed moleskin coat, a moleskin coat dyed red!—Cut up crazy!

400

Rented hotel ballrooms for victory celebrations, wouldn't cancel them when it—turned out—defeat. . . .

MAGGIE THE CAT! Ha ha!

[*Big Daddy nods.*]

—But Skipper, he had some fever which came back on him which doctors couldn't explain and I got that injury—turned out to be just a shadow on the X-ray plate—and a touch of bursitis. . . .

I lay in a hospital bed, watched our games on TV, saw Maggie on the bench next to Skipper when he was hauled out of a game for stumbles, fumbles!—Burned me up the way she hung on his arm!—Y'know, I think that Maggie had always felt sort of left out because she and me never got any closer together than two people just get in bed, which is not much closer than two cats on a—fence humping. . . .

So! She took this time to work on poor dumb Skipper. He was a less than average student at Ole Miss, you know that, don't you?!—Poured in his mind the dirty, false idea that what we were, him and me, was a frustrated case of that ole pair of sisters that lived in this room, Jack Straw and Peter Ochello!—He, poor Skipper, went to bed with Maggie to prove it wasn't true, and when it didn't work out, he thought it *was* true!—Skipper broke in two like a rotten stick—nobody ever turned so fast to a lush—or died of it so quick. . . .

—Now are you satisfied?

[*Big Daddy has listened to this story, dividing the grain from the chaff. Now he looks at his son.*]

BIG DADDY:
Are *you* satisfied?

401

BRICK:
With what?

BIG DADDY:
That half-ass story!

BRICK:
What's half-ass about it?

BIG DADDY:
Something's left out of that story. What did you leave out?

[*The phone has started ringing in the hall. As if it reminded him of something, Brick glances suddenly toward the sound and says:*]

BRICK:
Yes!—I left out a long-distance call which I had from Skipper, in which he made a drunken confession to me and on which I hung up!—last time we spoke to each other in our lives. . . .

[*Muted ring stops as someone answers phone in a soft, indistinct voice in hall.*]

BIG DADDY:
You hung up?

BRICK:
Hung up. Jesus! Well—

BIG DADDY:
Anyhow now!—we have tracked down the lie with which you're disgusted and which you are drinking to kill your disgust with, Brick. You been passing the buck. This disgust with mendacity is disgust with yourself.

You!—dug the grave of your friend and kicked him in it!—before you'd face truth with him!

402

BRICK:
His truth, not *mine!*

BIG DADDY:
His truth, okay! But you wouldn't face it with him!

BRICK:
Who *can* face truth? Can *you?*

BIG DADDY:
Now don't start passin' the rotten buck again, boy!

BRICK:
How about these birthday congratulations, these many, many happy returns of the day, when ev'rybody but you knows there won't be any!

[*Whoever has answered the hall phone lets out a high, shrill laugh; the voice becomes audible saying: "No, no, you got it all wrong! Upside down! Are you crazy?"*

[*Brick suddenly catches his breath as he realized that he has made a shocking disclosure. He hobbles a few paces, then freezes, and without looking at his father's shocked face, says:*]

Let's, let's—go out, now, and—

[*Big Daddy moves suddenly forward and grabs hold of the boy's crutch like it was a weapon for which they were fighting for possession.*]

BIG DADDY:
Oh, no, no! No one's going out! What did you start to say?

BRICK:
I don't remember.

BIG DADDY:
"Many happy returns when they know there won't be any"?

403

BRICK:

Aw, hell, Big Daddy, forget it. Come on out on the gallery and look at the fireworks they're shooting off for your birthday. . . .

BIG DADDY:

First you finish that remark you were makin' before you cut off. "Many happy returns when they know there won't be any"?—Ain't that what you just said?

BRICK:

Look, now. I can get around without that crutch if I have to but it would be a lot easier on the furniture an' glassware if I didn' have to go swinging along like Tarzan of th'—

BIG DADDY:

FINISH! WHAT YOU WAS SAYIN'!

[*An eerie green glow shows in sky behind him.*]

BRICK [*sucking the ice in his glass, speech becoming thick*]:
Leave th' place to Gooper and Mae an' their five little same little monkeys. All I want is—

BIG DADDY:

"LEAVE TH' PLACE," did you say?

BRICK [*vaguely*]:
All twenty-eight thousand acres of the richest land this side of the valley Nile.

BIG DADDY:

Who said I was "leaving the place" to Gooper or anybody? This is my sixty-fifth birthday! I got fifteen years or twenty years left in me! I'll outlive *you!* I'll bury you an' have to pay for your coffin!

BRICK:

Sure. Many happy returns. Now let's go watch the fireworks, come on, let's—

BIG DADDY:

Lying, have they been lying? About the report from th'—clinic? Did they, did they—find something?—*Cancer.* Maybe?

BRICK:

Mendacity is a system that we live in. Liquor is one way out an' death's the other. . . .

[*He takes the crutch from Big Daddy's loose grip and swings out on the gallery leaving the doors open.*

[*A song, "Pick a Bale of Cotton," is heard.*]

MAE [*appearing in door*]:
Oh, Big Daddy, the field hands are singin' fo' you!

BIG DADDY [*shouting hoarsely*]:
BRICK! BRICK!

MAE:

He's outside drinkin', Big Daddy.

BIG DADDY:
BRICK!

[*Mae retreats, awed by the passion of his voice. Children call Brick in tones mocking Big Daddy. His face crumbles like broken yellow plaster about to fall into dust.*

[*There is a glow in the sky. Brick swings back through the doors, slowly, gravely, quite soberly.*]

BRICK:

I'm sorry, Big Daddy. My head don't work any more and it's hard for me to understand how anybody could care if he lived or died or was dying or cared about anything but whether or not there was liquor left in the bottle and so I said what I said without thinking. In some ways I'm no better than the others, in some ways worse because I'm less alive. Maybe it's

405

being alive that makes them lie, and being almost *not* alive makes me sort of accidentally truthful—I don't know but—anyway—we've been friends . . .

—And being friends is telling each other the truth. . . .

[*There is a pause.*]

You told *me!* I told *you!*

[*A child rushes into the room and grabs a fistful of fire-crackers and runs out again.*]

CHILD [*screaming*]:
Bang, bang, bang, bang, bang, bang, bang, bang, bang!

BIG DADDY [*slowly and passionately*]:
CHRIST—DAMN—ALL—LYING SONS OF—LYING BITCHES!

[*He straightens at last and crosses to the inside door. At the door he turns and looks back as if he had some desperate question he couldn't put into words. Then he nods reflectively and says in a hoarse voice:*]

Yes, all liars, all liars, all lying dying liars!

[*This is said slowly, slowly, with a fierce revulsion. He goes on out.*]

—Lying! Dying! Liars!

[*His voice dies out. There is the sound of a child being slapped. It rushes, hideously bawling, through room and out the hall door.*

[*Brick remains motionless as the lights dim out and the curtain falls.*]

CURTAIN

ACT THREE

There is no lapse of time.
Mae enters with Reverend Tooker.

MAE:
Where is Big Daddy! Big Daddy?

BIG MAMA [*entering*]:
Too much smell of burnt fireworks makes me feel a little bit sick at my stomach.—Where is Big Daddy?

MAE:
That's what I want to know, where has Big Daddy gone?

BIG MAMA:
He must have turned in, I reckon he went to baid. . . .

[*Gooper enters.*]

GOOPER:
Where is Big Daddy?

MAE:
We don't know where he is!

BIG MAMA:
I reckon he's gone to baid.

GOOPER:
Well, then, now we can talk.

BIG MAMA:
What *is* this talk, *what* talk?

[*Margaret appears on gallery, talking to Dr. Baugh.*]

MARGARET [*musically*]:
My family freed their slaves ten years before abolition, my

407

great-great-grandfather gave his slaves their freedom five years before the war between the States started!

MAE:

Oh, for God's sake! Maggie's climbed back up in her family tree!

MARGARET [*sweetly*]:

What, Mae?—Oh, where's Big Daddy?!

[*The pace must be very quick. Great Southern animation.*]

BIG MAMA [*addressing them all*]:

I think Big Daddy was just worn out. He loves his family, he loves to have them around him, but it's a strain on his nerves. He wasn't himself tonight, Big Daddy wasn't himself, I could tell he was all worked up.

REVEREND TOOKER:

I think he's remarkable.

BIG MAMA:

Yaisss! Just remarkable. Did you all notice the food he ate at that table? Did you all notice the supper he put away? Why, he ate like a hawss!

GOOPER:

I hope he doesn't regret it.

BIG MAMA:

Why, that man—ate a huge piece of cawn-bread with molasses on it! Helped himself twice to hoppin' john.

MARGARET:

Big Daddy loves hoppin' john.—We had a real country dinner.

BIG MAMA [*overlapping Margaret*]:

Yais, he simply adores it! An' candied yams? That man put away enough food at that table to stuff a nigger *field* hand!

408

GOOPER [*with grim relish*]:
I hope he don't have to pay for it later on. . . .

BIG MAMA [*fiercely*]:
What's *that*, Gooper?

MAE:
Gooper says he hopes Big Daddy doesn't suffer tonight.

BIG MAMA:
Oh, shoot, Gooper says, Gooper says! Why should Big Daddy suffer for satisfying a normal appetite? There's nothin' wrong with that man but nerves, he's sound as a dollar! And now he knows he is an' that's why he ate such a supper. He had a big load off his mind, knowin' he wasn't doomed t'—what he thought he was doomed to. . . .

MARGARET [*sadly and sweetly*]:
Bless his old sweet soul. . . .

BIG MAMA [*vaguely*]:
Yais, bless his heart, where's Brick?

MAE:
Outside.

GOOPER:
—Drinkin' . . .

BIG MAMA:
I know he's drinkin'. You all don't have to keep tellin' *me* Brick is drinkin'. Cain't I see he's drinkin' without you continually tellin' me that boy's drinkin'?

MARGARET:
Good for you, Big Mama!

[*She applauds.*]

409

BIG MAMA:

Other people *drink* and *have* drunk an' will *drink,* as long as they make that stuff an' put it in bottles.

MARGARET:

That's the truth. I never trusted a man that didn't drink.

MAE:

Gooper never drinks. Don't you trust Gooper?

MARGARET:

Why, Gooper don't you drink? If I'd known you didn't drink, I wouldn't of made that remark—

BIG MAMA:

Brick?

MARGARET:

—at least not in your presence.

[*She laughs sweetly.*]

BIG MAMA:

Brick!

MARGARET:

He's still on the gall'ry. I'll go bring him in so we can talk.

BIG MAMA [*worriedly*]:

I don't know what this mysterious family conference is about.

[*Awkward silence. Big Mama looks from face to face, then belches slightly and mutters, "Excuse me. . . ." She opens an ornamental fan suspended about her throat, a black lace fan to go with her black lace gown and fans her wilting corsage, sniffing nervously and looking from face to face in the uncomfortable silence as Margaret calls "Brick?" and Brick sings to the moon on the gallery.*]

I don't know what's wrong here, you all have such long faces! Open that door on the hall and let some air circulate through here, will you please, Gooper?

MAE:
I think we'd better leave that door closed, Big Mama, till after the talk.

BIG MAMA:
Reveren' Tooker, will *you* please open that door?!

REVEREND TOOKER:
I sure will, Big Mama.

MAE:
I just didn't think we ought t' take any chance of Big Daddy hearin' a word of this discussion.

BIG MAMA:
I swan! Nothing's going to be said in Big Daddy's house that he cain't hear if he wants to!

GOOPER:
Well, Big Mama, it's—

[*Mae gives him a quick, hard poke to shut him up. He glares at her fiercely as she circles before him like a burlesque ballerina, raising her skinny bare arms over her head, jangling her bracelets, exclaiming:*]

MAE:
A breeze! A breeze!

REVEREND TOOKER:
I think this house is the coolest house in the Delta.—Did you all know that Halsey Banks' widow put air-conditioning units in the church and rectory at Friar's Point in memory of Halsey?

411

[*General conversation has resumed; everybody is chatting so that the stage sounds like a big bird-cage.*]

GOOPER:

Too bad nobody cools your church off for you. I bet you sweat in that pulpit these hot Sundays, Reverend Tooker.

REVEREND TOOKER:

Yes, my vestments are drenched.

MAE [*at the same time to Dr. Baugh*]:

You think those vitamin B$_{12}$ injections are what they're cracked up t' be, Doc Baugh?

DOCTOR BAUGH:

Well, if you want to be stuck with something I guess they're as good to be stuck with as anything else.

BIG MAMA [*at gallery door*]:

Maggie, Maggie, aren't you comin' with Brick?

MAE [*suddenly and loudly, creating a silence*]:

I have a strange feeling, I have a peculiar feeling!

BIG MAMA [*turning from gallery*]:

What feeling?

MAE:

That Brick said somethin' he shouldn't of said t' Big Daddy.

BIG MAMA:

Now what on earth could Brick of said t' Big Daddy that he shouldn't say?

GOOPER:

Big Mama, there's somethin'—

MAE:

NOW, WAIT!

[*She rushes up to Big Mama and gives her a quick hug and kiss. Big Mama pushes her impatiently off as the Reverend Tooker's voice rises serenely in a little pocket of silence:*]

REVEREND TOOKER:
Yes, last Sunday the gold in my chasuble faded into th' purple. . . .

GOOPER:
Reveren' you must of been preachin' hell's fire last Sunday!

[*He guffaws at this witticism but the Reverend is not sincerely amused. At the same time Big Mama has crossed over to Dr. Baugh and is saying to him:*]

BIG MAMA [*her breathless voice rising high-pitched above the others*]:

In my day they had what they call the Keeley cure for heavy drinkers. But now I understand they just take some kind of tablets, they call them "Annie Bust" tablets. But *Brick* don't need to take *nothin'*.

[*Brick appears in gallery doors with Margaret behind him.*]

BIG MAMA [*unaware of his presence behind her*]:
That boy is just broken up over Skipper's death. You know how poor Skipper died. They gave him a big, big dose of that sodium amytal stuff at his home and then they called the ambulance and give him another big, big dose of it at the hospital and that and all of the alcohol in his system fo' months an' months an' months just proved too much for his heart. . . . I'm scared of needles! I'm more scared of a needle than the knife. . . . I think more people have been needled out of this world than—

[*She stops short and wheels about.*]

413

OH!—here's Brick! My precious baby—

[*She turns upon Brick with short, fat arms extended, at the same time uttering a loud, short sob, which is both comic and touching.*

[*Brick smiles and bows slightly, making a burlesque gesture of gallantry for Maggie to pass before him into the room. Then he hobbles on his crutch directly to the liquor cabinet and there is absolute silence, with everybody looking at Brick as everybody has always looked at Brick when he spoke or moved or appeared. One by one he drops ice cubes in his glass, then suddenly, but not quickly, looks back over his shoulder with a wry, charming smile, and says:*]

BRICK:
I'm sorry! Anyone else?

BIG MAMA [*sadly*]:
No, son. I *wish* you wouldn't!

BRICK:
I wish I didn't have to, Big Mama, but I'm still waiting for that click in my head which makes it all smooth out!

BIG MAMA:
Aw, Brick, you—BREAK MY HEART!

MARGARET [*at the same time*]:
Brick, go sit with Big Mama!

BIG MAMA:
I just cain't *staiiiiiiii-nnnnnd*—it. . . .

[*She sobs.*]

MAE:
Now that we're all assembled—

GOOPER:
We kin talk. . . .

BIG MAMA:
Breaks my heart. . . .

MARGARET:
Sit with Big Mama, Brick, and hold her hand.

[*Big Mama sniffs very loudly three times, almost like three drum beats in the pocket of silence.*]

BRICK:
You do that, Maggie. I'm a restless cripple. I got to stay on my crutch.

[*Brick hobbles to the gallery door; leans there as if waiting.*

[*Mae sits beside Big Mama, while Gooper moves in front and sits on the end of the couch, facing her. Reverend Tooker moves nervously into the space between them; on the other side, Dr. Baugh stands looking at nothing in particular and lights a cigar. Margaret turns away.*]

BIG MAMA:
Why're you all *surroundin'* me—like this? Why're you all starin' at me like this an' makin' signs at each other?

[*Reverend Tooker steps back startled.*]

MAE:
Calm yourself, Big Mama.

BIG MAMA:
Calm you'self, *you'self*, Sister Woman. How could I calm myself with everyone starin' at me as if big drops of blood had broken out on m'face? What's this all about, annh! What?

[*Gooper coughs and takes a center position.*]

415

GOOPER:
Now, Doc Baugh.

MAE:
Doc Baugh?

BRICK [*suddenly*]:
SHHH!—

[*Then he grins and chuckles and shakes his head regret-fully.*]

—Naw!—that wasn't th' click.

GOOPER:
Brick, shut up or stay out there on the gallery with your liquor! We got to talk about a serious matter. Big Mama wants to know the complete truth about the report we got today from the Ochsner Clinic.

MAE [*eagerly*]:
—on Big Daddy's condition!

GOOPER:
Yais, on Big Daddy's condition, we got to face it.

DOCTOR BAUGH:
Well. . . .

BIG MAMA [*terrified, rising*]:
Is there? Something? Something that I? Don't—Know?

[*In these few words, this startled, very soft, question, Big Mama reviews the history of her forty-five years with Big Daddy, her great, almost embarrassingly true-hearted and simple-minded devotion to Big Daddy, who must have had something Brick has, who made himself loved so much by the "simple expedient" of not loving enough to disturb his*

416

charming detachment, also once coupled, like Brick's, with virile beauty.

[*Big Mama has a dignity at this moment: she almost stops being fat.*]

DOCTOR BAUGH [*after a pause, uncomfortably*]:
Yes?—Well—

BIG MAMA:
I!!!—want to—*knowwwwwww. . . .*

[*Immediately she thrusts her fist to her mouth as if to deny that statement.*

[*Then, for some curious reason, she snatches the withered corsage from her breast and hurls it on the floor and steps on it with her short, fat feet.*]

—*Somebody must be lyin'!*—*I want to know!*

MAE:
Sit down, Big Mama, sit down on this sofa.

MARGARET [*quickly*]:
Brick, go sit with Big Mama.

BIG MAMA:
What is it, what is it?

DOCTOR BAUGH:
I never have seen a more thorough examination than Big Daddy Pollitt was given in all my experience with the Ochsner Clinic.

GOOPER:
It's one of the best in the country.

MAE:
It's *THE* best in the country—bar *none!*

417

[*For some reason she gives Gooper a violent poke as she goes past him. He slaps at her hand without removing his eyes from his mother's face.*]

DOCTOR BAUGH:
Of course they were ninety-nine and nine-tenths percent sure before they even started.

BIG MAMA:
Sure of what, sure of what, sure of—*what?—what!*

[*She catches her breath in a startled sob. Mae kisses her quickly. She thrusts Mae fiercely away from her, staring at the doctor.*]

MAE:
Mommy, be a brave girl!

BRICK [*in the doorway, softly*]:
"*By the light, by the light,
Of the sil-ve-ry mo-ooo-n . . .*"

GOOPER:
Shut up!—Brick.

BRICK:
—Sorry. . . .

[*He wanders out on the gallery.*]

DOCTOR BAUGH:
But now, you see, Big Mama, they cut a piece off this growth, a specimen of the tissue and—

BIG MAMA:
Growth? You told Big Daddy—

DOCTOR BAUGH:
Now wait.

418

BIG MAMA [*fiercely*]:
You told me and Big Daddy there wasn't a thing wrong with
him but—

MAE:
Big Mama, they always—

GOOPER:
Let Doc Baugh talk, will yuh?

BIG MAMA:
—little spastic condition of—

[*Her breath gives out in a sob.*]

DOCTOR BAUGH:
Yes, that's what we told Big Daddy. But we had this bit of
tissue run through the laboratory and I'm sorry to say the
test was positive on it. It's—well—malignant. . . .

[*Pause.*]

BIG MAMA:
—Cancer?! Cancer?!

[*Dr. Baugh nods gravely.*]

[*Big Mama gives a long gasping cry.*]

MAE and GOOPER:
Now, now, now, Big Mama, you had to know. . . .

BIG MAMA:
WHY DIDN'T THEY CUT IT OUT OF HIM? HANH?
HANH?

DOCTOR BAUGH:
Involved too much, Big Mama, too many organs affected.

419

MAE:
Big Mama, the liver's affected and so's the kidneys, both! It's gone way past what they call a—

GOOPER:
A surgical risk.

MAE:
—Uh-huh. . . .

[*Big Mama draws a breath like a dying gasp.*]

REVEREND TOOKER:
Tch, tch, tch, tch, tch!

DOCTOR BAUGH:
Yes, it's gone past the knife.

MAE:
That's why he's turned yellow, Mommy!

BIG MAMA:
Git away from me, git away from me, Mae!

[*She rises abruptly.*]

I want Brick! Where's Brick? Where is my only son?

MAE:
Mama! Did she say "*only* son"?

GOOPER:
What does that make *me?*

MAE:
A sober responsible man with five precious children!—*Six!*

BIG MAMA:
I want Brick to tell me! Brick! Brick!

MARGARET [*rising from her reflections in a corner*]:
Brick was so upset he went back out.

BIG MAMA:
Brick!

MARGARET:
Mama, let *me* tell you!

BIG MAMA:
No, no, leave me alone, you're not my blood!

GOOPER:
Mama, I'm your son! Listen to *me!*

MAE:
Gooper's your son, Mama, he's your first-born!

BIG MAMA:
Gooper never liked Daddy.

MAE [*as if terribly shocked*]:
That's not TRUE!

[*There is a pause. The minister coughs and rises.*]

REVEREND TOOKER [*to Mae*]:
I think I'd better slip away at this point.

MAE [*sweetly and sadly*]:
Yes, Doctor Tooker, you go.

REVEREND TOOKER [*discreetly*]:
Goodnight, goodnight, everybody, and God bless you all . . .
on this place. . . .

[*He slips out.*]

DOCTOR BAUGH:
That man is a good man but lacking in tact. Talking about
people giving memorial windows—if he mentioned one
memorial window, he must have spoke of a dozen, and say-

421

ing how awful it was when somebody died intestate, the legal
wrangles, and so forth.

[*Mae coughs, and points at Big Mama.*]

DOCTOR BAUGH:
Well, Big Mama. . . .

[*He sighs.*]

BIG MAMA:
It's all a mistake, I know it's just a bad dream.

DOCTOR BAUGH:
We're gonna keep Big Daddy as comfortable as we can.

BIG MAMA:
Yes, it's just a bad dream, that's all it is, it's just an awful
dream.

GOOPER:
In my opinion Big Daddy is having some pain but won't
admit that he has it.

BIG MAMA:
Just a dream, a bad dream.

DOCTOR BAUGH:
That's what lots of them do, they think if they don't admit
they're having the pain they can sort of escape the fact of
it.

GOOPER [*with relish*]:
Yes, they get sly about it, they get real sly about it.

MAE:
Gooper and I think—

GOOPER:
Shut up, Mae!—Big Daddy ought to be started on morphine.

BIG MAMA:
Nobody's going to give Big Daddy morphine.

DOCTOR BAUGH:
Now, Big Mama, when that pain strikes it's going to strike mighty hard and Big Daddy's going to need the needle to bear it.

BIG MAMA:
I tell you, nobody's going to give him morphine.

MAE:
Big Mama, you don't want to see Big Daddy suffer, you know you—

[*Gooper standing beside her gives her a savage poke.*]

DOCTOR BAUGH [*placing a package on the table*]:
I'm leaving this stuff here, so if there's a sudden attack you all won't have to send out for it.

MAE:
I know how to give a hypo.

GOOPER:
Mae took a course in nursing during the war.

MARGARET:
Somehow I don't think Big Daddy would want Mae to give him a hypo.

MAE:
You think he'd want *you* to do it?

[*Dr. Baugh rises.*]

GOOPER:
Doctor Baugh is goin'.

423

DOCTOR BAUGH:
Yes, I got to be goin'. Well, keep your chin up, Big Mama.

GOOPER [*with jocularity*]:
She's gonna keep *both* chins up, aren't you Big Mama?

[*Big Mama sobs.*]

Now stop that, Big Mama.

MAE:
Sit down with me, Big Mama.

GOOPER [*at door with Dr. Baugh*]:
Well, Doc, we sure do appreciate all you done. I'm telling you, we're surely obligated to you for—

[*Dr. Baugh has gone out without a glance at him.*]

GOOPER:
—I guess that doctor has got a lot on his mind but it wouldn't hurt him to act a little more human. . . .

[*Big Mama sobs.*]

Now be a brave girl, Mommy.

BIG MAMA:
It's not true, I know that it's just not true!

GOOPER:
Mama, those tests are infallible!

BIG MAMA:
Why are you so determined to see your father daid?

MAE:
Big Mama!

MARGARET [*gently*]:
I know what Big Mama means.

MAE [*fiercely*]:
Oh, do you?

MARGARET [*quietly and very sadly*]:
Yes, I think I do.

MAE:
For a newcomer in the family you sure do show a lot of understanding.

MARGARET:
Understanding is needed on this place.

MAE:
I guess you must have needed a lot of it in your family, Maggie, with your father's liquor problem and now you've got Brick with his!

MARGARET:
Brick does not have a liquor problem at all. Brick is devoted to Big Daddy. This thing is a terrible strain on him.

BIG MAMA:
Brick is Big Daddy's boy, but he drinks too much and it worries me and Big Daddy, and, Margaret, you've got to cooperate with us, you've got to cooperate with Big Daddy and me in getting Brick straightened out. Because it will break Big Daddy's heart if Brick don't pull himself together and take hold of things.

MAE:
Take hold of *what* things, Big Mama?

BIG MAMA:
The place.

[*There is a quick violent look between Mae and Gooper.*]

425

GOOPER:
Big Mama, you've had a shock.

MAE:
Yais, we've all had a shock, but . . .

GOOPER:
Let's be realistic—

MAE:
—Big Daddy would never, would *never,* be foolish enough to—

GOOPER:
—put this place in irresponsible hands!

BIG MAMA:
Big Daddy ain't going to leave the place in anybody's hands; Big Daddy is *not* going to die. I want you to get that in your heads, all of you!

MAE:
Mommy, Mommy, Big Mama, we're just as hopeful an' optimistic as you are about Big Daddy's prospects, we have faith in *prayer*—but nevertheless there are certain matters that have to be discussed an' dealt with, because otherwise—

GOOPER:
Eventualities have to be considered and now's the time. . . . Mae, will you please get my briefcase out of our room?

MAE:
Yes, honey.

[*She rises and goes out through the hall door.*]

GOOPER [*standing over Big Mama*]:
Now Big Mom. What you said just now was not at all true and you know it. I've always loved Big Daddy in my own

426

quiet way. I never made a show of it, and I know that Big Daddy has always been fond of me in a quiet way, too, and he never made a show of it neither.

[*Mae returns with Gooper's briefcase.*]

MAE:
Here's your briefcase, Gooper, honey.

GOOPER [*handing the briefcase back to her*]:
Thank you. . . . Of ca'use, my relationship with Big Daddy is different from Brick's.

MAE:
You're eight years older'n Brick an' always had t'carry a bigger load of th' responsibilities than Brick ever had t'carry. He never carried a thing in his life but a football or a highball.

GOOPER:
Mae, will y' let me talk, please?

MAE:
Yes, honey.

GOOPER:
Now, a twenty-eight thousand acre plantation's a mighty big thing t'run.

MAE:
Almost singlehanded.

[*Margaret has gone out onto the gallery, and can be heard calling softly to Brick.*]

BIG MAMA:
You never had to run this place! What are you talking about? As if Big Daddy was dead and in his grave, you had to run it?

Why, you just helped him out with a few business details and had your law practice at the same time in Memphis!

MAE:

Oh, Mommy, Mommy, Big Mommy! Let's be fair! Why, Gooper has given himself body and soul to keeping this place up for the past five years since Big Daddy's health started failing. Gooper won't say it, Gooper never thought of it as a duty, he just did it. And what did Brick do? Brick kept living in his past glory at college! Still a football player at twenty-seven!

MARGARET [*returning alone*]:

Who are you talking about, now? Brick? A football player? He isn't a football player and you know it. Brick is a sport's announcer on TV and one of the best-known ones in the country!

MAE:

I'm talking about what he was.

MARGARET:

Well, I wish you would just stop talking about my husband.

GOOPER:

I've got a right to discuss my brother with other members of MY OWN family which don't include *you*. Why don't you go out there and drink with Brick?

MARGARET:

I've never seen such malice toward a brother.

GOOPER:

How about his for me? Why, he can't stand to be in the same room with me!

MARGARET:

This is a deliberate campaign of vilification for the most dis-

428

gusting and sordid reason on earth, and I know what it is! It's *avarice, avarice, greed, greed!*

BIG MAMA:
Oh, I'll scream! I will scream in a moment unless this stops!

[*Gooper has stalked up to Margaret with clenched fists at his sides as if he would strike her. Mae distorts her face again into a hideous grimace behind Margaret's back.*]

MARGARET:
We only remain on the place because of Big Mom and Big Daddy. If it is true what they say about Big Daddy we are going to leave here just as soon as it's over. Not a moment later.

BIG MAMA [*sobs*]:
Margaret. Child. Come here. Sit next to Big Mama.

MARGARET:
Precious Mommy. I'm sorry, I'm so sorry, I—!

[*She bends her long graceful neck to press her forehead to Big Mama's bulging shoulder under its black chiffon.*]

GOOPER:
How beautiful, how touching, this display of devotion!

MAE:
Do you know why she's childless? She's childless because that big beautiful athlete husband of hers won't go to bed with her!

GOOPER:
You jest won't let me do this in a nice way, will yah? Aw right—Mae and I have five kids with another one coming! I don't give a goddam if Big Daddy likes me or don't like me or did or never did or will or will never! I'm just appealing

429

to a sense of common decency and fair play. I'll tell you the truth. I've resented Big Daddy's partiality to Brick ever since Brick was born, and the way I've been treated like I was just barely good enough to spit on and sometimes not even good enough for that. Big Daddy is dying of cancer, and it's spread all through him and it's attacked all his vital organs including the kidneys and right now he is sinking into uremia, and you all know what uremia is, it's poisoning of the whole system due to the failure of the body to eliminate its poisons.

MARGARET [*to herself, downstage, hissingly*]:
Poisons, poisons! Venomous thoughts and words! In hearts and minds!—That's poisons!

GOOPER [*overlapping her*]:
I am asking for a square deal, and I expect to get one. But if I don't get one, if there's any peculiar shenanigans going on around here behind my back, or before me, well, I'm not a corporation lawyer for nothing, I know how to protect my own interests.—*OH! A late arrival!*

[*Brick enters from the gallery with a tranquil, blurred smile, carrying an empty glass with him.*]

MAE:
Behold the conquering hero comes!

GOOPER:
The fabulous Brick Pollitt! Remember him?—Who could forget him!

MAE:
He looks like he's been injured in a game!

GOOPER:
Yep, I'm afraid you'll have to warm the bench at the Sugar Bowl this year, Brick!

[*Mae laughs shrilly.*]

Or was it the Rose Bowl that he made that famous run in?

MAE:
The punch bowl, honey. It was in the punch bowl, the cut-glass punch bowl!

GOOPER:
Oh, that's right, I'm getting the bowls mixed up!

MARGARET:
Why don't you stop venting your malice and envy on a sick boy?

BIG MAMA:
Now you two hush, I mean it, hush, all of you, hush!

GOOPER:
All right, Big Mama. A family crisis brings out the best and the worst in every member of it.

MAE:
That's the truth.

MARGARET:
Amen!

BIG MAMA:
I *said, hush!* I won't tolerate any more catty talk in my house.

[*Mae gives Gooper a sign indicating briefcase.*

[*Brick's smile has grown both brighter and vaguer. As he prepares a drink, he sings softly:*]

BRICK:
Show me the way to go home,

431

I'm tired and I wanta go to bed,
I had a little drink about an hour ago—

GOOPER [*at the same time*]:
Big Mama, you know it's necessary for me t'go back to Memphis in th' mornin' t'represent the Parker estate in a lawsuit.

[*Mae sits on the bed and arranges papers she has taken from the briefcase.*]

BRICK [*continuing the song*]:
Wherever I may roam,
On land or sea or foam.

BIG MAMA:
Is it, Gooper?

MAE:
Yaiss.

GOOPER:
That's why I'm forced to—to bring up a problem that—

MAE:
Somethin' that's too important t' be put off!

GOOPER:
If Brick was sober, he ought to be in on this.

MARGARET:
Brick is present; we're here.

GOOPER:
Well, good. I will now give you this outline my partner, Tom Bullitt, an' me have drawn up—a sort of dummy—trusteeship.

MARGARET:
Oh, that's it! You'll be in charge an' dole out remittances, will you?

GOOPER:

This we did as soon as we got the report on Big Daddy from th' Ochsner Laboratories. We did this thing, I mean we drew up this dummy outline with the advice and assistance of the Chairman of the Boa'd of Directors of th' Southern Plantahs Bank and Trust Company in Memphis, C. C. Bellowes, a man who handles estates for all th' prominent fam'lies in West Tennessee and th' Delta.

BIG MAMA:

Gooper?

GOOPER [*crouching in front of Big Mama*]:

Now this is not—not final, or anything like it. This is just a preliminary outline. But it does provide a basis—a design—a —possible, feasible—*plan!*

MARGARET:

Yes, I'll bet.

MAE:

It's a plan to protect the biggest estate in the Delta from irresponsibility an'—

BIG MAMA:

Now you listen to me, all of you, you listen here! They's not goin' to be any more catty talk in my house! And Gooper, you put that away before I grab it out of our hand and tear it right up! I don't know what the hell's in it, and I don't want to know what the hell's in it. I'm talkin' in Big Daddy's language now; I'm his *wife,* not his *widow,* I'm still his *wife!* And I'm talkin' to you in his language an'—

GOOPER:

Big Mama, what I have here is—

MAE:

Gooper explained that it's just a plan. . . .

BIG MAMA:

I don't care what you got there. Just put it back where it came from, an' don't let me see it again, not even the outside of the envelope of it! Is that understood? Basis! Plan! Preliminary! Design! I say—what is it Big Daddy always says when he's disgusted?

BRICK [*from the bar*]:
Big Daddy says "crap" when he's disgusted.

BIG MAMA [*rising*]:
That's right—*CRAP!* I say *CRAP* too, like Big Daddy!

MAE:
Coarse language doesn't seem called for in this—

GOOPER:
Somethin' in me is *deeply outraged* by hearin' you talk like this.

BIG MAMA:
Nobody's goin' to take nothin'!—till Big Daddy lets go of it, and maybe, just possibly, not—not even then! No, not even then!

BRICK:
You can always hear me singin' this song,
Show me the way to go home.

BIG MAMA:
Tonight Brick looks like he used to look when he was a little boy, just like he did when he played wild games and used to come home all sweaty and pink-cheeked and sleepy, with his —red curls shining. . . .

[*She comes over to him and runs her fat shaky hand through his hair. He draws aside as he does from all physical contact and continues the song in a whisper, opening the*

434

ice bucket and dropping in the ice cubes one by one as if he were mixing some important chemical formula.]

BIG MAMA [*continuing*]:
Time goes by so fast. Nothin' can outrun it. Death commences too early—almost before you're half acquainted with life— you meet with the other. . . .

Oh, you know we just got to love each other an' stay together, all of us, just as close as we can, especially now that such a *black* thing has come and moved into this place without invitation.

[*Awkwardly embracing Brick, she presses her head to his shoulder.*

[*Gooper has been returning papers to Mae who has restored them to briefcase with an air of severely tried patience.*]

GOOPER:
Big Mama? Big Mama?

[*He stands behind her, tense with sibling envy.*]

BIG MAMA [*oblivious of Gooper*]:
Brick, you hear me, don't you?

MARGARET:
Brick hears you, Big Mama, he understands what you're saying.

BIG MAMA:
Oh, Brick, son of Big Daddy! Big Daddy does so love you! Y'know what would be his fondest dream come true? If before he passed on, if Big Daddy has to pass on, you gave him a child of yours, a grandson as much like his son as his son is like Big Daddy!

435

MAE [*zipping briefcase shut: an incongruous sound*]:
Such a pity that Maggie an' Brick can't oblige!

MARGARET [*suddenly and quietly but forcefully*]:
Everybody listen.

[*She crosses to the center of the room, holding her hands rigidly together.*]

MAE:
Listen to what, Maggie?

MARGARET:
I have an announcement to make.

GOOPER:
A sports announcement, Maggie?

MARGARET:
Brick and I are going to—*have a child!*

[*Big Mama catches her breath in a loud gasp.*]

[*Pause. Big Mama rises.*]

BIG MAMA:
Maggie! Brick! This is too good to believe!

MAE:
That's right, too good to believe.

BIG MAMA:
Oh, my, my! This is Big Daddy's dream, his dream come true!
I'm going to tell him right now before he—

MARGARET:
We'll tell him in the morning. Don't disturb him now.

BIG MAMA:
I want to tell him before he goes to sleep, I'm going to tell

436

him his dream's come true this minute! And Brick! A child will make you pull yourself together and quit this drinking!

[*She seizes the glass from his hand.*]

The responsibilities of a father will—

[*Her face contorts and she makes an excited gesture; bursting into sobs, she rushes out, crying.*]

I'm going to tell Big Daddy right this minute!

[*Her voice fades out down the hall.*

[*Brick shrugs slightly and drops an ice cube into another glass. Margaret crosses quickly to his side, saying something under her breath, and she pours the liquor for him, staring up almost fiercely into his face.*]

BRICK [*coolly*]:
Thank you, Maggie, that's a nice big shot.

[*Mae has joined Gooper and she gives him a fierce poke, making a low hissing sound and a grimace of fury.*]

GOOPER [*pushing her aside*]:
Brick, could you possibly spare me one small shot of that liquor?

BRICK:
Why, help yourself, Gooper boy.

GOOPER:
I will.

MAE [*shrilly*]:
Of course we know that this is—

GOOPER:
Be still, Mae!

437

MAE:
I won't be still! I know she's made this up!

GOOPER:
God damn it, I said to shut up!

MARGARET:
Gracious! I didn't know that my little announcement was going to provoke such a storm!

MAE:
That woman isn't *pregnant!*

GOOPER:
Who said she was?

MAE:
She did.

GOOPER:
The doctor didn't. Doc Baugh didn't.

MARGARET:
I haven't gone to Doc Baugh.

GOOPER:
Then who'd you go to, Maggie?

MARGARET:
One of the best gynecologists in the South.

GOOPER:
Uh huh, uh huh!—I see. . . .

[*He takes out pencil and notebook.*]

—May we have his name, please?

MARGARET:
No, you may not, Mister Prosecuting Attorney!

MAE:
He doesn't have any name, he doesn't exist!

MARGARET:
Oh, he exists all right, and so does my child, Brick's baby!

MAE:
You can't conceive a child by a man that won't sleep with you unless you think you're—

[*Brick has turned on the phonograph. A scat song cuts Mae's speech.*]

GOOPER:
Turn that off!

MAE:
We know it's a lie because we hear you in here; he won't sleep with you, we hear you! So don't imagine you're going to put a trick over on us, to fool a dying man with a—

[*A long drawn cry of agony and rage fills the house. Margaret turns phonograph down to a whisper.*

[*The cry is repeated.*]

MAE [*awed*]:
Did you hear that, Gooper, did you hear that?

GOOPER:
Sounds like the pain has struck.

MAE:
Go see, Gooper!

GOOPER:
Come along and leave these lovebirds together in their nest!

[*He goes out first. Mae follows but turns at the door, contorting her face and hissing at Margaret.*]

439

MAE:
Liar!

[*She slams the door.*

[*Margaret exhales with relief and moves a little unsteadily
to catch hold of Brick's arm.*]

MARGARET:
Thank you for—keeping still . . .

BRICK:
OK, Maggie.

MARGARET:
It was gallant of you to save my face!

BRICK:
—It hasn't happened yet.

MARGARET:
What?

BRICK:
The click. . . .

MARGARET:
—the click in your head that makes you peaceful, honey?

BRICK:
Uh-huh. It hasn't happened. . . . I've got to make it happen
before I can sleep. . . .

MARGARET:
—I—know what you—mean. . . .

BRICK:
Give me that pillow in the big chair, Maggie.

MARGARET:
I'll put it on the bed for you.

BRICK:

No, put it on the sofa, where I sleep.

MARGARET:

Not tonight, Brick.

BRICK:

I want it on the sofa. That's where I sleep.

[*He has hobbled to the liquor cabinet. He now pours down three shots in quick succession and stands waiting, silent. All at once he turns with a smile and says:*]

There!

MARGARET:

What?

BRICK:

The *click.* . . .

[*His gratitude seems almost infinite as he hobbles out on the gallery with a drink. We hear his crutch as he swings out of sight. Then, at some distance, he begins singing to himself a peaceful song.*

[*Margaret holds the big pillow forlornly as if it were her only companion, for a few moments, then throws it on the bed. She rushes to the liquor cabinet, gathers all the bottles in her arms, turns about undecidedly, then runs out of the room with them, leaving the door ajar on the dim yellow hall. Brick is heard hobbling back along the gallery, singing his peaceful song. He comes back in, sees the pillow on the bed, laughs lightly, sadly, picks it up. He has it under his arm as Margaret returns to the room. Margaret softly shuts the door and leans against it, smiling softly at Brick.*]

MARGARET:

Brick, I used to think that you were stronger than me and I

441

didn't want to be overpowered by you. But now, since you've taken to liquor—you know what?—I guess it's bad, but now I'm stronger than you and I can love you more truly!

Don't move that pillow. I'll move it right back if you do!

—Brick?

[*She turns out all the lamps but a single rose-silk-shaded one by the bed.*]

I really have been to a doctor and I know what to do and—Brick?—this is my time by the calendar to conceive!

BRICK:
Yes, I understand, Maggie. But how are you going to conceive a child by a man in love with his liquor?

MARGARET:
By locking his liquor up and making him satisfy my desire before I unlock it!

BRICK:
Is that what you've done, Maggie?

MARGARET:
Look and see. That cabinet's mighty empty compared to before!

BRICK:
Well, I'll be a son of a—

[*He reaches for his crutch but she beats him to it and rushes out on the gallery, hurls the crutch over the rail and comes back in, panting.*

[*There are running footsteps. Big Mama bursts into the room, her face all awry, gasping, stammering.*]

BIG MAMA:
Oh, my God, oh, my God, oh, my God, where is it?

MARGARET:
Is this what you want, Big Mama?

[*Margaret hands her the package left by the doctor.*]

BIG MAMA:
I can't bear it, oh, God! Oh, Brick! Brick, baby!

[*She rushes at him. He averts his face from her sobbing kisses. Margaret watches with a tight smile.*]

My son, Big Daddy's boy! Little Father!

[*The groaning cry is heard again. She runs out, sobbing.*]

MARGARET:
And so tonight we're going to make the lie true, and when that's done, I'll bring the liquor back here and we'll get drunk together, here, tonight, in this place that death has come into. . . .

—What do you say?

BRICK:
I don't say anything. I guess there's nothing to say.

MARGARET:
Oh, you weak people, you weak, beautiful people!—who give up.—What you want is someone to—

[*She turns out the rose-silk lamp.*]

—take hold of you.—Gently, gently, with love! And—

[*The curtain begins to fall slowly.*]

443

I *do* love you, Brick, I *do!*

BRICK [*smiling with charming sadness*]:
Wouldn't it be funny if that was true?

THE CURTAIN COMES DOWN

THE END

NOTE OF EXPLANATION

Some day when time permits I would like to write a piece about the influence, its dangers and its values, of a powerful and highly imaginative director upon the development of a play, before and during production. It does have dangers, but it has them only if the playwright is excessively malleable or submissive, or the director is excessively insistent on ideas or interpretations of his own. Elia Kazan and I have enjoyed the advantages and avoided the dangers of this highly explosive relationship because of the deepest mutual respect for each other's creative function: we have worked together three times with a phenomenal absence of friction between us and each occasion has increased the trust.

If you don't want a director's influence on your play, there are two ways to avoid it, and neither is good. One way is to arrive at an absolutely final draft of your play before you let your director see it, then hand it to him saying, Here it is, take it or leave it! The other way is to select a director who is content to put your play on the stage precisely as you conceived it with no ideas of his own. I said neither is a good way, and I meant it. No living playwright, that I can think of, hasn't something valuable to learn about his own work from a director so keenly perceptive as Elia Kazan. It so happened that in the case of *Streetcar,* Kazan was given a script that was completely finished. In the case of *Cat,* he was shown the first typed version of the play, and he was excited by it, but he had definite reservations about it which were concentrated in the third act. The gist of his reservations can be listed as three points: one, he felt that Big Daddy was too vivid and important a character to disappear from the play except as an offstage cry after the second act curtain; two, he felt that the character of Brick should undergo some apparent mutation as a result of the virtual vivisection that he undergoes in his interview with his father in Act Two. Three, he felt that the character of Margaret, while he understood that I sympathized with her and liked her myself, should be, if possible, more clearly sympathetic to an audience.

It was only the third of these suggestions that I embraced wholeheartedly from the outset, because it so happened that Maggie the Cat had become steadily more charming to me as I worked on her characterization. I didn't want Big Daddy to reappear in Act Three and I felt that the moral paralysis of Brick was a root thing in his tragedy, and to show a dramatic progression would obscure the meaning of that tragedy in him and because I don't believe that a conversation, however revelatory, ever effects so immediate a change in the heart or even conduct of a person in Brick's state of spiritual disrepair.

However, I wanted Kazan to direct the play, and though these suggestions were not made in the form of an ultimatum, I was fearful that I would lose his interest if I didn't re-examine the script from his point of view. I did. And you will find included in this published script the new third act that resulted from his creative influence on the play. The reception of the playing-script has more than justified, in my opinion, the adjustments made to that influence. A failure reaches fewer people, and touches fewer, than does a play that succeeds.

It may be that *Cat* number one would have done just as well, or nearly, as *Cat* number two; it's an interesting question. At any rate, with the publication of both third acts in this volume, the reader can, if he wishes, make up his own mind about it.

TENNESSEE WILLIAMS

446

EDITOR'S NOTE

Unlike the other dramatic material in this volume, the Broadway version of Act Three of *Cat on a Hot Tin Roof* includes directions for the stage, adapted from the production script. The positions and movements of the actors, their entrances and exits, are noted in abbreviated form, and always from a view *opposite* the audience. Thus a direction reading *"Brick XDSR on gallery"* might be rendered *"Brick, on the gallery, crosses downstage to the right*—"downstage" meaning *toward* the audience, and "right" referring to the part of the stage on the audience's *left*. The other common abbreviations used here in combination are: *C* (center, centerstage), *L* (left, stage left), *D* (downstage), *U* or *US* (upstage).

ACT THREE
AS PLAYED IN NEW YORK PRODUCTION

Big Daddy is seen leaving as at the end of Act II.

BIG DADDY [*shouts, as he goes out DR on gallery*]:
ALL—LYIN'—DYIN'—LIARS! LIARS! LIARS!

[*After Big Daddy has gone, Margaret enters from DR on gallery, into room through DS door. She X to Brick at LC.*]

MARGARET:
Brick, what in the name of God was goin' on in this room?

[*Dixie and Trixie rush through the room from the hall, L to gallery R, brandishing cap pistols, which they fire repeatedly, as they shout: "Bang! Bang! Bang!"*]

[*Mae appears from DR gallery entrance, and turns the children back UL, along gallery. At the same moment, Gooper, Reverend Tooker and Dr. Baugh enter from L in the hall.*]

MAE:
Dixie! You quit that! Gooper, will y'please git these kiddies t'baid? Right now?

[*Gooper and Reverend Tooker X along upper gallery. Dr. Baugh holds, UC, near hall door. Reverend Tooker X to Mae near section of gallery just outside doors, R.*]

GOOPER [*urging the children along*]:
Mae—you seen Big Mama?

MAE:
Not yet.

[*Dixie and Trixie vanish through hall, L.*]

449

REVEREND TOOKER [*to Mae*]:
Those kiddies are so full of vitality. I think I'll have to be startin' back to town.

[*Margaret turns to watch and listen.*]

MAE:
Not yet, Preacher. You know we regard you as a member of this fam'ly, one of our closest an' dearest, so you just got t'be with us when Doc Baugh gives Big Mama th' actual truth about th' report from th' clinic.

[*Calls through door:*]

Has Big Daddy gone to bed, Brick?

[*Gooper has gone out DR at the beginning of the exchange between Mae and Reverend Tooker.*]

MARGARET [*replying to Mae*]:
Yes, he's gone to bed.

[*To Brick:*]

Why'd Big Daddy shout "liars"?

GOOPER [*off DR*]:
Mae!

[*Mae exits DR. Reverend Tooker drifts along upper gallery.*]

BRICK:
I didn't lie to Big Daddy. I've lied to nobody, nobody but myself, just lied to myself. The time has come to put me in Rainbow Hill, put me in Rainbow Hill, Maggie, I ought to go there.

MARGARET:
Over my dead body!

[*Brick starts R. She holds him.*]

Where do you think you're goin'?

[*Mae enters from DR on gallery, X to Reverend Tooker, who comes to meet her.*]

BRICK [*X below to C*]:
Out for some air, I want air—

GOOPER [*entering from DR to Mae, on gallery*]:
Now, where is that old lady?

MAE:
Cantcha find her, Gooper?

[*Reverend Tooker goes out DR.*]

GOOPER [*X to Doc above hall door*]:
She's avoidin' this talk.

MAE:
I think she senses somethin'.

GOOPER [*calls off L*]:
Sookey! Go find Big Mama an' tell her Doc Baugh an' the Preacher've got tó go soon.

MAE:
Don't let Big Daddy hear yuh!

[*Brings Dr. Baugh to R on gallery.*]

REVEREND TOOKER [*off DR, calls*]:
Big Mama.

SOOKEY and DAISY [*running from L to R in lawn, calling*]:
Miss Ida! Miss Ida!

[*They go out UR.*]

451

GOOPER [calling off upper gallery]:
Lacey, you look downstairs for Big Mama!

MARGARET:
Brick, they're going to tell Big Mama the truth now, an' she needs you!

[Reverend Tooker appears in lawn area, UR, X C.]

DOCTOR BAUGH [to Mae, on R gallery]:
This is going to be painful.

MAE:
Painful things can't always be avoided.

DOCTOR BAUGH:
That's what I've noticed about 'em, Sister Woman.

REVEREND TOOKER [on lawn, points off R]:
I see Big Mama!

[Hurries off L. and reappears shortly in hall.]

GOOPER [hurrying into hall]:
She's gone round the gall'ry to Big Daddy's room. Hey, Mama!

[Off:]

Hey, Big Mama! Come here!

MAE [calls]:
Hush, Gooper! Don't holler, go to her!

[Gooper and Reverend Tooker now appear together in hall. Big Mama runs in from DR, carrying a glass of milk. She X past Dr. Baugh to Mae, on R gallery. Dr. Baugh turns away.]

BIG MAMA:
Here I am! What d'you all want with me?

GOOPER [*steps toward Big Mama*]:
Big Mama, I told you we got to have this talk.

BIG MAMA:
What talk you talkin' about? I saw the light go on in Big
Daddy's bedroom an' took him his glass of milk, an' he just
shut the shutters right in my face.

[*Steps into room through R door.*]

When old couples have been together as long as me an' Big
Daddy, they, they get irritable with each other just from too
much—devotion! Isn't that so?

[*X below wicker seat to RC area.*]

MARGARET [*X to Big Mama, embracing her*]:
Yes, of course it's so.

[*Brick starts out UC through hall, but sees Gooper and
Reverend Tooker entering, so he hobbles through C out DS
door and onto gallery.*]

BIG MAMA:
I think Big Daddy was just worn out. He loves his fam'ly. He
loves to have 'em around him, but it's a strain on his nerves.
He wasn't himself tonight, Brick—

[*XC toward Brick. Brick passes her on his way out, DS.*]

Big Daddy wasn't himself, I could tell he was all worked up.

REVEREND TOOKER [*USC*]:
I think he's remarkable.

BIG MAMA:
Yaiss! Just remarkable.

[*Faces US, turns, X to bar, puts down glass of milk.*]

453

Did you notice all the food he ate at that table?

[*XR a bit.*]

Why he ate like a hawss!

GOOPER [*USC*]:
I hope he don't regret it.

BIG MAMA [*turns US toward Gooper*]:
What! Why that man ate a huge piece of cawn bread with molassess on it! Helped himself twice to hoppin' john!

MARGARET [*X to Big Mama*]:
Bid Daddy loves hoppin' john. We had a real country dinner.

BIG MAMA:
Yais, he simply adores it! An' candied yams. Son—

[*X to DS door, looking out at Brick. Margaret X above Big Mama to her L.*]

That man put away enough food at that table to stuff a field hand.

GOOPER:
I hope he don't have to pay for it later on.

BIG MAMA [*turns US*]:
What's that, Gooper?

MAE:
Gooper says he hopes Big Daddy doesn't suffer tonight.

BIG MAMA [*turns to Margaret, DC*]:
Oh, shoot, Gooper says, Gooper says! Why should Big Daddy suffer for satisfyin' a nawmal appetite? There's nothin' wrong with that man but nerves; he's sound as a dollar! An' now he knows he is, an' that's why he ate such a supper. He had a big

load off his mind, knowin' he wasn't doomed to—what—he
thought he was—doomed t'—

[*She wavers.*]

[*Margaret puts her arms around Big Mama.*]

GOOPER [*urging Mae forward*]:
MAE!

[*Mae runs forward below wicker seat. She stands below
Big Mama, Margaret above Big Mama. They help her to
the wicker seat. Big Mama sits. Margaret sits above her.
Mae stands behind her.*]

MARGARET:
Bless his ole sweet soul.

BIG MAMA:
Yes—bless his heart.

BRICK [*DS on gallery, looking out front*]:
Hello, moon, I envy you, you cool son of a bitch.

BIG MAMA:
I want Brick!

MARGARET:
He just stepped out for some fresh air.

BIG MAMA:
Honey! I want Brick!

MAE:
Bring li'l Brother in here so we cin talk.

[*Margaret rises, X through DS door to Brick on gallery.*]

BRICK [*to the moon*]:
I envy you—you cool son of a bitch.

455

MARGARET:
Brick, what're you doin' out here on the gall'ry, baby?

BRICK:
Admirin' an' complimentin' th' man in the moon.

[*Mae X to Dr. Baugh on R gallery. Reverend Tooker and Gooper move R UC, looking at Big Mama.*]

MARGARET [*to Brick*]:
Come in, baby. They're gettin' ready to tell Big Mama the truth.

BRICK:
I can't witness that thing in there.

MAE:
Doc Baugh, d'you think those vitamin B$_{12}$ injections are all they're cracked up t'be?

[*Enters room to upper side, behind wicker seat.*]

DOCTOR BAUGH [*X to below wicker seat*]:
Well, I guess they're as good t'be stuck with as anything else.

[*Looks at watch; X through to LC.*]

MARGARET [*to Brick*]:
Big Mama needs you!

BRICK:
I can't witness that thing in there!

BIG MAMA:
What's wrong here? You all have such long faces, you sit here waitin' for somethin' like a bomb—to go off.

GOOPER:
We're waitin' for Brick an' Maggie to come in for this talk.

MARGARET [*X above Brick, to his R*]:
Brother Man an' Mae have got a trick up their sleeves, an' if
you don't go in there t'help Big Mama, y'know what I'm
goin' to do—?

BIG MAMA:
Talk. Whispers! Whispers!

[*Looks out DR.*]

Brick! . . .

MARGARET [*answering Big Mama's call*]:
Comin', Big Mama!

[*To Brick.*]

I'm going' to take every dam' bottle on this place an' pitch
it off th' levee into th' river!

BIG MAMA:
Never had this sort of atmosphere here before.

MAE [*sits above Big Mama on wicker seat*]:
Before what, Big Mama?

BIG MAMA:
This occasion. What's Brick an' Maggie doin' out there now?

GOOPER [*X DC, looks out*]:
They seem to be havin' some little altercation.

[*Brick X toward DS step. Maggie moves R above him to
portal DR. Reverend Tooker joins Dr. Baugh, LC.*]

BIG MAMA [*taking a pill from pill box on chain at her
wrist*]:

Give me a little somethin' to wash this tablet down with.
Smell of burnt fireworks always makes me sick.

457

[*Mae X to bar to pour glass of water. Dr. Baugh joins her. Gooper X to Reverend Tooker, LC.*]

BRICK [*to Maggie*]:
You're a live cat, aren't you?

MARGARET:
You're dam' right I am!

BIG MAMA:
Gooper, will y'please open that hall door—an' let some air circulate in this stiflin' room?

[*Gooper starts US, but is restrained by Mae who X through C with glass of water. Gooper turns to men DLC.*]

MAE [*X to Big Mama with water, sits above her*]:
Big Mama, I think we ought to keep that door closed till after we talk.

BIG MAMA:
I swan!

[*Drinks water. Washes down pill.*]

MAE:
I just don't think we ought to take any chance of Big Daddy hearin' a word of this discussion.

BIG MAMA [*hands glass to Mae*]:
What discussion of what? Maggie! Brick! Nothin' is goin' to be said in th' house of Big Daddy Pollitt that he can't hear if he wants to!

[*Mae rises, X to bar, puts down glass, joins Gooper and the two men, LC.*]

BRICK:
How long are you goin' to stand behind me, Maggie?

458

MARGARET:
Forever, if necessary.

[*Brick X US to R gallery door.*]

BIG MAMA:
Brick!

[*Mae rises, looks out DS, sits.*]

GOOPER:
That boy's gone t'pieces—he's just gone t'pieces.

DOCTOR BAUGH:
Y'know, in my day they used to have somethin' they called
the Keeley cure for drinkers.

BIG MAMA:
Shoot!

DOCTOR BAUGH:
But nowadays, I understand they take some kind of tablets that
kill their taste for the stuff.

GOOPER [*turns to Dr. Baugh*]:
Call 'em antibust pills.

BIG MAMA:
Brick don't need to take nothin'. That boy is just broken up
over Skipper's death. You know how poor Skipper died. They
gave him a big, big dose of that sodium amytal stuff at his
home an' then they called the ambulance an' give him another
big, big dose of it at th' hospital an' that an' all the alcohol
in his system fo' months an' months just proved too much for
his heart an' his heart quit beatin'. I'm scared of needles! I'm
more scared of a needle than th' knife—

[*Brick has entered the room to behind the wicker seat. He*

459

rests his hand on Big Mama's head. Gooper has moved a bit URC, facing Big Mama.]

BIG MAMA:
Oh! Here's Brick! My precious baby!

[Dr. Baugh X to bar, puts down drink. Brick X below Big Mama through C to bar.]

BRICK:
Take it, Gooper!

MAE [*rising*]:
What?

BRICK:
Gooper knows what. Take it, Gooper!

[Mae turns to Gooper URC. Dr. Baugh X to Reverend Tooker. Margaret, who has followed Brick US on R gallery before he entered the room, now enters room, to behind wicker seat.]

BIG MAMA [*to Brick*]:
You just break my heart.

BRICK [*at bar*]:
Sorry—anyone else?

MARGARET:
Brick, sit with Big Mama an' hold her hand while we talk.

BRICK:
You do that, Maggie. I'm a restless cripple. I got to stay on my crutch.

[Mae sits above Big Mama. Gooper moves in front, below, and sits on couch, facing Big Mama. Reverend Tooker closes in to RC. Dr. Baugh XDC, faces upstage, smoking cigar. Margaret turns away to R doors.]

460

BIG MAMA:

Why're you all *surroundin'* me?—like this? Why're you all starin' at me like this an' makin' signs at each other?

[*Brick hobbles out hall door and X along R gallery.*]

I don't need nobody to hold my hand. Are you all crazy? Since when did Big Daddy or me need anybody—?

[*Reverend Tooker moves behind wicker seat.*]

MAE:

Calm yourself, Big Mama.

BIG MAMA:

Calm you'self *you'self*, Sister Woman! How could I calm myself with everyone starin' at me as if big drops of blood had broken out on m'face? What's all this about annh! What?

GOOPER:

Doc Baugh—

[*Mae rises.*]

Sit down, Mae—

[*Mae sits.*]

—Big Mama wants to know the complete truth about th' report we got today from the Ochsner Clinic!

[*Dr. Baugh buttons his coat, faces group at RC.*]

BIG MAMA:

Is there somethin'—somethin' that I don't know?

DOCTOR BAUGH:

Yes—well . . .

BIG MAMA [*rises*]:

I—want to—*knowwwww!*

[*X to Dr. Baugh.*]

Somebody must be lyin'! *I want to know!*

[*Mae, Gooper, Reverend Tooker surround Big Mama.*]

MAE:
Sit down, Big Mama, sit down on this sofa!

[*Brick has passed Margaret Xing DR on gallery.*]

MARGARET:
Brick! Brick!

BIG MAMA:
What is it, what is it?

[*Big Mama drives Dr. Baugh a bit DLC. Others follow, surrounding Big Mama.*]

DOCTOR BAUGH:
I never have seen a more thorough examination than Big Daddy Pollitt was given in all my experience at the Ochsner Clinic.

GOOPER:
It's one of th' best in th' country.

MAE:
It's *THE* best in th' country—bar none!

DOCTOR BAUGH:
Of course they were ninety-nine and nine-tenths per cent certain before they even started.

BIG MAMA:
Sure of what, sure of what, sure of what—*what!?*

MAE:
Now, Mommy, be a brave girl!

BRICK [*on DR gallery, covers his ears, sings*]:
"*By the light, by the light, of the silvery moon!*"

GOOPER [*breaks DR. Calls out to Brick*]:
Shut up, Brick!

[*Returns to group LC.*]

BRICK:
Sorry . . .

[*Continues singing.*]

DOCTOR BAUGH:
But now, you see, Big Mama, they cut a piece off this growth,
a specimen of the tissue, an'——

BIG MAMA:
Growth? You told Big Daddy——

DOCTOR BAUGH:
Now, wait——

BIG MAMA:
You told me an' Big Daddy there wasn't a thing wrong with
him but——

MAE:
Big Mama, they always——

GOOPER:
Let Doc Baugh talk, will yuh?

BIG MAMA:
——little spastic condition of——

REVEREND TOOKER [*throughout all this*]:
Shh! Shh! Shh!

[*Big Mama breaks UC, they all follow.*]

DOCTOR BAUGH:
Yes, that's what we told Big Daddy. But we had this bit of tissue run through the laboratory an' I'm sorry t'say the test was positive on it. It's malignant.

[*Pause.*]

BIG MAMA:
Cancer! Cancer!

MAE:
Now now, Mommy—

GOOPER [*at the same time*]:
You had to know, Big Mama.

BIG MAMA:
Why didn't they cut it out of him? Hanh? Hannh?

DOCTOR BAUGH:
Involved too much, Big Mama, too many organs affected.

MAE:
Big Mama, the liver's affected, an' so's the kidneys, both. It's gone way past what they call a—

GOOPER:
—a surgical risk.

[*Big Mama gasps.*]

REVEREND TOOKER:
Tch, tch, tch.

DOCTOR BAUGH:
Yes, it's gone past the knife.

MAE:
That's why he's turned yellow!

[*Brick stops singing, turns away UR on gallery.*]

464

BIG MAMA [*pushes Mae DS*]:
Git away from me, git away from me, Mae!

[*XDSR.*]

I want Brick! Where's Brick! *Where's my only son?*

MAE [*a step after Big Mama*]:
Mama! Did she say "only" son?

GOOPER [*following Big Mama*]:
What does that make me?

MAE [*above Gooper*]:
A sober responsible man with five precious children—*six!*

BIG MAMA:
I want Brick! Brick! Brick!

MARGARET [*a step to Big Mama above couch*]:
Mama, let *me* tell you.

BIG MAMA [*pushing her aside*]:
No, no, leave me alone, you're not my blood!

[*She rushes onto the DS gallery.*]

GOOPER [*X to Big Mama on gallery*]:
Mama! I'm your son! Listen to me!

MAE:
Gooper's your son, Mama, he's your first-born!

BIG MAMA:
Gooper never liked Daddy!

MAE:
That's not true!

465

REVEREND TOOKER [*UC*]:
I think I'd better slip away at this point. Good night, good night everybody, and God bless you all—on this place.

[*Goes out through hall.*]

DOCTOR BAUGH [*XDR to above DS door*]:
Well, Big Mama—

BIG MAMA [*leaning against Gooper, on lower gallery*]:
It's all a mistake, I know it's just a bad dream.

DOCTOR BAUGH:
We're gonna keep Big Daddy as comfortable as we can.

BIG MAMA:
Yes, it's just a bad dream, that's all it is, it's just an awful dream.

GOOPER:
In my opinion Big Daddy is havin' some pain but won't admit that he has it.

BIG MAMA:
Just a dream, a bad dream.

DOCTOR BAUGH:
That's what lots of 'em do, they think if they don't admit they're havin' the pain they can sort of escape th' fact of it.

[*Brick X US on R gallery. Margaret watches him from R doors.*]

GOOPER:
Yes, they get sly about it, get real sly about it.

MAE [*X to R of Dr. Baugh*]:
Gooper an' I think—

GOOPER:

Shut up, Mae!—Big Mama, I really do think Big Daddy should be started on morphine.

BIG MAMA [*pulling away from Gooper*]:

Nobody's goin't to give Big Daddy morphine!

DOCTOR BAUGH:

Now, Big Mama, when that pain strikes it's goin' to strike mighty hard an' Big Daddy's goin' t'need the needle to bear it.

BIG MAMA [*X to Dr. Baugh*]:

I tell you, nobody's goin' to give him morphine!

MAE:

Big Mama, you don't want to see Big Daddy suffer, y'know y'—

DOCTOR BAUGH [*X to bar*]:

Well, I'm leavin' this stuff here

[*Puts packet of morphine, etc., on bar.*]

so if there's a sudden attack you won't have to send out for it.

[*Big Mama hurries to L side bar.*]

MAE [*X C, below Dr. Baugh*]:

I know how to give a hypo.

BIG MAMA:

Nobody's goin' to give Big Daddy morphine!

GOOPER [*X C*]:

Mae took a course in nursin' durin' th' war.

MARGARET:

Somehow I don't think Big Daddy would want Mae t'give him a hypo.

MAE [*to Margaret*]:
You think he'd want *you* to do it?

DOCTOR BAUGH:
Well—

GOOPER:
Well, Doc Baugh is goin'—

DOCTOR BAUGH:
Yes, I got to be goin'. Well, keep your chin up, Big Mama.

[*X to hall.*]

GOOPER [*as he and Mae follow Dr. Baugh into the hall*]:
She's goin' to keep her ole chin up, aren't you, Big Mama?

[*They go out L.*]

Well, Doc, we sure do appreciate all you've done. I'm telling
you, we're obligated—

BIG MAMA:
Margaret!

[*XRC.*]

MARGARET [*meeting Big Mama in front of wicker seat*]:
I'm right here, Big Mama.

BIG MAMA:
Margaret, you've got to cooperate with me an' Big Daddy to
straighten Brick out now—

GOOPER [*off L, returning with Mae*]:
I guess that Doctor has got a lot on his mind, but it wouldn't
hurt him to act a little more human—

BIG MAMA:
—because it'll break Big Daddy's heart if Brick don't pull
himself together an' take hold of things here.

[*Brick XDSR on gallery.*]

MAE [*UC, overhearing*]:
Take hold of what things, Big Mama?

BIG MAMA [*sits in wicker chair, Margaret standing behind chair*]:
The place.

GOOPER [*UC*]:
Big Mama, you've had a shock.

MAE [*X with Gooper to Big Mama*]:
Yais, we've all had a shock, but—

GOOPER:
Let's be realistic—

MAE:
Big Daddy would not, would *never*, be foolish enough to—

GOOPER:
—put this place in irresponsible hands!

BIG MAMA:
Big Daddy ain't goin' t'put th' place in anybody's hands, Big Daddy is *not* goin' t'die! I want you to git that into your haids, all of you!

[*Mae sits above Big Mama, Margaret turns R to door, Gooper X L C a bit.*]

•MAE:
Mommy, Mommy, Big Mama, we're just as hopeful an' optimistic as you are about Big Daddy's prospects, we have faith in prayer—but nevertheless there are certain matters that have to be discussed an' dealt with, because otherwise—

GOOPER:
Mae, will y'please get my briefcase out of our room?

469

MAE:
Yes, honey.

[*Rises, goes out through hall L.*]

MARGARET [*X to Brick on DS gallery*]:
Hear them in there?

[*X back to R gallery door.*]

GOOPER [*stands above Big Mama. Leaning over her*]:
Big Mama, what you said just now was not at all true, an' you
know it. I've always loved Big Daddy in my own quiet way.
I never made a show of it. I know that Big Daddy has always
been fond of me in a quiet way, too.

[*Margaret drifts UR on gallery. Mae returns, X to Gooper's
L with briefcase.*]

MAE:
Here's your briefcase, Gooper, honey.

[*Hands it to him.*]

GOOPER [*hands briefcase back to Mae*]:
Thank you. Of ca'use, my relationship with Big Daddy is
different from Brick's.

MAE:
You're eight years older'n Brick an' always had t'carry a bigger
load of th' responsibilities than Brick ever had t'carry; he
never carried a thing in his life but a football or a highball.

GOOPER:
Mae, will y'let me talk, please?

MAE:
Yes, honey.

GOOPER:

Now, a twenty-eight thousand acre plantation's a mighty big thing t'run.

MAE:

Almost single-handed!

BIG MAMA:

You never had t'run this place, Brother Man, what're you talkin' about, as if Big Daddy was dead an' in his grave, you had to run it? Why, you just had t'help him out with a few business details an' had your law practice at the same time in Memphis.

MAE:

Oh, Mommy, Mommy, Mommy! Let's be fair! Why, Gooper has given himself body and soul t'keepin' this place up fo' the past five years since Big Daddy's health started fallin'. Gooper won't say it, Gooper never thought of it as a duty, he just did it. An' what did Brick do? Brick kep' livin' in his past glory at college!

[Gooper places a restraining hand on Mae's leg; Margaret drifts DS in gallery.]

GOOPER:

Still a football player at twenty-seven!

MARGARET *[bursts into UR door]*:

Who are you talkin' about now? Brick? A football player? He isn't a football player an' you know it! Brick is a sports announcer on TV an' one of the best-known ones in the country!

MAE *[breaks UC]*:

I'm talkin' about what he was!

471

MARGARET [*X to above lower gallery door*]:
Well, I wish you would just stop talkin' about my husband!

GOOPER [*X to above Margaret*]:
Listen, Margaret, I've got a right to discuss my own brother with other members of my own fam'ly, which don't include *you!*

[*Pokes finger at her; she slaps his finger away.*]

Now, why don't you go on out there an' drink with Brick?

MARGARET:
I've never seen such malice toward a brother.

GOOPER:
How about his for me? Why can't he stand to be in the same room with me!

BRICK [*on lower gallery*]:
That's the truth!

MARGARET:
This is a deliberate campaign of vilification for the most disgusting and sordid reason on earth, and I know what it is! *It's avarice, avarice, greed, greed!*

BIG MAMA:
Oh, I'll scream, I will scream in a moment unless this stops! Margaret, child, come here, sit next to Big Mama.

MARGARET [*X to Big Mama, sits above her*]:
Precious Mommy.

[*Gooper X to bar.*]

MAE:
How beautiful, how touchin' this display of devotion! Do you know why she's childless? She's childless because that big,

472

beautiful athlete husband of hers won't go to bed with her, that's why!

[*X to L of bed, looks at Gooper.*]

GOOPER:
You jest won't let me do this the nice way, will yuh? Aw right—

[*X to above wicker seat.*]

I don't give a goddam if Big Daddy likes me or don't like me or did or never did or will or will never! I'm just appealin' to a sense of common decency an' fair play! I'm tellin' you th' truth—

[*X DS through lower door to Brick on DR gallery.*]

I've resented Big Daddy's partiality to Brick ever since th' goddam day you were born, son, an' th' way I've been treated, like I was just barely good enough to spit on, an' sometimes not even good enough for that.

[*X back through room to above wicker seat.*]

Big Daddy is dyin' of cancer an' it's spread all through him an' it's attacked all his vital organs includin' the kidneys an' right now he is sinkin' into uremia, an' you all know what uremia is, it's poisonin' of the whole system due to th' failure of th' body to eliminate its poisons.

MARGARET:
Poisons, poisons, venomous thoughts and words! In hearts and minds! That's poisons!

GOOPER:
I'm askin' for a square deal an' by God I expect to get one. But if I don't get one, if there's any peculiar shenanigans

473

goin' on around here behind my back, well I'm not a corporation lawyer for nothin!

[*XDS toward lower gallery door, on apex.*]

I know how to protect my own interests.

[*Rumble of distant thunder.*]

BRICK [*entering the room through DS door*]:
Storm comin' up.

GOOPER:
Oh, a late arrival!

MAE [*X through C to below bar, LCO*]:
Behold, the conquerin' hero comes!

GOOPER [*X through C to bar, following Brick, imitating his limp*]:
The fabulous Brick Pollitt! Remember him? Who could forget him?

MAE:
He looks like he's been injured in a game!

GOOPER:
Yep, I'm afraid you'll have to warm th' bench at the Sugar Bowl this year, Brick! Or was it the Rose Bowl that he made his famous run in.

[*Another rumble of thunder, sound of wind rising.*]

MAE [*X to L of Brick, who has reached the bar*]:
The punch bowl, honey, it was the punch bowl, the cut-glass punch bowl!

GOOPER:
That's right! I'm always gettin' the boy's *bowls* mixed up!

[*Pats Brick on the butt.*]

MARGARET [*rushes at Gooper, striking him*]:

Stop that! You stop that!

[*Thunder.*]

[*Mae X toward Margaret from L of Gooper, flails at Margaret; Gooper keeps the women apart. Lacey runs through the US lawn area in a raincoat.*]

DAISY and SOOKEY [*off UL*]:
Storm! Storm comin! Storm! Storm!

LACEY [*running out UR*]:
Brightie, close them shutters!

GOOPER [*X onto R gallery, calls after Lacey*]:
Lacey, put the top up on my Cadillac, will yuh?

LACEY [*off R*]:
Yes, sur, Mistah Pollit!

GOOPER [*X to above Big Mama*]:
Big Mama, you know it's goin' to be necessary for me t'go back to Memphis in th' mornin' t'represent the Parker estate in a lawsuit.

[*Mae sits on L side bed, arranges papers she removes from briefcase.*]

BIG MAMA:
Is it, Gooper?

MAE:
Yaiss.

GOOPER:
That's why I'm forced to—to bring up a problem that—

MAE:
Somethin' that's too important t' be put off!

GOOPER:
If Brick was sober, he ought to be in on this. I think he ought
to be present when I present this plan.

MARGARET [*UC*]:
Brick is present, we're present!

GOOPER:
Well, good. I will now give you this outline my partner, Tom
Bullit, an' me have drawn up—a sort of dummy—trustee-
ship!

MARGARET:
Oh, that's it! You'll be in charge an' dole out remittances,
will you?

GOOPER:
This we did as soon as we got the report on Big Daddy from
th' Ochsner Laboratories. We did this thing, I mean we drew
up this dummy outline with the advice and assistance of the
Chairman of the Boa'd of Directors of th' Southern Plantuhs
Bank and Trust Company in Memphis, C. C. Bellowes, a man
who handles estates for all th' prominent fam'lies in West
Tennessee and th' Delta!

BIG MAMA:
Gooper?

GOOPER [*X behind seat to below Big Mama*]:
Now this is not—not final, or anything like it, this is just a
preliminary outline. But it does provide a—basis—a design—
a—possible, feasible—*plan!*

[*He waves papers Mae has thrust into his hand, US.*]

476

MARGARET [*XDL*]:
Yes, I'll bet it's a plan!

[*Thunder rolls. Interior lighting dims.*]

MAE:
It's a plan to protect the biggest estate in the Delta from irresponsibility an'—

BIG MAMA:
Now you listen to me, all of you, you listen here! They's not
goin' to be no more catty talk in my house! And Gooper,
you put that away before I grab it out of your hand and tear
it right up! I don't know what the hell's in it, and I don't want
to know what the hell's in it. I'm talkin' in Big Daddy's
language now, I'm his *wife,* not his *widow,* I'm still his *wife!*
And I'm talkin' to you in his language an'—

GOOPER:
Big Mama, what I have here is—

MAE:
Gooper explained that it's just a plan . . .

BIG MAMA:
I don't care what you got there, just put it back where it come
from an' don't let me see it again, not even the outside of the
envelope of it! Is that understood? Basis! Plan! Preliminary!
Design!—I say—what is it that Big Daddy always says when
he's disgusted?

[*Storm clouds race across sky.*]

BRICK [*from bar*]:
Big Daddy says "crap" when he is disgusted.

BIG MAMA [*rising*]:
That's right—*CRAPPPP!* I say *CRAP* too, like Big Daddy!

477

[*Thunder rolls.*]

MAE:
Coarse language don't seem called for in this—

GOOPER:
Somethin' in me is *deeply outraged* by this.

BIG MAMA:
Nobody's goin' to do nothin'! till Big Daddy lets go of it, and maybe just possibly not—not even then! No, not even then!

[*Thunder clap. Glass crash, off L.*

[*Off UR, children commence crying. Many storm sounds, L and R: barnyard animals in terror, papers crackling, shutters rattling. Sookey and Daisy hurry from L to R in lawn area. Inexplicably, Daisy hits together two leather pillows. They cry, "Storm! Storm!" Sookey waves a piece of wrapping paper to cover lawn furniture. Mae exits to hall and upper gallery. Strange man runs across lawn, R to L.*

[*Thunder rolls repeatedly.*]

MAE:
Sookey, hurry up an' git that po'ch fu'niture covahed; want th' paint to come off?

[*Starts DR on gallery.*

[*Gooper runs through hall to R gallery.*]

GOOPER [*yells to Lacey, who appears from R*]:
Lacey, put mah car away!

LACEY:
Cain't, Mistah Pollit, you got the kevs!

[*Exit US.*]

GOOPER:
Naw, you got 'em, man.

[*Exit DR. Reappears UR, calls to Mae:*]

Where th' keys to th' car, honey?

[*Runs C.*]

MAE [*DR on gallery*]:
You got 'em in your pocket!

[*Exit DR.*

[*Gooper exits UR. Dog howls. Daisy and Sookey sing off UR to comfort children. Mae is heard placating the children.*

[*Storm fades away.*

[*During the storm, Margaret X and sits on couch, DR. Big Mama X DC.*]

BIG MAMA:
BRICK! Come here, Brick, I need you.

[*Thunder distantly.*

[*Children whimper, off L Mae consoles them. Brick X to R of Big Mama.*]

BIG MAMA:
Tonight Brick looks like he used to look when he was a little boy just like he did when he played wild games in the orchard back of the house and used to come home when I hollered myself hoarse for him! all—sweaty—and pink-cheeked—an' sleepy with his curls shinin'—

[*Thunder distantly.*

479

[*Children whimper, off L Mae consoles them. Dog howls, off.*]

Time goes by so fast. Nothin' can outrun it. Death commences too early—almost before you're half-acquainted with life—you meet with the other. Oh, you know we just got to love each other, an' stay together all of us just as close as we can, specially now that such a *black* thing has come and moved into this place without invitation.

[*Dog howls, off.*]

Oh, Brick, son of Big Daddy, Big Daddy does so love you. Y'know what would be his fondest dream come true? If before he passed on, if Big Daddy has to pass on ...

[*Dog howls, off.*]

You give him a child of yours, a grandson as much like his son as his son is like Big Daddy. . . .

MARGARET:
I know that's Big Daddy's dream.

BIG MAMA:
That's his dream.

BIG DADDY [*off DR on gallery*]:
Looks like the wind was takin' liberties with this place.

[*Lacey appears UL, X to UC in lawn area; Brightie and Small appear UR on lawn. Big Daddy X onto the UR gallery.*]

LACEY:
Evenin', Mr. Pollitt.

BRIGHTIE and SMALL:
Evenin', Cap'n. Hello, Cap'n.

MARGARET [*X to R door*]:
Big Daddy's on the gall'ry.

BIG DADDY:
Stawm crossed th' river, Lacey?

LACEY:
Gone to Arkansas, Cap'n.

[*Big Mama has turned toward the hall door at the sound of Big Daddy's voice on the gallery. Now she X's DSR and out the DS door onto the gallery.*]

BIG MAMA:
I can't stay here. He'll see somethin' in my eyes.

BIG DADDY [*on upper gallery, to the boys*]:
Stawm done any damage around here?

BRIGHTIE:
Took the po'ch off ole Aunt Crawley's house.

BIG DADDY:
Ole Aunt Crawley should of been settin' on it. It's time fo' th' wind to blow that ole girl away!

[*Field hands laugh, exit, UR. Big Daddy enters room, UC, hall door.*]

Can I come in?

[*Puts his cigar in ash tray on bar.*

[*Mae and Gooper hurry along the upper gallery and stand behind Big Daddy in hall door.*]

MARGARET:
Did the storm wake you up, Big Daddy?

481

BIG DADDY:

Which stawm are you talkin' about—th' one outside or th' hullaballoo in here?

[*Gooper squeezes past Big Daddy.*]

GOOPER [*X toward bed, where legal papers are strewn*]: 'Scuse me, sir . . .

[*Mae tries to squeeze past Big Daddy to join Gooper, but Big Daddy puts his arm firmly around her.*]

BIG DADDY:

I heard some mighty loud talk. Sounded like somethin' important was bein' discussed. What was the powwow about?

MAE [*flustered*]:

Why—nothin', Big Daddy . . .

BIG DADDY [*XDLC, taking Mae with him*]:

What is that pregnant-lookin' envelope you're puttin' back in your briefcase, Gooper?

GOOPER [*at foot of bed, caught, as he stuffs papers into envelope*]:

That? Nothin', suh—nothin' much of anythin' at all . . .

BIG DADDY:

Nothin'? It looks like a whole lot of nothing!

[*Turns US to group:*]

You all know th' story about th' young married couple—

GOOPER:

Yes, sir!

BIG DADDY:

Hello, Brick—

BRICK:
Hello, Big Daddy.

[*The group is arranged in a semicircle above Big Daddy, Margaret at the extreme R, then Mae and Gooper, then Big Mama, with Brick at L.*]

BIG DADDY:
Young married couple took Junior out to th' zoo one Sunday, inspected all of God's creatures in their cages, with satisfaction.

GOOPER:
Satisfaction.

BIG DADDY [*XUSC, face front*]:
This afternoon was a warm afternoon in spring an' that ole elephant had somethin' else on his mind which was bigger'n peanuts. You know this story, Brick?

[*Gooper nods.*]

BRICK:
No, sir, I don't know it.

BIG DADDY:
Y'see, in th' cage adjoinin' they was a young female elephant in heat!

BIG MAMA [*at Big Daddy's shoulder*]:
Oh, Big Daddy!

BIG DADDY:
What's the matter, preacher's gone, ain't he? All right. That female elephant in the next cage was permeatin' the atmosphere about her with a powerful and excitin' odor of female fertility! Huh! Ain't that a nice way to put it, Brick?

483

BRICK:

Yes, sir, nothin' wrong with it.

BIG DADDY:

Brick says the's nothin' wrong with it!

BIG MAMA:

Oh, Big Daddy!

BIG DADDY [*XDSC*]:

So this ole bull elephant still had a couple of fornications left in him. He reared back his trunk an' got a whiff of that elephant lady next door!—began to paw at the dirt in his cage an' butt his head against the separatin' partition and, first thing y'know, there was a conspicuous change in his *profile*—very *conspicuous!* Ain't I tellin' this story in decent language, Brick?

BRICK:

Yes, sir, too ruttin' decent!

BIG DADDY:

So, the little boy pointed at it and said, "What's that?" His Mam said, "Oh, that's—nothin'!"—His Papa said, "She's spoiled!"

[*Field-hands sing off R, featuring Sookey: "I Just Can't Stay Here by Myself," through following scene.*

[*Big Daddy X to Brick at L.*]

BIG DADDY:

You didn't laugh at that story, Brick.

[*Big Mama X DRC crying. Margaret goes to her. Mae and Gooper hold URC.*]

BRICK:

No, sir, I didn't laugh at that story.

[*On the lower gallery, Big Mama sobs. Big Daddy looks toward her.*]

BIG DADDY:

What's wrong with that long, thin woman over there, loaded with diamonds? Hey, what's-your-name, what's the matter with you?

MARGARET [*X toward Big Daddy*]:

She had a slight dizzy spell, Big Daddy.

BIG DADDY [*ULC*]:

You better watch that, Big Mama. A stroke is a bad way to go.

MARGARET [*X to Big Daddy at C*]:

Oh, Brick, Big Daddy has on your birthday present to him, Brick, he has on your cashmere robe, the softest material I have ever felt.

BIG DADDY:

Yeah, this is my soft birthday, Maggie. . . .

Not my gold or my silver birthday, but my soft birthday, everything's got to be soft for Big Daddy on this soft birthday.

[*Maggie kneels before Big Daddy C. As Gooper and Mae speak, Big Mama X USRC in front of them, hushing them with a gesture.*]

GOOPER:

Maggie, I hate to make such a crude observation, but there is somethin' a little indecent about your—

MAE:

Like a slow-motion football tackle—

MARGARET:

Big Daddy's got on his Chinese slippers that I gave him, Brick. Big Daddy, I haven't given you my big present yet, but now

485

I will, now's the time for me to present it to you! I have an announcement to make!

MAE:
What? What kind of announcement?

GOOPER:
A sports announcement, Maggie?

MARGARET:
Announcement of life beginning! A child is coming, sired by Brick, and out of Maggie the Cat! I have Brick's child in my body, an' that's my birthday present to Big Daddy on this birthday!

[*Big Daddy looks at Brick who X behind Big Daddy to DS portal, L.*]

BIG DADDY:
Get up, girl, get up off your knees, girl.

[*Big Daddy helps Margaret rise. He X above her, to her R, bites off the end of a fresh cigar, taken from his bathrobe pocket, as he studies Margaret.*]

Uh-huh, this girl has life in her body, that's no lie!

BIG MAMA:
BIG DADDY'S DREAM COME TRUE!

BRICK:
JESUS!

BIG DADDY [*X R below wicker seat*]:
Gooper, I want my lawyer in the mornin'.

BRICK:
Where are you goin', Big Daddy?

BIG DADDY:
Son, I'm goin' up on the roof to the belvedere on th' roof to look over my kingdom before I give up my kingdom—twenty-eight thousand acres of th' richest land this side of the Valley Nile!

[*Exit through R doors, and DR on gallery.*]

BIG MAMA [*following*]:
Sweetheart, sweetheart, sweetheart—can I come with you?

[*Exits DR.*

[*Margaret is DSC in mirror area.*]

GOOPER [*X to bar*]:
Brick, could you possibly spare me one small shot of that liquor?

BRICK [*DLC*]:
Why, help yourself, Gooper boy.

GOOPER:
I will.

MAE [*X forward*]:
Of course we know that this is a lie!

GOOPER [*drinks*]:
Be still, Mae!

MAE [*X to Gooper at bar*]:
I won't be still! I know she's made this up!

GOOPER:
God damn it, I said to shut up!

MAE:
That woman isn't pregnant!

487

GOOPER:
Who said she was?

MAE:
She did!

GOOPER:
The doctor didn't. Doc Baugh didn't.

MARGARET [*X R to above couch*]:
I haven't gone to Doc Baugh.

GOOPER [*X through to L of Margaret*]:
Then who'd you go to, Maggie?

[*Offstage song finishes.*]

MARGARET:
One of the best gynecologists in the South.

GOOPER:
Uh-huh, I see—

[*Foot on end of couch, trapping Margaret:*]

May we have his name please?

MARGARET:
No, you may not, Mister—Prosecutin' Attorney!

MAE [*X to R of Margaret, above*]:
He doesn't have any name, he doesn't exist!

MARGARET:
He does so exist, and so does my baby, Brick's baby!

MAE:
You can't conceive a child by a man that won't sleep with you unless you think you're—

[*Forces Margaret onto couch, turns away C.*

[*Brick starts C for Mae.*]

He drinks all the time to be able to tolerate you! Sleeps on the sofa to keep out of contact with you!

GOOPER [*X above Margaret, who lies face down on couch*]:
Don't try to kid us, Margaret—

MAE [*X to bed, L side, rumpling pillows*]:
How can you conceive a child by a man that won't sleep with you? How can you conceive? How can you? How can you!

GOOPER [*sharply*]:
MAE!

BRICK [*X below Mae to her R, takes hold of her*]:
Mae, Sister Woman, how d'you know that I don't sleep with Maggie?

MAE:
We occupy the next room an' th' wall between isn't soundproof.

BRICK:
Oh . . .

MAE:
We hear the nightly pleadin' and the nightly refusal. So don't imagine you're goin' t'put a trick over on us, to fool a dyin' man with—a—

BRICK:
Mae, Sister Woman, not everybody makes much noise about love. Oh, I know some people are huffers an' puffers, but others are silent lovers.

GOOPER [*behind seat, R*]:
This talk is pointless, completely.

489

BRICK:

How d'y'know that we're not silent lovers?

Even if y'got a peep-hole drilled in the wall, how can y'tell if sometime when Gooper's got business in Memphis an' you're playin' scrabble at the country club with other ex-queens of cotton, Maggie and I don't come to some temporary agreement? How do you know that—?

[*He X above wicker seat to above R end couch.*]

MAE:

Brick, I never thought that you would stoop to her level, I just never dreamed that you would stoop to her level.

GOOPER:

I don't think Brick will stoop to her level.

BRICK [*sits R of Margaret on couch*]:

What is your level? Tell me your level so I can sink or rise to it.

[*Rises.*]

You heard what Big Daddy said. This girl has life in her body.

MAE:

That is a lie!

BRICK:

No, truth is something desperate, an' she's got it. Believe me, it's somethin' desperate, an' she's got it.

[*X below seat to below bar.*]

An' now if you will stop actin' as if Brick Pollitt was dead an' buried, invisible, not heard, an' go on back to your peephole in the wall—I'm drunk, and sleepy—not as alive as Maggie, but still alive. . . .

490

[*Pours drink, drinks.*]

GOOPER [*picks up briefcase from R foot of bed*]:
Come on, Mae. We'll leave these love birds together in their nest.

MAE:
Yeah, nest of lice! Liars!

GOOPER:
Mae—Mae, you jes' go on back to our room—

MAE:
Liars!

[*Exits through hall.*]

GOOPER [*DR above Margaret*]:
We're jest goin' to wait an' see. Time will tell.

[*X to R of bar.*]

Yes, sir, little brother, we're just goin' to wait an' see!

[*Exit, hall.*

[*The clock strikes twelve.*

[*Maggie and Brick exchange a look. He drinks deeply, puts his glass on the bar. Gradually, his expression changes. He utters a sharp exhalation.*

[*The exhalation is echoed by the singers, off UR, who commence vocalizing with "Gimme a Cool Drink of Water Fo' I Die," and continue till end of act.*]

MARGARET [*as she hears Brick's exhalation*]:
The click?

[*Brick looks toward the singers, happily, almost gratefully. He XR to bed, picks up his pillow, and starts toward head*

491

of couch, DR, Xing above wicker seat. Margaret seizes the pillow from his grasp, rises, stands facing C, holding the pillow close. Brick watches her with growing admiration. She moves quickly USC, throwing pillow onto bed. She X to bar. Brick counters below wicker seat, watching her. Margaret grabs all the bottles from the bar. She goes into hall, pitches the bottles, one after the other, off the platform into the UL lawn area. Bottles break, off L. Margaret re-enters the room, stands UC, facing Brick.]

Echo Spring has gone dry, and no one but me could drive you to town for more.

BRICK:
Lacey will get me—

MARGARET:
Lacey's been told not to!

BRICK:
I could drive—

MARGARET:
And you lost your driver's license! I'd phone ahead and have you stopped on the highway before you got halfway to Ruby Lightfoot's gin mill. I told a lie to Big Daddy, but we can make that lie come true. And then I'll bring you liquor, and we'll get drunk together, here, tonight, in this place that death has come into! What do you say? What do you say, baby?

BRICK [*X to L side bed*]:
I admire you, Maggie.

[Brick sits on edge of bed. He looks up at the overhead light, then at Margaret. She reaches for the light, turns it out; then she kneels quickly beside Brick at foot of bed.]

492

MARGARET:

Oh, you weak, beautiful people who give up with such grace. What you need is someone to take hold of you—gently, with love, and hand your life back to you, like something gold you let go of—and I can! I'm determined to do it—and nothing's more determined than a cat on a tin roof—is there? Is there, baby?

[*She touches his cheek, gently.*]

CURTAIN

SUDDENLY LAST SUMMER

TO ANNE MEACHAM

Suddenly Last Summer, with *Something Unspoken*, were presented together under the collective title of *Garden District* at the York Theatre on First Avenue in New York on January 7, 1958, by John C. Wilson and Warner Le Roy. It was directed by Herbert Machiz; the stage set was designed by Robert Soule and the costumes by Stanley Simmons. Lighting was by Lee Watson and the incidental music was by Ned Rorem. *Something Unspoken* was added to the 1953 edition of *27 Wagons Full of Cotton and Other Plays.*

CAST OF CHARACTERS

MRS. VENABLE	HORTENSE ALDEN
DR. CUKROWICZ	ROBERT LANSING
MISS FOXHILL	DONNA CAMERON
MRS. HOLLY	ELEANOR PHELPS
GEORGE HOLLY	ALAN MIXON
CATHARINE HOLLY	ANNE MEACHAM
SISTER FELICITY	NANON-KIAM

Hortense Alden as Mrs. Venable, Robert Lansing as
Dr. Cukrowicz and Anne Meacham as Catherine Holly
in SUDDENLY LAST SUMMER. *Photo by Friedman-Abeles*

SCENE ONE

The set may be as unrealistic as the decor of a dramatic ballet. It represents part of a mansion of Victorian Gothic style in the Garden District of New Orleans on a late afternoon, between late summer and early fall. The interior is blended with a fantastic garden which is more like a tropical jungle, or forest, in the prehistoric age of giant fern-forests when living creatures had flippers turning to limbs and scales to skin. The colors of this jungle-garden are violent, especially since it is steaming with heat after rain. There are massive tree-flowers that suggest organs of a body, torn out, still glistening with undried blood; there are harsh cries and sibilant hissings and thrashing sounds in the garden as if it were inhabited by beasts, serpents and birds, all of savage nature. . . .

The jungle tumult continues a few moments after the curtain rises; then subsides into relative quiet, which is occasionally broken by a new outburst.

A lady enters with the assistance of a silver-knobbed cane. She

501

has light orange or pink hair and wears a lavender lace dress, and over her withered bosom is pinned a starfish of diamonds.

She is followed by a young blond Doctor, all in white, glacially brilliant, very, very good looking, and the old lady's manner and eloquence indicate her undeliberate response to his icy charm.

MRS. VENABLE:

Yes, this was Sebastian's garden. The Latin names of the plants were printed on tags attached to them but the print's fading out. Those ones there—[*She draws a deep breath.*]—are the oldest plants on earth, survivors from the age of the giant fern-forests. Of course in this semitropical climate—[*She takes another deep breath.*]—some of the rarest plants, such as the Venus's-flytrap—you know what this is, Doctor? The Venus's-flytrap?

DOCTOR:

An insectivorous plant?

MRS. VENABLE:

Yes, it feeds on insects. It has to be kept under glass from early fall to late spring and when it went under glass, my son, Sebastian, had to provide it with fruit flies flown in at great expense from a Florida laboratory that used fruit flies for experiments in genetics. Well, I can't do that, Doctor. [*She takes a deep breath.*] I can't, I just can't do it! It's not the expense but the—

DOCTOR:

Effort.

MRS. VENABLE:

Yes. So goodbye, Venus's-flytrap—like so much else.... Whew! ... [*She draws breath.*]—I don't know why, but—! I already feel I can lean on your shoulder, Doctor—Cu?—Cu?

DOCTOR:

Cu-kro-wicz. It's a Polish word that means sugar, so let's make it simple and call me Doctor Sugar.

[*He returns her smile.*]

MRS. VENABLE:

Well, now, Doctor Sugar, you've seen Sebastian's garden.

[*They are advancing slowly to the patio area.*]

DOCTOR:

It's like a well-groomed jungle. . . .

MRS. VENABLE:

That's how he meant it to be, nothing was accidental, every-thing was planned and designed in Sebastian's life and his— [*She dabs her forehead with her handkerchief which she had taken from her reticule.*]—work!

DOCTOR:

What was your son's work, Mrs. Venable?—besides this garden?

MRS. VENABLE:

As many times as I've had to answer that question! D'you know it still shocks me a little?—to realize that Sebastian Venable the poet is still unknown outside of a small coterie of friends, including his mother.

DOCTOR:

Oh.

MRS. VENABLE:

You see, strictly speaking, his *life* was his occupation.

DOCTOR:

I see.

MRS. VENABLE:

No, you *don't* see, yet, but before I'm through, you will.—

503

Sebastian was a poet! That's what I meant when I said his life was his work because the work of a poet is the life of a poet and—vice versa, the life of a poet is the work of a poet, I mean you can't separate them, I mean—well, for instance, a salesman's work is one thing and his life is another—or can be. The same thing's true of—doctor, lawyer, merchant, *thief*! —But a poet's life is his work and his work is his life in a special sense because—oh, I've already talked myself breathless and dizzy.

[*The Doctor offers his arm.*]

Thank you.

DOCTOR:

Mrs. Venable, did your doctor okay this thing?

MRS. VENABLE [*breathless*]:

What thing?

DOCTOR:

Your meeting this girl that you think is responsible for your son's death?

MRS. VENABLE:

I've waited months to face her because I couldn't get to St. Mary's to face her—I've had her brought here to my house. I won't collapse! She'll collapse! I mean her lies will collapse —not my truth—not the truth. . . . *Forward march, Doctor Sugar!*

[*He conducts her slowly to the patio.*]

Ah, we've *made* it, *ha ha*! I didn't know that I was so weak on my pins! Sit down, Doctor. I'm not afraid of using every last ounce and inch of my little, leftover strength in doing just what I'm doing. I'm devoting all that's left of my life, Doctor, to the defense of a dead poet's reputation. Sebastian had no public name as a poet, he didn't want one, he refused to have one. He *dreaded, abhorred*!—false values that come from being publicly known, from fame, from personal— exploitation. . . . Oh, he'd say to me: "Violet? Mother?— You're going to outlive me!!"

DOCTOR:
What made him think that?

MRS. VENABLE:
Poets are always clairvoyant!—And he had rheumatic fever when he was fifteen and it affected a heart-valve and he wouldn't stay off horses and out of water and so forth. . . . "Violet? Mother? You're going to live longer than me, and then, when I'm gone, it will be yours, in your hands, to do whatever you please with!"—Meaning, of course, his future recognition!—That he *did* want, he wanted it after his death when it couldn't disturb him; then he did want to offer his work to the world. All right. Have I made my point, Doctor? Well, here is my son's work, Doctor, here's his life going *on*!

[*She lifts a thin gilt-edged volume from the patio table as if elevating the Host before the altar. Its gold leaf and lettering catch the afternoon sun. It says* Poem of Summer. *Her face suddenly has a different look, the look of a visionary, an exalted religieuse. At the same instant a bird sings clearly and purely in the garden and the old lady seems to be almost young for a moment.*]

DOCTOR [*reading the title*]:
Poem of Summer?

MRS. VENABLE:
Poem of Summer, and the date of the summer, there are twenty-five of them, he wrote one poem a year which he printed himself on an eighteenth-century hand press at his— atelier in the—French—Quarter—so no one but he could see it. . . .

[*She seems dizzy for a moment.*]

DOCTOR:
He wrote one poem a year?

MRS. VENABLE:
One for each summer that we traveled together. The other nine months of the year were really only a preparation.

DOCTOR:
Nine months?

MRS. VENABLE:
The length of a pregnancy, yes. . . .

DOCTOR:
The poem was hard to deliver?

MRS. VENABLE:
Yes, even with me! *Without* me, *impossible*, Doctor!—he wrote no poem last summer.

DOCTOR:
He died last summer?

MRS. VENABLE:
Without me he died last summer, that was his last summer's poem.

[*She staggers; he assists her toward a chair. She catches her breath with difficulty.*]

One long-ago summer—now, why am I thinking of this?—my son, Sebastian, said, "Mother?—Listen to this!"—He read me Herman Melville's description of the Encantadas, the Galapagos Islands. Quote—take five and twenty heaps of cinders dumped here and there in an outside city lot. Imagine some of them magnified into mountains, and the vacant lot, the sea. And you'll have a fit idea of the general aspect of the Encantadas, the Enchanted Isles—extinct volcanos, looking

much as the world at large might look—after a last con-
flagration—end quote. He read me that description and said
that we had to go there. And so we did go there that summer
on a chartered boat, a four-masted schooner, as close as possible to the sort of a boat that Melville must have sailed
on. . . . We saw the Encantadas, but on the Encantadas we
saw something Melville *hadn't* written about. We saw the
great sea turtles crawl up out of the sea for their annual
egg-laying. . . . Once a year the female of the sea turtle crawls
up out of the equatorial sea onto the blazing sand-beach of a
volcanic island to dig a pit in the sand and deposit her eggs
there. It's a long and dreadful thing, the depositing of the eggs
in the sand pits, and when it's finished the exhausted female
turtle crawls back to the sea half dead. She never sees her
offspring, but we did. Sebastian knew exactly when the sea
turtle eggs would be hatched out and we returned in time for
it. . . .

DOCTOR:
You went back to the—?

MRS. VENABLE:
Terrible Encantadas, those heaps of extinct volcanos, in time
to witness the hatching of the sea turtles and their desperate
flight to the sea!

[*There is a sound of harsh bird-cries in the air. She looks
up.*]

—The narrow beach, the color of caviar, was all in motion!
But the sky was in motion, too. . . .

DOCTOR:
The sky was in motion, too?

MRS. VENABLE:
—Full of flesh-eating birds and the noise of the birds, the
horrible savage cries of the—

DOCTOR:
Carnivorous birds?

MRS. VENABLE:
Over the narrow black beach of the Encantadas as the just-hatched sea turtles scrambled out of the sand pits and started their race to the sea. . . .

DOCTOR:
Race to the sea?

MRS. VENABLE:
To escape the flesh-eating birds that made the sky almost as black as the beach!

[*She gazes up again: we hear the wild, ravenous, harsh cries of the birds. The sound comes in rhythmic waves like a savage chant.*]

And the sand all alive, all alive, as the hatched sea-turtles made their dash for the sea, while the birds hovered and swooped to attack and hovered and—swooped to attack! They were diving down on the hatched sea turtles, turning them over to expose their soft undersides, tearing the undersides open and rending and eating their flesh. Sebastian guessed that possibly only a hundredth of one per cent of their number would escape to the sea. . . .

DOCTOR:
What was it about this spectacle on the beach that fascinated your son?

MRS. VENABLE:
My son was looking for—

[*Stops short: continues evasively—*]

Let's just say he was interested in sea turtles.

DOCTOR:
You started to say that your son was looking for something.

508

MRS. VENABLE:

[*defiantly*]

All right, I started to say that my son was looking for God and I stopped myself because I was afraid that if I said he was looking for God, you'd say to yourself, "Oh, a pretentious young crack pot!"—which Sebastian was not. All poets look for God, all good poets do, and they have to look harder for Him than priests do since they don't have the help of such famous guidebooks and well-organized expeditions as priests have with their scriptures and churches. All right! Well, now I've said it, my son was looking for God. I mean for a clear image of Him. He spent that whole blazing equatorial day in the crow's nest of the schooner watching that thing on the beach of the Endantadas till it was too dark to see it, and when he came back down the rigging, he said, Well, now I've seen Him!—and he meant God . . .

DOCTOR:

I see.

MRS. VENABLE:

For several days after that he had a fever, he was delirious with it. I took command of the ship and we sailed north by east into cooler waters . . .

[*Miss Foxhill comes out silently on rubber-soled white oxfords, and waits to be noticed. She carries a water glass.*]

Next? India, China!—In the Himalayas—

[*Notices Miss Foxhill.*]

What? Oh, elixir of—ha!—Isn't it kind of the drugstore to keep me alive!

[*Tosses down medicine with a wry face and dismisses Miss Foxhill with a slight gesture.*]

Where was I?

DOCTOR:
In the Himalayas.

MRS. VENABLE:
Oh yes, that long-ago summer. .... In the Himalayas he almost entered a Buddhist monastery, had gone so far as to shave his head and eat just rice out of a wood bowl on a grass mat. He'd promised those sly Buddhist monks that he would give up the world and himself and all his worldly possessions to their mendicant order.—Well, I cabled his father, "For God's sake notify bank to freeze Sebastian's accounts!"—I got back this cable from my late husband's lawyer: "Mr. Venable critically ill Stop Wants you Stop Needs you Stop Immediate return advised most strongly. Stop. Cable time of arrival. . . ."

DOCTOR:
Did you go back to your husband?

MRS. VENABLE:
I made the hardest decision of my life. I stayed with my son. I got him through that crisis too. In less than a month he got up off the filthy grass mat and threw the rice bowl away—and booked us into Shepheard's Hotel in Cairo and the Ritz in Paris—. And from then on, oh, we—still lived in a—world of light and shadow. . . .

[*She turns vaguely with empty glass. He rises and takes it from her.*]

But the shadow was almost as luminous as the light.

DOCTOR:
Don't you want to sit down now?

MRS. VENABLE:
Yes, indeed I do, before I fall down.

[*He assists her into wheelchair.*]

—Are your hindlegs still on you?

DOCTOR [*still concerned over her agitation*]:
—My what? Oh—hind legs!—Yes . . .

MRS. VENABLE:

Well, then you're not a donkey, you're certainly not a donkey because I've been talking the hindlegs off a donkey—several donkeys. . . . But I had to make it clear to you that the world lost a great deal too when I lost my son last summer. . . . You would have liked my son, he would have been charmed by you. My son, Sebastian, was not a family snob or a money snob but he was a snob, all right. He was a snob about personal charm in people, he insisted upon good looks in people around him, and, oh, he had a perfect little court of young and beautiful people around him always, wherever he was, here in New *Orleans* or New York or on the Riviera or in Paris and Venice, he always had a little entourage of the beautiful and the talented and the young!

DOCTOR:

Your son was young, Mrs. Venable?

MRS. VENABLE:

Both of us were young, and stayed young, Doctor.

DOCTOR:

Could I see a photograph of your son, Mrs. Venable?

MRS. VENABLE:

Yes, indeed you could, Doctor. I'm glad that you asked to see one. I'm going to show you not one photograph but two. Here. Here is my son, Sebastian, in a Renaissance pageboy's costume at a masked ball in Cannes. Here is my son, Sebastian, in the same costume at a masked ball in Venice. These two pictures were taken twenty years apart. Now which is the older one, Doctor?

DOCTOR:

This photograph looks older.

MRS. VENABLE:

The photograph looks older but not the subject. It takes character to refuse to grow old, Doctor—successfully to refuse to. It calls for discipline, abstention. One cocktail before dinner, not two, four, six—a single lean chop and lime juice on a salad in restaurants famed for rich dishes.

[*Foxhill comes from the house.*]

FOXHILL:

Mrs. Venable, Miss Holly's mother and brother are—

[*Simultaneously Mrs. Holly and George appear in the window.*]

GEORGE:

Hi, Aunt Vi!

MRS. HOLLY:

Violet, dear, we're here.

FOXHILL:

They're here.

MRS. VENABLE:

Wait upstairs in my upstairs living room for me.

[*To Miss Foxhill:*]

Get them upstairs. I don't want them at that window during this talk.

[*To the Doctor:*]

Let's get away from the window.

[*He wheels her to stage center.*]

DOCTOR:

Mrs. Venable? Did your son have a—well—what kind of a *personal*, well, *private* life did—

MRS. VENABLE:
That's a question I wanted you to ask me.

DOCTOR:
Why?

MRS. VENABLE:
I haven't heard the girl's story except indirectly in a watered-down version, being too ill to go to hear it directly, but I've gathered enough to know that it's a hideous attack on my son's moral character which, being dead, he can't defend himself from. I have to be the defender. Now. Sit down. Listen to me . . .

[*The Doctor sits.*]

. . . before you hear whatever you're going to hear from the girl when she gets here. My son, Sebastian, was chaste. Not c-h-a-s-e-d! Oh, he was chased in that way of spelling it, too, we had to be very fleet-footed I can tell you, with his looks and his charm, to keep ahead of pursuers, every kind of pursuer!—I mean he was c-h-a-s-t-e!—Chaste. . . .

DOCTOR:
I understood what you meant, Mrs. Venable.

MRS. VENABLE:
And you *believe* me, don't you?

DOCTOR:
Yes, but—

MRS. VENABLE:
But *what*?

DOCTOR:
Chastity at—what age was your son last summer?

MRS. VENABLE:
Forty, maybe. We really didn't count birthdays. . . .

513

DOCTOR:
He lived a celibate life?

MRS. VENABLE:
As strictly as if he'd *vowed* to! This sounds like vanity, Doctor, but really I was actually the only one in his life that satisfied the demands he made of people. Time after time my son would let people go, dismiss them!—because their, their, their!—*attitude* toward him was—

DOCTOR:
Not as pure as—

MRS. VENABLE:
My son, Sebastian, demanded! We were a famous couple. People didn't speak of Sebastian and his mother or Mrs. Venable and her son, they said "Sebastian and Violet, Violet and Sebastian are staying at the Lido, they're at the Ritz in Madrid. Sebastian and Violet, Violet and Sebastian have taken a house at Biarritz for the season," and every appearance, every time we appeared, attention was centered on *us*! —*everyone else*! *Eclipsed*! Vanity? Ohhhh, no, Doctor, you can't call it that—

DOCTOR:
I didn't call it that.

MRS. VENABLE:
—It wasn't *folie de grandeur*, it was grandeur.

DOCTOR:
I see.

MRS. VENABLE:
An attitude toward life that's hardly been known in the world since the great Renaissance princes were crowded out of their palaces and gardens by successful shopkeepers!

514

DOCTOR:
I see.

MRS. VENABLE:
Most people's lives—what are they but trails of debris, each day more debris, more debris, long, long trails of debris with nothing to clean it all up but, finally, death. . . .

[*We hear lyric music.*]

My son, Sebastian, and I constructed our days, each day, we would—carve out each day of our lives like a piece of sculpture.—Yes, we left behind us a trail of days like a gallery of sculpture! But, last summer—

[*Pause: the music continues.*]

I can't forgive him for it, not even now that he's paid for it with his life!—he let in this—*vandal*! This—

DOCTOR:
The girl that—?

MRS. VENABLE:
That you're going to meet here this afternoon! Yes. He admitted this vandal and with her tongue for a hatchet she's gone about smashing our legend, the memory of—

DOCTOR:
Mrs. Venable, what do you think is her reason?

MRS. VENABLE:
Lunatics don't have reason!

DOCTOR:
I mean what do you think is her—motive?

MRS. VENABLE:
What a question!—We put the bread in her mouth and the clothes on her back. People that like you for that or even forgive you for it are, are—*hen's teeth,* Doctor. The role of

515

the benefactor is worse than thankless, it's the role of a victim, Doctor, a sacrificial victim, yes, they want your blood, Doctor, they want your blood on the altar steps of their *outraged, outrageous* egos!

DOCTOR:
Oh. You mean she resented the—

MRS. VENABLE:
Loathed!—They can't shut her up at St. Mary's.

DOCTOR:
I thought she'd been there for months.

MRS. VENABLE:
I mean keep her *still* there. She *babbles*! They couldn't shut her up in Cabeza de Lobo or at the clinic in Paris—she babbled, babbled!—smashing my son's reputation.—On the *Berengaria* bringing her back to the States she broke out of the stateroom and babbled, babbled; even at the airport when she was flown down here, she babbled a bit of her story before they could whisk her into an ambulance to St. Mary's. This is a reticule, Doctor. [*She raises a cloth bag.*] A catchall, carry-all bag for an elderly lady which I turned into last summer. . . . Will you open it for me, my hands are stiff, and fish out some cigarettes and a cigarette holder.

[*He does.*]

DOCTOR:
I don't have matches.

MRS. VENABLE:
I think there's a table-lighter on the table.

DOCTOR:
Yes, there is,

[*He lights it, it flames up high.*]

My Lord, what a torch!

MRS. VENABLE [*with a sudden, sweet smile*]:
"So shines a good deed in a naughty world," Doctor—
Sugar. . . .

[*Pause. A bird sings sweetly in the garden.*]

DOCTOR:
Mrs. Venable?

MRS. VENABLE:
Yes?

DOCTOR:
In your letter last week you made some reference to a, to a—
fund of some kind, an endowment fund of—

MRS. VENABLE:
I wrote you that my lawyers and bankers and certified public
accountants were setting up the Sebastian Venable Memorial
Foundation to subsidize the work of young people like you
that are pushing out the frontiers of art and science but have
a financial problem. You have a financial problem, don't you,
Doctor?

DOCTOR:
Yes, we do have that problem. My work is such a *new* and
radical thing that people in charge of state funds are naturally
a little scared of it and keep us on a small budget, so small
that—. We need a separate ward for my patients, I need
trained assistants, I'd like to marry a girl I can't afford to
marry!—But there's also the problem of getting right patients,
not just—criminal psychopaths that the state turns over to us
for my operation!—because it's—well—risky. . . . I don't want
to turn you against my work at Lion's View but I have to be
honest with you. There is a good deal of risk in my operation.
Whenever you enter the brain with a foreign object . . .

MRS. VENABLE:
Yes.

517

DOCTOR:
—Even a needle-thin knife . . .

MRS. VENABLE:
Yes.

DOCTOR:
—In a skilled surgeon's fingers . . .

MRS. VENABLE:
Yes.

DOCTOR:
—There is a good deal of risk involved in—the operation. . . .

MRS. VENABLE:
You said that it pacifies them, it quiets them down, it suddenly makes them peaceful.

DOCTOR:
Yes. It does that, that much we already know, but—

MRS. VENABLE:
What?

DOCTOR:
Well, it will be ten years before we can tell if the immediate benefits of the operation will be lasting or—passing or even if there'd still be—and this is what haunts me about it!—any possibility, afterwards, of—reconstructing a—totally sound person, it may be that the person will always be limited afterwards, relieved of acute disturbances but—*limited,* Mrs. Venable. . . .

MRS. VENABLE:
Oh, but what a blessing to them, Doctor, to be just peaceful, to be just suddenly—peaceful. . . .

[*A bird sings sweetly in the garden.*]

After all that horror, after those nightmares: just to be able

518

to lift up their eyes and see—[*She looks up and raises a hand to indicate the sky.*]—a sky not as black with savage, devouring birds as the sky that we saw in the Encantadas, Doctor.

DOCTOR:
—Mrs. Venable? I can't guarantee that a lobotomy would stop her—*babbling*!!

MRS. VENABLE:
That may be, maybe not, but after the operation, who would *believe* her, Doctor?

[*Pause: faint jungle music.*]

DOCTOR [*quietly*]:
My God. [*Pause.*]—Mrs. Venable, suppose after meeting the girl and observing the girl and hearing this story she babbles—I still shouldn't feel that her condition's—intractable enough! to justify the risks of—suppose I shouldn't feel that non-surgical treatment such as insulin shock and electric shock and—

MRS. VENABLE:
SHE'S HAD ALL THAT AT SAINT MARY'S!! Nothing else is left for her.

DOCTOR:
But if I disagreed with you? [*Pause.*]

MRS. VENABLE:
That's just part of a question: finish the question, Doctor.

DOCTOR:
Would you still be interested in my work at Lion's View? I mean would the Sebastian Venable Memorial Foundation still be interested in it?

MRS. VENABLE:
Aren't we always more interested in a thing that concerns us personally, Doctor?

DOCTOR:
Mrs. Venable!!

[*Catharine Holly appears between the lace window curtains.*]

You're such an innocent person that it doesn't occur to you, it obviously hasn't even occurred to you that anybody less innocent than you are could possibly interpret this offer of a subsidy as—well, as sort of a *bribe?*

MRS. VENABLE [*laughs, throwing her head back*]:
Name it that—I don't care—. There's just two things to remember. She's a destroyer. My son was a *creator!*—Now if my honesty's shocked you—pick up your little black bag without the subsidy in it, and run away from this garden!—Nobody's heard our conversation but you and I, Doctor Sugar. . . .

[*Miss Foxhill comes out of the house and calls.*]

MISS FOXHILL:
Mrs. Venable?

MRS. VENABLE:
What is it, what do you want, Miss Foxhill?

MISS FOXHILL:
Mrs. Venable? Miss Holly is here, with—

[*Mrs. Venable sees Catharine at the window.*]

MRS. VENABLE:
Oh, my God. There she is, in the window!—I told you I didn't want her to enter my house again, I told you to meet them at the door and lead them around the side of the house to the garden and you didn't listen. I'm not ready to face her. I have to have my five o'clock cocktail first, to fortify me. Take my chair inside. Doctor? Are you still here? I thought you'd run out of the garden. I'm going back through the

garden to the other entrance. Doctor? Sugar? You may stay in the garden if you wish to or run out of the garden if you wish to or go in this way if you wish to or do anything that you wish to but I'm going to have my five o'clock daiquiri, *frozen!*—before I face her. . . .

[*All during this she has been sailing very slowly off through the garden like a stately vessel at sea with a fair wind in her sails, a pirate's frigate or a treasure-laden galleon. The young Doctor stares at Catharine framed by the lace window curtains. Sister Felicity appears beside her and draws her away from the window. Music: an ominous fanfare. Sister Felicity holds the door open for Catharine as the Doctor starts quickly forward. He starts to pick up his bag but doesn't. Catharine rushes out, they almost collide with each other.*]

CATHARINE:
Excuse me.

DOCTOR:
I'm sorry. . . .

[*She looks after him as he goes into the house.*]

SISTER FELICITY:
Sit down and be still till your family come outside.

DIM OUT

SCENE TWO

*Catharine removes a cigarette from a lacquered box on the
table and lights it. The following quick, cadenced lines are
accompanied by quick, dancelike movement, almost formal, as
the Sister in her sweeping white habit, which should be
starched to make a crackling sound, pursues the girl about the
white wicker patio table and among the wicker chairs: this
can be accompanied by quick music.*

SISTER:
What did you take out of that box on the table?

CATHARINE:
Just a cigarette, Sister.

SISTER:
Put it back in the box.

CATHARINE:
Too late, it's already lighted.

522

SISTER:
Give it here.

CATHARINE:
Oh, please, let me smoke, Sister!

SISTER:
Give it here.

CATHARINE:
Please, Sister Felicity.

SISTER:
Catharine, give it here. You know that you're not allowed to smoke at Saint Mary's.

CATHARINE:
We're not at Saint Mary's, this is an afternoon out.

SISTER:
You're still in my charge. I can't permit you to smoke because the last time you smoked you dropped a lighted cigarette on your dress and started a fire.

CATHARINE:
Oh, I did not start a fire. I just burned a hole in my skirt because I was half unconscious under medication. [*She is now back of a white wicker chair.*]

SISTER [*overlapping her*]:
Catharine, give it here.

CATHARINE:
Don't be such a bully!

SISTER:
Disobedience has to be paid for later.

CATHARINE:
All right, I'll pay for it later.

SISTER [*overlapping*]:
Give me that cigarette or I'll make a report that'll put you

523

right back on the violent ward, if you don't. [*She claps her hands twice and holds one hand out across the table.*]

CATHARINE [*overlapping*]:
I'm not being violent, Sister.

SISTER [*overlapping*]:
Give me that cigarette, I'm holding my hand out for it!

CATHARINE:
All right, take it, here, take it!

[*She thrusts the lighted end of the cigarette into the palm of the Sister's hand. The Sister cries out and sucks her burned hand.*]

SISTER:
You burned me with it!

CATHARINE:
I'm sorry, I didn't mean to.

SISTER [*shocked, hurt*]:
You deliberately burned me!

CATHARINE [*overlapping*]:
You said give it to you and so I gave it to you.

SISTER [*overlapping*]:
You stuck the lighted end of that cigarette in my hand!

CATHARINE [*overlapping*]:
I'm *sick*, I'm *sick*!—of being *bossed* and *bullied*!

SISTER [*commandingly*]:
Sit down!

[*Catharine sits down stiffly in a white wicker chair on fore-stage, facing the audience. The Sister resumes sucking the burned palm of her hand. Ten beats. Then from inside the house the whirr of a mechanical mixer.*]

CATHARINE:

There goes the Waring Mixer, Aunt Violet's about to have her five o'clock frozen daiquiri, you could set a watch by it! [*She almost laughs. Then she draws a deep, shuddering breath and leans back in her chair, but her hands remain clenched on the white wicker arms.*]—We're in Sebastian's garden. *My God, I can still cry!*

SISTER:

Did you have any medication before you went out?

CATHARINE:

No. I didn't have any. Will you give me some, Sister?

SISTER [*almost gently*]:

I can't. I wasn't told to. However, I think the doctor will give you something.

CATHARINE:

The young blond man I bumped into?

SISTER:

Yes. The young doctor's a specialist from another hospital.

CATHARINE:

What hospital?

SISTER:

A word to the wise is sufficient....

[*The Doctor has appeared in the window.*]

CATHARINE [*rising abruptly*]:

I knew I was being watched, he's in the window, staring out at me!

SISTER:

Sit down and be still. Your family's coming outside.

CATHARINE [*overlapping*]:

LION'S VIEW, IS IT! DOCTOR?

[*She has advanced toward the bay window. The Doctor draws back, letting the misty white gauze curtains down to obscure him.*]

SISTER [*rising with a restraining gesture which is almost pitying*]:

Sit down, dear.

CATHARINE:

IS IT LION'S VIEW? DOCTOR?!

SISTER:

Be still. . . .

CATHARINE:

WHEN CAN I STOP RUNNING DOWN THAT STEEP WHITE STREET IN CABEZA DE LOBO?

SISTER:

Catharine, dear, sit down.

CATHARINE:

I loved him, Sister! Why wouldn't he let me save him? I tried to hold onto his hand but he struck me away and ran, ran, ran in the wrong direction, Sister!

SISTER:

Catharine, dear—be still.

[*The Sister sneezes.*]

CATHARINE:

Bless you, Sister. [*She says this absently, still watching the window.*]

SISTER:

Thank you.

CATHARINE:

The Doctor's still at the window but he's too blond to hide

526

behind window curtains, he catches the light, he shines through them. [*She turns from the window.*]—We were *going* to blonds, blonds were next on the menu.

SISTER:
Be still now. Quiet, dear.

CATHARINE:
Cousin Sebastian said he was famished for blonds, he was fed up with the dark ones and was famished for blonds. All the travel brochures he picked up were advertisements of the blond northern countries. I think he'd already booked us to—Copenhagen or—Stockholm.—Fed up with dark ones, famished for light ones: that's how he talked about people, as if they were—items on a menu.—"That one's delicious-looking, that one is appetizing," or "that one is *not* appetizing"—I think because he was really nearly half-starved from living on pills and salads. . . .

SISTER:
Stop it!—Catharine, be still.

CATHARINE:
He liked me and so I loved him. . . . [*She cries a little again.*] If he'd kept hold of my hand I could have saved him!—Sebastian suddenly said to me last summer: "Let's fly north, little bird—I want to walk under those radiant, cold northern lights—I've never *seen* the aurora borealis!"—Somebody said once or wrote, once: "We're all of us children in a vast kindergarten trying to spell God's name with the wrong alphabet blocks!"

MRS. HOLLY [*offstage*]:
Sister?

[*The Sister rises.*]

CATHARINE [*rising*]:
I think it's *me* they're calling, they call *me* "Sister," Sister!

527

SCENE THREE

The Sister resumes her seat impassively as the girl's mother and younger brother appear from the garden. The mother, Mrs. Holly, is a fatuous Southern lady who requires no other description. The brother, George, is typically good looking, he has the best "looks" of the family, tall and elegant of figure. They enter.

MRS. HOLLY:
Catharine, dear! Catharine—

[*They embrace tentatively.*]

Well, well! Doesn't she look fine, George?

GEORGE:
Uh huh.

CATHARINE:
They send you to the beauty parlor whenever you're going to have a family visit. Other times you look awful, you can't

528

have a compact or lipstick or anything made out of metal because they're afraid you'll swallow it.

MRS. HOLLY [*giving a tinkly little laugh*]:
I think she looks just splendid, don't you, George?

GEORGE:
Can't we talk to her without the nun for a minute?

MRS. HOLLY:
Yes, I'm sure it's all right to. Sister?

CATHARINE:
Excuse me, Sister Felicity, this is my mother, Mrs. Holly, and my brother, George.

SISTER:
How do you do.

GEORGE:
How d'ya do.

CATHARINE:
This is Sister Felicity. . . .

MRS. HOLLY:
We're so happy that Catharine's at Saint Mary's! So very grateful for all you're doing for her.

SISTER [*sadly, mechanically*]:
We do the best we can for her, Mrs. Holly.

MRS. HOLLY:
I'm sure you do. Yes, well—I wonder if you would mind if we had a little private chat with our Cathie?

SISTER:
I'm not supposed to let her out of my sight.

MRS. HOLLY:
It's just for a minute. You can sit in the hall or the garden

529

and we'll call you right back here the minute the private part of the little talk is over.

[*Sister Felicity withdraws with an uncertain nod and a swish of starched fabric.*]

GEORGE [*to Catharine*]:
Jesus! What are you up to? Huh? Sister? Are you trying to RUIN us?!

MRS. HOLLY:
GAWGE! WILL YOU BE QUIET. You're upsetting your sister!

[*He jumps up and stalks off a little, rapping his knee with his zipper-covered tennis racket.*]

CATHARINE:
How elegant George looks.

MRS. HOLLY:
George inherited Cousin Sebastian's wardrobe but everything else is in probate! Did you know that? That everything else is in probate and Violet can keep it in probate just as long as she wants to?

CATHARINE:
Where is Aunt Violet?

MRS. HOLLY:
George, come back here!

[*He does, sulkily.*]

Violet's on her way down.

GEORGE:
Yeah. Aunt Violet has an elevator now.

MRS. HOLLY:
Yais, she has, she's had an elevator installed where the back

530

stairs were, and, Sister, it's the cutest little thing you ever did see! It's paneled in Chinese lacquer, black an' gold Chinese lacquer, with lovely bird-pictures on it. But there's only room for two people at a time in it. George and I came down on foot.—I think she's havin' her frozen daiquiri now, she still has a frozen daiquiri promptly at five o'clock ev'ry afternoon in the world . . . in warm weather. . . . Sister, the horrible death of Sebastian just about *killed* her!—She's now slightly better . . . but it's a question of time.—Dear, you know, I'm sure that you understand, why we haven't been out to see you at Saint Mary's. They said you were too disturbed, and a family visit might disturb you more. But I want you to know that nobody, absolutely nobody in the city, knows a thing about what you've been through. Have they, George? Not a thing. Not a soul even knows that you've come back from Europe. When people enquire, when they question us about you, we just say that you've stayed abroad to study something or other. [*She catches her breath.*] Now. Sister?—I want you to please be *very* careful what you say to your Aunt Violet about what happened to Sebastian in Cabeza de Lobo.

CATHARINE:
What do you want me to say about what—?

MRS. HOLLY:
Just don't repeat that same fantastic story! For my sake and George's sake, the sake of your brother and mother, don't repeat that horrible story again! Not to Violet! Will you?

CATHARINE:
Then I am going to have to tell Aunt Violet what happened to her son in Cabeza de Lobo?

MRS. HOLLY:
Honey, that's why you're here. She has *INSISTED* on hearing it straight from YOU!

531

GEORGE:
You were the only witness to it, Cathie.

CATHARINE:
No, there were others. That *ran.*

MRS. HOLLY:
Oh, Sister, you've just had a little sort of a—*nightmare* about it! Now, listen to me, will you, Sister? Sebastian has left, has BEQUEATHED!—to you an' Gawge in his *will*—

GEORGE [*religiously*]:
To each of us, fifty grand, each!—AFTER! TAXES!—GET IT?

CATHARINE:
Oh, yes, but if they give me an injection—I won't have any choice but to tell exactly what happened in Cabeza de Lobo last summer. Don't you see? I won't have any choice but to tell the truth. It makes you tell the truth because it shuts something off that might make you able not to and *everything* comes out, decent or *not* decent, you have no control, but always, always the truth!

MRS. HOLLY:
Catharine, darling. I don't know the full story, but surely you're not too sick in your *head* to know in your *heart* that the story you've been telling is just—too—

GEORGE [*cutting in*]:
Cathie, Cathie, you got to forget that story! Can'tcha? For *your* fifty grand?

MRS. HOLLY:
Because if Aunt Vi contests the will, and we know she'll contest it, she'll keep it in the courts forever!—We'll be—

GEORGE:
It's in PROBATE NOW! And'll never get out of probate

until you drop that story—we can't afford to hire lawyers good enough to contest it! So if you don't stop telling that crazy story, we won't have a pot to—cook *greens* in!

[*He turns away with a fierce grimace and a sharp, abrupt wave of his hand, as if slapping down something. Catharine stares at his tall back for a moment and laughs wildly.*]

MRS. HOLLY:
Catharine, don't laugh like that, it scares me, Catharine.

[*Jungle birds scream in the garden.*]

GEORGE [*turning his back on his sister*]:
Cathie, the money is all tied up.

[*He stoops over sofa, hands on flannel knees, speaking directly into Catharine's face as if she were hard of hearing. She raises a hand to touch his cheek affectionately; he seizes the hand and removes it but holds it tight.*]

If Aunt Vi decided to contest Sebastian's will that leaves us all of this cash?!—Am I coming through to you?

CATHARINE:
Yes, little brother, you are.

GEORGE:
You see, Mama, she's crazy like a coyote!

[*He gives her a quick cold kiss.*]

We won't get a single damn penny, honest t' God we won't! So you've just GOT to stop tellin' that story about what you say happened to Cousin Sebastian in Cabeza de Lobo, even if it's what it *couldn't* be, TRUE!—You got to drop it, Sister, you can't tell such a story to civilized people in a civilized up-to-date country!

MRS. HOLLY:
Cathie, why, why, why!—did you invent such a tale?

533

CATHARINE:

But, Mother, I DIDN'T invent it. I know it's a hideous story but it's a true story of our time and the world we live in and what did truly happen to Cousin Sebastian in Cabeza de Lobo. . . .

GEORGE:

Oh, then you are going to tell it. Mama, she *IS* going to tell it! Right to Aunt Vi, and lose us a hundred thousand! —Cathie? You are a BITCH!

MRS. HOLLY:

GAWGE!

GEORGE:

I repeat it, a bitch! She isn't crazy, Mama, she's no more crazy than I am, she's just, just—PERVERSE! Was ALWAYS!— perverse. . . .

[*Catharine turns away and breaks into quiet sobbing.*]

MRS. HOLLY:

Gawge, Gawge, apologize to Sister, this is no way for you to talk to your sister. You come right back over here and tell your sweet little sister you're sorry you spoke like that to her!

GEORGE [*turning back to Catharine*]:

I'm sorry, Cathie, but you know we NEED that money! Mama and me, we—Cathie? I got *ambitions*! And, Cathie, I'm YOUNG!—I *want* things, I *need* them, Cathie! So will you please think about ME? Us?

MISS FOXHILL [*offstage*]:

Mrs. Holly? Mrs. Holly?

MRS. HOLLY:

Somebody's callin' fo' me. Catharine, Gawge put it very badly but you know that it's TRUE! WE DO HAVE TO GET

534

WHAT SEBASTIAN HAS LEFT US IN HIS WILL, DEAR-
EST! AND YOU WON'T LET US DOWN? PROMISE?
YOU WON'T? LET US DOWN?

GEORGE [*fiercely shouting*]: HERE COMES AUNT VI!
Mama, Cathie, Aunt Violet's—here is Aunt Vi!

SCENE FOUR

Mrs. Venable enters downstage area. Entrance music.

MRS. HOLLY:
Cathie! Here's Aunt Vi!

MRS. VENABLE:
She sees me and I see her. That's all that's necessary. Miss Foxhill, put my chair in this corner. Crank the back up a little.

[*Miss Foxhill does this business.*]

More. More. Not that much!—Let it back down a little. All right. Now, then. I'll have my frozen daiquiri, now. . . . Do any of you want coffee?

GEORGE:
I'd like a chocolate malt.

MRS. HOLLY:
Gawge!

MRS. VENABLE:
This isn't a drugstore.

MRS. HOLLY:
Oh, Gawge is just being Gawge.

MRS. VENABLE:
That's what I *thought* he was being!

[*An uncomfortable silence falls. Miss Foxhill creeps out like a burglar. She speaks in a breathless whisper, presenting a cardboard folder toward Mrs. Venable.*]

MISS FOXHILL:
Here's the portfolio marked Cabeza de Lobo. It has all your correspondence with the police there and the American consul.

MRS. VENABLE:
I asked for the *English transcript*! It's in a separate—

MISS FOXHILL:
Separate, yes, here it is!

MRS. VENABLE:
Oh . . .

MISS FOXHILL:
And here's the report of the private investigators and here's the report of—

MRS. VENABLE:
Yes, yes, yes! Where's the doctor?

MISS FOXHILL:
On the phone in the library!

MRS. VENABLE:
Why does he choose such a moment to make a phone-call?

MISS FOXHILL:
He didn't make a phone-call, he received a phone-call from—

537

MRS. VENABLE:
Miss Foxhill, why are you talking to me like a burglar!?

[*Miss Foxhill giggles a little desperately.*]

CATHARINE:
Aunt Violet, she's frightened.—Can I move? Can I get up and move around till it starts?

MRS. HOLLY:
Cathie, Cathie, dear, did Gawge tell you that he received bids from every good fraternity on the Tulane campus and went Phi Delt because Paul Junior did?

MRS. VENABLE:
I see that he had the natural tact and good taste to come here this afternoon outfitted from head to foot in clothes that belonged to my son!

GEORGE:
You gave 'em to me, Aunt Vi.

MRS. VENABLE:
I didn't know you'd parade them in front of me, George.

MRS. HOLLY [*quickly*]:
Gawge, tell Aunt Violet how grateful you are for—

GEORGE:
I found a little Jew tailor on Britannia Street that makes alterations so good you'd never guess that they weren't cut *out* for me to *begin* with!

MRS. HOLLY:
AND so reasonable!—Luckily, since it seems that Sebastian's wonderful, wonderful bequest to Gawge an' Cathie is going to be tied up a while!?

GEORGE:
Aunt Vi? About the will?

538

[*Mrs. Holly coughs.*]

I was just wondering if we can't figure out some way to, to—

MRS. HOLLY:

Gawge means to EXPEDITE it! To get through the red tape quicker?

MRS. VENABLE:

I understand his meaning. Foxhill, get the Doctor.

[*She has risen with her cane and hobbled to the door.*]

MISS FOXHILL [*exits calling*]:

Doctor!

MRS. HOLLY:

Gawge, no more about money.

GEORGE:

How do we know we'll ever see her again?

[*Catharine gasps and rises; she moves downstage, followed quickly by Sister Felicity.*]

SISTER [*mechanically*]:

What's wrong, dear?

CATHARINE:

I think I'm just dreaming this, it doesn't seem real!

[*Miss Foxhill comes back out, saying:*]

FOXHILL:

He had to answer an urgent call from Lion's View.

[*Slight, tense pause.*]

MRS. HOLLY:

Violet! *Not* Lion's View!

[*Sister Felicity had started conducting Catharine back to the patio; she stops her, now.*]

SISTER:
Wait, dear.

CATHARINE:
What for? I know what's coming.

MRS. VENABLE [*at same time*]:
Why? Are you all prepared to put out a thousand a month plus extra charges for treatments to keep the girl at St. Mary's?

MRS. HOLLY:
Cathie? Cathie, dear?

[*Catharine has returned with the Sister.*]

Tell Aunt Violet how grateful you are for her makin' it possible for you to rest an' recuperate at such a sweet, sweet place as St. Mary's!

CATHARINE:
No place for lunatics is a sweet, sweet place.

MRS. HOLLY:
But the food's good there. Isn't the food good there?

CATHARINE:
Just give me written permission not to eat fried grits. I had yard privileges till I refused to eat fried grits.

SISTER:
She lost yard privileges because she couldn't be trusted in the yard without constant supervision or even with it because she'd run to the fence and make signs to cars on the highway.

CATHARINE:
Yes, I did, I did that because I've been trying for weeks to get a message out of that "sweet, sweet place."

MRS. HOLLY:
What message, dear?

CATHARINE:
I got panicky, Mother.

MRS. HOLLY:
Sister, I don't understand.

GEORGE:
What're you scared of, Sister?

CATHARINE:
What they might do to me now, after they've done all the rest!—That man in the window's a specialist from Lion's View! We get newspapers. I know what they're . . .

[*The Doctor comes out.*]

MRS. VENABLE:
Why, Doctor, I thought you'd left us with just that little black bag to remember you by!

DOCTOR:
Oh, no. Don't you remember our talk? I had to answer a call about a patient that—

MRS. VENABLE:
This is Dr. Cukrowicz. He says it means "sugar" and we can call him "Sugar"—

[*George laughs.*]

He's a specialist from Lion's View.

CATHARINE [*cutting in*]:
WHAT DOES HE SPECIALIZE IN?

MRS. VENABLE:
Something new. When other treatments have failed.

[*Pause. The jungle clamor comes up and subsides again.*]

CATHARINE:
Do you want to bore a hole in my skull and turn a knife in my brain? Everything else was done to me!

541

[*Mrs. Holly sobs. George raps his knee with the tennis racket.*]

You'd have to have my mother's permission for that.

MRS. VENABLE:
I'm paying to keep you in a private asylum.

CATHARINE:
You're not my legal guardian.

MRS. VENABLE:
Your mother's dependent on me. All of you are!—Financially. . . .

CATHARINE:
I think the situation is—clear to me, now. . . .

MRS. VENABLE:
Good! In that case. . . .

DOCTOR:
I think a quiet atmosphere will get us the best results.

MRS. VENABLE:
I don't know what you mean by a quiet atmosphere. She shouted, I didn't.

DOCTOR:
Mrs. Venable, let's try to keep things on a quiet level, now. Your niece seems to be disturbed.

MRS. VENABLE:
She has every reason to be. She took my son from me, and then she—

CATHARINE:
Aunt Violet, you're not being fair.

MRS. VENABLE:
Oh, aren't I?

CATHARINE [*to the others*]:
She's not being fair.

[*Then back to Mrs. Venable*:]

Aunt Violet, you know why Sebastian asked me to travel with him.

MRS. VENABLE:
Yes, I *do* know why!

CATHARINE:
You weren't able to travel. You'd had a—[*She stops short.*]

MRS. VENABLE:
Go on! *What* had I had? Are you afraid to say it in front of the Doctor? She meant that I had a stroke.—I DID NOT HAVE A STROKE!—I had a slight aneurism. You know what that is, Doctor? A little vascular convulsion! Not a hemorrhage, just a little convulsion of a blood vessel. I had it when I discovered that she was trying to take my son away from me. Then I had it. It gave a little temporary—muscular —contraction.—To one side of my face. . . . [*She crosses back into main acting area.*] These people are not blood relatives of mine, they're my dead husband's relations. I always detested these people, my dead husband's sister and—her two worthless children. But I did more than my duty to keep their heads above water. To please my son, whose weakness was being excessively softhearted, I went to the expense and humiliation, yes, public humiliation, of giving this girl a debut which was a fiasco. Nobody liked her when I brought her out. Oh, she had some kind of—notoriety! She had a sharp tongue that some people mistook for wit. A habit of laughing in the faces of decent people which would infuriate them, and also reflected adversely on me and Sebastian, too. But, he, Sebastian, was amused by this girl. While I was disgusted, sickened. And halfway through the season, she was dropped off the

543

party lists, yes, dropped off the lists in spite of my position. Why? Because she'd lost her head over a young married man, made a scandalous scene at a Mardi Gras ball, in the middle of the ballroom. Then everybody dropped her like a hot—rock, but—[*She loses her breath.*] My son, Sebastian, still felt sorry for her and took her with him last summer instead of me. . . .

CATHARINE [*springing up with a cry*]:
I can't change truth, I'm not God! I'm not even sure that He could, I don't think God can change truth! How can I change the story of what happened to her son in Cabeza de Lobo?

MRS. VENABLE [*at the same time*]:
She was in love with my son!

CATHARINE [*overlapping*]:
Let me go back to Saint Mary's. Sister Felicity, let's go back to Saint—

MRS. VENABLE [*overlapping*]:
Oh, no! That's not where you'll go!

CATHARINE [*overlapping*]:
All right, *Lion's View* but don't ask me to—

MRS. VENABLE [*overlapping*]:
You *know* that you were!

CATHARINE [*overlapping*]:
That I was *what*, Aunt Violet?

MRS. VENABLE [*overlapping*]:
Don't call me "Aunt," you're the niece of my dead husband, not me!

MRS. HOLLY [*overlapping*]:
Catharine, Catharine, don't upset your—Doctor? Oh, Doctor!

[*But the Doctor is calmly observing the scene, with detach-*

544

ment. The jungle-garden is loud with the sounds of its feathered and scaled inhabitants.]

CATHARINE:
I don't want to, I didn't want to come here! I know what she thinks, she thinks I murdered her son, she thinks that I was responsible for his death.

MRS. VENABLE:
That's right. I told him when he told me that he was going with you in my place last summer that I'd never see him again and I never did. And only you know why!

CATHARINE:
Oh, my God, I—

[She rushes out toward garden, followed immediately by the Sister.]

SISTER:
Miss Catharine, Miss Catharine—

DOCTOR *[overlapping]*:
Mrs. Venable?

SISTER *[overlapping]*:
Miss Catharine?

DOCTOR *[overlapping]*:
Mrs. Venable?

MRS. VENABLE:
What?

DOCTOR:
I'd like to be left alone with Miss Catharine for a few minutes.

MRS. HOLLY:
George, talk to her, George.

[George crouches appealingly before the old lady's chair, peering close into her face, a hand on her knee.]

545

GEORGE:
Aunt Vi? Cathie can't go to Lion's View. Everyone in the Garden District would know you'd put your niece in a state asylum, Aunt Vi.

MRS. VENABLE:
Foxhill!

GEORGE:
What do you want, Aunt Vi?

MRS. VENABLE:
Let go of my chair. Foxhill? Get me away from these people!

GEORGE:
Aunt Vi, listen, think of the talk it—

MRS. VENABLE:
I can't get up! Push me, push me away!

GEORGE [*rising but holding chair*]:
I'll push her, Miss Foxhill.

MRS. VENABLE:
Let go of my chair or—

MISS FOXHILL:
Mr. Holly, I—

GEORGE:
I got to talk to her.

[*He pushes her chair downstage.*]

MRS. VENABLE:
Foxhill!

MISS FOXHILL:
Mr. Holly, she doesn't want you to push her.

GEORGE:
I know what I'm doing, leave me alone with Aunt Vi!

546

MRS. VENABLE:
Let go me or I'll *strike* you!

GEORGE:
Oh, Aunt Vi!

MRS. VENABLE:
Foxhill!

MRS. HOLLY:
George—

GEORGE:
Aunt Vi?

[*She strikes at him with her cane. He releases the chair and Miss Foxhill pushes her off. He trots after her a few steps, then he returns to Mrs. Holly, who is sobbing into a handkerchief. He sighs, and sits down beside her, taking her hand. The scene fades as light is brought up on Catharine and the Sister in the garden. The Doctor comes up to them. Mrs. Holly stretches her arms out to George, sobbing, and he crouches before her chair and rests his head in her lap. She strokes his head. During this: the Sister has stood beside Catharine, holding onto her arm.*]

CATHARINE:
You don't have to hold onto me. I can't run away.

DOCTOR:
Miss Catharine?

CATHARINE:
What?

DOCTOR:
Your aunt is a very sick woman. She had a stroke last spring?

CATHARINE:
Yes, she did, but she'll never admit it. . . .

547

DOCTOR:
You have to understand why.

CATHARINE:
I do, I understand why. I didn't want to come here.

DOCTOR:
Miss Catharine, do you hate her?

CATHARINE:
I don't understand what hate is. How can you hate anybody
and still be sane? You see, I still think I'm sane!

DOCTOR:
You think she did have a stroke?

CATHARINE:
She had a slight stroke in April. It just affected one side, the
left side, of her face . . . but it was disfiguring, and after that,
Sebastian couldn't use her.

DOCTOR:
Use her? Did you say use her?

[*The sounds of the jungle-garden are not loud but ominous.*]

CATHARINE:
Yes, we all use each other and that's what we think of as love,
and not being able to use each other is what's—*hate.* . . .

DOCTOR:
Do you hate her, Miss Catharine?

CATHARINE:
Didn't you ask me that, once? And didn't I say that I didn't
understand hate. A ship struck an iceberg at sea—everyone
sinking—

DOCTOR:
Go on, Miss Catharine!

548

CATHARINE:
But that's no reason for everyone drowning for hating everyone drowning! Is it, Doctor?

DOCTOR:
Tell me: what was your feeling for your cousin Sebastian?

CATHARINE:
He liked me and so I loved him.

DOCTOR:
In what way did you love him?

CATHARINE:
The only way he'd accept:—a sort of motherly way. I tried
to save him, Doctor.

DOCTOR:
From what? Save him from what?

CATHARINE:
Completing!—a sort of!—*image*!—he had of himself as a
sort of!—*sacrifice* to a!—*terrible* sort of a—

DOCTOR:
—God?

CATHARINE:
Yes, a—*cruel* one, Doctor!

DOCTOR:
How did you feel about that?

CATHARINE:
Doctor, my feelings are the sort of feelings that you have in
a dream. . . .

DOCTOR:
Your life doesn't seem real to you?

CATHARINE:

Suddenly last winter I began to write my journal in the third person.

[He grasps her elbow and leads her out upon forestage. At the same time Miss Foxhill wheels Mrs. Venable off, Mrs. Holly weeps into a handkerchief and George rises and shrugs and turns his back to the audience.]

DOCTOR:

Something happened last winter?

CATHARINE:

At a Mardi Gras ball some—some boy that took me to it got too drunk to stand up! *[A short, mirthless note of laughter.]* I wanted to go home. My coat was in the cloakroom, they couldn't find the check for it in his pockets. I said, "Oh, hell, let it go!"—I started out for a taxi. Somebody took my arm and said, "I'll drive you home." He took off his coat as we left the hotel and put it over my shoulders, and then I looked at him and—I don't think I'd ever even seen him before then, really!—He took me home in his car but took me another place first. We stopped near the Duelling Oaks at the end of Esplanade Street. . . . Stopped!—I said, "What for?"—He didn't answer, just struck a match in the car to light a cigarette in the car and I looked at him in the car and I knew "what for"!—I think I got out of the car before he got out of the car, and we walked through the wet grass to the great misty oaks as if somebody was calling us for help there!

[Pause. The subdued, toneless bird-cries in the garden turn to a single bird song.]

DOCTOR:

After that?

CATHARINE:

I lost him.—He took me home and said an awful thing to

me. "We'd better forget it," he said, "my wife's expecting a child and—."—I just entered the house and sat there thinking a little and then I suddenly called a taxi and went right back to the Roosevelt Hotel ballroom. The ball was still going on. I thought I'd gone back to pick up my borrowed coat but that wasn't what I'd gone back for. I'd gone back to make a scene on the floor of the ballroom, yes, I didn't stop at the cloak-room to pick up Aunt Violet's old mink stole, no, I rushed right into the ballroom and spotted him on the floor and ran up to him and beat him as hard as I could in the face and chest with my fists till—Cousin Sebastian took me away.— After that, the next morning, I started writing my diary in the third person, singular, such as "She's still living this morning," meaning that *I* was. . . . —"WHAT'S NEXT FOR HER? GOD KNOWS!"—I couldn't go out any more. —However one morning my Cousin Sebastian came in my bedroom and said: "Get up!"—Well . . . if you're still alive after dying, well then, you're obedient, Doctor.—I got up. He took me downtown to a place for passport photos. Said: "Mother can't go abroad with me this summer. You're going to go with me this summer instead of Mother."—If you don't believe me, read my journal of Paris!—"She woke up at daybreak this morning, had her coffee and dressed and took a brief walk—"

DOCTOR:
Who did?

CATHARINE:
She did. *I* did—from the Hotel Plaza Athénée to the Place de l'Étoile as if pursued by a pack of Siberian wolves! [*She laughs her tired, helpless laugh.*]—Went right through all stop signs—couldn't wait for green signals.—"Where did she think she was going? Back to the Duelling Oaks?"—Everything chilly and dim but his hot, ravenous mouth! on—

551

DOCTOR:
Miss Catharine, let me give you something.

[*The others go out, leaving Catharine and the Doctor onstage.*]

CATHARINE:
Do I have to have the injection again, this time? What am I going to be stuck with this time, Doctor? I don't care. I've been stuck so often that if you connected me with a garden hose I'd make a good sprinkler.

DOCTOR [*preparing needle*]:
Please take off your jacket.

[*She does. The Doctor gives her an injection.*]

CATHARINE:
I didn't feel it.

DOCTOR:
That's good. Now sit down.

[*She sits down.*]

CATHARINE:
Shall I start counting backwards from a hundred?

DOCTOR:
Do you like counting backwards?

CATHARINE:
Love it! Just love it! One hundred! Ninety-nine! Ninety-eight! Ninety-seven. Ninety-six. Ninety—five—. Oh!—I already feel it! How funny!

DOCTOR:
That's right. Close your eyes for a minute.

[*He moves his chair closer to hers. Half a minute passes.*]

Miss Catharine? I want you to give me something.

CATHARINE:
Name it and it's yours, Doctor Sugar.

DOCTOR:
Give me all your resistance.

CATHARINE:
Resistance to what?

DOCTOR:
The truth. Which you're going to tell me.

CATHARINE:
The truth's the one thing I have never resisted!

DOCTOR:
Sometimes people just think they don't resist it, but still do.

CATHARINE:
They say it's at the bottom of a bottomless well, you know.

DOCTOR:
Relax.

CATHARINE:
Truth.

DOCTOR:
Don't talk.

CATHARINE:
Where was I, now? At ninety?

DOCTOR:
You don't have to count backwards.

CATHARINE:
At ninety something?

DOCTOR:
You can open your eyes.

CATHARINE:
Oh, I do feel funny!

553

[Silence, pause.]

You know what I think you're doing? I think you're trying to hypnotize me. Aren't you? You're looking so straight at me and doing something to me with your eyes and your—eyes. . . . Is that what you're doing to me?

DOCTOR:

Is that what you *feel* I'm doing?

CATHARINE:

Yes! I feel so peculiar. And it's not just the drug.

DOCTOR:

Give me all your resistance. See. I'm holding my hand out. I want you to put yours in mine and give me all your resistance. Pass all of your resistance out of your hand to mine.

CATHARINE:

Here's my hand. But there's no resistance in it.

DOCTOR:

You are totally passive.

CATHARINE:

Yes, I am.

DOCTOR:

You will do what I ask.

CATHARINE:

Yes, I will try.

DOCTOR:

You will tell the true story.

CATHARINE:

Yes, I will.

DOCTOR:

The absolutely true story. No lies, nothing not spoken. Everything told, exactly.

554

CATHARINE:

Everything. Exactly. Because I'll have to. Can I—can I stand up?

DOCTOR:

Yes, but be careful. You might feel a little bit dizzy.

[*She struggles to rise, then falls back.*]

CATHARINE:

I can't get up! Tell me to. Then I think I could do it.

DOCTOR:

Stand up.

[*She rises unsteadily.*]

CATHARINE:

How funny! Now I can! Oh, I do feel dizzy! Help me, I'm—

[*He rushes to support her.*]

—about to fall over. . . .

[*He holds her. She looks out vaguely toward the brilliant, steaming garden. Looks back at him. Suddenly sways toward him, against him.*]

DOCTOR:

You see, you lost your balance.

CATHARINE:

No, I didn't. I did what I wanted to do without you telling me to.

[*She holds him tight against her.*]

Let me! Let! Let! Let me! Let me, let me, oh, let me. . . .

[*She crushes her mouth to his violently. He tries to disengage himself. She presses her lips to his fiercely, clutching his body against her. Her brother George enters.*]

555

Please hold me! I've been so lonely. It's lonelier than death, if I've gone mad, it's lonelier than death!

GEORGE [*shocked, disgusted*]:
Cathie!—you've got a hell of a nerve.

[*She falls back, panting, covers her face, runs a few paces and grabs the back of a chair. Mrs. Holly enters.*]

MRS. HOLLY:
What's the matter, George? Is Catharine ill?

GEORGE:
No.

DOCTOR:
Miss Catharine had an injection that made her a little unsteady.

MRS. HOLLY:
What did he say about Catharine?

[*Catharine has gone out into the dazzling jungle of the garden.*]

SISTER [*returning*]:
She's gone into the garden.

DOCTOR:
That's all right, she'll come back when I call her.

SISTER:
It may be all right for you. You're not responsible for her.

[*Mrs. Venable has re-entered.*]

MRS. VENABLE:
Call her now!

DOCTOR:
Miss Catharine! Come back.

[*To the Sister:*]

Bring her back, please, Sister!

[*Catharine enters quietly, a little unsteady.*]

Now, Miss Catharine, you're going to tell the true story.

CATHARINE:
Where do I start the story?

DOCTOR:
Wherever you think it started.

CATHARINE:
I think it started the day he was born in this house.

MRS. VENABLE:
Ha! You see!

GEORGE:
Cathie.

DOCTOR:
Let's start later than that. [*Pause.*] Shall we begin with last summer?

CATHARINE:
Oh. Last summer.

DOCTOR:
Yes. Last summer.

[*There is a long pause. The raucous sounds in the garden fade into a bird song which is clear and sweet. Mrs. Holly coughs. Mrs. Venable stirs impatiently. George crosses downstage to catch Catharine's eye as he lights a cigarette.*]

CATHARINE:
Could I—?

MRS. VENABLE:
Keep that boy away from her!

GEORGE:
She wants to smoke, Aunt Vi.

557

CATHARINE:
Something helps in the—hands. . . .

SISTER:
Unh unh!

DOCTOR:
It's all right, Sister. [*He lights her cigarette.*] About last summer: how did it begin?

CATHARINE:
It began with his kindness and the six days at sea that took me so far away from the—Duelling Oaks that I forgot them, nearly. He was affectionate with me, so sweet and attentive to me, that some people took us for a honeymoon couple until they noticed that we had—separate staterooms, and—then in Paris, he took me to Patou and Schiaparelli's—*this* is from Schiaparelli's! [*Like a child, she indicates her suit.*]—bought me so many new clothes that I gave away my old ones to make room for my new ones in my new luggage to—travel. . . . I turned into a peacock! Of course, so was *he* one, too. . . .

GEORGE:
Ha Ha!

MRS. VENABLE:
Shh!

CATHARINE:
But then I made the mistake of responding too much to his kindness, of taking hold of his hand before he'd take hold of mine, of holding onto his arm and leaning on his shoulder, of appreciating his kindness more than he wanted me to, and, suddenly, last summer, he began to be restless, and—oh!

DOCTOR:
Go on.

CATHARINE:
The Blue Jay notebook!

DOCTOR:
Did you say notebook?

MRS. VENABLE:
I know what she means by that, she's talking about the school composition book with a Blue Jay trademark that Sebastian used for making notes and revisions on his *Poem of Summer*. It went with him everywhere that he went, in his jacket pocket, even his dinner jacket. I have the one that he had with him last summer. *Foxhill! The Blue Jay notebook!*

[*Miss Foxhill rushes in with a gasp.*]

It came with his personal effects shipped back from Cabeza de Lobo.

DOCTOR:
I don't quite get the connection between new clothes and so forth and the Blue Jay notebook.

MRS. VENABLE:
I HAVE IT!—Doctor, tell her I've found it.

[*Miss Foxhill hears this as she comes back out of house: gasps with relief, retires.*]

DOCTOR:
With all these interruptions it's going to be awfully hard to—

MRS. VENABLE:
This is important. I don't know why she mentioned the Blue Jay notebook but I want you to see it. Here it is, here! [*She holds up a notebook and leafs swiftly through the pages.*] Title? *Poem of Summer*, and the date of the summer— 1935. After that: *what? Blank pages, blank pages,* nothing but *nothing!*—last summer. . . .

DOCTOR:
What's that got to do with—?

MRS. VENABLE:

His destruction? I'll tell you. A poet's vocation is something that rests on something as thin and fine as the web of a spider, Doctor. That's all that holds him *over!*—out of destruction. . . . Few, very few are able to do it alone! Great help is needed! I *did* give it! She *didn't*.

CATHARINE:

She's right about that. I failed him. I wasn't able to keep the web from—breaking. . . . I saw it breaking but couldn't save or—repair it!

MRS. VENABLE:

There now, the truth's coming out. We had an agreement between us, a sort of contract or covenant between us which he broke last summer when he broke away from me and took her with him, not me! When he was frightened and I knew when and what of, because his hands would shake and his eyes looked in, not out, I'd reach across a table and touch his hands and say not a word, just look, and touch his hands with my hand until his hands stopped shaking and his eyes looked out, not in, and in the morning, the poem would be continued. *Continued until it was finished!*

[*The following ten speeches are said very rapidly, overlapping.*]

CATHARINE:

I—couldn't!

MRS. VENABLE:

Naturally not! He was *mine*! I *knew* how to help him, I *could*! You didn't, you couldn't!

DOCTOR:

These interruptions—

MRS. VENABLE:

I would say "You *will*" and he *would*, I—!

CATHARINE:
Yes, you see, I failed him! And so, last summer, we went to Cabeza de Lobo, we flew down there from where he gave up writing his poem last summer....

MRS. VENABLE:
Because he'd broken our—

CATHARINE:
Yes! Yes, something had broken, that string of pearls that old mothers hold their sons by like a—sort of a—sort of—*umbilical* cord, *long—after* ...

MRS. VENABLE:
She means that I held him back from—

DOCTOR:
Please!

MRS. VENABLE:
Destruction!

CATHARINE:
All I know is that suddenly, last summer, he wasn't young any more, and we went to Cabeza de Lobo, and he suddenly switched from the evenings to the beach. . . .

DOCTOR:
From evenings? To beach?

CATHARINE:
I mean from the evenings to the afternoons and from the fa—fash—

[*Silence*: *Mrs. Holly draws a long, long painful breath. George stirs impatiently.*]

DOCTOR:
Fashionable! Is that the word you—?

561

CATHARINE:
Yes. Suddenly, last summer Cousin Sebastian changed to the afternoons and the beach.

DOCTOR:
What beach?

CATHARINE:
In Cabeza de Lobo there is a beach that's named for Sebastian's name saint, it's known as La Playa San Sebastian, and that's where we started spending all afternoon, every day.

DOCTOR:
What kind of beach was it?

CATHARINE:
It was a big city beach near the harbor.

DOCTOR:
It was a big public beach?

CATHARINE:
Yes, public.

MRS. VENABLE:
It's little statements like that that give her away.

[*The Doctor rises and crosses to Mrs. Venable without breaking his concentration on Catharine.*]

After all I've told you about his fastidiousness, can you accept such a statement?

DOCTOR:
You mustn't interrupt her.

MRS. VENABLE [*overlapping him*]:
That Sebastian would go every day to some dirty free public beach near a harbor? A man that had to go out a mile in a boat to find water fit to swim in?

562

DOCTOR:

Mrs. Venable, no matter what she says you have to let her say it without any more interruptions or this interview will be useless.

MRS. VENABLE:

I won't speak again. I'll keep still, if it kills me.

CATHARINE:

I don't want to go on. . . .

DOCTOR:

Go on with the story. Every afternoon last summer your Cousin Sebastian and you went out to this free public beach?

CATHARINE:

No, it wasn't the free one, the free one was right next to it, there was a fence between the free beach and the one that we went to that charged a small charge of admission.

DOCTOR:

Yes, and what did you do there?

[*He still stands beside Mrs. Venable and the light gradually changes as the girl gets deeper into her story: the light concentrates on Catharine, the other figures sink into shadow.*]

Did anything happen there that disturbed you about it?

CATHARINE:

Yes!

DOCTOR:

What?

CATHARINE:

He bought me a swim-suit I didn't want to wear. I laughed. I said, "I can't wear that, it's a scandal to the jay birds!"

DOCTOR:
What did you mean by that? That the suit was immodest?

CATHARINE:
My God, yes! It was a one-piece suit made of white lisle, the water made it transparent! [*She laughs sadly at the memory of it.*] —I didn't want to swim in it, but he'd grab my hand and drag me into the water, all the way in, and I'd come out looking naked!

DOCTOR:
Why did he do that? Did you understand why?

CATHARINE:
—Yes! To attract!—Attention.

DOCTOR:
He wanted you to attract attention, did he, because he felt you were moody? Lonely? He wanted to shock you out of your depression last summer?

CATHARINE:
Don't you understand? I was PROCURING for him!

[*Mrs. Venable's gasp is like the sound that a great hooked fish might make.*]

She used to do it, *too*.

[*Mrs. Venable cries out.*]

Not consciously! She didn't *know* that she was procuring for him in the smart, the fashionable places they used to go to before last summer! Sebastian was shy with people. She wasn't. Neither was I. We both did the same thing for him, made contacts for him, but she did it in nice places and in decent ways and I had to do it the way that I just told you! —Sebastian was lonely, Doctor, and the empty Blue Jay notebook got bigger and bigger, so big it was big and empty as

564

that big empty blue sea and sky. . . . I knew what I was doing. I came out in the French Quarter years before I came out in the Garden District. . . .

MRS. HOLLY:
Oh, Cathie! Sister . . .

DOCTOR:
Hush!

CATHARINE:
And before long, when the weather got warmer and the beach so crowded, he didn't need me any more for that purpose. The ones on the free beach began to climb over the fence or swim around it, bands of homeless young people that lived on the free beach like scavenger dogs, hungry children. . . . So now he let me wear a decent dark suit. I'd go to a faraway empty end of the beach, write postcards and letters and keep up my— third-person journal till it was—five o'clock and time to meet him outside the bathhouses, on the street. . . . He would come out, *followed.*

DOCTOR:
Who would follow him out?

CATHARINE:
The homeless, hungry young people that had climbed over the fence from the free beach that they lived on. He'd pass out tips among them as if they'd all—shined his shoes or called taxis for him. . . . Each day the crowd was bigger, noisier, greedier!—Sebastian began to be frightened.—At last we stopped going out there. . . .

DOCTOR:
And then? After that? After you quit going out to the public beach?

CATHARINE:
Then one day, a few days after we stopped going out to the

beach—it was one of those white blazing days in Cabeza de Lobo, not a blazing hot *blue* one but a blazing hot *white* one.

DOCTOR:

Yes?

CATHARINE:

We had a late lunch at one of those open-air restaurants on the sea there.—Sebastian was white as the weather. He had on a spotless white silk Shantung suit and a white silk tie and a white panama and white shoes, white—white lizard skin—pumps! He—[*She throws back her head in a startled laugh at the recollection.*]—kept touching his face and his throat here and there with a white silk handkerchief and popping little white pills in his mouth, and I knew he was having a bad time with his heart and was frightened about it and that was the reason we hadn't gone out to the beach. . . .

[*During the monologue the lights have changed, the surrounding area has dimmed out and a hot white spot is focused on Catharine.*]

"I think we ought to go north," he kept saying, "I think we've done Cabeza de Lobo, I think we've done it, don't you?" *I* thought we'd done it!—but I had learned it was better not to seem to have an opinion because if I did, well, Sebastian, well, you know Sebastian, he always preferred to do what no one else wanted to do, and I always tried to give the impression that I was agreeing reluctantly to his wishes . . . it was a—game. . . .

SISTER:

She's dropped her cigarette.

DOCTOR:

I've got it, Sister.

[*There are whispers, various movements in the penumbra. The Doctor fills a glass for her from the cocktail shaker.*]

CATHARINE:

Where was I? Oh, yes, that five o'clock lunch at one of those fish places along the harbor of Cabeza de Lobo, it was between the city and the sea, and there were naked children along the beach which was fenced off with barbed wire from the restaurant and we had our table less than a yard from the barbed wire fence that held the beggars at bay. . . . There were naked children along the beach, a band of frightfully thin and dark naked children that looked like a flock of plucked birds, and they would come darting up to the barbed wire fence as if blown there by the wind, the hot white wind from the sea, all crying out, *"Pan, pan, pan!"*

DOCTOR [*quietly*]:

What's *pan*?

CATHARINE:

The word for bread, and they made gobbling noises with their little black mouths, stuffing their little black fists to their mouths and making those gobbling noises, with frightful grins!—Of course we were sorry that we had come to this place but it was too late to go. . . .

DOCTOR [*quietly*]:

Why was it "too late to go"?

CATHARINE:

I told you Cousin Sebastian wasn't well. He was popping those little white pills in his mouth. I think he had popped in so many of them that they had made him feel weak. . . . His, his!—eyes looked—dazed, but he said: "Don't look at those little monsters. Beggars are a social disease in this country. If you look at them, you get sick of the country, it spoils the whole country for you. . . ."

DOCTOR:

Go on.

CATHARINE:
I'm going on. I have to wait now and then till it gets clearer. Under the drug it has to be a vision, or nothing comes. . . .

DOCTOR:
All right?

CATHARINE:
Always when I was with him I did what he told me. I didn't look at the band of naked children, not even when the waiters drove them away from the barbed wire fence with sticks!— Rushing out through a wicket gate like an assault party in war!—and beating them screaming away from the barbed wire fence with the sticks. . . . Then! [*Pause.*]

DOCTOR:
Go on, Miss Catherine, what comes next in the vision?

CATHARINE:
The, the the!—band of children began to—serenade us. . . .

DOCTOR:
Do what?

CATHARINE:
Play for us! On instruments! Make music!—if you could call it music. . . .

DOCTOR:
Oh?

CATHARINE:
Their, their—instruments were—instruments of percussion!— Do you know what I mean?

DOCTOR [*making a note*]:
Yes. Instruments of percussion such as—*drums*?

CATHARINE:
I stole glances at them when Cousin Sebastian wasn't looking,

568

and as well as I could make out in the white blaze of the sand-beach, the instruments were tin cans strung together.

DOCTOR [*slowly, writing*]:
Tin—cans—strung—together.

CATHARINE:
And, and, and, and—and!—bits of metal, other bits of metal that had been flattened out, made into—

DOCTOR:
What?

CATHARINE:
Cymbals! You know? *Cymbals*?

DOCTOR:
Yes. Brass plates hit together.

CATHARINE:
That's right, Doctor.—Tin cans flattened out and clashed together!—Cymbals. . . .

DOCTOR:
Yes. I understand. What's after that, in the vision?

CATHARINE [*rapidly, panting a little*]:
And others had paper bags, bags made out of—coarse paper! —with something on a string inside the bags which they pulled up and down, back and forth, to make a sort of a—

DOCTOR:
Sort of a—?

CATHARINE:
Noise like—

DOCTOR:
Noise like?

CATHARINE [*rising stiffly from chair*]:
Ooompa! Oompa! Oooooompa!

569

DOCTOR:
Ahhh . . . a sound like a *tuba*?

CATHARINE:
That's right!—they made a sound like a tuba. . . .

DOCTOR:
Oompa, oompa, oompa, like a tuba.

[*He is making a note of the description.*]

CATHARINE:
Oompa, oompa, oompa, like a—

[*Short pause.*]

DOCTOR:
—Tuba. . . .

CATHARINE:
All during lunch they stayed at a—a fairly *close—distance.* . . .

DOCTOR:
Go on with the vision, Miss Catharine.

CATHARINE [*striding about the table*]:
Oh, I'm going on, nothing could stop it now!!

DOCTOR:
Your Cousin Sebastian was *entertained* by this—*concert*?

CATHARINE:
I think he was *terrified* of it!

DOCTOR:
Why was he terrified of it?

CATHARINE:
I think he recognized some of the musicians, some of the boys,
between childhood and—older. . . .

DOCTOR:
What did he do? Did he do anything about it, Miss Catharine?
—Did he complain to the manager about it?

CATHARINE:
What manager? *God?* Oh, *no!*—The manager of the fish
place on the beach? Haha!—No!—You don't understand my
cousin!

DOCTOR:
What do you mean?

CATHARINE:
*He! —accepted! —all! —*as —how! —things! —are! —And
thought nobody had any right to complain or interfere in any
way whatsoever, and even though he knew that what was
awful was awful, that what was wrong was wrong, and my
Cousin Sebastian was certainly never sure that anything was
wrong!—He thought it unfitting to ever take any action about
anything whatsoever!—except to go on doing as something in
him directed. . . .

DOCTOR:
What did something in him direct him to do?—I mean on
this occasion in Cabeza de Lobo.

CATHARINE:
After the salad, before they brought the coffee, he suddenly
pushed himself away from the table, and said, "They've got to
stop that! Waiter, make them stop that. I'm not a well man,
I have a heart condition, it's making me sick!"—This was the
first time that Cousin Sebastian had ever attempted to correct
a human situation!—I think perhaps that *that* was his—fatal
error. . . . It was then that the waiters, all eight or ten of
them, charged out of the barbed wire wicket gate and beat the
little musicians away with clubs and skillets and anything
hard that they could snatch from the kitchen!—Cousin Sebastian left the table. He stalked out of the restaurant after throwing a handful of paper money on the table and he fled from
the place. I followed. It was all white outside. White hot, a

571

blazing white hot, hot blazing white, at five o'clock in the afternoon in the city of—Cabeza de Lobo. It looked as if—

DOCTOR:
It looked as if?

CATHARINE:
As if a huge white bone had caught on fire in the sky and blazed so bright it was white and turned the sky and everything under the sky white with it!

DOCTOR:
—White . . .

CATHARINE:
Yes—white . . .

DOCTOR:
You followed your Cousin Sebastian out of the restaurant onto the hot white street?

CATHARINE:
Running up and down hill. . . .

DOCTOR:
You ran up and down hill?

CATHARINE:
No, no! *Didn't!*—move either *way!*—at first, we were—

[*During this recitation there are various sound effects. The percussive sounds described are very softly employed.*]

I rarely made any suggestion but *this* time I *did.* . . .

DOCTOR:
What did you suggest?

CATHARINE:
Cousin Sebastian seemed to be paralyzed near the entrance of the café, so I said, "Let's go." I remember that it was a very wide and steep white street, and I said, "Cousin Sebastian,

572

down that way is the waterfront and we are more likely to find a taxi near there. . . . Or why don't we go back in?—and have them *call* us a taxi! Oh, let's do! Let's do *that*, that's better!" And he said, "*Mad*, are you *mad*? Go back in that filthy place? Never! That gang of kids shouted vile things about me to the waiters!" "Oh," I said, "then let's go down toward the docks, down there at the bottom of the hill, let's not try to climb the hill in this dreadful heat." And Cousin Sebastian shouted, "Please shut up, let me handle this situation, will you? I want to handle this thing." And he started up the steep street with a hand stuck in his jacket where I knew he was having a pain in his chest from his palpitations. . . . But he walked faster and faster, in panic, but the faster he walked the louder and closer it got!

DOCTOR:
What got louder?

CATHARINE:
The music.

DOCTOR:
The music again.

CATHARINE:
The oompa-oompa of the—following band.—They'd somehow gotten through the barbed wire and out on the street, and they were following, following!—up the blazing white street. The band of naked children pursued us up the steep white street in the sun that was like a great white bone of a giant beast that had caught on fire in the sky!—Sebastian started to run and they all screamed at once and seemed to fly in the air, they outran him so quickly. I screamed. I heard Sebastian scream, he screamed just once before this flock of black plucked little birds that pursued him and overtook him halfway up the white hill.

DOCTOR:
And you, Miss Catharine, what did *you* do, then?

CATHARINE:
Ran!

DOCTOR:
Ran where?

CATHARINE:
Down! Oh, I ran down, the easier direction to run was down, down, down, down!—The hot, white, blazing street, screaming out "Help" all the way, till—

DOCTOR:
What?

CATHARINE:
—Waiters, police, and others—ran out of buildings and rushed back up the hill with me. When we got back to where my Cousin Sebastian had disappeared in the flock of featherless little black sparrows, he—he was lying naked as they had been naked against a white wall, and this you won't believe, nobody *has* believed it, nobody *could* believe it, nobody, nobody on earth could possibly believe it, and I don't *blame* them!—They had *devoured* parts of him.

[*Mrs. Venable cries out softly.*]

Torn or cut parts of him away with their hands or knives or maybe those jagged tin cans they made music with, they had torn bits of him away and stuffed them into those gobbling fierce little empty black mouths of theirs. There wasn't a sound any more, there was nothing to see but Sebastian, what was left of him, that looked like a big white-paper-wrapped bunch of red roses had been *torn, thrown, crushed!*—against that blazing white wall. . . .

[*Mrs. Venable springs with amazing power from her wheel-*

chair, stumbles erratically but swiftly toward the girl and tries to strike her with her cane. The Doctor snatches it from her and catches her as she is about to fall. She gasps hoarsely several times as he leads her toward the exit.]

MRS. VENABLE [*offstage*]:
Lion's View! State asylum, cut this hideous story out of her brain!

[*Mrs. Holly sobs and crosses to George, who turns away from her, saying:*]

GEORGE:
Mom, I'll quit school, I'll get a job, I'll—

MRS. HOLLY:
Hush son! Doctor, can't you say something?

[*Pause. The Doctor comes downstage. Catharine wanders out into the garden followed by the Sister.*]

DOCTOR [*after a while, reflectively, into space*]:
I think we ought at least to consider the possibility that the girl's story could be true. . . .

THE END